Thomas Jefferson

Alexander Hamilton

by John S. Pancake

Professor of History, University of Alabama

Barron's Educational Series, Inc.
Woodbury, New York

All inquiries should be addressed to:
Barron's Educational Series, Inc.
113 Crossways Park Drive
Woodbury, New York 11797

Library of Congress Catalog Card No. 74-750

International Standard Book No. 0–8120–0463–9

PRINTED IN THE UNITED STATES OF AMERICA

Library of Congress Cataloging in Publication Data

Pancake, John S.
 Thomas Jefferson and Alexander Hamilton
 (Shapers of history)

 SUMMARY: Short biographies of two members of
President Washington's first cabinet emphasizing the
contrast between Hamilton's concern for the public
interest and Jefferson's for individual freedom.
 Bibliography: p.
 1. Jefferson, Thomas, Pres. U.S., 1743-1826.
2. Hamilton, Alexander, 1757-1804. [1. Jefferson,
Thomas, Pres. U.S., 1743-1826. 2. Hamilton, Alexander,
1757-1804. 3. Statesmen, American] I. Title.

E332.P24   973.4'092'2 [B]   [920]   74-750

ISBN 0-8120-0463-9

This book is for

A.D.H.

Table of Contents

Editor's Foreword

THE SHAPERS OF HISTORY SERIES presents a collection of short biographies of statesmen who have made significant contributions to the world in which we live, The series also includes some duo-biographies of two historic figures of the same nation and the same period, who have interacted as opponents or else as colleagues in the same political or social movement.

A unique feature of the Series is a chapter in each biography entitled "The Verdict of History" which surveys the history of the public image of the statesman as produced by historians, essayists, poets, and others since his death, with citations to the writings of these various authors. This chapter is followed by a concluding chapter summing up the author's own appraisal of the man and his times.

John S. Pancake, the author of the present duo-biography, was born in Staunton, Virginia. He graduated from Hampden-Sydney College in 1942 and served in the United States Navy during the Second World War. He earned his doctorate of philosophy at the University of Virginia in 1949 and now serves as Professor of History at the University of Alabama. He is also the author of a biography of Samuel Smith who represented Maryland in Congress for forty years and who commanded the defenses at Baltimore in 1814 when Francis Scott Key wrote the national anthem.

Professor Pancake has written an objective duo-biography of two great statesmen who confronted each other in President Washington's first cabinet. Although Professor Pancake was born and educated in the South and oriented toward Jeffersonian ideology, he is as fair toward Alexander Hamilton as toward Jefferson. Throughout the duo-biography the author properly contrasts Hamilton's concern for the "good of society" or the public interest with Jefferson's concern for the freedom of the individual.

KENNETH COLEGROVE

Author's Preface

THIS BOOK, perhaps more than most, owes a great deal to the massive historical excavations of other scholars, and I have tried to acknowledge them in the bibliography and notes. I am particularly indebted to biographies by Dumas Malone, Merrill S. Peterson, Broadus Mitchell, and John C. Miller. I have also cited in the first note of some chapters the works of scholars who were particularly valuable to me and who would be helpful to the reader who wishes to pursue these particular subjects further. I do not thereby claim to have selected everyone's choice for preeminence, although I do not believe that anyone would deny the merits of these works. For example, from the wealth of scholarship on the diplomacy of the 1790's, I chose Alexander De Conde because he related diplomacy to domestic politics in a way that was especially useful. I have avoided manuscript sources and have tried to use materials available in most university libraries.

Some hard choices had to be made because the limited nature of this book made it necessary to omit much that was fascinating and perhaps significant about Jefferson and Hamilton. My judgement was based, in general, on a desire to include what seemed to be most revealing in making comparisons and contrasts between the two, and at the same time to prevent their remarkable personalities from being lost in the parade of events and the welter of ideas and theories.

If there is a single recurrent theme which emerges from this study, it is the search for a balance between Hamilton's orderly and secure society—what he called the "public good" —and Jefferson's free and uninhibited individual. There was a parallel search for the balance between colonies' (later states') desire for a large degree of autonomy and the need for imperial (national) centralization to achieve collective security and prosperity—in short, the federal problem. The conflict between Jefferson and Hamilton was part of the unceasing political struggle in the United States which produces a compromise between extremes and which represents the essence of American democracy.

Anyone who has said, "I wrote a book," doesn't know what he is talking about. *We* wrote this book, and this includes: Ruth Kibbey, who typed the final manuscript; Bill Björk, Bob Griffin, Larry and Caterina Sutley, and Ken Valliere, students—in the very best sense of the word—who assisted with the research; library staffs at the University of Alabama, Auburn University, Washington and Lee University, the University of Virginia, and the Library of Congress; Dr. Kenneth Colegrove, the consulting editor, who helped me avoid many pitfalls and corrected many errors. My colleague at the University of Alabama, Professor Robert Mitchell, generously took time to read the manuscript, but I absolve him of any blame for errors of fact or judgement, which are mine alone.

I am also very grateful to the University of Alabama Research Committee for making it possible for me to take leaves of absence from my teaching duties and thereby making this book possible.

UNIVERSITY OF ALABAMA   JOHN PANCAKE

I Virginia and The West Indies

THEY WERE OPPOSITES in many ways. Thomas Jefferson's roots were deep in the soil and culture of Virginia, the oldest English community in the New World. Alexander Hamilton was an immigrant to the American Continent who left his West Indian home with scarcely a backward glance. The young Jefferson's life seemed to lie before him like a blueprint. There was a family estate, an established social order, a way of life to which his orderly mind and temperament easily adapted. Hamilton was a young man in a hurry. His mercurial personality and energetic enthusiasm were often brought to focus fortuitously, but a remarkably mature judgement enabled him to fit his life to circumstance.

The America of these two young men was on the fringe of the civilization and consciousness of Western Europe. Virginia was old only by New World standards, and to the average Englishman America was a half-savage land inhabited by inferior peoples about whom he knew little and cared less. By the time the generation of Jefferson and Hamilton came to an end, a new nation had been formed and a new philosophy was taking shape which was vastly different in its promise from the traditions of the Old World.

Mr. Henry and the Stamp Act

"Caesar had his Brutus, Charles the First his Cromwell, and George the Third ———" The resonant voice of the

1

speaker was interrupted by indignant cries of "Treason, Sir! Treason!" "—George the Third may profit by their example," the rolling voice continued. "If this be treason, make the most of it!"

Standing among the listeners just outside the chamber of the Virginia House of Burgesses was a tall, slender, red-headed law student. Thomas Jefferson listened with vast admiration to the oratory of Patrick Henry, the tempestuous representative from Hanover County whose clothes were not quite proper and who seemed attracted to people of the common sort.[1]

The year was 1765, and Mr. Henry had introduced seven resolutions opposing the Stamp Act, a tax on legal and commercial paper recently passed by Parliament. A "rump" session of the Burgesses rejected two of the most vehement of the resolutions but passed the other five—and regretted it as soon as the torrential eloquence of the delegate from Hanover ebbed. After all, the idea that Parliament's power to tax the colony "has a manifest tendency to destroy British as well as American freedom," was pretty strong stuff.[2] No matter, Mr. Henry had already seen to it that all seven resolutions were in the mails. They appeared in colonial newspapers as far away as Boston.

There is reason to doubt that the scene just described was quite as dramatic as Jefferson and his young companion John Tyler reported it in later years. But there is no doubt that the Virginia Resolves triggered an unprecedented explosion of opposition to British authority. Nor is there any doubt that young Jefferson was in sympathy with the opposition and tremendously impressed by Patrick Henry's powerful eloquence. The two had been acquainted for several years prior to the Stamp Act crisis, and their paths crossed frequently in the ensuing decades. Jefferson greatly admired Henry's genius in the service of the Revolutionary cause, but the orderly scholar in him was somewhat critical of Henry's intellectual laziness.[3]

At twenty-two Jefferson had already developed a discipline of mind which was remarkable among the young gentry who frequented Williamsburg. Along with Tyler, John Page, and Dabney Carr, he danced at the Raleigh Tavern and frequented its Apollo Room, where he undoubtedly did his share of gambling and acquired a connoisseur's taste for good wine. He dressed fastidiously, as a member of the gentry should, and was an excellent horseman, as any man who travelled at all in Virginia had to be.[4] But he never strayed from his fixed conviction that the human mind could penetrate any secret of the universe if its freedom to inquire were unfettered and its intelligence properly trained. The diligence with which he pursued this conviction grew out of no Calvinistic self-discipline or sense of duty. His curiosity—his zest for inquiry into almost any subject—was rooted in a desire for the only kind of power he ever craved—the power of knowledge.

Peter Jefferson

The intellectual maturity of the young Jefferson might argue that his background was a remarkable one. Yet Jefferson's early years and upbringing were not unusual unless it was unusual to be born in America and in Virginia.

His father was the scion of a family which had been in America for three generations. Peter Jefferson was not a member of the Virginia aristocracy, but he numbered Randolphs, Eppeses, and Pages among his friends and acquaintances. He was magistrate of Goochland County, and when Albemarle was separated from Goochland, Peter Jefferson became justice of the peace, a judge of the court of chancery, and a member of the House of Burgesses. These were positions which came to him as the leading citizen of the county and were regarded as public duties rather than the result of political ambition. He served two terms in the Assembly in 1754 and 1755 but did not stand for reelection.

He also gained local fame as the senior surveyor for the Crown. He and an associate Joshua Fry surveyed part of the vast Fairfax domain in northern Virginia, and in 1749 they extended the Virginia–North Carolina boundary almost a hundred miles beyond the original one the second William Byrd had laid twenty years before.[5]

Peter Jefferson, in short, was a member of the gentry. He came from western—but not frontier—Virginia, and if his land holdings were somewhat modest, it was not thought strange that this rising young planter courted and married Jane Randolph. She was the daughter of Isham Randolph, a sea captain who was also a large landholder in Goochland County. Her grandparents were William and Mary Randolph of Turkey Island whose descendents married Marshalls, Lees, Carters, Nelsons, Blands, and Carrs.[6]

It was probably in 1741, about five years after his marriage that Peter Jefferson took his family to Shadwell, a modest home he had built on the Rivanna River near the hamlet of Charlottesville. Thomas Jefferson was born here on April 13, 1743, but within little more than two years the family moved to Tuckahoe, the home of a close friend William Randolph, Jane's first cousin. Randolph had died at the age of thirty-three and in his will had charged Peter Jefferson with the responsibility of raising his children. Most of young Tom's early memories were of Tuckahoe where his father was master but not owner. When the boy was nine, the family moved back to Shadwell, and five years later Peter Jefferson died.[7]

Thomas Jefferson in later life always spoke of his father with admiration and respect but rarely with affection.[8] Peter Jefferson was frequently away from home on his surveying trips or attending to public duties. When the family moved back to Shadwell in 1751, Tom was either left at Tuckahoe or shortly returned there to study under a tutor, for his father was determined that his son would have a good education. The tutor was that James Maury who was afterward embroiled in the Parson's Cause, a case which marked Patrick Henry's rise to political prominence. From him young Jefferson received a basic knowledge of the classics, but Maury also emphasized what he called "the Mother Tongue." [9] The young man of seventeen who arrived at Williamsburg in 1760 to complete his studies at the College of William and Mary had received a sound elementary education and was socially well connected. Peter Jefferson's ambition for his son was on the way to realization.

Education in Virginia

The genius of the mind and spirit which marks men like Thomas Jefferson does not develop spontaneously from native ability. It must be nurtured and inspired. The College of William and Mary was passing through an upheaval when Jefferson arrived in Williamsburg in 1760. This coincidence of circumstances resulted in his having only one professor for more than half of his college career.

William Small had been appointed in 1758 as professor of natural philosophy, and by the time of Jefferson's arrival he was also teaching physics, metaphysics, and mathematics. The departure of two more professors added rhetoric, logic, ethics, and moral philosophy to his teaching duties. Yet this remarkable man responded to the burden by displaying not only a wide range of knowledge but a singular ability to communicate with his students. Jefferson considered him the most important influence on his education with the exception of George Wythe. Jefferson later observed that Small "proba-

bly fixed the destiny of my life . . . and from his conversation
I got my first views of the expansion of science & of the
system of things in which we are placed." [10]

It was Small who introduced Jefferson to George Wythe
and persuaded the eminent lawyer to accept him as a law
student. Although he was only thirty-five years old, Wythe
was already acknowledged as an outstanding member of the
Virginia bar. In choosing to study law, Jefferson was following the well-established custom of upper-class Virginians.
Knowledge of the law was highly desirable for a large landholder, which Jefferson knew he would be, and a good practice provided a cash income to supplement his profits as a
planter. Wythe's broad and liberal mind had encompassed
the classics as well as the law. The pupil was directed to works
of Greek and Latin as well as to that classic of English legal
scholars, *The Institutes of the Laws of England.* He observed
his teacher as a brilliant lawyer before the General Court and
as a respected member of the House of Burgesses. [11]

Wythe introduced his pupil to Governor Francis Fauquier,
and the dinner conversations at the palace were notable for
their learned and scientific flavor, "more rational and philosophical" than any Jefferson had heard elsewhere, he later
noted, possibly with exaggeration. Tom was proficient
enough to add his violin to the musical group which consisted
of the governor, Peyton Randolph and his brother John,
Robert Carter, and Jefferson's intimate friend John Page. [12]
Governor Fauquier was indeed a patron of the arts and the
sciences, and here Jefferson may well have discovered that
the scholar and the aristocrat could be combined into the
"complete gentleman."

William Small, George Wythe, and Francis Fauquier,
then, were the three major influences on young Thomas Jefferson. In their company his mind was broadened and disciplined. He learned that knowledge was a stimulant to further

inquiry more often than an end in itself. He was part of a society which prided itself on its polish and elegance, its good manners, and its generosity. If it contained a considerable strain of conservatism in economic and political matters, it prided itself on intellectual pursuits and a certain modernity of spirit. Jefferson did not accept its code uncritically, and he deplored some of its false values and snobbish inequalities, but he was "in all respects a gentleman. His distinction lies in the fact that he became a great deal more." [13]

West Indian Boyhood

"I contemn the grov'ling and condition of a Clerk or the like, to which my Fortune, &c. condemns me and would willingly risk my life tho' not my Character to exalt my Station." [14] This querulous complaint with its note of bombast might seem ordinary enough except that the writer was only fourteen years old. Alexander Hamilton was doing very well indeed considering the fact that he was orphaned, and his relatives and friends, while sympathetic to the young man's plight, could do little to help him.

The exception was Nicholas Cruger of the mercantile firm of Beckman and Cruger, Christiansted, on the island of St. Croix. Hamilton's mother had managed to support her two sons on the slender income from a shop which she ran, but her death in 1768 left them destitute. Cruger not only employed young Alexander but became his patron and friend, and the friendship remained a close one until Cruger's death in 1801. [15] The firm in which Hamilton was employed was a small one although it had a loose partnership with Cruger's father and brothers in New York and another brother in Curaçao. Unlike his brothers, Cruger supported the American cause during the Revolution and in later years moved his business to New York.

St. Croix, one of the Virgin Islands, was about twenty miles long and about five miles wide. Its 50,000 acres were intensely cultivated, and in 1769 its population was about 24,000, the slaves outnumbering the whites about twelve to one. Its principal product, exported by Beckman and Cruger, was sugar, and its imports were food, lumber, and livestock. Except for the administrative officials, who were Danish, its white population was almost entirely English and Scottish. The blue waters of the snug harbor at Christiansted set against the green hills which overlooked it provided an idyllic setting for the elegance of the members of the planter aristocracy who were, nonetheless, never quite free of two great fears—a slave revolt and hurricanes.

The slender, handsome youth who "grov'led" as a clerk at Cruger's was a highly intelligent lad. He had presumably picked up an education of sorts from the usual tutors and from his relatives. The business correspondence which he conducted for Cruger was polished and proficient, and the easy facility with which he later mastered a diversity of subjects as a formal student indicates that he had probably done a good deal of studying on his own.

In the fall of 1771 Nicholas Cruger became ill and went to New York, presumably for medical treatment. It was a mark of Hamilton's precocious talent that Cruger appointed the sixteen-year-old lad to conduct the firm's affairs during his absence. The young deputy kept his employer informed of his dealings with planters, ships captains, and merchants. Worms in a cargo of flour indicated that "it could not have been very new when twas shipd." A certain Captain Newton "seems rather to want experience" and another ship's master "talks largely of Dangers & difficultys upon the Coast but no doubt exaggerates." [16] When Cruger returned to Christiansted in the spring of 1772, he was presumably well pleased with Hamilton's work.

In any event, it was Cruger who took the decisive step in Hamilton's career. With the help of generous gentlemen of the island, he decided to underwrite Hamilton's education in New York. Whether the merchant was impressed with his business acumen or by his budding literary talent—young Alexander gained local fame by publishing an outrageously sensational account of a hurricane of that year [17]—Hamilton took ship for the mainland in the fall of 1772. He never returned to St. Croix.

The Bar Sinister

There is no indication that Hamilton was unhappy as a boy, and as a man he was noted rather for his high spirits and conviviality. Yet there was a shadow over his early life which could not have failed to haunt his mind in later years. His grandmother Mary Fawcett married a man some years older than she and then was separated from her husband after more than twenty years of marriage. Her daughter Rachael, Alexander's mother, was married at the age of sixteen to a Danish Jew John Lavien, a merchant of St. Croix who was several years older than she. It may have been that the disparity in ages made the marriage an unhappy one. In any event, within five years Lavien had had Rachael imprisoned briefly for adultery and the two had separated. In 1759 Lavien sued his wife for divorce in St. Croix, and she did not contest. The divorce deprived her of the right to remarry under Danish law. [18]

Some years prior to the divorce Rachael had begun living with James Hamilton, a well-born but irresponsible Scot. Alexander was born in 1755 probably either on the island of St. Kitts or nearby Nevis. The date 1755, two years earlier than usually given for Hamilton's birth date, is accepted on the basis of evidence presented by Professor Broadus Mitch-

ell. The key document is the record of the probate court in
Christiansted when Hamilton's mother died in 1768, and her
meagre estate was settled. Hamilton's uncle by marriage
James Lytton testified that the boy was thirteen years old.[19]

The legally adulterous relationship of Alexander's parents
seems to have attracted little notice or notoriety, for such
arrangements were frequent in the West Indies. Given the
stringency of English divorce laws, which required that di-
vorces could only be granted in England, it was both expensive and time consuming to legalize a marriage separation.
The union between Rachael and James Hamilton lasted for
fifteen years, and though it ended in separation, this was
probably due to the inability of the ne'er-do-well father to
provide for his family.[20] Alexander kept up a dutiful, if sporadic, correspondence with his father, and in later years the
son helped his unfortunate parent financially and even made
plans for the elder Hamilton to join him in America. These
never materialized, and James Hamilton died in St. Vincent
in 1799.[21] James Lytton, Rachael's brother-in-law, was a
prosperous and respected planter on St. Croix, and he seems
to have been genuinely attached to the little family. Had his
own fortunes not deteriorated it seems certain that he would
have aided them substantially. Peter Lytton, his son, became
the legal guardian of Rachael's two sons at her death.[22]

Alexander probably served a business apprenticeship in his
mother's shop in Christiansted. He was a slender, almost frail
youngster, but he had inherited the good looks and attractive
personality of his mother and grandmother. From time to
time he submitted poems and essays for publication in the
local paper, including his account of the hurricane of 1772.
The promptness with which the local gentry subscribed to
the fund for young Hamilton's education suggests that he was
regarded as a young man of great promise.

King's College

Hamilton landed in Boston in October of 1772. This "hotbed of the American Revolution" was comparatively quiet. The public indignation generated by the Boston "Massacre" of 1770 had cooled, and, indeed, Samuel Adams, the incendiary leader of the local Sons of Liberty, was in despair. Times were prosperous, and the British government was so perverse as to do nothing that would arouse the colonial radicals. To a professional revolutionary like Sam Adams this was highly frustrating.

Hamilton continued to New York, his ultimate destination, and arrived about the first of November. Here he went to the mercantile firm of Lawrence Kortwright, a New York friend of Nicholas Cruger, through whom Alexander's expenses were to be paid. He was turned over to Hercules Mulligan, a brother of one of Kortwright's partners, and thus he became acquainted with the colorful Irishman who was later to become a part of General Washington's espionage system in New York during the war.[23]

It was evident that Hamilton would need to correct some deficiencies, notably in Latin and Greek, before he attempted college. He therefore became a pupil at Tappan Reeve's famous academy in Elizabethtown, New Jersey. His teacher was Francis Barber who held both bachelor's and master's degrees from Princeton. This brilliant young scholar was a major influence on Hamilton's first formal education. He and Barber became close friends and the latter had a distinguished career in the War of Independence.[24]

Like Jefferson, Hamilton moved in a circle of distinguished men who must have had a salutary influence on the development of his ideas. William Livingston, a leader of the Revolutionary movement in New Jersey and still later a member of the Constitutional Convention of 1787, had already delivered polemic shots at Tories, the Church of England, and the royal governor in the New York press. Elias Boudinot was well known in New Jersey as a distinguished lawyer, patron of education, and man of liberal views.[25]

Hamilton worked prodigiously at his studies, and at the end of a year he announced that he was ready for college. His friend Hercules Mulligan accompanied him to Princeton and introduced him to President John Witherspoon. After examining the young candidate, Dr. Witherspoon pronounced him acceptable, whereupon Hamilton made the unusual request that he "be permitted to advance from Class to Class with as much rapidity as his exertions would enable him to do." Here, indeed, was a young man in a hurry. Two weeks later Alexander was informed that the trustees of the college had refused his request.[26]

Shortly afterward, in the fall of 1773, Hamilton enrolled at King's College in New York, probably as a "private" student since his name does not appear on the official list of admissions until the academic year 1774–75. He had no special kind of education in mind and appears to have been chiefly interested in anatomy and mathematics. He pursued his studies with the intensity which was becoming characteristic of him but found time to form a circle of friends that included Ned Stevens, a boyhood friend from the West Indies, Robert Troup, and Henry Nicoll. These formed a sort of seminar for the improvement of writing and debating, and much of their discussion centered on the growing colonial resistance to Parliament's Tea Act which, in its turn, inspired the famous Boston Tea Party in December, 1773.

It is not certain exactly when Hamilton began writing newspaper pieces for the radical cause since such articles were usually anonymous. His earliest known effort was a pamphlet titled *A Full Vindication of the Measures of the Congress* (the

First Continental Congress which met in the fall of 1774), and it was dated December 15, 1774. By this time Hamilton had already delivered a rousing speech at a gathering of Whigs in "The Fields" (City Hall Park) in July, 1774. The famous New York radical Alexander McDougall presided, and the youthful speaker urged resistance to the Intolerable Acts, striking a nationalistic note which was to be a Hamilton hallmark. "Our brethren . . . ," he said, "are now suffering in the common cause of these Colonies." [27] Hamilton never graduated from King's, but he had become an accomplished revolutionary.

History has a way of dealing with men, of making them appear to be pawns of a larger destiny. The question whether great men make great events of history or whether there are only great challenges which ordinary men are called upon to meet is an ancient and unresolved argument. But one would hesitate to predict that ordinary times would have created in Alexander Hamilton a talent for political philosophy or made Thomas Jefferson a man of action.

II The Young Rebels*

THE STAMP ACT and its aftermath is a well-known episode in the history of the American Revolution, and justly so, for it represented the first real resistance by the colonists to British authority. It is true that James Otis had made an eloquent protest over the writs of assistance, or general search warrants, which had been issued in 1760, and there had been some grumbling over the Revenue Act of 1764, sometimes called the Sugar Act. But the Stamp Act was important in that it raised the constitutional question embodied in that famous phrase, "taxation without representation is tyranny!" The opposition first voiced by Patrick Henry was echoed throughout the colonies and even provoked the calling of an inter-colonial Stamp Act Congress. Boycotts were invoked against goods imported from England, and underground groups styling themselves the Sons of Liberty made their initial appearance. Both the nature of the opposition and the unanimity with which it was voiced were unprecedented in the imperial relationship between Britain and her American colonies.

The Stamp Act was no casual whim of its author George Grenville, who became head of the Cabinet in 1763. Grenville

* For this chapter see especially Edward S. Morgan, *The Birth of the Republic, 1763–1789;* and Merrill Jensen, *The Founding of a Nation.*

14

is not one of the great names in the history of British statesmanship, but neither was he the oafish tyrant depicted so often in American history books of an earlier time. He took office at the end of the Seven Years' War, the climax of a series of conflicts which made Britain a colossus among the powers of Europe. But the victory had been expensive. Britain staggered under a burden of debt whose annual interest was more than the combined indebtedness of all the thirteen colonies.

Grenville was a fairly capable administrator, and when he examined the situation of the American colonies, he found to his dismay that their administrative cost was about four times greater than the income derived from them. Moreover, the home government had reimbursed the colonies for the expenses they had incurred during the recent war. To Grenville it seemed only logical that the colonies should pay their own way. He sought advice from Benjamin Franklin, then acting as a colonial agent in England, as well as from some of the royal governors. After due deliberation, he recommended, and Parliament passed, the Stamp Act. The storm of protest which it aroused bewildered him as well as others on both sides of the Atlantic. In fact, Jefferson's fellow Virginian and sometime revolutionary Richard Henry Lee solicited the aid of Dr. Franklin to secure his appointment as a stamp master, a request which was hastily withdrawn.

In considering the course of the Revolutionary movement, it should be noted that at no time, either in the imposition of the Stamp Act or in subsequent efforts, did Parliament attempt to raise revenue for any purpose except to defray the cost of colonial administration. Nor should it be forgotten that the colonies and their attendant problems were comparatively insignificant within the framework of British politics of the 1760's. When the Stamp Act was voted in the House of Commons, there was only token opposition—although

Isaac Barre significantly noted that Parliament should beware of offending "those sons of liberty" in America. Colonial radicals always seized upon such expressions of sympathy in the belief that they were indicative of widespread support for their cause in the homeland. In this they were greatly mistaken. In short, it was indifference as much as tyranny that lost Britain her thirteen American colonies.

At the time of the Stamp Act crisis there was no thought of separation from Great Britain. Such an idea would have horrified even a radical like Patrick Henry, not only in 1765 but for some years to come. When men talked about "liberty" and "freedom," they were voicing what they considered to be their rights as British citizens. They felt that these rights were as fully protected by legal and historical precedent as if they were residents of England. But their allegiance was to the Crown, not to Parliament. The legal point they raised in 1765, and subsequently, was that since they were not represented in Parliament it had no legislative authority over them. They could only be taxed by their colonial assembly, over whose members they could exercise direct control at election time.

When Parliament, responding to colonial pressure, repealed the Stamp Act in 1766, it passed the Declaratory Act which insisted on Parliament's own legislative supremacy. Thus it rejected the colonial concept of their federal relationship to the imperial government of Great Britian. The failure to resolve this problem was at the root of the final separation from Britain. It should be noted that the federal problem did not end with American independence.

Lawyer and Planter

It took Thomas Jefferson an unusually long time to become a lawyer. He began his studies under George Wythe in 1762 and was not examined for admission to the bar until 1767. It may be that Wythe was so demanding of his young assistant that Jefferson's own study was delayed. "I always was of the opinion," Jefferson wrote later, "that the placing of a youth to study with an attorney was rather a prejudice than a help. We are all too apt by shifting on them our business, to encroach on that time which should be devoted to their studies. The only help youth wants is direction." [1] Undoubtedly Jefferson studied much more than the law, and he was also spending a good deal of time at Shadwell. He was the head of a family which consisted of his mother, three sisters, and a brother. Most of all, Jefferson was predominately a farmer rather than a lawyer, and in 1766 he began his *Garden Book* which along with the *Farm Book* became as detailed a record of his farming as a ship captain's log of a sea voyage.

These and other intimate and meticulous records expose his personal life in a way that could never be learned otherwise. His account of his daily expenses shows that he loved the curiosities of traveling magicians and animal exhibitions as much as the theatre. He tells us that he laid aside his violin after the Revolution, but his account book shows continued purchases of strings for many years thereafter. A refracting telescope, a backgammon board, eighty-nine bottles of wine "carried off or broke," admission charge to a puppet show, a fine mare, powder for his servant Jupiter's wig—in short, a bewildering array of interests and fancies.[2]

At about the time he began to practice law, Jefferson also started plans for his own home. The site of Monticello was located, as the name indicated, on a small mountaintop which was part of Peter Jefferson's original holding. The visitor of today can readily see why Jefferson was attracted to it. The rolling hills of the Virginia Piedmont fall away to the Tidewater to the east, and to the west rises the blue and purple wall of the Blue Ridge. The move was hastened by the destruction of Shadwell by fire in 1770. Although no one was injured, all of Jefferson's personal papers and books were destroyed, a loss which he felt keenly. By the fall of 1770 he had moved into a single room at Monticello which was later referred to as the "southeast pavillion." [3] The construction of Monticello was to take years and was a constant and delightful preoccupation for much of Jefferson's lifetime.

It was to this crude beginning of a home that Jefferson finally brought a bride in the winter of 1772. It was unusual for a man to be twenty-eight years old and still a bachelor, but Jefferson seems to have had only one serious affair before this. When a young student of twenty-one, he thought of marrying Rebecca Burwell, but he was so "abominably indolent" that the young lady accepted another proposal.[4]

Jefferson first met Martha Skelton in Williamsburg in 1770. She was the widowed daughter of John Wayles and Martha Eppes and some five years younger than Jefferson. He was a frequent visitor at The Forest, the Wayles' home, for more than a year. His marriage took place on New Year's Day, 1772, and the following September their first child, also named Martha, was born. Although the press of events in the years that followed often kept him from his family, there is no doubt that Jefferson and his pretty, sprightly wife formed a deep love affair that lasted until her untimely death in 1782.[5]

The Townshend Acts

At the time of his marriage Jefferson had already assumed those public duties which were expected of a leading citizen. He was a justice of the peace, a member of the county court, and chief militia officer of Albemarle County, this position entitling him to be called "colonel." The death of his friend Francis Fauquier and the appointment of a new governor Lord Botetourt necessitated the election of new burgesses in

December, 1768. Jefferson was chosen a delegate from Albemarle, and mid-spring, 1769, found him in Williamsburg to attend to the odds and ends of his law practice before the opening of the legislative session.

It was a notable gathering which Jefferson joined. Patrick Henry was back from Hanover, as were older and more dignified members like President Peyton Randolph, Robert Carter Nicholas, treasurer of the colony, and Richard Bland, the noted constitutional scholar whom Jefferson described as looking like an old parchment. He also probably met for the first time the big, dignified man from Fairfax, George Washington.

Jefferson himself, at two inches over six feet, was probably as tall as any of the members. His hair was reddish above hazel eyes and an upturned nose and his slender figure moved diffidently among his friends and acquaintances. He was not a handsome man but very likeable, although inclined to a certain shyness with strangers.[6]

The new session of the assembly was not an auspicious occasion for the newly arrived governor Norborne Berkeley, Lord Botetourt. The British government was still trying to solve the problem of raising colonial revenue, and the best it could do was a series of duties on lead, paper, glass, tea, and other imports from Britain. Collectively known as the Townshend Acts, after the cynical and bibulous chancellor of the exchequer, they had been enacted by Parliament in 1767. Now, two years later, they were no more acceptable to the colonies than the Stamp Act. Massachusetts had issued a circular letter, calling on the colonies to unite in resisting them. In New York a factional fight between the radicals and the more conservative Whig property owners and merchants had resulted in a defeat for the radicals and had driven one of their leaders William Livingston into temporary retirement in New Jersey where he became the mentor of young

Alexander Hamilton. In Virginia the General Court had defied the Crown by refusing writs of assistance to Attorney-General John Randolph and persisted in its refusal even after Randolph confronted them with an affirmative opinion of their legality from the Lord Chief Justice of England himself. The writs of assistance were general search warrants authorized for the enforcement of the Townshend Acts, and they aroused almost as much opposition as the duties themselves.[7]

Peyton Randolph had already sent an encouraging letter to Boston acknowledging receipt of the Massachusetts Circular Letter. Lord Botetourt, an amiable gentleman for whom Virginians never lost their liking, was probably not surprised at the Assembly's action. That body reiterated its statement of the previous year when it had declared that its members were "the sole constitutional representatives of His Majesty's most dutiful and loyal subjects, the people of Virginia." [8] Governor Botetourt, acting under instructions, dissolved the assembly and ordered new elections. The members promptly adjourned to the Apollo Room of the Raleigh Tavern and drew up Articles of Association—the first document of this sort that Jefferson ever signed. The Association was a pledge to support nonimportation and nonconsumption of a long list of British goods until Parliament should repeal the Townshend duties.[9] Similar resolutions were passed in other colonies, but unlike the economic pressure of the Stamp Act boycotts, they had little effect. When the Townshend Acts were repealed in 1770, it was primarily because they had not been successful in raising the anticipated amount of revenue. Parliament retained the tax on tea as a face-saving measure to affirm its legislative authority.

Thus, Jefferson's first session as a legislator lasted exactly ten days. However, when the new elections were held and the Burgesses reconvened in the fall of 1769 with their membership practically unchanged, they received an announcement from the governor that Parliament intended to repeal the obnoxious duties. Nothing was said about tea. In the summer of 1770 Jefferson signed another Association agreement, this one supposedly strengthened by the creation of local committees who were to investigate violators and "publish an account of their conduct." [10] This seems to have had little effect, but the news that Parliament had indeed repealed the Townshend Acts gave the colonies a distinct feeling that they had won another round in their struggle for local prerogative.

Jefferson became more absorbed in his law practice, and the work at Shadwell and Monticello claimed much of his attention. The death of Lord Botetourt in October, 1770, was sincerely mourned by Virginians, but the arrival of his successor Lord Dunmore in the fall of 1771 occasioned only routine notice. The new prime minister in England, Lord North, appeared to be following a policy of drift, and the cause of radicalism in America sank into apathy. Jefferson, apparently absorbed in wedded bliss, did not attend the legislative session of 1772.[11]

The Dispute Over Tea

During most of 1773 Governor Dunmore kept the Assembly prorogued, thinking perhaps to spare himself from its contentiousness. He seems to have had a full measure of the haughtiness and arrogance of a Scottish peer, with and none of the amiability and charm which had been the saving grace of Fauquier and Botetourt. A brief session in the spring of 1773 to deal with counterfeiting of the colonial currency produced a few resolutions, but the governor "thought them so insignificant that I took no notice of them." [12] One of these created a standing committee of correspondence of which Jefferson was a member. He and several other young burgesses had planned the passage of the resolution at the Ra-

leigh Tavern. Although it was worded innocuously, its purpose was to pave the way for an intercolonial information
service such as Sam Adams had already created in Massachusetts.[13] The colonial press had proven to be something less
than satisfactory as a means of disseminating reliable information and virtually useless in coordinating Whig strategy.
The committees of correspondence, it was hoped, would answer these needs. If the governor thought this "so insignificant," Massachusetts and the other colonies did not. The
Boston committee ordered three hundred copies of the Virginia resolutions printed, and by the end of the year only
three colonies had failed to follow the example of Virginia
and Massachusetts in organizing committees.[14]

By the time the delegates reconvened in Williamsburg in
the spring of 1774, the whole complexion of the Revolutionary movement had changed and Sam Adams was back in
business. Parliament had passed the East India Company
Act, more familiarly known as the "Tea Act," which was
designed to accomplish a double purpose. The East India
Company, a giant corporation through which Britain controlled vast territories and resources in India, had fallen on
evil times. The Tea Act conferred upon it an exclusive and
direct monopoly of the sale of tea in the colonies. It also
reduced the tax so that the company could undersell even the
illegal tea smuggled from Holland. Thus, Lord North hoped
that the East India Company could be helped and that revenues from the sale of tea would increase the income from the
colonies.

It should be noted that the Tea Act was a minor bill which
was submerged in the much larger struggle for Parliamentary
control of the East India Company, and its passage provoked
little discussion. But American merchants professed themselves aghast at this encroachment on the spirit of free enterprise. They were supported by popular leaders who saw in

the act a renewed attempt to assert Parliamentary authority. After all, tea was the coffee and Coke of eighteenth-century America, and people at all levels of society were drawn into the controversy. Quickly the word went out through the committees of correspondence that every effort was to be made to block the landing and sale of tea consignments. In Boston Sam Adams directed the Sons of Liberty in a raid which was made famous in history as the "Boston Tea Party." In Philadelphia the Whigs warned the captain of the tea ship that they would "heave him keel, and see that his bottom was well-fired," and in Baltimore the tea ship *Peggy Stewart* was burned to the water line.[15]

But American indignation over the Tea Act was nothing compared with the rude shock of the home government's retaliation. This took the form of four acts of Parliament, collectively called the Intolerable or Coercive Acts. The Boston Port Bill closed down all shipping into the city until the tea was paid for. The Massachusetts Government Act and the Administration of Justice Act, respectively, concentrated governmental powers of the colony in the hands of the governor and altered procedures for change of venue which allowed accused persons to be tried outside the colony. The Quartering Act allowed commanders to take over private buildings to use as barracks for their troops.[16]

It was against a background of furious indignation aroused by the Coercive Acts that Jefferson joined the other delegates in Williamsburg in the spring of 1774, at which time the House of Burgesses resolved to declare a day of fasting and prayer to demonstrate their sympathy for Massachusetts. Governor Dunmore promptly dissolved the Assembly, and Jefferson and his fellow Whigs just as promptly signed another Association agreement and directed the committee of correspondence to join in the general call for an intercolonial congress.[17]

A Summary View

During the remainder of the summer, Governor Dunmore was off to the west fighting Indians in a little war which history has named for him. His absence made it impossible for the legislature to meet, but it also allowed a gathering of Whigs in the capital in August, 1774, to send representatives to the proposed colonial Congress. Delegates to the Williamsburg "convention" had been chosen and instructed by meetings of freeholders in the counties. Jefferson was elected by the Albemarle voters and had prepared a set of resolutions which he hoped to present to the Virginia convention for approval as the basis for their instructions to the Congress. But a violent attack of dysentery laid him low and prevented his arrival at Williamsburg. He forwarded the resolutions to Peyton Randolph, the presiding officer, but the convention never acted upon them. Nevertheless, someone among the radicals had them printed under the title of *A Summary View of the Rights of British America.*[18]

The invalid author immediately became famous throughout the colonies. The *Summary View* received wider attention than any revolutionary writing of Jefferson except the Declaration of Independence. One reason for this was the fact that the radicals among the Whigs badly needed a spokesman since most of the views expressed in the resolutions, circular letters, and the like expressed the views of the moderates. These latter firmly believed in the injustice of specific acts of Parliament such as the Stamp Act and the Coercive Acts. But they insisted that the political structure of the empire must provide for a supreme legislature. Jefferson denied this.

> The inhabitants of the several states of British America are subject to the laws which they adopted at their first settlement, and to such others as have been since made

by their respective Legislatures duly constituted and appointed with their own consent. That no other Legislature whatever may rightfully exercise authority over them, and that these privileges they hold as the common rights of mankind. . . .[19]

Thus read the "Resolutions of the Freeholders of Albemarle County." Jefferson probably intended this as an introduction to the detailed *Summary View,* which itself declared that "the British Parliament have no right to exercise authority over us."

Nor did Jefferson confine himself to attacking Parliament. He included the King in his detailed history of usurpations, charging him with unwarranted vetoes of colonial acts, use of troops, dissolution of legislatures, and so on, for more than one-third of the document. This was boldness indeed. Even the radicals had hesitated to attack George III, for it was their loyalty to the Crown that bound them to the empire. To denounce the King was to skirt the edge of treason, and Whig opinion, particularly moderate opinion, was not yet ready to close the door to conciliation.[20] Jefferson was ahead of his time—but only by two years.

The Student Radical

"Perhaps before long, your tables, and chairs, and platters, and dishes, and knives and forks, and everything else would be taxed. Nay, I don't know but what they would find means to tax you for every child you got, and for every kiss your daughters received from their sweethearts, and God knows, that would ruin you." [21] Young Alexander Hamilton thus combined rhetoric and broad humor in his first public effort against the Tory opposition. The time was December, 1774, and Hamilton was halfway through his second year at King's

College. The occasion for the pamphlet was to defend the work of the First Continental Congress, which had met at Philadelphia the previous autumn to determine what was to be done about the situation of the colonies in general and the Coercive Acts in particular.

The opposition to the Tea Act would have aroused considerable ire in England in any event, but the "Boston Tea Party" had damned Massachusetts completely. Not only had British authority been flouted, but property had been destroyed. Even the most ardent friends of America were dismayed by the rashness of the Sons of Liberty. "Sanctity of property" was no idle phrase either in England or in America.

In the historical context of the late nineteenth and early twentieth centuries, when "private property" sometimes had an illiberal connotation and "propertied interests" were considered inimical to popular rights, it may have been forgotten that the philosophers of the Enlightenment linked property with the other basic human rights. John Locke spoke of "life, liberty, *and* property," and he considered that each was necessary to the enjoyment of the other two.[22] American moderates who had supported the Whig cause up to now were apprehensive over such displays of violence as the Boston Tea Party.

The closing of the port of Boston was the severest treatment yet meted out by the home government. Yet it is indicative of the strength of Tory and moderate Whig sentiment that Boston's call for another economic association met with considerable apathy even in Massachusetts. Only when the news of the other Coercive Acts arrived did the Whig resistance movement begin to gain ground.

The severity of the Coercive Acts was a shock to the colonies. After all, defiance to the home government for over a decade had been marked by a succession of retreats. Even acts of violence like the burning of the *Gaspée* in 1772 had attracted only passing notice in England. What the colonies failed to realize was that, after years of frustrating effort, George III had finally constructed a political organization which would do his bidding. The ministry of Lord North was now able to give some attention to the American colonial problem, and it controlled a sufficient majority in the House of Commons to put its policies into effect. It was this abrupt demonstration of purpose that shocked the colonies, not into submission, but to a determination and unity which they otherwise might never have attained.[23]

The occasion of Hamilton's first public speech at "The Fields" was an attempt of the New York radicals to gain support for Virginia's call for a congress. Alexander McDougall and Isaac Sears used different techniques from those of the Virginia leaders. A city of more than 20,000 people could provide a crowd to listen to passionate oratory or be fired to mob action. Hamilton's speech to the assembled crowd was extemporaneous, sparked by youthful enthusiasm and impetuosity. It was probably not a very good speech, but the good-humored crowd applauded and the Whig leaders welcomed him to the radical ranks. In rural Virginia the radicals moved in a more sedate and dignified manner. Thus, while McDougall insisted that the delegates to Congress must be chosen at a mass meeting of the "mechanics" of New York, Peyton Randolph, lately speaker of the House of Burgesses, presided over a decorous convention at Williamsburg whose members had been elected in the counties.[24]

The First Continental Congress met in the fall of 1774. Its membership was almost evenly split between moderates and radicals, and its work may seem insignificant compared to its successor's. It addressed a petition to the King, but it also enacted resolutions for nonimportation, nonexportation and nonconsumption of British goods, and it set up a Continental Association of committees for their enforcement. Finally, it voted to meet again within a year to determine what further measures should be taken. The First Continental Congress was a milestone in the revolutionary movement because for the first time most American leaders agreed to a single policy-making body. Its existence had no legal sanction, but in effect, it legislated, it set up a machinery of enforcement, and it provided for its own continuity. In a limited way its members had set up a governmental body which rivalled that of Parliament.[25]

The Young Propagandist

Alexander Hamilton's first active part in the Revolution was as the author of several tracts in the newspaper war between Whigs and Tories. This was the first revolution in history in which newspaper propaganda played a major role, and the Whigs dominated the colonial press. Hamilton's *A Full Vindication of the Measures of Congress* (1774) was prompted by a condemnation of that body which appeared under the signature of "A Westchester Farmer." The author was no farmer but an Anglican missionary and physician named Samuel Seabury who was one of the most effective of the Tory pamphleteers.

Seabury noted that the measures adopted by the Continental Congress were an attempt at commercial blackmail designed to coerce Britain. Not only would Britain retaliate by enacting ruinous duties against the colonies and enforcing them with her fleet, said Seabury, but she would find other sources to replace American products. The idea that the colonies could coerce the mother country was ridiculous. He denounced the Association as a scheme of the merchants to restrict the market and raise prices.

"The Farmer" then struck two shrewd blows at the Whig action. He pointed out that the Congress had not taken "one step that tended toward peace." Radicals like Jefferson and Adams were always fearful of losing the support of moderate Whigs, who wanted justice but within the framework of the empire. Their innate loyalty to the Crown made the moderates shy away from independence. "The Farmer" charged that the belligerent action of the Congress was closing off the possibility of reconciliation. "If I must be enslaved," he exhorted, "let it be by a King at least, not by a parcel of lawless, upstart Committee-men." [26] Finally he pointed out that the real victims would be the farmers, for it was their crops which would be restricted by nonexportation. He thus appealed to the overwhelmingly rural population who, he said, were being victimized by the urban rabble.

Hamilton at once assailed "The Farmer" for evading the principal issue: "Whether we shall preserve that security to our lives and properties, which the law of nature, the genius of the British Constitution, and our charters afford us." The Tea Act, the original cause of the present crisis, represented the crux of the matter, "and that principle is . . . [Parliament's] *right to tax us in all cases whatsoever.*" [27]

To the charge that Congress had gone too far in its actions, the young pamphleteer noted, "What petitions can we offer that have not been offered? The right of America and the injustice of Parliamentary pretensions have been repeatedly stated, both in and out of Parliament." Far from inviting a conflict, Congress had "no resource but in a restriction of our trade, or in a resistance *vi et armis.* Our Congress, therefore, have imposed what restraint they thought necessary." [28]

Hamilton published another pamphlet, *The Farmer Refuted,* in the latter part of February, 1775. It was a long, turgid, and rambling polemic which occupies eighty-four pages in Syrett's *Papers,* but it contains some interesting points. Hamilton deals here with the idea that the colonies' tie to Britain was through the Crown "by virtue of a compact

between us and the kings of Great Britain . . . and it is from
these covenants [colonial charters] that the duty of protection
on their part, and the duty of allegiance on ours, arise." [29]

It is also interesting, in the light of Hamilton's later national outlook, that there is scarcely a reference to New York,
but a constant use of "America," "the American continent,"
and one enthusiastic reference to "the boundless extent of
territory we possess . . . the luxuriance and fertility of our
soil, the variety of our products, the rapidity [of the growth]
of our population, the industry of our country men and the
commodiousness of our ports." [30]

The Farmer Refuted is also replete with quotations from
Blackstone, Hume, and the economist Postlethwayt (along
with some far-fetched historical analogies) indicating that the
propagandist had not completely submerged the student.

Hamilton's vehement eloquence in the Whig cause belied
his academic surroundings, for King's and its president Dr.
Myles Cooper held strong Tory views. Two incidents in the
spring of 1775 may have had an influence on Hamilton's later
aversion to mob violence. He somehow learned that the local
Sons of Liberty planned a march on Dr. Cooper's home.
Accompanied by his young friend Robert Troup, he hurried
to warn Dr. Cooper and helped the venerable clergyman to
escape just as the mob appeared. [31]

Sometime later another mob attacked the newspaper office
of James Rivington, one of the few Tory editors in New York.
His press was destroyed and Rivington himself was finally
forced to flee to England. Hamilton deplored "such commo-
tion as the present" although he seems to have been concerned more about the fact that the action was taken by the
local Liberty boys instead of under the direction of Congress.
But he instinctively felt that despite the need to suppress
Rivington, "yet I cannot help condemning this step." [32]

By the early part of 1775, the student and the writer had

become part-time soldier. Tension between England and the colonies mounted and finally exploded in the battles at Lexington and Concord in mid–April, 1775. New York began to make preparations in anticipation of the outbreak of hostilities. Hamilton and several of his friends, including Hercules Mulligan, began drilling with a military company under Major Edward Fleming. The group eventually was incorporated into an artillery company and Hamilton obtained an appointment as captain in the New York militia, thanks to the influence of his friend Colonel Alexander McDougall.[33]

So far as can be determined Hamilton and his gunners saw no action and performed only routine duty, although it seems clear that he trained his men well and earned a reputation as a diligent and responsible officer. By the spring of 1776 the twenty-year-old captain had abandoned his studies at King's. The war had been going on for more than a year although the fighting had been sporadic. The colonies were frantically organizing their citizen army under the command of George Washington, and Great Britain was slowly mobilizing its ponderous war machine to crush the American "rabble in arms."

We call the young men of the Revolution the Founding Fathers, thereby paying deference to the grandeur of their accomplishment and a wisdom which we associate with ancient statesmen. Or it may be that the traditional paintings, like John Trumbull's "Declaration of Independence," have created in our mind's eye a picture of elderly philosophers hoary with age and responsibility.

But revolutions are the business of young men, for they require energy and youthful idealism and a certain recklessness that is willing to gamble with such stakes as "lives . . . fortunes, and . . . sacred honor." George Washington was a patriarchial forty-four years old when he took command of the American army. Nathanael Greene was thirty-four when he was commissioned a major general. John Hancock was thirty-nine when he signed the Declaration of Independence. Thomas Jefferson was thirty-three when he wrote it. Alexander Hamilton went to war when he was twenty-one.

III "We Hold These Truths..."*

THE AMERICAN RADICALS were rapidly approaching the point of no return. The severity of the Coercive Acts appeared to strengthen both their determination and their unity. If George III had hoped to "divide and conquer" by aiming the acts principally at Massachusetts, the united front presented by the First Continental Congress might well have given him pause. The committees of correspondence did their work well, and Virginia, along with the rest, affirmed its unwavering support of New England's resistance.

In London Parliamentary leaders argued that the recalcitrant Americans must be brought into complete submission. For them there was no middle ground. There were many Americans who stubbornly resisted the movement toward independence, but they just as stubbornly refused to accept complete subjugation to Parliamentary will. They insisted that a way could be found to preserve their liberties within the framework of the British imperial system. In this group lay, perhaps, the salvation of the empire. But as the year 1775 began, events on both sides of the Atlantic made their position less and less tenable until at last they had to choose between America and England.

* For this chapter see especially Carl Becker, *The Declaration of Independence.*

The Second Continental Congress

An attack of dysentery, which had unheroically felled Jefferson in the late summer of 1774 and prevented him from being chosen to the First Continental Congress, subsided sufficiently to allow him to be elected to another Virginia Convention which met in Richmond in March, 1775. The move to the inland city, which eventually became the state capital, was doubtless dictated by the delegates' desire to avoid the fulminations of Governor Dunmore who was becoming increasingly belligerent in the face of the succession of illegal assemblies and their provocative resolutions.[1]

The meeting in Richmond went far to confirm the governor's fears. A resolution to put the colony "in a posture of defence," that is, to raise an armed force, was passed in the last week of March. In the debate over the resolution Patrick Henry gave his greatest performance. He swept the opposition aside with a furious denunciation which began, "Gentlemen cry peace, peace—when there is no peace," and ended with, "Give me liberty, or give me death!" It was just twenty-six days before the battle of Lexington. The ringing phrases so moved the reticient Jefferson that he himself rose to speak in Henry's support—a rare occasion indeed.[2]

On the following day the convention voted to suspend the courts of the colony and elected delegates to the second meeting of Congress. Jefferson was chosen as an alternate for Peyton Randolph who was not only burdened with the responsibility of presiding over the convention but was in poor health. Foreseeing a lengthy absence from Virginia, Jefferson went home to attend to the sale of his tobacco crops and order his other business affairs, which had not been going well and for which he never seemed to have enough time.[3] It was a harbinger of his whole life. Although he was an enthusiastic and skillful farmer, Jefferson's frequent absences from Monticello made it impossible for him either to be financially successful or to gratify his deep-rooted desire to cultivate his land. The year before he had laid out a garden on the southeast slope of Monticello. It was not completed until after he had retired from the presidency thirty-five years later.[4]

By June 1 Jefferson was back in Williamsburg, impatient to go on to Philadelphia. However Peyton Randolph had one more task for him. Governor Dunmore, in desperation, had reconvened the assembly at Williamsburg and presented to it a message from the ministry. The essence of Lord North's proposal was that those colonies which would provide the necessary revenue from their own resources would not be taxed by Parliament. The proposal was made in complete bad faith, for it still required the colonies to furnish revenue at the request of the mother country. But of greater consequence, it preceded two Restraining Acts which interdicted the trade of New England and five other colonies. When the proposal was discussed in Parliament, William Pitt had denounced it as "mere verbiage . . . puerile mockery," and predicted that it would "be spurned in America."[5]

The Virginia Assembly did just that, and Jefferson was chosen to draw up the necessary resolutions. He went, as usual, directly to the core of the problem. "To render perpetual our exemption from an unjust taxation, we must saddle ourselves with a perpetual tax adequate to the expectations and subject to the disposal of Parliament alone. . . . It is not merely the mode of raising, but the freedom of granting our Money for which we have contended." Jefferson also exposed the basic deceit of North's proposal. "At the very time of requiring from us grants of Money they are making disposition to invade us with large Armaments by Sea and land."[6] Behind the open profession of continued loyalty to the Crown, Jefferson clearly revealed his consciousness of an emerging American state. "We consider ourselves as bound in Honor as well as Interest to share one general Fate with our Sister Colonies, and should hold ourselves base Deserters of that Union, to which we have acceded, were we to agree to Measures distinct and apart from them." [7]

Jefferson did not wait for the passage of his resolutions but left for Philadelphia the day after the committee had completed its work. There he was welcomed by the other Virginia delegates, their enthusiasm perhaps enhanced by the fact that Jefferson brought part of their back pay.[8] He found Congress deep in the task of making preparations for armed resistance. Its members were well aware that the outbreak of fighting would do much to cement the union of the colonies. Fourteen thousand New England militia had swarmed to the vicinity of Boston following Lexington and Concord. In other colonies thousands of young men like Alexander Hamilton had joined "drill companies" of volunteers. At no time during the War of Independence was there such militant fervor as in the early summer of 1775.

Jefferson's colleague George Washington had been appointed to bring order out of this enthusiastic chaos, and the big Virginian departed for Boston a few days after Jefferson's arrival. Congress was careful as always to justify its actions, for if sympathy in England was ebbing, American support must be maintained. Jefferson was soon put to work as a member of a committee to draw up a statement explaining the reasons for America's armed resistance. He was well known as the author of the *Summary View,* but another committee member John Dickinson, leader of the moderate group in Congress, was even better known as the author of the *Letters from a Pennsylvania Farmer.* Jefferson drafted a set of resolutions and submitted it to the committee, but its members thought its tone too radical. Dickinson then completely reworked Jefferson's draft although many of his sentences and paragraphs were retained intact. The composite result was *The Declaration . . . of the Causes and Necessity for Taking Up Arms.* Dickinson's revisions actually did little to alter the forcefulness of Jefferson's draft but improved the language. Indeed its most eloquent appeal was in Dickinson's words: "Our cause is just. Our union is perfect. Our internal Resources are great. . . . [We are] with one Mind resolved to die Freeman rather than to live Slaves." [9]

If Jefferson's feelings were hurt, he probably recovered. His pen was soon at work again, this time in a committee to reply to Lord North's proposal. Since he had done the job for Virginia already, his colleagues Benjamin Franklin, Richard Henry Lee, and John Adams were glad to have him repeat the performance for Congress. His resolutions were approved on June 25.[10]

This may well have been the first episode in the long association between Jefferson and John Adams. Less radical and impetuous than his cousin Samuel, John nonetheless was impatient that Congress "declare themselves for or against something." The crusty New Englander was immediately drawn to Jefferson who was, he said, "a silent member of Congress," and thus a relief from many delegates who variously possessed "the vanity of the ape, the tameness of the ox, or the stupid servility of the ass." [11]

"Open and Avowed Rebellion . . ."

Congress adjourned on August 1, and Jefferson had a brief respite. He travelled to Richmond where he reported to the Virginia Convention and was reelected for the next session of Congress. In his absence Virginia had become an armed camp. The royal governor had retired to a British man-of-war in Hampton Roads and had issued blustering proclamations declaring martial law and attempting to recruit Loyalists.

One proclamation offered freedom to all slaves who would join his forces, and thus was the Earl of Dunmore damned forever in Virginia.

Jefferson's homecoming at Monticello was bleak. His infant daughter Jane died a few days after his arrival, and both his mother and daughter Martha were in poor health. A return trip to Philadelphia in September was saddened by the death of Peyton Randolph, and the ensuing weeks were not only marked by dull routine or inactivity but by an increasing anxiety for his family. "I have never received the scrip of a pen from any mortal in Virginia since I left it . . ." he wrote early in November. "If anything has happened, for god's sake let me know it." He was back at Monticello early in the new year where he found his daughter somewhat improved, but his mother's health steadily declining. Jane Jefferson died on the last day of March, 1776. Jefferson himself fell victim to one of those vicious migraine headaches which were to plague him throughout his life. Altogether he remained at Monticello for four months and did not return to Philadelphia until May, 1776.[12]

During this period several events took place which determined the course of the revolutionary movement. By November, 1775, the colonies received the news of the King's answer to the petition of Congress. George III had declared the colonies to be in a state of "open and avowed rebellion" and ordered "the suppression of such rebellion."[13] Parliament had followed in December with a sweeping Prohibitory Act which interdicted all American trade and declared that American ships and their cargoes were to be treated as if they "were the ships and effects of open enemies."[14] The effect of these events was crucial. It was now apparent that the position of moderates like Dickinson and Joseph Galloway was virtually hopeless. It was no longer possible for Americans to maintain their liberties within the framework of the Empire. The home government had said, in effect, "You must end all resistance and then we shall make a settlement on our terms." In short, if Americans wished to retain their liberties, the only road left open led to independence.

This argument was made with devastating effect by Thomas Paine in his pamphlet *Common Sense.* Paine directed his attack against the symbol of loyalty to Great Britain— George III. The king, he declared, was primarily responsible for the loss of American freedom. Paine minced no words: "the wretch, that with the pretended title of FATHER OF HIS PEOPLE can unfeelingly hear of their slaughter, and composedly sleep with their blood upon his soul." [15]

One hundred and twenty thousand copies of the pamphlet were circulated in the early part of 1776, one of which Jefferson received in February. More than any single piece of writing, *Common Sense* stirred popular sentiment for independence. Yet Congress delayed. When Jefferson returned to Philadelphia in mid-May, he found the members still hesitating despite the urgings of Richard Henry Lee, the Adamses, and Jefferson's old friend, George Wythe.[16] The reason for Congressional reluctance was that the delegates felt that, whatever might be their own best judgement, they could not act without instructions from home. It was also important to get as nearly a unanimous vote as possible. It must be borne in mind that, as in all revolutions, the revolutionaries were in the minority. It would be fatal if this minority failed to present a united front to the Tory opposition.

During the spring of 1776, then, the struggle for independence took place in the colonies. Radicals urged "rump" governments to issue specific instructions to their Congressional delegations. In March South Carolina led the way by giving its delegation authority to use its own judgement, and Georgia shortly afterward issued similar instructions. The North Carolina provincial congress was the first to direct its

members to "approve independence." On May 15 the Virginia Convention instructed its delegates "to propose . . . to
declare the United Colonies free and independent States." [17]

"The Second Day of July . . ."

A casual visitor to the meeting of Congress on the morning
of June 7 would have listened with boredom as the delegates
considered payment of damages to one Charles Walker whose
sloop had been seized by the Continental Navy; a South
Carolina resolution concerning the raising of troops; a
proposed investigation of defective powder sold to Congress. Then Richard Henry Lee offered a resolution that
"these United Colonies are, and of a right ought to be,
free and independent States." John Adams appropriately
seconded. The next morning Congress began the great debate.[18]

As June came to an end, "Every Post and every Day rolls
in upon Us. Independence like a Torrent." [19] John Dickinson
vainly attempted to stem the tide. Like many Americans, he
could not renounce his deep-rooted loyalty to Britain. In the
final debate in July he made a last eloquent plea, and although
he finally cast his lot with America, he could not bring himself to sign the Declaration of Independence.[20] On 2 July
twelve colonies voted approval of the Lee Resolution. John
Adams wrote his wife the next day, "The second day of July
1776 . . . ought to be solemnized with pomp and parade, and
illuminations from one end of this continent to the other from
this time forward forever more." [21] Americans have done just
that ever since—but on the wrong day.

Congress had foreseen the need for a statement justifying
the resolution for independence. On June 11 it had appointed
a committee consisting of Jefferson, John Adams, Dr. Franklin, Roger Sherman of Connecticut, and Robert Livingston

of New York. "The committee . . . desired me to do it," Jefferson tersely noted, "It was accordingly done and being approved by them, I reported it to the house on Friday the 28th of June when it was ordered to lie on the table." [22]

After the Lee Resolution had passed, Congress took up the debate on Jefferson's report. During the three days of discussion, Jefferson sat characteristically silent but writhing inwardly. He was self-consciously vain about his writing, and any suggested changes caused him a good deal of chagrin. His friend John Adams defended every word of the document, but Congress insisted on some deletions. His charge that George III had been responsible for the importation of slaves was struck, and the final paragraph was changed to paraphrase the Lee Resolution. But what emerged was the basic document as Jefferson had composed it. [23]

The heart of the Declaration is the second paragraph. Here Jefferson stated the distilled essence of the relationship of men to their government and the justification for America's separation from Britain. As Jefferson himself affirmed in later years, his intention was "not to find out new principles, or new arguments, never before thought of, not merely to say things which had never been said before; but to place before mankind the common sense of the subject . . . to be an expression of the American mind." But that single paragraph was grounded in a whole philosophy which had been shaped over more than a century. [24]

The Law of Nature

The Age of Reason or the Enlightenment began a revolution in scientific thinking and knowledge. This scientific spirit was perhaps best exemplified by the work of Sir Isaac Newton, not necessarily because he was the greatest of the thinkers of the period, but because he was the one most universally recognized and honored. His great reputation may also be explained by the fact that he dealt with light and gravity, two things with which people were most familiar and yet which were the most difficult to explain except as phenomena created by a divine being.

Newton's *Principia* was published in 1686. Here was explained, on a rational and scientific basis, the action of light passing through a prism, and the mathematical formula which revealed not only what caused an apple to fall from a tree but the force which positioned the planets in the heavens and indeed gave order to the whole universe. With the possible exception of Charles Darwin, no scientist in modern times has so caught the popular imagination as Newton. Not many people understood his intricate formula, and popular simplifications such as Benjamin Martin's *A Plain and Familiar Introduction to Newtonian Philosophy* and Count Algarotti's *Il Newtonianismo per le dame* far outsold the massive *Principia*.

The important thing was that Newton had seemingly opened the way to the secrets of the universe. Natural phenomena had previously been explained as mystic emanations of the Creator's divine purpose, impenetrable by the mind of man. The rational and logical explanations of Newton made it apparent that there were "natural laws" which governed the universe and that any intelligent man had only to observe them to comprehend a system for the world.

It required only a logical progression to conclude that if there were principles which governed the world of nature there must be other "laws," equally discernable, which governed the world of economics, government, and indeed the whole social order. In short, what the eighteenth century called "Newtonian philosophy" embraced not only the natural sciences but what the twentieth century calls the social sciences. Jefferson himself believed that there was no secret of the universe which could not be unlocked by the human mind.[25]

No problem was more intriguing to the philosophers of the Enlightenment than man's relationship to the government of his society. In medieval times this relationship was based on a conception of God as the supreme ruler, who made his will known to the Pope, who in turn revealed it to the various monarchs. The Reformation and the rise of nation-states had eliminated the papacy from this hierarchy so that kings ruled directly under the authority of God. Thus was established the "divine right of monarchy" in which the people are subject to the king and the king is accountable to God.

But the rational philosophers posed the question: what happens if a bad king becomes ruler? It is true that he will ultimately be punished by a just God, but this will come only at the final judgement. Surely a benevolent God did not intend that man must wait until Judgement Day to be relieved of the tyranny of an evil despot. Seventeenth-century thinkers believed that there was an instrument through which God's will could be known, and this was man's reason. (If one rejected the existence of God, as many *philosophes* did, then it was "nature" which was the source of reason; Jefferson paid deference to both beliefs by using the phrase "the laws of nature and nature's God.") Refining their thinking still further, they concluded that there existed a compact between the king and the people, the one to protect his subjects and the other to be obedient. But there was another compact between God on the one hand and the king and the people on the other. Under this compact the people had a covenant to see to it that the king ruled righteously according to God's will and to resist the king if he did not. How did they know when the king had broken his covenant? Through reason, which was the God-given guide to natural law *(We hold these truths to be self-evident . . .)*

The Right of Revolution

Jefferson and his colleagues were thoroughly conversant with these ideas through their absorption in the "elementary books of public right, as Aristotle, Cicero, Locke, Sidney, etc." [26] Locke in particular was of interest to the Americans because he had formulated his natural rights doctrine to justify the Glorious Revolution of 1688. It should perhaps be noted that the French *philosophes* did not take up the idea of political "natural law" until well into the eighteenth century. Certainly Jefferson read Voltaire and Rousseau, but his revolutionary ideas were traditonally English in origin.

In his *Treatise of Civil Government* Locke postulated a theoretical state of nature in which men, possessed of equal God-given rights, are guided by natural law and so are free from compulsion. The only law is the law of reason. *(". . . that all men are created equal, that they are endowed by their Creator with certain unalienable Rights, that among these are Life, Liberty and the pursuit of happiness.")* In reality, however, there are always evil men who will try to destroy the rights of the rest. This creates an intolerable situation since each man must be constantly alert to protect his life and his possessions. It is therefore decided that a few men will be appointed to watch over the interests of all. Thus, "one divests himself of his liberty, and puts on the bonds of civil society, . . . by agreeing with other men to join and unite into a community for their comfortable, safe, and peaceable living." [27] It follows that "there wants an established, settled, known law, received and allowed by common consent to be the standard of right and wrong." [28] *("That to secure these rights, Governments are instituted among men, deriving their just powers from the consent of the governed.")*

In essence, then, the colonies had been living under the kind of government which Locke had described. It was a government of laws and rested upon the consent of the governed. When "a single person or prince sets up his own arbitrary will in place of the laws which are the will of the society" [29] the governed may call him to account, as Charles I and James II could attest. *(. . . whenever any Form of Government becomes destructive of these ends, it is the Right of the People to alter or abolish it.)*

Of what, then, were the colonists complaining? How did they justify their separation from the Empire?

At the time of the Stamp Act the colonists had objected to "taxation without representation." Did this mean that Parliament could legislate in other areas? The colonists had undoubtedly accepted Parliamentary legislation since 1607 and had even agreed to acts which involved the payment of a duty. For a time the colonists attempted to distinguish between "external" and "internal" taxes which were for the purpose of raising revenue. These latter, they maintained, could only be levied by their own colonial legislatures in which they were represented. This argument was swept away by "Champagne Charley" Townshend's duties on colonial imports.

More to the point was the insistence by the Tories that the colonies were indeed represented. An English member of Parliament considered that he represented not only the district from which he had been elected but the whole Empire, including the American colonies. This "virtual representation" was in sharp contrast to the colonial notion that a "representative" must be a resident of the district from which he came and should speak and vote for the people of that district, even against his own best judgement. Witness the reluctance of members of Congress to vote for the Lee Resolution until they had received specific instructions. Here is provided an example of what is basic to an understanding of the revolution. Though Englishmen and Americans spoke the same language, the words had different meanings. English institutions transplanted to the New World environment became distinctly American. The gap between New York and London was more than 2,500 miles of ocean. In short, by 1776 many colonists were thinking of themselves more as Americans than as Englishmen. And it was to this intuitive conclusion that their reasoning led them.

Dr. Benjamin Franklin, that venerable observer of the human race, was slow to express his view, but he went to the heart of the matter when he concluded in 1768 that "no middle ground can be maintained. . . . Parliament has a power to make *all laws* for us, or it has a power to make *no laws* for us." By 1770 he had made up his mind. "That the colonies originally were constituted distinct States, and intended to be continued as such is clear to me. . . . Parliament has usurped an authority of making laws." [30] Hamilton stated the point with precision five years later when he noted that there existed only a "compact between us and the kings of Great Britain." [31]

It is obvious why the Whig moderates, in professing loyalty to the Crown, aimed their shots at Parliament. It is equally obvious why Thomas Paine and Thomas Jefferson, in presenting the case for independence, attacked George III. He represented the only legal tie with the Empire, the only party to the compact as the colonies conceived it. To dissolve the compact it was only necessary to discredit the King, to convict him of the charge of tyranny. *(The history of the present King of Great Britain is a history of repeated injuries and usurpations, all having in direct object the establishment of an absolute Tyranny over these States.)*

"Prudence, indeed, will dictate," wrote Jefferson, "that Governments long established should not be changed for light and transient causes. . . . But when a long train of abuses and usurpations . . . evinces a design to reduce them under an absolute Despotism, it is their right, it is their duty, to throw off such government. . . . To prove this, let the facts be submitted to a candid world."

Jefferson then presented "the facts," twenty-eight charges against the King: George III "has plundered our seas, ravaged our coasts, burnt our towns, and destroyed the lives of our people. He is at this time transporting large armies of foreign mercenaries to complete the works of death, desolation and tyranny, already begun with circumstances of Cruelty & perfidy scarcely paralleled in the most barbarous ages; . . . He has excited domestic insurrections amongst us, and endeavored to bring on the inhabitants of our frontiers the merciless Indian savages, whose known rule of warfare is an undistinguished destruction of all ages, sexes and conditions." If the mind boggles at Jefferson's version of the causes of the American Revolution it should be remembered that, as Carl Becker has said, Thomas Jefferson was not writing history, he was making it.[12] This was a lawyer arraigning the accused before the bar of world opinion. "Gentlemen of the jury," the young Virginian seems to be saying, "look upon this criminal."

Finally, the Declaration closed with the words, "And for the support of this Declaration, with a firm reliance in the protection of Divine Providence, we mutually pledge to each other our Lives, our Fortunes, and our sacred Honor." This may strike the modern reader as eighteenth-century bombast. Yet if the revolution failed, it would be the fifty-five men whose signatures appeared on this document who would be the first rebels hunted down as traitors and who might die in disgrace on the gallows. Lives, fortune, and honor were indeed the stakes in the game.

The Declaration of Independence was designed, of course, as propaganda. It was offered because "a decent respect to the opinion of mankind requires that they should declare the causes which impel them to the separation," in other words, to enlist support at home and in Europe. But history has made a great deal more of it. Within a generation it was quoted in support of the revolutions in Latin America, and freedom fighters throughout the world have appealed to its principles as a basic statement of the rightful relationship of men to their government.

Conservative minds in every generation in American history have been alarmed at the self-evident truths held up to them by abolitionists, working men, poor men, and black men. The Declaration has achieved the universal appeal that Jefferson had hoped for when he himself called it one of the three great achievements of his life. Carl Becker may have said the final word:

> It is to these principles—for a generation somewhat obscured, it must be confessed, by the Shining Sword and the Almighty Dollar, by the lengthening shadow of Imperialism and the soporific haze of Historic Rights and the Survival of the Fittest—it is to these principles, these "glittering generalities," that the minds of men are turning again in this day of desolation as a refuge from the cult of efficiency and from faith in "that which is just by the judgement of experience." [33]

These words were written in 1918.

IV In the Service of the Nation[*]

ALEXANDER HAMILTON was twenty-one years old in the year that the United States was born. A psychologist, arguing from the premise that the environment and experience of youth are important determinants of adult attitudes, could perhaps readily understand why Hamilton was never anything but an American. He never thought of returning to the West Indies and never afterward expressed any nostalgia for the scenes of his boyhood. His student days at King's College were scarcely sufficient to create any deep-rooted loyalty to New York. The fact that he eventually became a resident of that state was undoubtedly due to the fact that he married a daughter of one of its great families. Having no local ties of his own, he was willing to accept those of his wife. Thus, unlike most Americans, Hamilton was not drawn by an older history and tradition as John Adams was to Massachusetts or Jefferson to Virginia. When Hamilton joined the army he committed to it the enthusiastic fealty of youth, and he always afterward identified himself with the nation which it served.

* For general military history see especially Douglas Southall Freeman, *George Washington, A Biography,* vols. IV and V. Hereafter cited as Freeman, Washington. See also Christopher Ward, *The War of the Revolution.* Hereafter cites as Ward, *Revolution.*

The Aide-de-Camp

Exactly when young Hamilton first came to the attention
of the commander in chief is difficult to say. The Continental
Line of the American army, which consisted of men who had
enlisted for three years or for the duration of the war, was
the national army created by Congress. It was a comparatively small organization, and Washington was acquainted
with many of the officers of lower rank. If he did not know
Hamilton by sight, he had probably come across his name
in reports of subordinate commanders. In the discouraging
campaigns of 1776, which saw the British occupy New York
and drive Washington out of New Jersey, Hamilton performed capably and well.

The gloomy record of American defeats was somewhat
offset by two brilliant little victories at Trenton and Princeton
in a two-week period that bridged the New Year of 1777.
Hamilton's artillery company was part of the cannonade
which broke the Hessian defense at Trenton, and he was
almost constantly in action until after the battle of Princeton.
Whether or not a shot from Hamilton's battery actually
crashed through the wall of Nassau Hall and smashed a
portrait of George II, as legend has it, he was virtually without a command after the battle. By the time the army was
ready to go into winter quarters, desertions, sickness, and
casualties had reduced his company to two officers and thirty
men.[1]

He joined Washington's staff on March 1, 1777, and was
promoted to the rank of lieutenant colonel.[2] Along with half
a dozen or more young officers, Hamilton soon became en-
grossed in the headquarters work of the commander in chief.
The members of Washington's staff were a hard-working
group, most of them in their twenties, with all the enthusiasm
which young men can generate working closely together for

a cause to which they are dedicated. Intimate friendships were formed among Hamilton, John Laurens, Richard Meade, and Robert Harrison. Yet there was little time for fun and games. "Aides-de-Camp are persons in whom entire confidence must be placed. It requires men of Abilities," wrote the commander in chief. "I give in to no kind of amusement myself, consequently those about me can have none." He did not expect his "family" to be military experts, but he did require that they "write a good Letter, write quick, are methodical, and diligent." The unending problems of poorly organized militia, hospitals for the sick and wounded, and departments of supply and intelligence required "persons that can think for me, as well as execute orders." [3]

There was occasional relief from the grind of official business. Some officers' ladies, including Martha Washington, visited at the headquarters in Morristown in the winter of 1776–77. One of them noted the "sensible Genteel polite" young Hamilton among the group of "sociable gentlemen who make the day pass with a great deal of satisfaction to the visitors." The general himself sometimes unbent to the extent of becoming "the chatty agreeable companion." [4]

Hamilton's position on Washington's staff and his relationship with the commanding general are easy to exaggerate. His later prominence as Secretary of the Treasury and President Washington's close advisor led contemporaries to see in this earlier relationship more significance than was warranted. Such Hamilton admirers as General Philip Schuyler, his father-in-law; Henry Knox, the first Secretary of War; and Timothy Pickering, Knox's successor have left the impression that Hamilton dominated the staff and that Washington relied heavily on him for ideas as well as his abilities as a secretary. One contemporary, for example, related that whenever dispatches arrived in the middle of the night one heard "the calm deep tones of that voice, so well remembered . . .

the command of the chief to his . . . watchful attendant, 'Call
Colonel Hamilton!' " [5] If a real emergency existed the general
would have undoubtedly called Tench Tilghman, the big
Marylander who was ten years older than Hamilton and
senior officer of the staff, or Robert Harrison, the indispensable staff secretary. The fact that Hamilton was present at
conferences with the French high command when the French
forces came to America was simply because he spoke the
language. The further suggestion that Hamilton supplied the
ideas as well as the language of Washington's dispatches is
a claim advanced only by later historians. [6] Certainly a young
man as brilliant as Hamilton contributed a great deal to the
work of Washington's staff; certainly he was chosen for mis-
sions which were particularly suited to his talents; and just
as certainly Hamilton's performance of his duties was superior. But it is hard to believe that he was Washington's alter
ego and confidant.

The admiration of the young colonel for his chief was
boundless, and he thoroughly understood the American strategy of indirection. In his own correspondence he enthusiastically defended Washington's actions and decisions and expressed impatience with those who could not discern that in
"our Fabian conduct" was the "truest policy." He bitterly
denounced the "folly, caprice, . . . want of foresight, com-
prehension and dignity" of Congress which, as he saw it,
seemed determined to thwart the efforts of the commanding
general. [7] In fact, such outspoken language later brought on
an attack from the Reverend William Gordon, the self-styled
historian of the Revolution. He accused the young colonel
of casting treasonous aspersions on Congress. Hamilton, who
should have known better, countered with the charge that
Gordon was a black-hearted scoundrel, whereupon that gentleman took refuge in his ministerial cloth and demanded that
Hamilton be brought to account. Washington coldly invited

the righteous cleric to produce witnesses for a court-martial or else hold his peace, and there the matter ended.[8]

The Rabble in Arms

Hamilton found himself immersed in the details and complexities of Washington's headquarters. There were problems which were inevitable in a revolutionary army that had to be created from nothing. There was no cadre of trained soldiers from a peacetime establishment upon which to build. The Continental Line was a "regular" army only in the sense that it was composed of men with long-term enlistments. Their initial training was brief and rudimentary. Indeed, it might be said that most of their training came all too quickly in the form of experience acquired in battle, where mistakes brought not merely reprimands, but defeat, death, or capture. From Howe's evacuation of Boston in the early summer of 1776 until the battle of Monmouth two years later, Washington's army earned not a single solid victory. Trenton and Princeton involved the overrunning of British outposts, not encounters with a major enemy army.

If Americans believed themselves capable of taking on British regulars in 1775, they were soon sadly disillusioned. As a nation of farmers in a frontier land, they were probably more familiar with firearms than most Englishmen, but they soon discovered that there was more to war than loading and firing a musket. The close-ordered ranks of red coats with their mechanical parade-ground precision may have provoked American derision in pre-war days, but the awesome British phalanx which crashed through Washington's lines at Brooklyn Heights and the Brandywine sent them flying in terrified retreat. It was not until that crusty old Prussian Baron von Steuben became drill master of the army that Americans comprehended the fact that massed ranks meant massed firepower, and that "Indian style" fighting with a smoothbore musket, whose maximum effective range was seventy-five yards and which took a half a minute to reload, was not effective against a disciplined enemy.[9]

It was these circumstances which in great measure determined Washington's strategy. As Hamilton noted, independence could not be risked "upon a single cast of the die. The loss of one general engagement may effectually ruin us." [10] Washington clearly understood that as long as the army survived the Revolution could survive. He did not as clearly perceive the fact that he was not committed to the defense of strategic lines or geographic points. European military science, which was so intricately tied to military fortresses and populous cities, was too deeply imbedded in the eighteenth-century thinking. Military texts on strategy were eagerly read not only by the officers but by many of the enlisted men. Thus, the capture of the "rebel capital" Philadelphia in 1777 was not followed by the collapse of the American cause, yet Washington continued to be preoccupied with plans to recapture it. It was left for General Nathanael Greene to demonstrate in the southern campaign of 1781 that rebel armies have only to avoid complete conquest in order to win.

In addition to the recruitment and training of troops, there were the myriad problems which any army encounters but which were magnified by the lack of organizational experience in the revolutionary command. Guns, ammunition, and soldiers do not make an army. A service of supply must constantly feed and clothe it, and hospitals and medical service must care for its wounded and sick. Men become ill whether the army fights or not. In fact, there was more sickness in the winter camps, where the crowding of immobilized troops in inclement weather created more health problems than when the army was on the march. Not only was eighteenth-century medicine sheer quackery by modern standards, but very little was known of the science of military hygiene. Typhoid fever, diphtheria, and influenza scourged the camps of both armies and death came twice as often from disease as from combat.

There were equally frustrating problems peculiar to the American Revolution. The Second Continental Congress, which served as the governing body of the United States during the war, performed the executive as well as the legislative functions of government. Most of these functions were attempted by committees, although the Board of War had very little autonomy and most important questions were referred to Congress. Moreover, the members were men who had lately denounced the crimes committed by the soldiery of George III. The traditional American fear of standing armies was already taking root along with the firm conviction that such armies ought to be under civilian control. Though Washington held the title of commander in chief he found it necessary to defer to the wishes of Congress in matters ranging from strategic planning to the promotion of senior officers. On one occasion Congress planned an invasion of Canada only to have the scheme collapse of its own absurdity.[11]

Congress also frequently failed to promote officers recommended by Washington but was not at all hesitant about saddling him with foreign gentry whose influence, it was hoped, would arouse sympathy for the American cause abroad. Most of them were utterly useless; Lafayette, von Steuben, Johann de Kalb, and Thaddeus Kosciuszko were notable exceptions.[12]

Nor was this all. Although the Continental Line eventually provided a core of veterans, Washington was forced to rely heavily on manpower from state militia for any major campaign. The militia were recruited, trained and officered, and equipped under state control. Worst of all, the enlistments were usually for either 90 or 120 days. Although there were a few exceptions, most of these regiments refused to extend their enlistments even though the expiration might come on the eve of battle or the middle of a campaign. The states were as bad as Congress in failing to furnish equipment and supplies so that Washington found himself on occasion with "reenforcements" who were without arms. It was indeed a "rag, tag and bobtail" of an army.[13]

Hamilton was not long in learning and appreciating these problems. The correspondence which he prepared for the commander in chief contained appeals to Congress and to the states which constantly sounded a note of urgency or even desperation. In the spring of 1777 he wrote to Governor Patrick Henry of Virginia that "a strange, unaccountable languor seems . . . to prevail at a time, when the preservation of our rights and all that is dear, calls loudly for the most vigorous and active exertions."[14]

The Army is Tested

By the spring of 1777 British military leaders came to the realization that they were engaged in a full-scale war which required full-scale planning. A three-pronged attack on New York state was undertaken, the main thrust to be delivered from Canada by an invading army under the command of General John Burgoyne. Sir William Howe, the supreme commander of British forces in America, also decided to launch an attack against Philadelphia. This latter campaign was eminently successful, for Howe not only drew Washington away from New York and Burgoyne but defeated him decisively at the battle of the Brandywine. On September 26 the British occupied Philadelphia.

Howe's diversion, however, left Burgoyne without support.

With some help from Washington, the Americans were able to raise another army in the north under the command of General Philip Schuyler. This force successfully fended off a minor British attack from the west and prepared to face Burgoyne. At this juncture Congress intervened and replaced Schuyler with General Horatio Gates. It was claimed that Schuyler was unpopular with the New Englanders who comprised most of the northern force, although there were some who said that Gates had ingratiated himself with Congress. The American army met the British in a series of engagements in the vicinity of Saratoga, New York, and Burgoyne was forced to surrender his entire army on October 19, 1777. It was this astonishing and resounding victory which resulted in the formal alliance between the United States and France in February, 1778.

There were other and less fortunate repercussions from the victory at Saratoga. General Gates would have been less than human had he not responded to the shower of adulation and flattery which followed his victory over Burgoyne—although it was said in some quarters that the victory had really been won by Gates' hard-fighting subordinate Benedict Arnold. Hamilton observed the effects of Gates' triumph at first hand when Washington sent him as an emissary to the northern army to secure reenforcements for a projected attack against Howe in Philadelphia. Gates had ignored the commander in chief's written requests and seemed to believe that he held an independent command. Such was not the case, but it took all that Hamilton possessed in the way of tact and firmness to extricate two brigades from Gates.[15] The scene was thus laid for a series of unfortunate events which comprise what is known as the "Conway cabal." [16]

Thomas Conway was a vainglorious Frenchman who became a champion of Gates and allegedly characterized Washington's command as comprising "a weak General and bad counsellors." [17] The quotation was supposed to have been part of a letter from Conway to Gates, or so Washington was informed in the late fall of 1777. Shortly afterward, Conway was promoted to major general over the heads of a number of brigadiers, and Gates was made president of the Board of War. All this coincided with strong criticism of Washington's fitness for command among some members of Congress. The crowning affront was Conway's appearance at headquarters in Valley Forge as a newly appointed inspector general of the army.

These were presumably outward indications of a plot to supplant Washington with Gates. The officers of the headquarters' staff were furious, and none more so than Alexander Hamilton, who denounced Conway as "one of the vermin bred in the entrails of this chimera dire, and there does not exist a more villainous calumniator and incendiary." [18] Washington's innate sense of dignity and his dislike of any dissension which might weaken the country's cause were finally overridden by the conviction that his integrity and fitness for command had been seriously challenged. In the controversial correspondence which ensued, Washington, with the able assistance of Colonel Hamilton, cut through the tangle of charges and countercharges. He challenged Conway directly and so thoroughly discredited him that he resigned. Washington then forced the issue with Gates and wrung from him an apologetic declaration that "I am of no faction; and if any of my letters . . . convey any meaning, which in any construction is offensive to your Excellency, that was by no means the intention of the writer." [19] By facing down Gates, Washington inferentially challenged his critics, and the reaction made it clear that the soldiers in camp at Valley Forge were right when they toasted, *"Washington* or no Army." [20]

With the country's faith in the commander in chief thus affirmed, the army took the field in the summer of 1778 in high spirits. It could now regard itself as a veteran army, for to its skills had been added the rigorous drills conducted by General von Steuben, and it was ready to meet the enemy on something like equal terms. Washington chose as its mission the destruction of the British army as it withdrew from Philadelphia to New York. Sir Henry Clinton, who had succeeded Howe as the British commander, had decided to abandon Philadelphia. The line of his retreat to New York was across New Jersey to Sandy Hook. Washington hoped to strike the British on the march and instructed General Charles Lee to lead an advance force which would attack the enemy column and bring it to bay. The troops performed well and claimed a victory on the field, but tactics miscarried and the opportunity to strike a decisive blow was lost. Young Hamilton was in the thick of the fight, rallying troops, carrying orders for the commanding general, seeming to bear a charmed life as he moved through the hail of enemy fire. Finally his horse was shot from under him, and the fall injured him sufficiently to remove him from action.[21]

Washington blamed the lost opportunity on General Lee, and on the battlefield he charged Lee with failure to execute his orders to engage the enemy. Hamilton subsequently supported the charge in his testimony at Lee's court-martial. Lee was convicted, and the army knew him no more. He published a *Vindication* in which he charged that Hamilton was one of the "idolatrous Sett of Toad-Eaters" who would say anything to support their leader.[22] The air was soon thick with charges and insults, and Hamilton nearly fought a duel with one of Lee's former aides. His friend, John Laurens, challenged Lee to a duel, and Hamilton acted as his second in an affair in which the general was slightly wounded. Whether for his bravery in action or for his role as self-appointed defender of Washington's honor, Hamilton became known at headquarters as the "Little Lion."[23]

The Winning of Independence

Monmouth was the last major engagement fought by Washington's army until the Yorktown campaign of 1781. Yet the staff duties were as onerous as ever. Although the British soon shifted their attention to the South, there were no assurances that Clinton would not take the offensive from New York. There were just enough small battles and minor actions to keep Washington apprehensive. The army still constituted a force in being; it still had to be clothed, fed, paid, and trained. Even the advent of French military and sea power seemed not to alter the balance decisively in favor of the United States. As 1779 slipped into 1780, Americans became more discouraged. Congress seemed even more dilatory and timeserving and the states less and less responsive to calls for support.

Then came a blow of the kind that Washington had dreaded—treason. On September 25, 1780, Washington, accompanied by Hamilton, was returning to headquarters in New Jersey from a conference with French General Rochambeau in Hartford. En route the commander planned a visit to the American fortress at West Point which guarded the upper Hudson River. He expected to have breakfast with its commander General Benedict Arnold and conduct an inspection of the fortifications. But Arnold was mysteriously absent when Washington arrived, and the commanding general inspected the fort without him.

In the middle of the afternoon dispatches revealing that Arnold had turned traitor arrived. John André, an officer from Clinton's headquarters, had been captured only a few miles from West Point. Papers on his person and his own subsequent testimony indicated that only the day before he had confirmed with Arnold a plan to betray West Point to the British. Arnold had unfortunately been notified of André's capture and had fled only a few moments before Washington's arrival. Colonel Hamilton was dispatched down river to attempt to cut off Arnold's escape, but it was too late. More in grief than in anger Washington exclaimed, "Whom can we now trust?"

It was a serious blow to the American cause. Arnold had been one of the finest generals in the army. Cantankerous and quarrelsome with his superiors, he was nonetheless an energetic driver and a hard fighter. He had been heroic in the actions at Saratoga but had quarrelled with Gates and accused him of cowardice. Delay in promotion, a wound that would not heal, and an extravagant mode of living which he could not afford had soured Arnold and turned him to treason. After the shock of the episode had passed, however, Washington was able to take a more optimistic view. "Traitors are the growth of every country," he observed, "and in a revolution of the present nature, it is more to be wondered at, that the catalogue is so small than that there have been found a few." [24]

Shortly after this black episode, Hamilton concluded a whirlwind courtship with the charming daughter of General Philip Schuyler. Elizabeth "has fine black eyes—is rather handsome and has every other requisite of the exterior to make a lover happy." Hamilton may have begun his courtship with an eye to the family's wealth and social position in New York. Certainly his future father-in-law looked with favor upon Hamilton's political views, and Hamilton's part in thwarting the ambitions of the "Hero of Saratoga" had not escaped the old general's notice. Yet there is no reason to doubt that the social prestige and position at which Hamilton aimed was accompanied by a deep and affectionate love for Betsey Schuyler. They were married on December 14, 1780. [25]

Hamilton did not intend to allow marital ties to divert him from military fame. He not only resumed his duties on

Washington's staff but asked the commander in chief to secure him a field command. This may have been rooted in the
boredom of headquarters routine or it may be that his long
association with Washington had begun to grate on him, for
the commanding general was not an easy taskmaster. There
was also his deep-seated ambition for distinction on the battlefield; he had remarked on the departure of another young
officer, James Monroe, that he would "find some employment, that will enable him to get knocked on the head in an
honorable way." [26] Doubtless all these factors had built up
in this restless, ambitious young man an explosive charge
with a very low ignition point.

The occasion came in the middle of February, 1781. Washington was in the midst of plans to secure the cooperation
of the French commanders, and the reduction of the staff by
absence and illness had created an unusual accumulation of
work for Hamilton. Washington summoned his young aide
and Hamilton delayed long enough to snap the commander's
patience. His angry reprimand concluded with "I must tell
you, Sir, you treat me with disrespect." "I am not conscious
of it, Sir," shot back Hamilton, "but since you have thought
it necessary to tell me so we part." Washington typically
recovered his composure at once and sent Tilghman to make
a move toward reconciliation—as close as he could come to
an apology. Hamilton refused this advance and rebuffed
subsequent attempts to gloss over the matter.[27] It is probable
that while Hamilton may have lost his temper he may also
have decided that the time had come to leave the staff. He
soon afterward asked Washington for a position in the line,
but there were other such requests of greater merit and precedence. The general therefore temporized, whereupon Hamilton petulantly submitted his resignation from the army.
Washington, whose patience must have been sorely tried,
finally secured for him a battalion in Lafayette's division. By

the end of July, 1781, Hamilton had secured his coveted field command.[28]

The military situation in the South was gradually improving from the doldrums into which it had sunk in 1780. The British had successfully seized Charleston, and an invading army under Lord Cornwallis had swept up through the Carolinas, smashing an American army under Gates at the battle of Camden. General Greene, who replaced Gates as commander of the Southern Department, had won a few minor successes and then had fought Cornwallis to a standstill at Guilford Court House in mid-March, 1781. The British commander then turned toward Virginia, and Greene, a true disciple of Washington's strategy of the indirect approach, did not challenge him but went back into the Carolinas to undo the work of conquest which Cornwallis had only imperfectly begun.

Although only lightly harassed by American forces in Virginia, Cornwallis finally thought it prudent to open a new line of supply and communication with British headquarters in New York. At the end of the summer of 1781 he withdrew to the Yorktown peninsula. The fortuitous arrival in the western Atlantic of Admiral de Grasse with a strong French naval force enabled Washington to plan a decisive stroke. In company with General Rochambeau and his troops, he proposed by a quick march to Virginia to concentrate an overwhelming force against Cornwallis while de Grasse sealed off the Chesapeake from British naval support. By late September the trap had closed on Cornwallis.

The seige of Yorktown, begun on September 28, was a rather dull affair. Colonel Hamilton found himself with the unglamorous task of commanding troops who were engaged in digging trench approaches, or parallels, by which artillery could be brought to bear on the enemy's fortifications. On one occasion he relieved the tedium by having his men mount the parapet of the trench and perform the manual of arms in full view—and range—of the enemy.[29] It gained Hamilton a dashing reputation among his fellow officers. There is no record of what his soldiers had to say about their needless exposure to fire, but it was undoubtedly profane.

For Hamilton the climax came on October 15 when he helped to lead a storming party against an enemy redoubt which had to be reduced to allow the siege lines to advance. It was a classic little action with the troops creeping upon the unsuspecting enemy and then charging with the bayonet. The position was overrun, and most of the enemy detachment was captured. The whole affair lasted less than fifteen minutes.[30]

With the enemy fortifications now enfiladed by American artillery fire, Cornwallis' situation became desperate. Convinced that there was no longer any hope of relief or escape, he surrendered his army on October 17.

Yorktown was the decisive battle of the war. By 1781 what had begun as the suppression of American rebels had become a war of major proportions. Britain faced not only France but Holland and Spain, and the Baltic states had joined with Russia in the League of Armed Neutrality which threatened to join the allies. The ministry of Lord North fell from power in England, and a new ministry took office pledged to end the costly conflict even if this meant conceding American independence.

The treaty of peace was two years in the future, but for Hamilton the war was over at Yorktown. Within a week he was hurrying home to Betsey, no doubt wondering whether independence and peace would be a blessing or a curse for a family man of twenty-six whose only profession was soldiering.

V In the Service of Virginia

EVEN BEFORE THE Second Continental Congress had voted for independence, Jefferson was anxious to be back in Williamsburg where a constitutional convention was forming the new state government. The end of British authority in America had only begun the Revolution, "for should a bad government be instituted for us in future it had been as well to have accepted . . . the bad one offered to us from beyond the water without the risk and expense of contest." [1] Britain's power must be replaced, and in America this problem had two dimensions: to create new governments in the colonies now become states; and to create a national government for the United States.

Both sentimentally and rationally, Jefferson concluded that the most pressing problem was to erect sound and viable governments in the states. Although his nascent nationalism was stronger than most, his first loyalty was to the Old Dominion simply because he was drawn by an older loyalty and tradition. He was convinced that the new nation could not exist unless it was built on a solid foundation of republicanism in the states. Jefferson recognized that a true revolution must uproot more than British government: it must sweep away the old order of privilege and aristocracy and establish a basis for popular government.

65

A Constitution for Virginia

In the middle of June, 1776, Jefferson had written to Edmund Pendleton, the president of the Virginia Convention, expressing his wish not to be reelected to Congress.[2] He realized, however, that the important work of securing acceptance of the Lee Resolution would detain him in Philadelphia. He therefore prepared a detailed plan for a constitution which he submitted for consideration *in absentia*. By the time it was presented by his old friend George Wythe, another plan, largely the work of George Mason, had already passed through committee and was being debated in the convention. Despite the absence of the author that body adopted several of Jefferson's proposals.[3]

His preamble, repeating most of the charges against George III's misrule which he had already set forth in the Declaration, was adopted virtually word for word. His suggestion that no person be allowed to hold more than one office in the government was also adopted. This was to prevent the concentration of power in a few persons by making them multiple office holders, a common practice of royal governors in colonial times. The barring of "Ministers of the Gospel of every Denomination" from serving in the assembly was probably another of Jefferson's suggestions, for it accorded with his strict notions about the separation of church and state.[4]

One of the most significant of his proposals was the sweeping assertion of Virginia's authority over the vast region known as the Old Northwest. This was the first positive claim that the state had made to an area which was included in her colonial charter of 1609 and which the colonial government had only occasionally recognized. However, Jefferson's further suggestion that the western territory should have "the same fundamental laws contained in this instrument, and

. . . be free and independent of this colony and all the world," was rejected.[5] Here was the essence of the idea that newly settled territory, "colonial" territory, should be accorded equal status with the "mother country." Jefferson later incorporated his concept into the Ordinance of 1784, and it remained the guiding principle of the Northwest Ordinance of 1787 which set the pattern for the formation of new states.

Whether Jefferson's presence in Williamsburg would have resulted in the adoption of more of his constitutional ideas is a question impossible to answer. Though he was an important and influential man, there was serious opposition to the liberalizing trend which he represented. The dual nature of the revolution was nowhere better illustrated than in Virginia. The revolt against England had included men of all classes, and the aristocracy of the colony was well represented by leaders like Pendleton, Mason, Landon Carter, and Thomas Nelson, Jr. But Jefferson wanted a real revolution, one which would embody the principles which he had in mind when he used phrases like "public liberty" and "rights of the people." Thus, where George Mason had proposed qualifications for voting and holding public office, Jefferson would have extended the franchise to all taxpayers. And when the requirement was finally set at a fifty-acre freehold, he proposed that the government give fifty acres of land to every landless adult male. In this way, he thought, the goal of truly popular government could be achieved.[6]

With the adoption of the Declaration of Independence by the Continental Congress, Jefferson was impatient to be gone from Philadelphia. He was therefore exasperated to learn that he had been reelected to Congress, although he had been next-to-last in the voting. This oddly sensitive young man read into the small vote cast for him a rebuke of his services rather than the compliment implied by his election in the face of his stated wish to resign.[7] It was characteristic of his reaction to criticism, whether real or fancied. In later years he learned to conceal his irritation in public, but to his intimate friends he occasionally gave way to outbursts of almost childish petulance at any imputation on his motives or suggestion that he had failed to do his duty.

He immediately sent Pendleton a letter of resignation, but since he was the only Virginia delegate left in Philadelphia, he was forced to await the arrival of Richard Henry Lee. It was not until the September 3 that he finally left the capital and hastened home. Monticello and Martha drew him like a magnet, and he arrived on September 9. A month later he was ready to go to Williamsburg as the delegate from Albemarle. An invitation to share George Wythe's home enabled him to take Martha with him.[8] Shortly after his arrival, he received a notice from Congress that he had been appointed, along with Benjamin Franklin and Silas Deane, as minister to France. With much reluctance he wrote that "circumstances very peculiar in the situation of my family . . . compel me to decline." [9] His friends knew that the "peculiar situation" was Martha's continued poor health. He was never far from her during the remainder of her life.

Jefferson now began a work which was especially congenial to his philosophical nature. Shortly after the convening of the General Assembly, he was appointed to a committee charged with revising the whole body of English and Virginia statutes which was to comprise the new laws for the state. It was a task for which he was eminently suited and he began it with obvious enthusiasm. No partisan political considerations intruded to divert him from the far-reaching purpose of striking at nascent aristocracy and building a firm foundation of republicanism.

Land and Liberty

Two legal features of English landholdings were, in Jefferson's opinion, primarily responsible for the creation and perpetuation of the Old World aristocracy. These were the law of entail which prevented an owner from disposing of an estate to anyone other than his descendants and the law of primogeniture which required that a propertied inheritance could be deeded only to the eldest son. By these two practices large estates in England had remained in the same family from generation to generation, immune even from seizure for the payment of debts. Primogeniture prevented the division of land among several heirs. Thus the legal structure tended to buttress the social system which maintained an almost impregnable aristocracy. America was as yet too young and her society too fluid for an upper class to have become thoroughly entrenched, but Jefferson saw danger for the future if such anachronisms were allowed to persist. He never implied that the Virginia aristocracy of his day had ruled badly, for this would have been untrue. But "the time for fixing every essential right on a legal basis is while our rulers are honest and ourselves united."

Soon after the opening of the session, therefore, Jefferson introduced a bill for the abolition of entail. Edmund Pendleton led the opposition, and his attempts to block or modify the measure bore the marks of an old master in debate and parliamentary maneuver. Jefferson and his supporters were finally successful, and despite the prevalence of sharp divisions and factionalism, Jefferson himself seems to have retained the friendship and regard of Pendleton and other conservatives.[10] There were to be more battles in the next three years—the most bitter of his whole career, according to Jefferson—yet this quiet, diffident man whose convictions could

provoke such storms of debate seldom aroused the rancour
or personal enmity of his opponents.

The abolition of the law of primogeniture came later and
was part of the larger task of the committee of revisors that
consisted of Jefferson, Pendleton, Mason, Wythe, and
Thomas Ludwell Lee. This group had the task of adapting
English and Virginia colonial law to form a new state law
code. Two members of the committee, Lee and Mason, resigned (Lee died shortly afterward), thus leaving three members to divide the work. Jefferson assumed the greatest burden, but one which he undoubtedly welcomed—that of
revising English common law along with the statutes of England down to the founding of Virginia in 1607. Wythe undertook the revision of British statutes after 1607, and Pendleton, the laws of Virginia itself. It was to take the committee
three years to prepare its report.[11]

The abolition of entail and primogeniture was only one
aspect of Jefferson's view of the relationship of the land to
popular government. It was not only necessary to prevent the
accumulation of large estates, but to make the vast resources
of land in America available to as many people as possible.
He wished to avoid the quitrent system and other colonial
impediments to frontier expansion. "I am against selling
lands at all," he wrote in 1776. He knew that the flood of
pioneers could not be stemmed but "by selling lands to them,
you will disgust them and cause an avulsion of them from
the common union. They will settle the lands in spite of
everybody." He realized that speculators would come in great
numbers, "but make them pay in settlers. A Foreigner who
brings a settler for every 100, or 200 acres of land to be
granted him pays a better price. . . . That settler will be
worth to the public 20 times as much every year, as . . . he
would in one paiment only." [12]

His concern for the small settlers encountered two obstacles. One was the fact that as the war progressed Virginia's financial resources were strained to the limit and the sale of western lands to speculators offered a source of revenue which the leaders of the state, many of whom were themselves speculators, were loath to forego. There was also increasing pressure from the small states to have the large states with extensive western territory cede their claims to the central government. Maryland led this struggle and for a time refused to ratify the Articles of Confederation until her demand was met.

When Jefferson and George Mason introduced bills to liberalize public land policy in 1778, they found the various propertied interests too much for them. The only thing they could salvage were provisions to protect "squatters" who filtered into the wilderness and occupied lands without title. These settlers were permitted to purchase their holdings at minimum prices, but no provisions were made to protect such people in the future.[13] By the end of the war, title to the western territory had passed to the Confederation government. Jefferson, as a member of Congress in 1784, had another opportunity to implement his policies.

His Ordinance of 1784 was a blueprint for the future development of the West.[14] He reiterated his earlier conviction that new states must be admitted to the union on an equal basis with the old and their people thus accorded first class citizenship. The touchstone of colonial discontent with British rule had been that the mother country failed to recognize their full rights as English citizens. Jefferson was determined that Americans on the frontier should never have such grounds for disaffection with their country, and he provided for some measure of self-government even in the earliest stages of development toward statehood: an elected territorial legislature; a representative in Congress; and a popularly elected constitutional convention when the territory was ready for admission as a state. Although it was superseded by the Northwest Ordinance of 1787, the Ordinance of 1784 embodied the basic framework and philosophy for creating new states for the next 175 years.

Crime and Slavery

Not the least of the reforms which Jefferson regarded as essential to the new America was the revision of the criminal code, and it constituted a major portion of his work as revisor of the English statutes. As in the cases of primogeniture and entail this was a matter of discarding an outmoded system. The brutal punishments prescribed under British law were the outgrowth of the belief that fear was an effective deterrent against crime. Already eighteenth-century humanitarians had protested against prescribing the death penalty for a wide range of offenses from murder to petty theft. As Jefferson pointed out, "the experience of all ages and countries hath shewn that cruel and sanguinary laws defeat their own purpose by engaging the benevolence of mankind to withhold prosecutions, to smother testimony, or to listen to it with bias, when, if the punishment were only proportioned to the injury, men would feel it their inclination as well as their duty to see the laws observed." He felt that the death penalty was "the last melancholy resort," and the revisions provided that it should be inflicted only for treason and murder.[15] He proposed to substitute "hard labour, in the public works, in punishment of their crimes," but he eventually came to believe that this would be degrading and have little effect upon reforming criminals.[16] Later nineteenth- and twentieth-century practice proved him to be prophetic.

His regard for criminals as persons was at variance with the eighteenth-century criminal code which was designed solely to punish and confine the offender. A person "committing an inferior injury, does not wholly forfeit the protection of his fellow-citizens, but, after suffering punishment in proportion to his offense is entitled to their protection from all greater pain." He proposed that prisoners be treated humanely and that prison conditions be maintained through inspection by "some person of discretion, humanity and attention." [17]

In dealing with punishments for some crimes, Jefferson was rather surprisingly an advocate of the principle of *lex talionis,* "an eye for an eye," which he found in English common law. In particular, the punishments for rape, sodomy, and polygamy—"if a man, by castration, if a woman, by cutting thro' the cartilege of her nose a hole of one half inch in diameter" —seem brutally out of character for this gentle philosopher.[18] But it should be remembered that Jefferson was an eighteenth-century man, and the eighteenth century was a brutal time. For all of the enlightenment of the *philosophes,* their society still condoned severe corporal punishment even among children and held life cheap, particularly among the lower classes. Jefferson was formulating the law of the land, and he was painfully aware that he was dealing with legislators whose visions were more limited than his own and who were answerable to public opinion. To expound a prophetic philosophy was one thing; to deal with the practicalities of a law code was another. It may be that Jefferson felt that the strictures on the death penalty and humane treatment of criminals were the limit of acceptance. He had already learned that politics was in large measure the art of attaining the possible. In these cases, his gauge of the temper of his colleagues was wrong, and the sections on the death penalty and treatment of prisoners were voted down, although the former was enacted twenty years later.

Another section of the revisions which met a similar fate, and for the same reason, was his attempt to abolish the slave trade. Jefferson and many of his colleagues believed that emancipation of slaves would eventually be attained, and Jefferson had proposed the elimination of the slave trade in his constitutional plan of 1776.[19] He now proposed not only to ban the importation of slaves from abroad but also from other states. This was the most that the committee of revisors believed would be acceptable by members of the assembly. They also discussed a scheme of gradual emancipation, such as was shortly adopted in many northern states, by which Negro children born after a certain date would be free. But, as Jefferson noted almost half a century later, "the public mind would not yet bear the proposition, nor will it bear it even to this day." [20]

Religious Liberty and Education

In his own mind Jefferson's great victory of this period was the statute which established religious freedom. The relationship of church and state had a long and stormy history dating back to the founding of the colonies. The Congregationalists in New England and the Anglicans in Virginia had constituted established churches; that is, there was only one religion which was recognized by law and supported by taxation. Infractions of religious discipline might be punished by law, and dissenters might be driven from a colony. In a land of such diverse peoples, many of whom came to America to escape some form of Old World intolerance, there was bound to be a crescendo of dissent. Roger Williams had been evicted from Massachusetts in 1635 for expounding the wildly radical view that a man's religious beliefs—or lack of them—were of no concern to the state. William Penn had established the principle of religious toleration in Pennsylvania, but political rights were limited to those of Christian belief.

Under the impact of the Age of Reason, state religions had given ground to the extent that colonial governments tolerated religious dissent. However, taxes were still levied for the support of a state religion in many colonies, and in a few only the established clergy could perform a legal marriage. Jefferson had always regarded religion as a private matter. His own study had led him to reject man-made doctrine and clergymen who posed as authorities of revealed religion. Throughout his career, this man who profoundly believed in the moral foundation of society was bitterly attacked as a freethinker, which he was, and an atheist, which he was not.

Unorthodox in his religious views, Jefferson had the utmost respect for those of other men. The only thing that Jefferson was intolerant of was intolerance, and his strictures upon the clergy stemmed from the fact that they, "having been secured against rivalship by fixed salaries, did not give themselves the trouble of acquiring influence over the people." [21] As for the laws, he believed that they should be confined to preventing one man from injuring another. "It does me no injury for my neighbour to say that there are twenty gods, or no god. It neither picks my pocket nor breaks my leg." [22]

At the time that Jefferson framed his bill, there was little actual restraint on the free practice of religion. The few common law punishments for heresy which remained were completely outmoded by the spirit of the times. Most of the controversy centered on the taxes levied for the support of the clergy and church property. Indeed, many of the dissenting religious groups wanted state support for their ministry as well as for the Anglican clergy. Jefferson intended to sever all connection between church and state, both the support of religion and the punishment of heresy. He did not deal in particulars but instead composed a sweeping and magnificent statement of the freedom of the human spirit. The preamble of the bill declared:

> Well aware that . . . Almighty God hath created the mind free, and manifested his supreme will that free it

shall remain by making it altogether insusceptible of restraint; that all attempts to influence it by temporal punishments, or burthens, or by civil incapacitations, tend only to beget habits of hypocrisy and meanness, and are a departure from the plan of the holy author of our religion, who being lord of both body and mind, yet chose not to propagate it by coercions on either, as was in his Almighty power to do, but to extend it by its influence on reason alone; that the impious presumption of legislators and rulers, civil as well as ecclesiastical, who, being themselves but fallible and uninspired men, have assumed dominion over the faith of others, setting up their own opinions and modes of thinking as the only true and infallible, and as such endeavoring to impose them on others, hath established and maintained false religions over the greatest part of the world and through all time; . . . that our civil rights have no dependence on our religious opinions, any more than our opinions in physics and geometry; that therefore the proscribing any citizen as unworthy the public confidence by laying upon him an incapacity of being called to offices of trust or emolument, unless he profess or renounce this or that religious opinion, is depriving him injuriously of those privileges and advantages to which . . . he has a natural right; . . . and finally, that truth is great and will prevail if left to herself; that she is the proper and sufficient antagonist to error, and has nothing to fear from the conflict unless by human interposition disarmed of her natural weapons, free argument and debate; errors ceasing to be dangerous when it is permitted freely to contradict them.[23]

It was undoubtedly because of the all-inclusive scope of this preamble that the assembly refused to enact the bill in 1779. It was not until 1786, when Jefferson was serving as minister to France, that his colleague James Madison guided the bill through the legislature to adoption. Jefferson was tremendously pleased to hear this news, for he had already circulated copies among his friends in Paris and reported to

Madison that it had "been received with infinite approbation . . . and propagated with enthusiasm." [24]

Up to this point the revisions of the code had dealt with the reform of existing law or the abolition of that which the revisors considered outmoded and archaic. In the bill "for the More General Diffusion of Knowledge" he planned a comprehensive structure for an educational system "to illuminate, as far as practicable, the minds of the people at large." [25] This man who abhorred aristocracy of property or birth was a firm believer in an intellectual aristocracy. "It is generally true that people will be happiest whose laws are best, and are best administered, and that the laws will be wisely formed, and honestly administered, in proportion as those who form and administer them are wise and honest; whence it becomes expedient for promoting the publick happiness that those persons, whom nature hath endowed with genius and virtue, should be rendered by a liberal education worthy to receive and able to guard the sacred deposit of rights and liberties of their fellow citizens." [26]

Yet Jefferson understood that it was necessary to educate the electorate as well. In spite of his faith in democracy he never deluded himself into thinking that the majority always decided wisely. But, as he noted in later years, "if we think them not enlightened enough to exercise their control with a wholesome discretion, the remedy is not to take it from them, but to inform their discretion by education." [27] Thus the problem was a dual one of creating "a natural aristocracy" which consisted of people of "virtue and talents" and also an educated citizenry.

This could be accomplished only by making education available to all "at the common expence of all"—in short, universal public education. [28] Almost alone among the statesmen of his time, Jefferson understood that the survival of popular government depended on education. "I hope the edu-

cation of the common people will be attended to," he once
wrote to Madison, "convinced that on their good sense we
may rely with the most security for the preservation of a due
degree of liberty." [29] This public purpose was the primary
object of the system which he proposed, and he remained an
apostle of enlightenment to the day of his death. When he
spoke of this as the most important work of his revisions, he
probably knew that his proposals would not be adopted by
the assembly, but he anticipated the time when public education would gain universal acceptance as part of the American
democratic dogma.

He proposed the creation of "hundreds," or school districts, which would provide three years of primary education
for everyone. At the secondary level the "grammar" schools,
embracing several counties, would provide for studies in lan-
guages, geography, higher mathematics, and science. Although the state would furnish buildings and grounds for
these schools, most of the students would pay their own
expenses. But here a select group of the superior students
from the "hundred" schools would be supported by the state,
and from these the most highly qualified would be sent to the
state university. Thus Jefferson envisaged a system which
would constantly produce a pool of people of superior education from whom government servants would be selected.

The capstone of the system, the state university, was to be
the College of William and Mary, and Jefferson had extensive
plans for renovating that somewhat archaic institution. Besides enlarging the faculty and curriculum, he proposed to
eliminate the professors of divinity and to add professors of
law, medicine, and modern language.[30] As governor he was
successful in bringing about some of these changes, but he
never did transform it into a truly public institution. It was
typical of the man that, having failed to accomplish his pur-

pose at William and Mary, he eventually created an institution which is still known as "Mr. Jefferson's university." [31]

Governor Jefferson

It was inevitable that Jefferson should become a candidate for governor. His rise to prominence, first in the Continental Congress and then in the Virginia assembly, had marked him as one of the half a dozen or so outstanding leaders of the Old Dominion. Patrick Henry, the most powerful political force in the state, had served three successive terms and was therefore ineligible for reelection in 1779. Richard Henry Lee's earlier popularity had waned when he championed the cause of paper money with disastrous results for the state's finances.

Jefferson was chosen by the assembly over two rivals who were long-time friends, Thomas Nelson, Jr. and John Page. Characteristically, both sincerely wished Jefferson well, and he assumed office on June 2, 1779.[32] It was a time of high hope, for the great victory at Saratoga two years before had been followed by the alliance with France. It appeared that the end of the struggle for independence was in sight.

The new governor was nevertheless soon overwhelmed by a profusion of problems. From the beginning he was hampered by constitutional restrictions which seemed at times to reduce him to the role of the legislature's administrative officer. This, in fact, was the intent of the framers of the state constitution. In the wave of enthusiasm for their newly acquired independence, most states, Virginia among them, wished to insure against that menace to colonial freedom —executive power.[33] Jefferson had been elected by the assembly for a term of one year. He was responsible to it and had no executive veto over its legislation. He was also supposed to be guided by a Council of State. These limitations, coupled with his own scrupulous observance of them, inhibited his exertion of executive leadership. There were critical times when he chafed under the limitations of his power and became exasperated at the dilatory half-measures of the assembly, yet he himself fell victim to the formality and routine of administrative procedure. When British forces later invaded the state and threatened the capital itself, Jefferson dutifully convened daily meetings of the Council of State and meticulously recorded the fact that not enough members were present to constitute a quorum.[34]

But this was in the future. Upon his accession to office Jefferson found that the two most serious problems were inflation of the state's currency and raising troops and supplies. The assembly had attempted a solution to the problem of finances by the usual expedient of issuing paper money. By the time Jefferson left office a total of over £12,000,000 had been printed and had become virtually worthless. The governor ruefully noted in 1780 that a bonnet for Martha cost 36 pounds. At the current exchange this meant about $180. When one considers that a laborer earned (and could live on) about $300 a year in normal times, the chaotic nature of wartime finance is well understood.[35]

Other alternatives were attempted to mitigate the problem. It was hoped that the sale of expropriated Loyalist property would provide income, but the legal processes involved and the fact that no one had the money to make purchases doomed this idea to failure. The assembly turned to the obvious alternative of taxation—a poll tax, a tax on slaves, carriages, and liquors. But such tax collectors as could be recruited soon found that most people believed—or professed to believe—that the war was being fought to end taxation. "No taxation without representation" had become "no taxation with or without representation." [36]

The military problem was almost as hopeless. If the state had no income, how could it pay for men and supplies? And military forces must be raised not only to defend the state but to support General Washington's army. By 1779 most of the volunteers and those who could be recruited had already enlisted in the Continental Line or were incorporated into the state militia. Virginia and the United States were no more able to raise sufficient volunteers to fight this first war than for subsequent wars. Slender as were his resources, the governor insisted that the national army be the principal recipient of military support. Jefferson was convinced that "the interest of this State is intimately blended, so perfectly the same with that of the others of the confederacy that the most effectual aid it can at any time receive, is where the general cause most needs it." [37] Like most states Virginia failed to meet its quotas of money and men required by Congress, but Jefferson attempted at least to render an accounting to the national government and to do his best with the limited resources available. The evidence seems to be that Virginia did rather better than most of the other states in supporting the national effort.[38]

At the beginning of 1780 the British decided to launch a concerted campaign against the southern states. The offensive began with an attack on Charleston, South Carolina, and by the middle of May General Benjamin Lincoln had been forced to surrender the city and an entire American army, including some 1,500 Virginia veterans. Spurred by this disaster the assembly voted authorization for the raising of additional levies of troops and ordered an additional £2,000,000 of paper money issued. Yet paper money and paper regiments were of little assistance to Jefferson as he set about raising military support for General Horatio Gates, whom Washington had sent south to reorganize the shattered American army. Of the 3,000 men authorized by the legislature, only

1,400 reached Gates' headquarters in South Carolina and most of these were without arms or equipment.[39]

The second disaster in the South came at the battle of Camden in mid-August, 1780. The British, moving northward from Charleston, completely routed Gates' army. The defeat was made all the more bitter by the fact that the Virginia forces had been the first to give way, fleeing ingloriously before the onslaught of the enemy. This was disheartening news indeed, for the troops represented strenous efforts in recruitment, and the loss of wagons, tents, and small arms was virtually irreparable. By the end of September Jefferson had determined to resign and only the urging of friends like George Mason and John Page persuaded him to continue at his post.[40] As he perhaps had foreseen, the remainder of his term was one of the most bitter and frustrating periods of his life.

The Enemy Invasion

Jefferson's first task was again to help rebuild the army of the southern department now commanded by General Nathanael Greene. Even a British raid on the lower James in the fall of 1780 failed to divert him from his purpose. He calmed the distracted and alarmed legislature and assured General Greene that troops and supplies were forthcoming. Greene visited the governor at the new capital in Richmond in the end of November, 1780, on his way south to repair the wreckage of the American army, and Jefferson's assurances gave him considerable encouragement. Greene left General von Steuben in Virginia to supervise the mustering and training of troops.[41]

Jefferson's first direct involvement in the war came in December. Benedict Arnold, the traitor who now served as a brigadier general in the British army, commanded a force which descended like a bolt of lightening upon eastern Virginia. He led his force of some 1,500 men up the James to the outskirts of Richmond. After destroying the foundry near the city, burning a quantity of tobacco, and destroying some government records, Arnold retired to the coast and the crisis passed. Governor Jefferson reacted to the emergency with energy but also in considerable confusion. His main efforts seemed to have been to remove government stores beyond the reach of the enemy, and he was partly successful. He also attempted to cooperate with General von Steuben, in which effort he was completely unsuccessful. He issued orders for mustering the militia of the surrounding counties but made no effort to command them himself. He seems to have assumed that von Steuben would take whatever military action was necessary.[42]

Some months later Jefferson was severely criticized for doing so little and doing it so belatedly. The criticism was justified, for he had never concerned himself about military matters and had no conception of the role of a military commander. It should be pointed out that he was badly served by his sources of information and did not learn of the presence of the enemy until Arnold was almost at Richmond. It might also be noted that no general in either army moved so swiftly or struck so hard as Benedict Arnold.

The January raid, however, was only a prelude to disaster in Virginia. Despite the temporary respite afforded by Arnold's withdrawal, he was soon reenforced by additional British contingents. General Washington detached a small force of Continental troops under the Marquis de Lafayette to meet the British threat, but it did not arrive until March. Meantime Jefferson continued to honor his commitment to General Greene. With von Steuben's aid he attempted to raise additional Continental enlistments while at the same time organizing and training the militia to defend the state. And always there was the critical matter of supplies. Soldiers must not only have guns but horses, wagons, tents, rum, (without which, it was supposed, no army could march a step), and food.[43] The state's desperate financial condition did not improve, and its currency was utterly worthless.

It was in this state of affairs that Jefferson came face to face with the grim reality that popular government was ill-suited to waging war. It was perhaps frustrating that the government which Jefferson had done so much to create should have its principles immediately put to the test in such trying circumstances as the war created. Bound as he was by both personal inclination and constitutional limitations, he refused either to assume extraordinary powers or even to exercise those given to him.

General von Steuben, who was finding it difficult to teach Americans the stern lessons of war, was highly annoyed when the governor refused to allow him to commandeer civilian laborers and slaves for the building of fortifications below Richmond. "The Executive have not . . . any power to call a freeman to labour even for the Public without his consent, nor a Slave without that of his Master," wrote the governor.[44] On another occasion when a transfer of troops was requested, he suggested to von Steuben "whether it might not be proper that you should order so many of them to be annexed to that regiment *as should be willing to join it.*" In still another instance he insisted that horses commandeered by the army be returned to their owners even though this entailed considerable expense and inconvenience.[45]

In March, 1781, Greene engaged the British General Cornwallis at Guilford Court House (Greensboro), North Carolina. Following the inconclusive battle, Cornwallis retired to Wilmington to refurbish his army. Greene, instead of following him or moving into Virginia, marched back into

South Carolina and began to mop up the lightly held British garrisons which Cornwallis had left in the wake of his north-ward march. This was sound strategy, for it was not long before the enemy control of the Carolinas had ended except for his bases in Wilmington and Charleston.

Virginia, however, was left completely exposed to a British invasion and by late May, 1781, Cornwallis had marched northward from Wilmington and joined forces with the Brit-ish in eastern Virginia. A small force of Continentals and militia under Lafayette could only harass and annoy the enemy. Cornwallis occupied Richmond, and the governor and the assembly fled westward. The state government col-lapsed completely as its fugitive members found sanctuary, first at Charlottesville, and then across the Blue Ridge in Staunton. On his last official day in office, June 4, 1781, Jefferson himself barely escaped capture by the pursuing Brit-ish. Since he had no sanction of power nor any indication from the "rump" assembly that he should do otherwise, he retired with his family to his wife's family home, Poplar Forest, in Bedford County. Despite later charges of derelic-tion of duty and other criticisms, Jefferson's exit from the governorship was perfectly honorable and correct, though somewhat ignominious. The forty remaining assemblymen finally met in Staunton and chose Thomas Nelson as his successor on June 12.[46]

It may be supposed that Jefferson's thoughts were not un-like those which he expressed in the only commentary on his governorship which appears in his *Autobiography:* "From the belief that under the pressure of the invasion which we were then laboring, the public would have more confidence in a Military chief, and . . . that the Military commander should be invested with the Civil power also, [so that] both might be wielded with more energy, promptitude and effect for the defence of the state, I resigned the administration." [47] He thus foresaw the ultimate solution to the problem of waging war in a democracy.

Thomas Jefferson, at the age of thirty-eight, had become one of the most famous men in America. He had been a notable member of the national congress, a legislator, and governor. Shortly after his retirement from this last position, he again refused a diplomatic mission, this one as a member of the peace delegation in Paris. His services as a lawmaker constituted the most creative phase of his career during the Revolution. No other eighteenth-century *philosophe* had such a rare opportunity to translate ideas into a constitution and a code of law.

Jefferson was thus a complete revolutionist. It was because of him and men like him that the American Revolution was the only one in modern times which succeeded. For only in America was the system which the revolution destroyed replaced by a government in which the ideals and principles of the revolutionaries were realized. It was to be more than a decade before the new nation achieved stability, but the same men who had instigated the revolt against Great Britain—Hamilton, Jefferson, Adams, and Washington—still guided its destinies.

VI Hamilton and the Rise of Nationalism[*]

ALEXANDER HAMILTON was twenty-six years old in 1781. He had no professional training, but this was not unusual in a day when formal education was not looked upon as a prerequisite for either social prestige or a successful career. Far more to his credit was the fact that he was a veteran of five years of honorable service in the army. This included a fine record in combat and an intimate association with General Washington, the most famous American of the day. He also counted among his friends such influential men as Robert and Gouverneur Morris, James Duane, and two rising young statesmen John Jay and James Madison. Although he seemed at first determined upon "renouncing public life altogether," within a year he was writing to John Laurens, "Quit your sword my friend, put on the toga. . . . We have fought side by side to make America free, let us hand in hand struggle to make her happy." [1]

Lessons in Finance

He is truly a very fine young gentleman the most agreeable in his conversation and manners . . . nor less remarkable for his intelligence and sweetness of temper.

[*] For this chapter see especially Burnett, *The Continental Congress.*

. . . His features are good, his eyes not only sprightly
and expressive but full of benignity. His attitude in sit-
ting is by connoisseurs esteemed graceful and he has a
method of waving his hand that announces the future
orator. He stands however rather awkwardly and as his
legs have not all the delicate slimness of his father's. It
is feared He may never excel as much in dancing. . . .
If he has any fault in manners, he laughs too much.[2]

Thus Hamilton, the doting father, described his seven-
month-old son in August, 1782. After Hamilton's return
from Yorktown, the little family had settled down in Albany.
"You cannot imagine how entirely domestic I am growing,"
Hamilton wrote to a friend. "I lose all taste for the pursuits
of ambition." [3] He decided that his future lay in the law, and
under the tutelage of his friend Robert Troup he began to
study for his bar examination. It was typical of Hamilton that
the preparation proceeded at a furious pace. As always, "time
is so precious to me that I could not put myself in the way
of any interruptions." In his day, as now, there were short
cuts, and he spent much of his time poring over a student's
manual especially written for candidates for the bar. The
driving energy so characteristic of Hamilton's whole life enabled him to be admitted to practice in July, 1782, and acquire
"the degree of Counsellor" by the end of October.[4]

Whatever may have been his original intentions, he soon
found himself in public office although one which would
hardly win him public acclaim. Robert Morris had asked him
to take the position of tax collector for the Confederation
government. Although the pay was small, Hamilton undertook the task largely out of his high regard for Morris. The
Superintendent of Finance was struggling mightily to rescue
the Congress from the deplorable financial state to which it
had been reduced by six years of war. In its fear of centralized
authority, Congress had at first delegated most of its execu-

tive functions to committees. Not until 1781 was the administration of fiscal affairs vested in a single officer. It was a monumental and thankless task that Morris, "The Financier of the Revolution," undertook.[5]

As Washington's aide Hamilton had lived for years with the chronic shortages of pay and supplies for the army. As collector for the central government he now viewed the other side of the coin. In July, 1782, he wrote to Morris from Albany that his efforts to secure support from the New York legislature for a new scheme of taxation seemed doomed to failure. "I found every man convinced that something was wrong, but few that were willing to recognize the mischief when defined and consent to the proper remedy." And a few weeks later he reported bitterly, "The inquiry constantly is what will *please* not what will *benefit* the people. In such a government there can be nothing but temporary expedient, fickleness and folly."[6]

Hamilton had begun his education while he was still in the army. His readings had included, among other items, the massive two volume *Universal Dictionary of Trade and Commerce* by the English economist Malachy Postlethwayt. He had thus learned from both his study and experience what seemed to him a universal truth: "There are men in all countries, the business of whose lives it is, to raise themselves above indigence, by every little art in their power. . . . When others, who have characters to support, and credit enough . . . to satisfy a moderate appetite for wealth . . . are found to be actuated by the same spirit, our contempt is mixed with indignation."[7] To the patriotic young officer who daily witnessed the sufferings and hardships of the army, the behavior of venal and selfish men seemed incomprehensible.

But to Hamilton the great enemy was lack of governmental credit and its companion—inflation. Congress issued paper money which it intended to back with income from the states.

It failed to reckon with the distaste of newly independent Americans for any form of taxation by the central government. The Congress which had usurped the power of Britain had inherited the imperial problem of raising money from the colonies, now become states. In many quarters the idea of taxation by Congress was as abhorrent as taxation by Parliament, and the framers of the Articles of Confederation were prudent enough to omit this from the list of the powers which it conferred upon the central government. Thus millions of dollars of paper money were issued, but quotas of revenue requested from the states were met halfheartedly or not at all. "An excess of the spirit of liberty which has made the particular states show a jealousy of all power, . . ." wrote Hamilton in 1780, "has led them to exercise a right of judging in the last resort of the measures recommended by Congress, and of acting according to their own opinions." [8]

Hamilton put forward several proposals to remedy the situation. One such was the establishment of a national bank, an idea which remained central to Hamilton's thinking throughout his career. In 1781 he had sent Morris a detailed outline for its organization and function.[9] The bank would be capitalized through the sale of stock, a large part of which would be purchased by the government with money obtained from foreign loans. Since hard money, or specie, was scarce, private investors would be allowed to make part of their payment "in landed security." This would provide a means by which a man whose chief wealth was in real estate might have his holdings "converted into Cash, which he may employ in loans, in profitable contracts, in beneficial purchases, in discounting bills of exchange and in other methods." Thus there would be a centralized financial institution whose notes would be the chief circulating medium of the country and which could extend credit to the government when needed. Also, "the bank will find its advantage in lending at moderate interest [to private individuals] . . . which will at the same time promote commerce and by a kind of mutual reaction the bank will assist commerce and commerce will assist the bank." [10]

The idea of a national bank was certainly not new to Morris or to others. In fact, Morris secured a charter from Congress late in 1781 for the Bank of North America. It rendered important services to the United States, but it never operated on the scale of a truly national bank. By 1784 the government was no longer a stockholder, and its charter was held from the state of Pennsylvania.[11] Hamilton's letter was important because it revealed the marvelous range of his knowledge of banking, government finance, and commerce—a knowledge acquired in hours of study sandwiched between his arduous duties as Washington's aide. It was equally obvious that Hamilton readily grasped the more subtle implications of the policies which he proposed. "Paper credit," he noted, "depends much on opinion and opinion is often guided by outside appearances;" and again, "Whatever serves to increase the apparent wealth of the bank will enhance its credit!"

Of greatest importance, "the tendency of a national bank is to increase public and private credit. The former gives power to the state for the protection of its rights and interests, and the latter facilitates and extends the operations of commerce among individuals." [13] If the people of wealth and property could be given a stake in the success of the government their support of the government would be assured. It was an axiom which Hamilton thus propounded early in his career and never forgot.

This led him to the other principal remedy for the deplorable state of the nation. "Congress must deal plainly with their constituents. They must tell them, that power without revenue is a bubble, that unless they give them substantial resources . . . they will not have enough . . . either to prose-

cute the war or to maintain the union in peace." The financial
stability of the government rested upon revenue and this was
part of a still larger problem inherent in the relationship of
the central government to the states. The fact was the Confederation government not only lacked necessary powers, taxation among them, but it lacked power—power to enforce its
will upon recalcitrant states and the people. "It has ever been
my opinion that Congress ought to have complete sovereignty
in all but the mere municipal law of each state;" he wrote
in 1781, "and I wish to see a convention of all the states, with
full power to alter & amend finally and irrevocably the present futile and senseless confederation." [14]

It was the goal which dominated Hamilton's consciousness
for the next seven years.

Congressman Hamilton

The Congress of the Confederation appeared to be the most
obvious vehicle through which Hamilton might realize his
ideas. In the summer of 1782 the New York legislature chose
him as a member of its delegation. His election was undoubtedly due in part to the influence of General Schuyler but the
position of Congressman was not considered to be very important. Nor was Hamilton himself very sanguine. "I am
going to throw away a few months more in public life," he
remarked on the eve of his departure for Philadelphia, "and
then I retire a simple citizen and a good paterfamilias." [15]
Whether this represented his real sentiments or not Hamilton
was never able to divert his mind from public affairs for very
long; and what the mind perceived the driving energy of the
man constantly sought to achieve. He arrived at the capital
on November 25, 1782.

He found a harried Congress struggling to find solutions
to a veritable nightmare of problems. The first flush of the

victory at Yorktown had worn off. Surely the war was won, but after more than a year British troops still occupied New York and Charleston, and there was no word of the signing of a treaty. The consent of all thirteen of the states had at last been secured to the Articles of Confederation, but it appeared that this was a hollow victory since the Confederation Congress had no more power than the old Continental Congress. Especially, it had no power to tax although it was beset with creditors. Private investors clamored for payment on government securities. Foreign governments like France and Holland were wary of extending more loans now that the humbling of Great Britian seemed to have been achieved. Perhaps most alarming of all was the army. Congress did not dare send it home, for if the peace negotiations should break down, it would be needed. Neither could Congress afford to keep it, for its officers and men had not been paid in months, and an army which is both unpaid and idle has a certain volcanic quality about it. Already, in 1781, there had been a minor mutiny of the Pennsylvania line—not militia malcontents but hard-bitten regulars—which was quelled with little difficulty. But how long could the soldiers' resentment be contained?

Finally, there was Congress itself. Many of its distinguished members had gone to other duties. Many more had been rendered ineligible by the provision that no member might serve more than three successive years. Congress' prestige was at a low ebb because of "an excess of the spirit of liberty, which has made the particular states show a jealousy of all power not in their own hands." [16] State politicians found it useful to denounce any proposal to increase Congressional power. "They think their own consequence connected with the power of the [state] government of which they are a part; and will endeavor to encrease the one as a means of encreasing the other." [17]

By the fall of 1782 Congress had reached an impasse. Desperate for revenue, it had proposed to levy a five-percent tariff, or impost, on manufactured goods coming into the United States. Since this would require an amendment to the Articles of Confederation, it was necessary to have the measure ratified by all thirteen states. By November, 1782, all states had given their approval except Rhode Island. Its legislature had uncompromisingly refused to acquiesence because it felt that an impost was placing an undue and discriminatory burden on the commercial states. Rhode Island wrapped herself in the cloak of state sovereignty and defied the power of Congress—which most of the states had been doing implicitly since 1776.[18]

Hamilton was appointed to a committee which was to consider what steps were to be taken. Another member of the committee was James Madison, a slight, diffident Virginian whose shy demeanor concealed a steel-trap mind of tremendous intellectual capacity and force. Madison was serving his third year in Congress, and his thinking was fully as nationalistic as Hamilton's. "The idea of erecting our national independence on the ruins of public faith and national honor," he exclaimed, "must be horrid to every mind which retained either honesty or pride." [19]

The committee's first task was to attempt to persuade Rhode Island to change its mind. Hamilton drew up a message to the state which was to be delivered by a Congressional delegation. Hamilton did not mince words: "[Congress] feel themselves unable to devise any other [means], that will be more efficacious, less exceptionable or more generally agreeable; and if this is refused they anticipate calamities of a most menacing nature." Altogether the tone was more threatening than conciliatory. The delegation never reached its destination because in the meantime it was learned that Virginia had withdrawn its ratification of the impost amendment.[20]

Hamilton and Madison were not done. The latter, more experienced than his young colleague, offered an omnibus proposal which was an eighteenth-century version of "log-rolling." In March, 1783, he proposed that the ratification of the tariff amendment be accompanied by and conditioned upon the assumption of the states' war debts by the national government; that requisitions, or requests for funds from the states, be based on population rather than land values; and that states with western lands be required to cede them to the national government at once. (Some had already agreed to do so but had delayed actual cession.) Thus the assumption of state debts and the land cessions "are to serve as sweeteners to those who oppose the impost." [21]

Having thus learned one lesson, Hamilton promptly ignored another. So determined was he that the bill should pass without alteration that he found himself in the company of the obstreperous Rhode Islanders voting against its final passage. So intent was he in wishing to enhance the prestige of Congress that he objected to the appointment of revenue collectors by the states.[22] Hamilton had yet to learn that politics was often the art of attaining the possible. The bill passed Congress, but its approval by the states was lost in the welter of confusion attending the arrival of news of the peace treaty and the general consensus that Congress' usefulness was at an end.

Despite the failures of the Confederation government, despite the "dangerous prejudices in the particular States," Hamilton clung to his goal of establishing the public credit of the national government. He vigorously opposed the idea of turning the problem of the national debt over to the states. When it was proposed that the army be dismissed and the troops turned back to their states to be paid, he dissented sharply. He insisted that the army had fought in the cause of the United States and Congress must settle its accounts.

Furthermore, to pay the army and not satisfy private creditors was a breach of faith which Congress could not in good conscience tolerate.[23]

There was a more powerful and more subtle reason for Hamilton's view. He had earlier noted that "a national debt if it is not excessive, will be to us a national blessing, it will be powerfull cement of our union." [24] This was particularly true now that the war was over and the most important cohesive force of the union of the states thus ended. More than ever there had to be a potent and influential group who had an economic stake in the national government, and therefore a motive to support and preserve it. If the states assumed the national debt, holders of public securities would no longer have such a stake in the Confederation.

The most critical problem facing Congress,—it daily became more acute—was still what to do with the army. As early as December, 1782, a delegation of senior officers headed by Hamilton's old acquaintance General Alexander McDougall, arrived in Philadelphia to present the army's case to Congress. Although their manner was respectful, it was ominously clear that they expected an answer. Hamilton's agile mind surveyed the situation and saw that there was a way to turn circumstances to the account of nationalism. The states were refractory. One small state, Rhode Island, had rendered Congress helpless. But was Congress indeed helpless? Did it not have ready at hand, literally, loaded guns "to produce a concurrence in the measures which the exigencies of affairs demand?" [25]

The Newburgh Plot

A revolution, of necessity, produces an army, for it is an essential instrument of the overthrow of the old order. In most revolutions the control of the army is a determinant factor in the direction which the revolution takes. Cromwell, Napoleon, Chiang Kai-shek, and Hitler immediately come to mind as men who used control of the army as the key to the "new order."

In the midst of his efforts to secure government revenue and establish public credit, Hamilton conceived of a combination of civilian creditors and unpaid soldiers whose combined pressure might force recalcitrant elements in Congress and in the states to yield. It has already been noted that when it was proposed that a special impost be raised for the army alone, Hamilton objected strenuously. This would have destroyed the support of civilian creditors who would, in the long run, be much more valuable in creating support for the national government. Nor did he lose sight of the fact that paying off the army would not restore public credit. To Hamilton the payment of the immediate obligations of the government was a means toward the larger objective of making the United States financially respectable, inspiring enough confidence to enable it to borrow from its citizens and from foreign countries.

The notion of using the threat of the army was not confined to Hamilton. Robert and Gouverneur Morris, General Henry Knox, and several others thought that extreme measures were necessary. In early February, 1783, Hamilton wrote a confidential letter to General Washington at his headquarters in Newburgh, New York. He pointed out the fact that "the state of our finances was perhaps never more critical," but that in this crisis Congress was "not governed by reason or foresight but by circumstances." What was to be done? "The claims of the army," suggested Hamilton, "urged with moderation, but with firmness . . . may add weight to the applications of Congress to the several states." This would be effective only if Washington would not "discountenance their endeavors to procure redress, but rather . . . *to take direction of them.* . . . This will enable you in case of extremity to guide the torrent, and bring order perhaps even good, out of confusion." Nor did he attempt to conceal the fact that it was more than just the army which caused him concern. "The great *desideratum* at present is the establishment of general funds, which alone can do justice to the Creditors of the United States, . . . restore public credit and supply the future wants of the government. This is the object of all men of sense; in this influence the army, properly directed, may co-operate." [26]

Washington did not answer Hamilton's letter for almost a month. When he did, it was obvious that he was laboring under great restraint. "The sufferings of a complaining Army on the one hand, and the inability of Congress and the tardiness of the States on the other, are forebodings of evil . . ." he admitted. But Hamilton's proposal he dismissed in a tone which left no doubt that the former aide was receiving a reprimand. "I shall give it as my opinion, that it would at this day be productive of Civil commotions and end in blood. Unhappy situation this! God forbid we should be involved in it." [27]

The commander in chief's apprehension was justified. On March 10 he was handed an anonymous petition calling for a meeting of officers to obtain redress for the army's grievances. This was accompanied by an appeal which called on the officers to insist upon satisfaction from Congress. The alternatives: "If peace, then nothing can separate you from your arms but death; if war . . . inviting the direction of your illustrious leader, you will retire to some unsettled country . . . and 'mock them when their fear cometh.' " In other words, if the treaty of peace were concluded without further military operations the army would refuse to lay down its arms; if the war continued it would set up a new country in the western wilderness and leave Congress to its fate. [28]

A second and more hastily drawn petition written by Major John Armstrong appeared in the camps. Although its tone was more respectful, it proposed that the officers appeal "from the *justice* to the fears of the government." [29]

Washington was appalled, but he well understood the deep-seated resentment of the army. He therefore issued an order authorizing a meeting, but he determined to bring the full weight of his prestige to bear to crush the incipient revolt. He decided not to preside at the meeting but to make a brief appeal to the officers and then leave them to deliberate. It was a dramatic moment when the big general strode into the assembly, for Washington hated such public appearances and rarely made them. He asked his audience for "one last act of patriotism" and urged them to "rely on the plighted faith of your country . . . and to express your utmost horror and detestation of the man who wishes . . . to overturn the liberties of our country, and who wishes to open the flood gates of civil discord and deluge our rising empire in blood." After he left the assembly the officers repudiated the incendiary petitions and voted confidence in Washington and Congress. The crisis had passed.[30] When Washington informed Hamilton of the appearances of the petitions—but before the officers' meeting of March 15—Hamilton obviously did not completely abandon hope for his scheme. "Your Excellency has in my opinion acted wisely," he wrote. "The best way is ever not to attempt to stem a torrent but to divert it." And a little later he was moved to add that "if no excesses take place I shall not be sorry that ill-humors have appeared. I shall not regret importunity, if temperate, from the army." In answer to Washington's surmise that the plot had orginated in the capital, Hamilton admitted that this was "partly true. I have myself urged in Congress the propriety of uniting . . . the public creditors, and the army . . . to prevail upon the states. . . . I have expressed the same sentiments out-of-doors." But he had never advocated extreme measures, simply "that Congress should adopt such a plan as would embrace the relief of all public creditors including the army. . . . I thought the discontent of the army might be turned to good account." But he closed with an expression of righteous indignation at "any combination of Force" which might lead to the "horrors of a civil war." [31]

When he received word of the collapse of the "mutiny," Hamilton noted with resignation, "Republican jealousy has in it a principle of hostility to an army whatever be their merits, whatever be their claims, to the gratitude of the community. It acknowledges their services with unwillingness and rewards them with reluctance." The army would have to submit to its fate. "I cannot myself enter into any views of coercion which some Gentlemen entertain, for I confess could force avail I should almost wish to see it employed." [32] Hamilton did not seem to grasp the fact that armies in revolt are seldom "temperate" or "moderate."

In the midst of all this, on March 12, came news that the United States and Great Britain had concluded preliminary peace negotiations. This was followed in a few days by news that France and Spain had also concluded agreements with Britain. Although these were not final treaties, no one doubted that the long war was over and that peace and independence had come at last. Washington must have been overwhelmed with the magnitude of his accomplishment, but he permitted himself to say only, "The News of a general Peace has filled my Mind with inexpressible satisfaction." [33]

On April 19, the day after Congress had passed Madison's "Omnibus" bill and eight years to the day after Lexington and Concord, Congress announced the end of hostilities. It authorized the commander in chief to grant "furloughs" to the soldiers, from which, of course, they were not expected to return. To Washington's urgent request for three months' pay for the army, the only response was the issue of paper certificates authorizing the states to pay the returning men. There were no farewell addresses, no parades, no final salutes. Congress had voted the soldiers their arms so the veterans simply slung their muskets and left for home. Thus was a shabby army shabbily dismissed by the cause it had served.[34]

There remained a final touch of irony. In June state troops stationed at Lancaster marched into Philadelphia, surrounded the State House, and confronted Congress with demands for pay. These were short-term militiamen and recruits of a sort that might start a good-sized riot but not a military revolt. When the Pennsylvania Executive Council refused to order out the militia to quell the mutineers, Congress, as Hamilton put it, was "in the power of a lawless armed banditti" and therefore unceremoniously adjourned to Princeton. Although the members were scheduled to reconvene on June 26, it was not until the end of July that a quorum from nine states finally assembled.[35]

Long before this Hamilton's patience had become exhausted. In May he had written to Governor Clinton that he wished to be replaced and only the crisis created by the "mutiny" detained him. He drew up a proposal for Congress calling for a constitutional convention, but a notation on the document told the story: "Resolutions intended to be submitted to Congress at Princeton . . . but abandoned for want of support." It was dated June 30, 1783. By the middle of August Hamilton was home in Albany "preparing to take leave of public life to enter into the practice of the law." [36]

Hamilton realized that New York City was about to become the most important commercial and business center in the United States. It was also being talked of as the national capital since it was doubtful that Congress would ever return to Philadelphia. Thus it was that, as the British army finally evacuated the city in November, 1783, Hamilton and his little family moved into residence at Number 57, Wall Street. This part of the city was still a fashionable residential district although many of the residents were lawyers who, like Hamilton, used their homes as offices. Robert Troup was a neighbor and lived and worked nearby. In the city which had been the headquarters of the British army for seven years, the erstwhile veteran soldier and former Congressman began his professional career. He was twenty–eight years old.

Attorney-At-Law

> I . . . do solemnly without any mental reservations or Equivocation whatsoever swear and declare and call God to witness That I renounce and adjure all allegiance to the King of Great Britain; and that I will bear true faith & allegiance to the State of New York, as a free Independent State, and that I will in all things to the best of my knowledge & ability. Do my duty as a good and faithful Subject of the said State ought to do. So help me God.

So swore Alexander Hamilton and "every attorney, solicitor and counsellor at law" in the state of New York under an act passed by the legislature.[37] It is ironic that revolutionary governments are always highly sensitive about the loyalty of their "subjects" and that repression of "the enemy" usually intensifies in direct ratio to the decrease in the need for internal security. So it seemed to Hamilton, and he deplored the large numbers of Loyalists who left the city with the British army. Yet many remained under the dubious assumption that they would be protected by the guarantees of the peace treaty. These people were, after all, Americans whose roots were as deep as many who had been patriots. For many and varied reasons they had decided to cast their lot with the new nation in the expectation that they would be accepted.

Governor Clinton and the legislature soon showed them their mistake. Those who had remained within the British lines, for whatever reason, were disenfranchised. Their rights could be restored only after they had taken a complicated oath that they had not been guilty of "aiding" the enemy. This aid might simply consist of selling supplies, renting property, or otherwise doing business with the British army of occupation. Such activities were also frequently the pretext for the seizure of Loyalist property.

Hamilton was throughly alarmed by what he regarded as "the subversion of all private security and genuine liberty." He had no sympathy for those who had actively opposed the American cause, but he feared that an indiscriminate witch hunt would result in injustice to "a large number of . . . fellow-citizens unheard, [and] untried." It would also permanently alienate a considerable number of potentially substantial people. "Make it the interest of those citizens, who, during the revolution, were opposed to us to be friends of the new government, by affording them not only protection, but participation in its privileges, and they will undoubtedly become its friends." He was anxious to salvage the ability and resources of the artisans, mechanics, "rich merchants and others who are called Tories." There was little danger that they would subvert the government "if they are allowed to be happy under the government of the society in which they live." [38]

Hamilton was also concerned because laws, such as New York had enacted, flouted the authority of the national government. The treaty between the United States and Great Britain contained specific provision that "there shall be no future Confiscations made nor any Prosecutions commenc'd against any Person or Persons for or by Reason of the Part, which he or they may have taken in the present War, and that no Person shall . . . suffer any future Loss or Damage, either in his Person Liberty or Property." [39] To Hamilton the treaty was binding on the states since "the act of confederation places the exclusive right of war and peace in the United States in Congress." Here Hamilton was making the fundamental point that when the states granted powers to the national government they must be bound by the exercise of that power "and ought religiously to observe it." [40]

He recognized also that if patriotism was not the "last refuge of the scoundrel" certainly there were "rash and unprincipled men" who "pretend to appeal to the spirit of Whiggism, while they endeavour to put in motion all the furious and dark passions of the human mind." [41] There was no doubt Hamilton had Governor Clinton and his party in mind when he observed that "there are some among us, who possess interest to shut their minds against . . . that moderation, which the real welfare of the community teaches." [42] Thus, early in his career, Hamilton set himself against George Clinton and all his works, not only because he was contemptuous of his demagoguery, but because the attack on the Loyalists was an attack on the class of wealthy and substantial people whom Hamilton believed were necessary to the nation's future. Moreover, to attack their property rights was to jeopardize the property rights of everyone.

The young attorney did more than protest. A considerable part of his law practice consisted of defending the former Loyalists in cases involving confiscations and property damages. It was well that Hamilton did not decide to pursue a political career at just this time, for his position was not only unpopular but led some of the most extreme "patriots" to question his own loyalty. Yet he gained a wide reputation in a litigation which, on the surface, seemed to be for a hopeless cause.

In February, 1784, Hamilton undertook the defense of Joshua Waddington, a British merchant who was being sued under a state Trespass Act. Waddington had operated a brewery on the property of Mrs. Elizabeth Rutgers in New York City during the British occupation. Mrs. Rutgers was suing in the Mayor's Court to recover damages of $8,000 in rent. Arrayed against Hamilton were his old friend Robert Troup and Egbert Benson, the attorney-general for the state of New York. The temper of the time being what it was, it seemed too much to expect that the British brewer could successfully plead against the patriot widow. *Rutgers* v. *Waddington* was a test case in more ways than one.[43]

Hamilton based his defense, first of all, on the ground that the war had created special circumstances under which international law applied. Citing Vattel, Grotius, and other authorities, he contended for the principle that the conqueror was entitled to the spoils of war. Counsel for the plaintiff argued that the War of Independence had been no ordinary war, but a civil war waged by an enemy who had pillaged and looted. No honest patriot would deny that America had fought against a tyrannical and brutal foe.

This gave Hamilton his opening for a countercharge. Surely his equally patriotic opponents would not deny that it was a war between the sovereign government of the United States and that of Great Britain. To do so would be to deny the validity of the Declaration of Independence and the legal existence of Congress. According to international law, the justice or the injustice of the war had no bearing on the rights of belligerents. He then moved to the principal point of his case. The treaty, he pointed out, was made by Congress under authority conferred upon it by the states in the Articles of Confederation. By the terms of the treaty, claims of citizens of both nations for war damages were reciprocally cancelled. If the United States was to maintain its dignity and prestige as a nation it must honor its obligations.[44]

Hamilton now postulated an altogether novel doctrine.

Where the law of a state conflicted with a treaty made under
the authority of the United States, the state law must give
way. Furthermore, the courts rather than the legislatures
were to determine whether such a conflict existed and, if such
were the case, declare the law invalid. Here was the concept
of judicial review, the power of the courts to determine
whether a legislative act was constitutional. Hamilton appealed to the Mayor's Court to make judicial history which
"will be handed down to posterity." [45]

It was clear that the court was impressed with Hamilton's
argument. It was equally clear that it was not prepared to
accept the revolutionary concept of judicial review. Obviously Governor Clinton and the legislature loomed larger
than posterity. Yet the court in effect acknowledged the validity of Hamilton's position concerning the precedence of national over state law. In ruling that Waddington was liable
for only a portion of the damages, it pointed out that the
conflict between the Trespass Act and the treaty was obviously not intended by the legislature. Thus it exercised the
function of judicial interpretation, but it was careful to acknowledge that "to set the *judicial* above the *legislative* . . .
would be subversive of all government." [46]

It should perhaps be noted that the state legislature later
made it painfully clear that the Mayor's Court had not by
any means correctly interpreted its intentions. It passed a
resolution censuring the court and reaffirmed the Trespass
Act. Hamilton, having made his point, advised his client to
settle out of court when Mrs. Rutgers filed an appeal. [47]

Hamilton further damned himself in the eyes of many of
his fellow citizens by representing British merchants in their
suits against Americans for prewar debts. Yet he left no doubt
that he intended to champion the rights of property, and in
the long run it was the group of substantial citizens called
"conservative" who supported the cause of nationalism and

public credit. In the meantime, "legislative folly has afforded so plentiful a harvest to us lawyers that we have scarcely a moment to spare from the substantial business of reaping." [48]

The Road to Philadelphia

When Alexander Hamilton had gone to Congress in the fall of 1782, he had carried with him a set of resolutions which he himself had drawn and the New York legislature had passed "proposing a Convention of the states to enlarge the powers of Congress and vest them with funds." A year later he was convinced that there seemed to be "little disposition either in or out of Congress to give solidity to our national system." Whatever nationalist sentiment had prevailed in New York had vanished and "the road to popularity in each state is to inspire jealousies of the power of Congress, though nothing can be more apparent than that they have no power." [49]

Next to the lack of revenue, the most persistent and obvious problem was the lack of control over interstate and foreign commerce. This was felt particularly by those states which had no deep-water ports and were therefore dependent on their neighbors for foreign imports. Both Connecticut and New Jersey, for example, were at the mercy of New York, which levied heavy tariffs on trade with its neighbors. So indignant was New Jersey, in fact, that in 1785 its House of Representatives refused to grant the annual requisition to Congress until New York had been brought to account. Although every state was delinquent in its payments, none had ever defied national authority so belligerently. Congress was so alarmed that it sent a special delegation to secure a repeal of the offending resolution. It is interesting to note that one of the delegates, Charles Pinckney, ended his appeal to the legislature by urging it to "instruct her delegates in Congress, to urge the calling of a general convention of the states, for the purpose of revising and amending the federal system." [50]

In addition to discriminating against their neighbors, states often enacted their own "navigation acts" in retaliation against foreign trade, especially that of Great Britain. For their part, most nations did not even attempt to conclude commercial agreements with the United States because they recognized that there was no way for Congress to enforce compliance. Instead, American vessels found themselves excluded from the profitable trade with the British West Indies, and American ship builders were barred from selling their vessels to British buyers. No wonder Hamilton observed that if "the constitution is slighted or explained away, upon every frivolous pretext, the future spirit of government will be feeble, distracted and arbitrary." [51]

Finally there were signs of deep sectional dissension. In Congress seven states indicated a willingness to allow Foreign Secretary John Jay to concede the navigation of the Mississippi in return for commercial concessions from Spain. But the five southern states, already deeply suspicious of the merchants of the northeast, were outraged. This seemed the final proof of their conviction that northern commercial interests were as perfidious as Albion had ever been. In August, 1786, James Monroe of Virginia reported talk of "a dismemberment of the States east of the Hudson from the Union." His suspicions were not unfounded, for Theodore Sedgewick of Massachusetts was writing at about the same time, "It well becomes the eastern and middle States, who are in interest one, seriously to consider what advantages result to them from their connection with the Southern States. They can give us nothing." And Timothy Bloodworth of North Carolina may have spoken the conviction of many when he remarked that "the Confederated compact is no more than a rope of sand." [52]

These suspicions of each other and of the national government on the part of the states had a debilitating effect upon Congress. As Hamilton discovered, to be a member of Congress automatically brought one under the suspicion of being subversive of the states. By the middle of the decade, only a few outstanding Americans like Jefferson and Madison were willing to risk their reputations by being reelected to the national legislature. Members of Congress frequently waited for weeks or even months for representatives of nine states to assemble—nine being the number necessary under the Articles of Confederation to enact legislation. Nor did it help matters that Congress moved the seat of government from Princeton to Annapolis to Trenton and, finally, to New York.

By 1785, then, the nationalist cause looked dark indeed. States were jealous of each other and of Congress. The national government itself seemed to have reached a level of impotence from which it would never recover.

In the spring of 1785 there occurred an episode whose importance was probably not realised by the participants. Virginia and Maryland had for some time been disputing the commercial and fishing rights along their mutual boundaries, the Potomac River and the Chesapeake Bay. At the insistence of James Madison, the two states appointed commissioners who met under the friendly aegis of General Washington at Mount Vernon. They reached a satisfactory and amicable agreement which was remarkable, not only for the mutual willingness to make concessions but for the declaration that the waterways were open to the trade of all Americans and to foreigners. The commissioners also suggested that future conferences be held among the states to discuss the commercial questions.

When the agreement came up for approval by the Virginia legislature, Madison saw an opportunity to utilize the situation for a broader purpose. Like Hamilton, he suffered from

his reputation as a "continentalist." He therefore induced
John Tyler to introduce a resolution naming Madison and
four others to "meet such commissioners as may be appointed
by the other states . . . to take into consideration the trade
of the United States . . . to consider how far a uniform
system . . . may be necessary to their common interest." [53]
The way was thus paved for the meeting of the Annapolis
Convention.

The news of the Virginia resolution reached New York at
a particularly fortuitous moment. The Clintonians were as
jealous as ever of Congressional power, but the state had
become aroused because British redcoats still occupied several forts on the American side of the Canadian boundary
in northern and western New York. In its eagerness to find
some means to retaliate against Great Britain, the legislature
forgot its anti-nationalistic sentiments long enough to appoint
Hamilton and Egbert Benson, a like-minded New York attorney, as delegates to the Annapolis meeting. [54]

When Hamilton reached the Maryland capital in September, 1786, he found that only a few of the delegates had
assembled, but one of them was Madison who had arrived
three days before him. Yet they found little that was encouraging in the small group representing only five states. "I
do not extend my views beyond commercial reform," wrote
Madison to Jefferson. "To speak the truth I almost despair
even of this." [55] Yet there was some satisfaction in the fact
that the delegates who did come were all nationalists and
were determined to make the most of the occasion. At Hamilton's suggestion they agreed to issue a call for another convention to consider not only commercial relations but the
whole question of revising the Articles of Confederation.
Hamilton was appointed to draft such a recommendation,
and its tone was typically vigorous and forthright. As on a
previous occasion, it was Madison who applied the brakes.

Instead of shocking—and thereby arousing—the opposition with a proposal to revise the Articles, the report simply pointed out that the commercial power would obviously affect other related powers. The suggested meeting would thus have to "devise such further provisions as shall appear to them necessary to render the constitution of the Federal Government adequate to the exigencies of the Union." [56]

Eight months later, on May 25, 1787, delegates from seven states opened the first session of the Constitutional Convention. Within a few days twelve states were represented, and the serious work of writing a constitution had begun.

It may be well to ask why, after years of seemingly insurmountable opposition, the cause of nationalism suddenly blossomed. After all, during 1786 it was a rare occasion when representatives of as many as nine states could be found in their seats in Congress.

Two events, one just before and one just after the Annapolis Convention, may help to explain the "miracle at Philadelphia." In August, 1786, Charles Pinckney of South Carolina presented to Congress a list of sweeping proposals for strengthening its powers. These included exclusive control over interstate and foreign commerce and the power to levy customs duties and to penalize those states which were delinquent in paying their requisitions. There was even a proposal to enforce the attendance of members of Congress. The boldness of these proposals carried with them a note of desperation. Only extreme measures, they seemed to imply, could save the situation. But the debate ended in the usual futile inaction. [57]

The second event was the outbreak of Shays' Rebellion in Massachusetts in September, 1786, almost simultaneously with the Annapolis meeting. A typical postwar boom for merchants and farmers had been followed by an equally typi-

cal bust which saw a sharp decline in prices and wages. As
in most depressions, the farmers were particularly hard-
pressed to pay their debts. Shays' Rebellion, a rising of farmers in western Massachusetts in defiance of attempts to fore-
close their mortgages, was a symptom of the deep economic
unrest which pervaded the whole country. Shays and his
followers were only the latest of a number of protesters—not
rabble, but respectable, impoverished farmers—who resorted
to violence not only in Massachusetts but also in Virginia,
Connecticut, and South Carolina. It is worth noting that
when Massachusetts appealed to Congress for help in quell-
ing the rebellion the answer was apathetic helplessness. It is
also noteworthy that the Shaysites won a victory at the polls
in Massachusetts at the next election.[58]

Thus the culmination of the movement for a constitutional
convention was not just a crisis of what Madison called "the
existing embarrassments and mortal diseases of the Confederacy." [59] It was also the essential failure of the states, the sort
of "despotism and iniquity of the Legislature" with which
Hamilton characterized the government of New York. It is
true that he called upon "those who are concerned for the
security of property" to correct the situation, but he thought
reform was as necessary in the states as in the national government. While Hamilton may have seen the struggle as a
conflict between "men of respectability" and those *"of the
levelling kind"* yet he tended to see the situation from the
point of view of the urban business interests.[60]

It should be remembered that property holders included
a large number of small farmers whose few hundred acres
were as precious to them as the holdings of the great planters.
In the political lexicon of the revolutionary philosophers,
property was joined with "life and liberty." The idea that
property was inherently hostile to liberty was characteristic
of the thinking of the industrial age of the late nineteenth and

twentieth centuries. John Locke insisted that property was necessary to the full enjoyment of life and liberty. Even Dan Shays and his rebels were aroused by what they regarded as illegal and unjust attempts to take their land away from them.

Thus, by 1786 there was a variety of ills which beset the nation, the magnitude of which might seem small compared with later crises in the national experience. But there seemed to be no remedies at either the state or national level through which solutions might be proposed and acted upon. The inadequacies of the states, "so frequent and so flagrant . . ." said James Madison, "contributed more to that uneasiness which produced the Convention . . . than those which accrued . . . from the inadequacy of the Confederation." [61] It was the overriding necessity for an orderly society, which for years had obsessed Hamilton and Morris and Washington, that accounted for the assembly at Philadelphia and its determination to bring about a revolution in the nature of American government.

VII Hamilton and the Constitution*

THE CONSTITUTIONAL CONVENTION of 1787 was the climax of the American Revolution. The vacuum of power created by the destruction of British imperial rule in 1783 had been only partially eliminated by the government under the Articles of Confederation. "You see alas what contempt we are falling into since the peace," observed Hamilton to the New York legislature in January, 1787. "You see to what our commerce is exposed on every side. You see us the laughing stock, the sport of foreign nations, and what may this lead to? I dread Sir, to think." [1] Not until the constitution produced by the convention of 1787 had been implemented, did Americans find a satisfactory answer to the question of what should replace British imperial rule.

A nineteenth-century historian John Fiske coined the phrase "the critical period" to describe the United States in the postwar years, and he elaborated on the theme by suggesting that the nation was on the verge of disruption and disintegration. More modern scholars have suggested that this "picture . . . of stagnation, ineptitude, bankruptcy, corruption, and disintegration . . . is at worst false and at best grossly distorted." To use a medical metaphor, the patient's condi-

* For this chapter see especially Clinton Rossiter, *1787: The Grand Convention*. Hereafter cited as Rossiter, *Grand Convention*.

tion was "serious" but not "critical." They have suggested that the United States has since suffered much more serious economic, diplomatic, and governmental crises than those of the 1780's.[2]

History seldom comes to conclusive judgements on such questions, but it should be pointed out that there was a conspicuous lack of institutional frameworks within which the difficulties of the United States in the 1780's could be managed. Neither state nor national governments nor private institutions possessed the necessary authority and prestige to cope with the multitude of problems. This is not to say that the nation's people were in a state of alarmed confusion or panic. A casual visitor in the busy towns or in the rural back country would have seen a tranquil citizenry going about its business with little apprehension for the future.

Yet it was this very apathy which aroused concern among the nationalists and impelled them along the road-to Philadelphia. They greatly feared that the nation would collapse, not so much from Daniel Shays' rebels or even from the predators of Europe, as from the inertia of a people who had neither the vision nor the boldness to grapple with the future. "Power must be granted, or civil Society cannot exist," Hamilton told the New York legislature. "The possibility of abuse is no argument against the *thing;* this possibility is incident to every species of power however placed or modified." And later, addressing the ratifying convention, he urged that "when . . . you have rendered your system as perfect as human forms can be; you must place confidence; you must give power." [3]

What course the history of the United States might have taken had the convention not met and completed its great work is a matter for speculation. The fact remains that the men who met in Philadelphia in the summer of 1787 believed, justifiably or not, "that this is the critical opportunity for establishing the prosperity of this country on a solid foundation." [4]

The Convention Assembles

It was ironic that Hamilton, as fervent a nationalist as could be found in America, should be resident in a state which was notable for its suspicion of centralized government. Early in 1787 a desperate Congress had once again gotten twelve states to agree to the levying of an impost by the national government. But New York was adamant. Despite Hamilton's exhortations, the legislature refused to bow to the tyranny of "King Cong." Yet Governor Clinton and his anti-federalist cohorts (i.e., those opposed to increasing the power of the central government) may have been reluctant to push their recalcitrance too far by refusing to elect delegates to the Philadelphia meeting. Despite his dominant position, Clinton sensed the danger of completely alienating such prominent nationalists as General Schuyler, John Jay, James Duane, Egbert Benson, and Philip Livingston. Or perhaps the governor thought that New York ought at least to have representatives to keep a watchful eye on the proceedings.

The New York legislature therefore voted to send a delegation to the convention, but one thoroughly representative of the state's anti-federalist sentiments. Only the powerful influence of Philip Schuyler in the state senate forced a compromise which allowed the general's favorite son-in-law to be selected. The two other delegates, John Lansing and Robert Yates, were staunch Clintonians, so that however eloquently Hamilton might plead the cause of nationalism in Philadelphia, he would not speak for New York. To make doubly sure, the legislature instructed the delegation to restrict themselves to "the sole and express purpose of revising the articles of Confederation." [5]

Hamilton arrived in Philadelphia on May 18, 1787, four days after the date set for the opening of the convention but a full week before a quorum of delegates assembled. He joined men from twelve states who eventually numbered fifty-five. Some of these arrived late and some departed early. Hamilton himself left Philadelphia before the convention had reached the halfway point in its deliberations, but he returned to sign the final report. [6]

These fifty-five "Founding Fathers" were no longer young revolutionary firebrands, but neither were they elder statesmen. In fact, their average age was forty-three, although almost all of them had achieved positions of prominence in the nation or in their states. As to their supernatural character, it should be borne in mind that the Revolutionary generation could have produced at least an additional half a hundred who were their equal in experience and talent.

Much has been written about the background and motives of the men who came to Philadelphia. Suggestions have been made that, collectively or individually, they were there to protect the interests of a social and economic class, or to enhance the welfare of their state and section, or that they were moved by some inner flame of national destiny. No doubt all these motives were present in varying degrees—the selfish and the honorable mixed in the minds of the delegates themselves—although the venerable George Mason vowed that he "would not, upon pecuniary motives, serve in this convention for a thousand pounds per day." [7]

It is perhaps more profitable to the understanding of the delegates and their work to note some more concrete characteristics. They were members of a generation of Americans who had more political sophistication than any other in the nation's history. All but a few had served in some official capacity in their state or colonial governments. Forty–two had served in Congress, at least half of them with considerable distinction. Half of them had helped to draft either state constitutions or state law codes. Three-fourths of them were serving their states in some capacity in 1787. Alexander Hamilton's record as war veteran and member of Congress and of his state legislature was not particularly distinguished in this company of men.[8] When they spoke of what Congress had or had not been capable of achieving, when they pointed to the inadequacies of the states in dealing with national problems, they spoke of things of which they had first-hand knowledge, and their colleagues who listened did not need proof of conditions they had all experienced. They were familiar with working examples of bicameral and unicameral legislatures, of single and multiple executives, of separation of powers and government by legislature only, of the centralized federalism of the British Empire, and of the decentralized government of the Confederation Congress. The contention of those who argue that the convention only fused together what was already a part of the American tradition is quite correct. But that tradition embraced a variety of experience which ran from Magna Carta through the charter of the Virginia Company to the Articles of Confederation.

It is also fair to say that a considerable number of the delegates were imbued with a sense of nationhood, a belief that the government of the United States had to be infused with more unity and energy in order to make its future secure. Some felt this more keenly than others, and only a handful, like Hamilton's colleagues Yates and Lansing, were completely hostile to the idea of greater centralization. In particular, the majority was determined that however limited the government's *powers* might be it must have *power*. And this

could only be achieved by freeing the central government
from its dependence on the states. As the work of the convention progressed, the delegates found themselves driven by two
other considerations. The first was that they must not adjourn until they had accomplished their work, until they had
a solid plan of government they could propose for public
approval. The second was an increasing awareness that whatever personal, sectional, or state axes there might be to grind,
the ultimate test was that "the plan must be accomodated to
the public mind." Pierce Butler of South Carolina reminded
his colleagues that Solon "gave the Athenians not the best
Govt. he could devise; but the best they wd. receive." The
framers were aware of how far they could go and, above all,
how far they could not go.[9]

Hamilton's advocacy of strong government was a matter
of both public and private record. As early as 1780 he had
proposed a government with "complete sovereignty in all that
relates to war, peace, trade, finance, and to the management
of foreign affairs," and he had urged an immediate "convention of all the states with full authority to conclude finally
upon a general confederation."[10] When he first appeared as
a member of Congress in 1782, he had carried with him
instructions from the New York legislature urging that such
a convention be called. In his efforts to secure more power
for the Confederation government, he had argued that the
taxing power was implicit in Congress' powers to raise armies
and wage war, thereby foreshadowing the "implied powers"
clause of the Constitution. In *Rutgers* v. *Waddington* he had
set forth the doctrine that a conflict between state statute and
an act of the general government must be resolved in favor
of the latter's supremacy. In short, there had been a constantly recurring theme from the beginning of Hamilton's
political career—"Congress ought to have complete au-

thority in all but the mere municipal law"—to the Annapolis Convention—"to render the constitution . . . adequate to the exigencies of the Union." [11]

Hamilton's Plan of the Union

The opening of the convention revealed that the delegates were struggling with a dilemma. Clearly the great majority of members believed that the Articles of Confederation were inadequate for the needs of the nation. Yet few had dared to say so when the state legislatures were electing them. North Carolina sent its representatives "for the purpose of revising the Federal Constitution." As noted, New York appointed Hamilton, Yates, and Lansing "for the sole and express purpose of revising the Articles of Confederation." Even in those states which had adopted the wording of the Annapolis Convention in instructing their delegates, it was widely assumed that "the federal Constitution" meant the Articles of Confederation and that to "render [it] adequate to the exigencies of the Union" did not mean abandoning the entire framework of the Confederation government.[12]

If they were to act with vigor and violate the spirit if not the letter of their instructions, it was obvious that the delegates would have to offer an alternative plan, one which would be both a comprehensive and an acceptable replacement of the Articles. And they could scarcely achieve this if they were exposed to the "licentious publications of their proceedings" which would undoubtedly result in "misrepresentations and mistakes." The convention therefore decided on secret deliberations and resolved that "nothing . . . be printed, or otherwise published or communicated." [13] Thus most of the compulsive orators were muzzled, honest doubts could be freely expressed about such sacrosanct principles as state sovereignty, and opinions vehemently defended in the early days of the proceedings could be gracefully abandoned as reason or compromise might dictate. It may appear surprising to modern Americans that this secrecy was not seriously challenged by the public, perhaps because the gentlemen of the press had not yet inserted the inalienable "right of the public to know" into their version of the Bill of Rights. It was perhaps understandable that Jefferson, far from the scene of action and impatient at the evasiveness of his confidant Madison should have pronounced this "tying up the tongues" as "abominable." [14]

The nationalist cat was let out of the bag when Edmund Randolph, the eloquent governor of Virginia, got the floor on May 29 and introduced a plan drawn up by James Madison, which he suggested as the basis for debate. After a lengthy exposition which took most of the day, Randolph introduced two resolutions, the substance of which was that "a Union of the States merely federal will not accomplish the objects . . . [of] common defence, security of liberty & genl. welfare," and "that a *national* Government ought to be established consisting of a *supreme* Legislative, Executive & Judiciary." These resolutions were adopted by a vote of six states to one. Lansing was absent from the convention so Hamilton's affirmative vote was cancelled by Yates' negative. [15]

For the next three weeks the work of the convention progressed rapidly, but Hamilton took little part in the proceedings. He confined himself to brief remarks proposing to give the executive an absolute negative on all laws and supporting proportionate representation in both houses of the legislative branch. [16] The strongest objections to the Virginia plan were the sweeping extent of the powers to be given to the national government and the failure to provide equal representation in at least one house of the legislative branch. An alternative plan was presented by William Paterson of New Jersey limit-

ing the granting of powers and providing for equal representation in the legislature. It should be noted, however, that the
New Jersey plan was not a recasting of the Articles of Confederation, for it contained a provision which foreshadowed the
"supreme powers" clause of Article VI of the final draft of
the Constitution: "All Acts of the U. States . . . and all
Treaties made . . . shall be the supreme law of the respective
States . . . and that the Judiciary of the several States shall
be bound thereby." [17]

Although these restraints on the states and even stronger
ones proposed in the Virginia plan went far beyond the
Confederation framework—and shocked anti-federalists like
Lansing, Yates, and the bibulous Luther Martin from Maryland—Hamilton was not satisfied. Virtually silent since the
convention began, he finally entered the debate on June 18
with a plan of his own.

His presentation consumed five hours, the entire "working
day." It was a curious interlude since his proposal was so
sweepingly nationalist in its approach, so breathtaking in its
scope, that it drew virtually no response from the delegates.
Hamilton's address could be lifted bodily from the record of
the convention, and there would be scarcely a hint of its
existence. Just prior to his speech John Dickinson had made
a motion to postpone "the 1st Resolution of Mr. Paterson's
plan." Twenty-four hours later Madison's notes for June 19
began, "The Substitute offered yesterday by Mr. Dickinson
being rejected. . . ." [18]

Hamilton's plan was notable for two characteristics. First,
it was his intention to reduce the states to a position of
complete subordination. Not only were state laws "contrary
to the Constitution or laws of the United States to be utterly
void" but state governors were to be appointed by the chief
executive of the national government. Here Hamilton was
revealed as the continentalist with not a vestige of state loy-

alty. His only concern was that they perform their function as subordinate administrative units and be rendered helpless to interfere with the central government.

Secondly, Hamilton's plan embodied a comprehensive grant of national authority. Far from dividing power between the federal government and the states, as Madison proposed, the legislative branch would have "unlimited power of passing *all laws* without exception." Under his plan, also, the president and senators were to be elected for life.[19]

Altogether it was an odd performance. Did Hamilton believe that the convention, some members of which were already boggling at the far-reaching authority of the Virginia plan, could be persuaded to go even farther and consent to the proposition that the "State sovereignties ought not to exist"? Perhaps not. He was aware that "it went beyond the ideas of most members." But he reminded them that the crucial question was, "Will such a plan be accepted out of doors?" Hamilton thought so. He saw "evils operating in the States which must soon cure the people of their fondness for democracies. . . . The people will in time be unshackled from their prejudices." It may be that he hoped to fire the delegates with something of his own fervid and daring spirit. "Our Situation is peculiar," he urged, *"It leaves us Room to dream."*[20]

Man and Government

On July 29, ten days after the presentation of his plan to the convention, Hamilton left Philadelphia and returned to New York. He may have felt that his position on the New York delegation was fruitless and useless, hamstrung as he was by the recalcitrant Yates and Lansing. He may have felt the need to look to his private affairs, and there are some indications that he was even now beginning his campaign to get acceptance in New York for whatever plan the delegates might propose. He certainly did not leave in a mood of petulance over the failure of the convention to accept his ideas. In those remaining days before his departure and in a few brief appearances in August, he was active in debate, supporting direct election of the lower house of the legislature, discussing the almost insoluble problem of the method of choosing the president, insisting that the Confederation Congress' approval must be sought for the new constitution—these and other suggestions clearly indicate that he was not sulking in defeat. He returned to Philadelphia on September 6 to be present during the concluding sessions and served on the Committee on Style which prepared the final draft of the Constitution. His last speech was an urgent appeal for all members to sign the document, and he himself recorded his signature, though "no man's ideas were more remote from the plan than [mine] were known to be." [21]

Yet Hamilton's part in the convention was a disappointing episode in his career. To have worked with such singleness of purpose to strengthen the government and then to contribute so little appeared completely out of character with his usual brilliance.

The Constitutional Convention marks not so much a turning point in Hamilton's career and his thinking as a vantage point from which to examine his political ideas. The fact that he subsequently became the foremost advocate of the ratification of the Constitution and one of the ablest practitioners of its powers and usages does not make the ideas which he expressed on June 18 any less sincere. In the confidential atmosphere of Independence Hall he unburdened his notions of what constituted good government, and if his listeners were shocked—some later claimed they were horrified—at his concept of "the American empire," it was perhaps because Hamilton had never previously matured his own thoughts or had the proper forum in which to express them.

Hamilton was primarily concerned with results rather than forms. It was thus impossible for him to conceive of good government which did not also possess energy and authority. As noted above, Hamilton believed that the states, with "internal interests adverse to those of the whole," were the most serious obstacles to this energy and therefore must be reduced to complete subordination.[22]

Yet the power had to be firmly rooted in a republican government, for "there are two objects in forming systems of government—safety for the people and energy in the administration." Republicanism, as defined in eighteenth-century America, meant "a government which derives all its powers directly or indirectly from . . . the people, and is administered by persons holding their offices . . . for a limited period, or during good behavior [i.e., for life]." Hamilton was later accused by Jefferson of being a monarchist and by others of being opposed to democracy. To Hamilton, as to many other eighteenth-century Americans, democracy sometimes "presented an ungovernable mob, not only incapable of every deliberation, but prepared for every enormity." [23] It was to guard against this kind of democracy, so recently observed in Shays' Rebellion, that Hamilton proposed life tenure for the president and members of the senate. "It will be objected probably, that such an Executive will be an *elective Monarch,*" Hamilton wryly told the convention. "He w[oul]d reply that *Monarch* is an indefinite term. . . . [The Virginia plan] wd. be a monarch for seven years." [24] In short, none of this was consistent with republicanism. In another time and country, indeed, Hamilton might have accepted the efficiency of enlightened despotism, and he often expressed admiration for the British constitutional monarchy. But Hamilton was fully aware that he was an American and that any proposal would have to fit the American context. He recalled in later years that when he delivered a final draft of his constitutional proposal to Madison at the close of the convention he felt that "the political principles of the people of this country would endure nothing but republican government" and that "the government should be so constructed as to give all energy and stability reconcilable with the principles of that theory." In short, "what may be good in Philadelphia may be bad at Paris, and ridiculous at [Saint] Petersburg." [25]

What, then, were the results which Hamilton expected from his government of energy and republicanism? The phrase most frequently used by Hamilton was "the public good." One can also find references to "the public interest," "the general happiness," "the common happiness," and half-a-dozen other phrases. This range of terms indicates that Hamilton himself might have difficulty explaining exactly what he meant, yet it was a deep-rooted conviction toward which all his efforts as a politician were directed. The public good was that which benefited society as a whole, yet it was more than the sum of individual interests, for Hamilton frequently called upon the people to sacrifice their own desires for "the national interest" or the "welfare of the community." But it also included the interests of the individual, and each member of society was better off for having obeyed the commands of the community as a whole.

Good government, then, was something from which all classes benefited, but the people at large rarely understood the measures which were necessary for the public good. This required far-ranging vision which only "the talented few" possessed. This national aristocracy of "disinterested, discreet, and temperate rulers" could be elevated to positions of leadership only through a restrained and filtered kind of republicanism which, while it rested in the will of the people, kept them from exerting much direct influence upon the leaders.[26] In Hamilton's plan the people voted for the electors, who in turn chose another group of electors, who made the final choice of the president. Thus the people would be two levels removed from the chief executive, yet the republican framework would be preserved. Moreover, as noted above, the president would have life tenure and would thereby be free to make wide-ranging policy decisions for the common good without the necessity of currying favor with the legislature or mending political fences, which he would otherwise find necessary if he had to stand for periodic reelection.[27]

The "talented few" who made up the leadership could always be found in sufficient numbers in a free society, although Hamilton was not as sure as Jefferson that these might come from any class of society and any walk of life. He believed that such men were more likely to be found among the aristocracy of birth and wealth.[28] If doubts were expressed that such men existed or that such a system made it easy to promote a tyrant into a position of leadership out of reach of popular control, Hamilton had only to point to the towering figure of General Washington and dare the opposition to imagine him as a despot. In fact, one of the most difficult tasks which the nationalists faced at Philadelphia, and later in the ratifying conventions, was the fear of a powerful president. Previous experience with colonial governors and George III had induced in many Americans an almost paranoiac aversion to executive prerogative. It is not too much to say that the conversion was possible only because it was obvious that what was being considered was not an abstract or theoretical public office but a very real person named George Washington.

It remained for Hamilton to prescribe just how the people were to be induced to support a government those high purpose they only dimly perceived or did not understand at all. Hamilton understood that this was the nub of the problem

—indeed, that this was what politics was all about. He had neither complete faith in the people nor did he find them altogether wanting in character and virtue. In one of his earliest political essays, *The Farmer Refuted* (1775), Hamilton noted, "Political writers . . . have established it as a maxim, that, in contriving any system of government . . . *every man must be supposed a knave.*"The more sophisticated Hamilton of *The Federalist* decided that "the supposition of universal venality in human nature is little less an error in political reasoning than the supposition of universal rectitude." He was, he insisted, "a man disposed to view human nature as it is, without either flattering its virtues or exaggerating its vices." Yet, on the whole, he thought that men were guided by their own self-interest. "By this interest, we must govern him, and by means of it, *make him cooperate to public good,* notwithstanding his insatiable avarice and ambition. Without this, we shall in vain boast of the advantages of *any constitution.* "[29] Self-interest might take the form of lust for money, position, or power, but it was by appealing to these individual and particular desires that people could be attracted to the support of government. And sound government would somehow reconcile these private interests and harmonize them into the public good. This was the essential test of successful politics.

The Federalist

"[Hamilton] does not agree with those persons who say they will vote against the report because they cannot get all parts of it to please them—He will take any system which promises to save America from the dangers with which she is threatened—"[30] This precisely expressed Hamilton's mood as he arrived home in New York on September 20, 1787. He had pledged his allegiance to the Constitution, and he intended to give his unstinted support to its adoption in New York. And when Hamilton unleashed the full force of his energy, it meant that any opponent would have little rest.

His enthusiasm for the new Constitution did not indicate a man of wavering principle. He had by no means abandoned his basic belief that what the nation needed was a government of power and energy. But if a coach-and-four were not available, Hamilton did not disdain to ride in a buggy if it carried him toward his goal. As always in his career, he never looked back in regret at past failures or engaged in recriminations about past error except as it might serve to point the proper course for the future. Hamilton had a hard streak of pragmatism which strongly suggested that the Constitution might become whatever a man might make of it—especially if that man were Alexander Hamilton. Certainly the overriding consideration was that failure to adopt the new government would result in "the wreck of the general Confederacy." [31] There was, then, no hesitation or doubt in his mind as Hamilton came home from an undistinguished performance to begin one of the brilliant episodes of his career.

The proponents of the Constitution in New York and throughout the country became known as the Federalists, and their opponents, by default, had to adopt the rather negative title of Anti-Federalists. Although the proposed new government did not embody a federal system as eighteenth-century American political scientists understood the term, it was hoped that the name would serve to allay the doubts of those who feared centralized power. It was also hoped that the use of this term by friends of the Constitution would indicate unanimity of opinion and a close-knit coordination of purpose which did not in fact exist. Only in individual states could one really find Federalists and Anti-Federalists aligned with enough cohesion to justify calling them political parties.

The idea for a series of pamplets known as *The Federalist* was undoubtedly Hamilton's. Pamphleteering was one of his favorite weapons of political warfare. He realized that the magnitude of the task of explaining the Constitution was too much for even his prolific pen. He therefore enlisted the support of James Madison, who was in New York faithfully attending the sessions of a moribund Confederation Congress. He also asked the help of William Duer, Gouverneur Morris, and John Jay. Only Jay responded, and after contributing five pieces, he was incapacitated by illness.[32]

All *The Federalist* essays were anonymously concealed behind the signature of "Publius"—so effectively, indeed, that there still remains some doubt as to exactly what contributions Hamilton and Madison made. Probably Hamilton wrote fifty-one of the pieces, Madison twenty-six, and Jay five. Three were written jointly by Hamilton and Madison.[33]

Hamilton began his work by detailing the weaknesses of the government of the Confederation. Most of his observations have already been noted and are not particularly interesting to the modern student. But they provided the needed ammunition with which to shoot down the arguments of the most persistent of the Anti-Federalists who saw no need to change the *status quo*. If Hamilton's shots were sometimes wide of the mark or if he seemed to be savagely beating a dead horse, it must be remembered that he was dashing off an average of five thousand words a week and was capable of eight thousand words in four days—all this, while attending to his law practice, serving as a trustee of King's College (which had changed its name to Columbia), and being a husband and father to his growing family.[34]

Hamilton's basic beliefs in man's relationship to government, the need for decisive power, and his continentalism are repeated but with considerably more restraint than his speeches in the Constitutional Convention. He insisted that such a government was possible without menacing individual liberty and without destroying the states.

Perhaps the most difficult idea for the public to understand was how a central government could be sovereign in a nation of sovereign states. (John C. Calhoun professed to be still puzzled fifty years later.) Madison devoted considerable space in his essays to this idea of "dual sovereignty," which was, after all, original with him. Hamilton supplemented Madison's scholarly analysis with a more simplified explanation. He pointed out that "the great and radical vice in the construction of the existing Confederation is in the principle of LEGISLATION for STATES or GOVERNMENTS, in their CORPORATE or COLLECTIVE CAPACITIES, as contradistinguished from the INDIVIDUALS of whom they consist." It was necessary to "extend the authority of the nation to the persons of the citizens." Both the central and the state governments, each in its separate area of power, would exercise authority directly on the individual. This device of dual sovereignty or dual citizenship was the unique contribution of the framers of the Constitution.[35]

Hamilton's most original contribution in *The Federalist* was his exposition of the doctrine of judicial review in essay Number 78. "The interpretation of the laws," he noted, "is the proper and peculiar function of the courts. A constitution is, in fact, and must be regarded by the judges as a fundamental law. It therefore belongs to them to ascertain its meaning as well as the meaning of any particular act proceeding from the legislative body. If there should happen to be an irreconcilable variance between the two . . . the constitution ought to be preferred to the statute . . ."

Did this not grant sweeping authority to judges appointed for life, and so beyond the reach of the people? Not so, said "Publius." The people's will is set forth in the Constitution, and the judges may not change what the people created.

Rather, the courts stand between the people and the legislature and make it impossible "for the representatives . . . to substitute their *will* to that of their constitutents." [36]

If this reasoning sounds somewhat specious, it nevertheless illustrates a fundamental facet of Hamilton's philosophy. The Constitution represented the kind of enduring policy which "the talented few" had designed at Philadelphia. One suspects that he was concerned that the Supreme Court guard the Constitution against both the legislators *and* the people, especially when the latter were "turbulent and changing." Whatever the validity of Hamilton's argument, the verdict of history would seem to be that if judicial review is not a logical deduction from the Constitution it is, as Judge Learned Hand has observed, "a practical condition upon its successful operation." [37]

Initially *The Federalist* was intended as a series of newspaper pieces to persuade readers in New York, where Hamilton faced the almost overwhelming opposition of Governor Clinton and his party. The New York *Independent Journal* published all eighty-five essays, and the other city papers printed them with varying regularity from late October, 1787, until the end of March, 1788. Thomas Greenleaf, editor of the *New York Journal* and supporter of the Anti-Federalists, noted that some of his readers were complaining about the regular appearance of "Publius" and discontinued the series after Number 16. Elsewhere in the states, *The Federalist* appeared at least once in sixteen newspapers, most of them in Massachusetts and Virginia, but except in New York, they did not receive wide circulation. [38]

All in all, *The Federalist* was not as effective as its authors had hoped. Louis Otto, the French chargé in New York probably correctly observed that "this work is of no use to learned people, and too sophisticated and too long for the ignorant." [39] It certainly did not significantly reduce the influence of the Clintonians. Probably its most important value at the time of its publication was its usefulness to Federalist leaders as a sort of handbook to guide them in informal discussions and debates, and especially in the ratifying conventions. "I executed your command respecting the first vol. of the Federalist," Hamilton wrote to Madison in mid-May of 1788. "I sent 40 of the common copies & twelve of the finer ones addressed to the care of Governor Randolph." [40]

The Federalist had its most enduring fame in the years after the crisis of ratification. Though hastily composed by the "Publius" coterie and shot through with faults and inconsistencies, it became an authoritative commentary on the Constitution which eminent lawyers did not hesitate to cite in their legal briefs. Chief Justice John Marshall never acknowledged any debt of gratitude to Hamilton by name, but after a perusal of his opinions in *Marbury* v. *Madison* and *McCulloch* v. *Maryland,* one can understand his statement that "the *Federalist* has always been considered as of great authority . . . and is appealed to by all parties, in the questions to which [the Constitution] has given birth." [41]

The Ratifying Convention

The climax of the struggle for ratification of the Constitution in New York was the convention which met at Poughkeepsie on June 17, 1788. Hamilton must have known that the opposition was formidable since it was only out of deference to his father-in-law that the legislature had elected him to the Constitutional Convention. It is therefore difficult to understand what moved him to write, shortly after his return from Philadelphia, that "the first impressions everywhere are in its favour." "Everywhere" was probably New York City where the new government had strong support. But the state had been notable for its lack of cooperation with Congress and, outside of New York City, provincial in its outlook. The influence of Governor Clinton was pervasive and Hamilton soon realized he was in a desperate fight.[42]

Clinton's initial strategy was to delay consideration of the question in order to see what the reaction in the other states would be. By February, 1788, six states had given their consent. The four small states, New Jersey, Connecticut, Delaware, and Georgia, were expected to embrace the new union eagerly. But the approval of Pennsylvania and Massachusetts, one to the south and one to the east, were powerful additions to the Federalist cause. In fact, from first to last, the greatest pressure on the New York Anti-Federalists came from outside the state.[43]

The Anti-Federalists in the state legislature, well aware that their strength lay in the rural votes of the upstate counties, had ordered that "all free male citizens of the age of twenty-one years upwards" should vote for delegates to the convention. Both parties had campaigned furiously and "Publius" had turned out twenty-nine numbers of *The Federalist* between February 1 and late April, when the election was held. Even Hamilton was shocked by the results announced early in June. Forty-nine Anti-Federalists had been elected to only nineteen Federalists. "I fear an eventual disunion and civil war," Hamilton wrote to Madison. "God grant that Virginia may accede." This appeared to be the only hope. "[The Anti-Federalists] are . . . afraid to reject the constitution." He directed Madison to send him the news of Virginia's action by an express rider (whose expenses Hamilton would pay).[44]

As the convention opened Hamilton and his Federalist colleagues, Jay, Benson, James Duane, and R. R. Livingston, began their pleas and exhortations. It was now their turn to delay, to draw out the proceedings until some wind of fortune would change the opinion of twelve of the members of the opposition. Clinton presided over the convention and thus removed himself from most of the debate. Livingston moved to consider the Constitution and all proposed changes clause by clause, and this was accepted. With copies of *The Federalist* in hand, the advocates of ratification prepared for long siege. Despite the importance of the question and the depth of feeling, most of the debates were conducted with good-tempered courtesy.[45]

One of the most difficult obstacles which Hamilton and his colleagues had to overcome was the Anti-Federalist fear of the subordination of state power. Hamilton vehemently insisted that the states "are absolutely necessary to the system. Their existence must form a leading principle in the most perfect constitution we could form. I insist, that it never can be the interest or desire of the national legislature, to destroy the state." Such sentiments were hardly consistent with his speech to the convention almost exactly a year before when he had advocated that "we must establish a general and national government, completely sovereign, and annihilate the state distinctions and state operations." These very words had been recorded by Hamilton's colleague in Philadelphia, Judge Robert Yates, and both Yates and Lansing were present at Poughkeepsie. Would they preserve the pledge of secrecy made at Philadelphia and allow Hamilton's eloquent plea to go unchallenged? They would not.[46]

Lansing "let fall some expressions which tended to shew an inconsistency in Col. Hamilton's conduct. . . . In the Federal Convention that gentleman had agreed strongly that the state governments ought to be subverted." A hot exchange between Hamilton and Lansing reached a boiling point when the latter "made an appeal to Judge Yates . . . for proof of Mr. Hamilton's expressions." For once, gentlemanly tempers had exploded and "produced some disorder . . . and the chairman was obliged to call to order. A motion for adjournment put an end to the altercation." In the next session the courtly Yates let Hamilton off the hook by testifying that "Col. Hamilton's design did not appear to him to point to a total extinguishment of the State governments." [47]

The first encouraging sign for the Federalists came on June 24 when word was received that New Hampshire had voted in favor of accepting the Constitution. Two weeks later came, presumably by Hamilton's express, the welcome news that Virginia had ratified. The Federalists were now able to apply pressure by pointing to the prospect of a union from which New York would be excluded. How could the state, for example, expect the new government to oust the British from the forts which they still occupied on Lake Champlain if it had no sanction from New York? It was even hinted that New York City might secede from the state and join the union. But the Anti-Federalists died hard. "We have gone to great lengths and have conceded enough, . . ." said George Clinton. "If convulsions and civil war are the consequence, I will go with my party." [48]

By the middle of July, although some adherents had been won, the majority still insisted on "conditional ratification." This meant that New York would enter the union only if certain amendments, primarily having to do with limitations on the power of the executive and judiciary, were added to the Constitution. Bolstered by Madison's insistence that New York "could not be received on that plan," since "the Constitution requires an adoption *in toto,* and *forever,*" Hamilton stepped up the pressure. In a crucial vote on July 25 that New York might "withdraw herself *from the Union*" if the amendments were not adopted, the motion was lost by a narrow vote of thirty-one to twenty-eight. The Anti-Federalists managed to salvage the concession that a circular letter calling for another constitutional convention be sent to the governors of all the states. On July 26 New York voted to enter the union unconditionally, and Hamilton had won the first great victory of his career.[49]

In the year which began in the summer of 1787 Hamilton gave wider expression to his political ideas than at any time in his life. It is perhaps a proper context in which to consider a quotation so often associated with this complex and baffling man. There are two detailed accounts of what Hamilton said on June 18, 1787, in presenting his constitutional plan to the convention. Two very intelligent and attentive men listened to the same words and left these two versions.[50]

Madison reported:

> The members most tenacious of republicanism . . . were as loud as any in declaiming agst. the vices of democracy. This progress of the public mind led him to anticipate the time, when others as well as himself would join in the praise bestowed by Mr. Necker on the British Constitution, namely that it is the only Govt. in the world "which unites public strength with individual security."—In every community where industry is encouraged, there will be a division of it into the few & the many. Hence separate interests will arise. There will be debtors & creditors &c. Give all power to the many, they will oppress the few. Give all power to the few, they will oppress the many. Both therefore ought to have power, that each may defend itself agst. the other.

Judge Yates reported:

> I am at a loss to know what must be done—I despair that a republican form of government can remove the difficulties. Whatever may be my opinion, I would hold it however unwise to change that form of government. I believe the British government forms the best model the world ever produced, and such has been its progress in the minds of the many, that this truth gradually gains ground. This government has for its object *public strength* and *individual security*. It is said with us to be

unattainable. If it was once formed it would maintain itself. All communities divide themselves into the few and the many. The first are the rich and well born, the other the mass of the people. The voice of the people has been said to be the voice of God; and however generally this maxim has been quoted and believed, it is not true in fact. The people are turbulent and changing; they seldom judge or determine right. Give therefore to the first class a distinct, permanent share in the government. They will check the unsteadiness of the second, and as they cannot receive any advantage by a change, they therefore will ever maintain good government. Can a democratic assembly, who annually revolve in the mass of the people, be supposed steadily to pursue the public good? Nothing but a permanent body can check the imprudence of democracy. Their turbulent and uncontrouling disposition requires checks.[49]

VIII Jefferson and France *

"I . . . HAVE RETIRED to my farm, my family and books," Jefferson wrote to Edmund Randolph in the early fall of 1781, "from which I think nothing will ever more separate me." [1] This hunger for the peace of Monticello was reiterated many times during Jefferson's career, and he felt it most keenly when he feared that he had failed. The Virginia Assembly, harried by the British all the way beyond the Blue Ridge to Staunton, had passed a resolution for "an enquirey . . . into the Conduct of the Executive for the last twelve Months." Young George Nicholas of Hanover county was the instigator, "the tool worked with by another hand. He was like the minners which go in and out of the fundament of the whale," the whale in this case being the ubiquitous Mr. Henry. [2] Jefferson's friends voted for the resolution, "Confident an Inquire would do you Honor," explained Archibald Cary. Jefferson arranged to have himself chosen as a delegate from Albemarle County in order to answer the charges in person. By the time the Assembly was ready to hear the accusations on December 12, 1781, the government was safely back in Richmond, Cornwallis had been defeated, and the atmosphere had changed considerably. The investigation, such as it was, was abandoned, and the assembly resolved "to declare the high

* For this chapter see especially Marie Kimball, *Jefferson: The Scene of Europe.*

139

opinion which they entertain of Mr. Jefferson's Ability, Rectitude, and Integrity as cheif [sic] Magistrate of this Common-
wealth." [3]

It was a justification of sorts, and Jefferson returned at once
to his seclusion in Albemarle. In the spring of 1782 young
James Monroe wrote anxiously, "It is publickly said here
[Richmond] that the people of your county inform'd you they
had frequently elected you in times of less difficulty and
danger . . . to please you, but that now they had call'd you
forth into publick office to serve themselves. . . . You should
not decline the service of your country." This was strong
language from a young man whom Jefferson had befriended
and who idolized him. But the reply to Monroe was that of
a man who had received "a wound on my spirit which will
only be cured by the all-healing grave." It was a long letter,
shot through with such phrases as "disapprobation of the
well-meaning but uninformed people;" "public service and
private misery;" and "asylum . . . for rest to the wearied." [4]

For Jefferson it was an unhappy time. A few days before
he wrote to Monroe, Martha Jefferson had borne her sixth
child, and it was soon evident that she was not recovering
properly. As Jefferson watched from her bedside, her condition gradually worsened. Her death on September 6, 1782,
induced a traumatic shock which confined Jefferson to his
room for three weeks. He finally emerged to take long rides
through the fields and woods of Monticello accompanied by
his nine-year-old daughter Martha, "a solitary witness to
many a violent burst of grief." [5]

For once the surroundings of Monticello palled on him,
and he took his household, which included the adopted children of Dabney Carr, his deceased brother-in-law, to visit
Colonel Archibald Cary. Here Jefferson supervised the chil-
drens' inoculation against smallpox, and it was here that he
received word that Congress had appointed him to join
Franklin and Adams in Paris to negotiate the treaty with

Britain. James Madison, then a member of Congress, noted impersonally that the appointment was made "in consequence of its being suggested that the death of Mrs. J. had probably changed the sentiments of Mr. J. with regard to public life." There seems to be little doubt as to who "suggested." Jefferson's good friend was not above practicing a bit of psychiatry with this recommendation for therapy. The patient responded. "I shall lose no time . . . in preparing for my departure," he wrote to Madison on November 26, 1782.[6]

Notes on Virginia

Among Jefferson's belongings when he prepared for his European journey was a copy of the only book he ever wrote. *Notes on the State of Virginia* was originally prepared as a reply to the request of the Marquis de Barbé-Marbois, secretary of the French mission, for information on America which his government had directed him to collect.

Over the years Jefferson had gathered odds and ends of "information of our country which might be of use in any station public or private." These were "on loose paper, bundled up without order," and the lengthy questionnaire which he received from Barbé-Marbois seemed an excellent occasion for organizing the material. The twenty-three questions provided a ready-made table of contents, and by the fall of 1781, thanks to his precipitate retirement from the governorship, Jefferson had sent a reply to the Frenchman which must have astounded him as much by its erudition as by its volume.[7]

Jefferson was far from satisfied with the first draft, and during the ensuing months and years, he was constantly revising and adding to the *Notes*. The work, in fact, was not published until 1785 when he was in France, and the English edition which he authorized did not appear until 1787.

The *Notes on Virginia* ranged through a breadth and depth

of information which today would be classified under geography, anthropology, biology, political science, and sociology. The modern reader, while recognizing the obvious errors which Jefferson shared with other eighteenth-century scientists, is perhaps most impressed by the versatility of his mind and by the amount of knowledge, particularly in the natural sciences, which came from first-hand observation. The deer and the panther, the great Natural Bridge in the Valley of Virginia, Indians, fossils, an extensive and meticulous list of plants—all these he described from his own knowledge of them.

The *Notes* are especially revealing because Jefferson did not have publication in mind when he prepared the manuscript. Furthermore, it was for a rather limited and non-American audience. He therefore expressed his ideas on a wide range of subjects without any sense of restraint, thereby affording a valuable insight into the evolution of many of his ideas. Jefferson was a true intellectual and philosopher, a man who avoided dogmatism and whose conclusions were always tentative.

He pointed out, for example, that an influx of immigrants from Europe "will bring with them the principles of governments they leave. . . . In proportion to their numbers, they will share with us the legislation. They will infuse into it their spirit . . . and render it a heterogeneous, incoherent, distracted mass." [8] Here was the kind of super-patriotism and fear of "foreign takeover" which characterized much of later American illiberalism. Yet one of Jefferson's most bitter political battles was against the Alien and Sedition Acts, and it was partly born of his sympathy for fugitives from the oppression of Europe.

At a time when the Industrial Revolution was coming to Europe, he insisted that "those who labour in the earth are the chosen people of God . . . whose breasts he has made his peculiar deposit for substantial and genuine virtue." He preferred to leave manufacturing to Europe. "The loss by the transportation of commodities across the Atlantic will be made up in the happiness and permanence of government." [9] But his report on foreign commerce in 1793 advocates "such . . . encouragement to manufactures as may induce the manufacturer to come himself into these States, where cheaper subsistence, equal laws, and a vent for his wares free of duty, may insure him the highest profits for his wares." [10]

Jefferson never lost his faith in the people as the great guardians of liberty. He deplored the fact that the Virginia constitution of 1776 had never been submitted to a ratifying convention, and in his own constitutional proposals, which he included as an appendix to the *Notes,* he advocated universal male suffrage. He opposed the county unit system of representation in Virginia which allowed the Tidewater to dominate the more populous western counties. Yet he was painfully aware of the deficiencies of the people. "From the conclusion of this war we shall be going down hill. . . . They will forget themselves, but in the sole faculty of making money, and will never think of uniting to effect a due respect for their rights." [11]

The question which perplexed Jefferson most of all was slavery. The institution confounded the most fundamental tenets of the philosophy of the Enlightenment: that the society of man was one in which human relationships were established by the rule of reason and that restraints upon man's freedom were those imposed by his own consent. "And can the liberties of a nation be thought secure when we have removed their only firm basis, a conviction in the minds of the people that these liberties are the gift of God? That they are not to be violated but with his wrath?" [12]

He could not reject the universally acknowledged scientific conclusion that the black man was inherently inferior to the white, but neither could he accept it. "I advance it therefore as a suspicion only, that the blacks, whether originally a distinct race, or made distinct by time and circumstances, are inferior to the whites in the endowments both of body and mind." But he was sure that, under the practical conditions of his time, the black population could not be incorporated into either government or society. The freed slaves must be "removed beyond the reach of mixture" through colonization.[13]

The *Notes on Virginia,* then, was a curious compilation of fact and speculation by a scientific philosopher who refused to write simply as an antiquarian. He was truly a child of the Age of Reason, endlessly fascinated by the experiment of human experience. But he could not view it with detachment, and he eagerly embraced every opportunity to alter its chemistry.

Doctor Franklin's Successor

The vagaries of eighteenth-century travel and the vacillation of Congress put an end to Jefferson's projected mission to Europe. There was an initial delay in getting British assurance of safe conduct, and he spent a pleasant month, January, 1783, in Philadelphia with his friend Madison. Then the winter ice closed on the *Romulus,* the French vessel on which he had booked passage. Congress, meantime, received news of the conclusion of the preliminary articles of peace with Great Britain and finally decided to cancel his mission.[14]

Jefferson made a leisurely return trip to Monticello by way of Richmond. There was much talk of a constitutional convention in Virginia, and when he reached home in the spring of 1783, he plunged into the drafting of a constitution, the one which appeared in the appendix of the *Notes on Virginia.* By the time he completed his work the mood for a convention had passed. He then began the task of cataloguing his library. Ever since the destructive fire at Shadwell in 1770 he had been buying books, and for the rest of his life he seemingly never satisfied his scholar's appetite. In 1783 there were already over 2,600 volumes in the collection which eventually became the nucleus of the Library of Congress.[15]

His official resumption of public life came with his election as delegate to Congress, and by late autumn he was on his way to Princeton where Congress had briefly settled after the mutinous militia had forced it out of Philadelphia. He had scarcely taken his seat when the government moved to Annapolis. Although he personally preferred the sophisticated atmosphere of Philadelphia (perhaps because his eldest daughter was in school there), Jefferson hoped that the nation's permanent capital would be located in or near Virginia, and during this brief period in Congress he made a detailed study of the possibility of a site on the Potomac. He was therefore thoroughly acquainted with the project long before he had a later momentous conversation with Alexander Hamilton.[16]

Jefferson found Congress in the same state of torpor and inactivity which had induced Hamilton to leave it a few months before. This was, incidentally, the closest point of approach for the two until they met as colleagues in Washington's cabinet seven years later. Even the arrival of the treaty which ended the war failed to stir Congress from its lethargy. It soon appeared that there would not be delegates from enough states (nine) to vote its approval before the expiration of the time limit set by its terms. Jefferson was chairman of the committee which recommended the formal ratification on January 14, 1784, when delegates from nine states finally had assembled. He may have hoped to bolster the authority of the national government when he inserted into the report the injunction that "those stipulations [were] entered into . . .

under the authority of that federal bond by which their existence as an independent people is bound up together . . . and
with that good faith which is every man's surest guide . . .
they carry into effect the said Definitive articles . . . sincerely, strictly and completely." Fortunately Britain did not
quibble over the fact that the ratification was several months
late in arriving.[17]

This time in Annapolis was exasperating, to say the least.
Only rarely were there enough delegates present to enact
legislation, so there was little to do but listen to interminable
and largely meaningless debates. Most of the debaters were
lawyers, Jefferson remarked wryly, "whose trade it is to question everything, yield nothing, & talk by the hour," and he
soon became convinced that "we should all retire." His study
of the multiple executive provided for in the Articles of
Confederation led him to conclude that there would have to
be "a single Arbiter for ultimate decision," since the quarrel-
ling and bickering in the Committee of the States "left the
government without any visible head." [18] Yet Jefferson did
not allow his pessimism to keep him from a conscientious
performance of his duty. He served on numerous committees
and drafted over thirty reports during his brief six-month
tenure. He renewed his acquaintance with young James
Monroe, and toward the end of his term they shared quarters
and a servant.[19]

Jefferson's most notable work in the Congress was his report on the administration of western lands, the basic elements of which were embodied in the Ordinance of 1784, as
previously mentioned. He was still concerned about slavery,
and his proposal to exclude it from the new territories after
1800 failed to pass Congress by a single vote. The idea of
prohibiting slavery expansion finally found limited expression
in the Northwest Ordinance of 1787, but the southern states

would not agree to a similar exclusion in the Old Southwest (later Alabama and Mississippi).[20]

Jefferson also drew up several of the reports of the "grand Committee of Congress" on finance and currency. Those dealing with the problems of the national debt and recommendations for current governmental operations are convincing evidence of the myth of Jefferson's naivité on questions of public finance. His principal contribution in these reports was the decimal monetary system based on the Spanish dollar unit. To argue that the monetary system of the United States was or was not original with Jefferson is beside the point. He recognized the merit of the proposal—as opposed to one of Robert Morris' which was theoretically more perfect but not nearly as practical—and he was in the necessary position to secure its adoption.[21]

By the spring of 1784 it became apparent that one of the most serious problems which Congress faced was its commercial relations with foreign nations. Here was one area, at least, in which the states did not vie with Congress for competence, although they showed little inclination to abide by such diplomatic agreements as the national government had already made. On May 7, 1784, Congress adopted a comprehensive set of instructions to its diplomatic representatives abroad. On the same day Jefferson was chosen as minister plenipotentiary to negotiate treaties with European nations. He replaced John Jay who was coming home to become secretary of foreign affairs. Jefferson's long-deferred visit to Europe was at last a reality.[22]

He did not bother to return to Monticello. He arranged for the care of his household through correspondence, placing much of the responsibility on his trusted friend Madison. He picked up Martha, who was usually called Patsy, from her school in Philadelphia. She was his favorite traveling companion and the apple of her father's eye, and he did not intend to leave her behind. Passage was arranged aboard a ship leaving from Boston, perhaps to afford Jefferson his first opportunity to visit New England. On July 5, 1784, he and Patsy boarded the brig *Ceres,* outward bound to Europe.[23]

The journey to Paris was relatively swift and uneventful. Jefferson set up housekeeping, first in rented rooms, and finally, in October, 1785, in a house on the Champs Elysées where his household could be comfortable and he could entertain as a diplomat and Virginia gentleman should. Patsy was placed in a convent and was soon chattering in French like a native. Colonel David Humphreys, formerly one of Washington's aides and later to follow a diplomatic career of his own, was secretary of the legation. William Short, a protégé whom Jefferson treated almost like the son he had never had, was his private secretary.[24]

Jefferson paid his respects to the head of the American mission Benjamin Franklin, but the great man's health was failing, and he was no longer the center of Parisian social life. No American ever made such an impact on Europe as this venerable philosopher of the New World. French society and the court at Versailles had been devastated by his wit and charm and learning. Jefferson was well aware of the difficulty of coming to Paris in the wake of "the greatest man and ornament of the age & country in which he lived." He later noted that "the succession to Dr. Franklin, at the court of France, was an excellent school of humility," and it was a mark of his respect that Jefferson always insisted that "no one can replace him . . . I am only his successor." [25]

The American Minister

In Paris Jefferson quickly renewed acquaintances with two old friends. One was Lafayette whom he had known in the dark days of the war. The other was John Adams, recently minister to Holland, who had assisted in the conclusion of the peace treaty and had remained to work on the commerical agreements. He had with him his children and his wife Abigail, and Jefferson was constantly in their company until Adams was sent to England a year later. Jefferson regarded Adams as "an old friend . . . in whose abilities and steadiness I always had great cause to confide." There was a mutual fondness for Abigail and the children, and these friendships, although severely tested in the political battles of the next three decades, survived for a lifetime. Jefferson often took young John Quincy to see the sights of Paris, and when, years later, the latter became President, his father wrote to Jefferson, "I call him our John, because, when you were . . . at Paris, he appeared to me to be almost as much your boy as mine." [26]

Through Lafayette, Jefferson found his way into the rich social world of Paris. He was sometimes to be found in the company of Madame Helvétius or strolling in the Bois de Boulogne with Madame de Corny. The Marquis de Chastellux introduced him to the great French naturalist, Buffon, with whom he discussed the flora and fauna of the New World. The Frenchman had an erroneous but dogmatic contempt for the small size of American animals, and some of Jefferson's American friends found themselves in receipt of disconcerting but urgent demands for large deer antlers and the carcass of an elk. (He got them, and displayed them triumphantly to Buffon.) [27]

He found time to draw up plans for the Virginia state capitol in consultation with the architect Charles Louis Clerisseau. He met the sculptor Houdon and arranged for him to go to America to take a life mask of Washington for a statue that stands today in the capitol in Richmond. Houdon also did busts of Franklin, Lafayette, John Paul Jones, and one of Jefferson himself. There was no end to his energy, the range of his curiosity, and the penetration of his observations. It was one of the happy times of his life, and especially so after his personal tragedies and the disappointments of public office.[28]

In the late summer of 1786 Jefferson met Maria Cosway. It was a brief romantic interlude, yet his deep attachment to this charming and artistic lady was more than an infatuation. She was the wife of an English artist, and Jefferson was almost constantly in her company for about two months. The affair was ended with one of the most remarkable letters Jefferson wrote—a debate between the head and the heart of a man of reason and of sentiment. At the close, the "heart" tells the "head": "Morals were too essential to the happiness of man to be risked on the incertain combinations of the head. [Nature] laid their foundation therefore in sentiment, not in science." [29]

And he still found time to be the American minister in France. Soon after his arrival in Paris, Jefferson met with Franklin and Adams to begin the task of negotiating treaties of commerce with the nations of Europe. Congress had outlined the basic elements of American policy and Jefferson drew up a "model treaty" based on its instructions. These concerned the treatment of neutrals and civilians by an occupying power; rules regarding contraband; and a basic principle which was American in origin, that goods and persons aboard a neutral vessel on the high seas were neutral. In other words, neutrality was determined by the nationality of the vessels, not that of the cargo or passengers (assuming that neither was of a military nature).[30]

The ministers were not naive enough to imagine that England or any other major sea power would agree to the principle that "free ships make free goods." But they did hope that this would appeal to small nations like Denmark, Holland,

and Sweden. They were soon disappointed. Such nations were reluctant to make diplomatic agreements with a new country whose national government possessed as little power as the Confederation Congress. Jefferson observed that "all respect for our government is annihilated on this side of the water, from an idea of its want of tone and energy." Two years later he added the corollary: "The politics of Europe render it indispensably necessary that with respect to everything external we be one nation only, firmly hooped together. Interior government is what each state should keep for itself." Hamilton himself could not have put it better.[31]

Adams and Franklin left Paris in the early summer of 1785, the former to his new assignment as minister to Great Britain, and the latter home to the United States after an absence of almost a decade. Jefferson was now the head of the ministry in Paris, and he diligently pressed the case for American commerce. French officials and the diplomats of other nations listened respectfully to his arguments and acknowledged their admiration both for the minister and the young nation which he represented, but they firmly refused to commit themselves. Early in 1786 he hastened to England in response to a summons from John Adams, who believed that an agreement might be reached with the Barbary States whose corsairs ravaged international shipping in the Mediterranean. The negotiations came to nothing, but Jefferson got his first taste of Barbary blackmail. Two decades later, when he was President, he was finally able to give vent to his indignation.[32]

Jefferson scored only two small successes in the course of his duties. In 1788, with Adams' help, he managed to make arrangements with the Dutch bankers in Amsterdam not only to put the American debt on a more satisfactory basis but also to get a new loan to take care of the needs of the American government for the next two years. Much of the credit was due to Adams, but Jefferson noted with satisfaction that "I am well informed that our credit is now the first at that exchange." [33]

He also succeeded in partially mitigating the evils of the tobacco monopoly which had existed between the French Farmers General and the American financier Robert Morris. In addition, he negotiated concessions on American trade in other articles. But the death of Vergennes, the chronic precarious state of the French government's finances, and the increasing internal political tensions combined to make governmental policies and ministerial promises of doubtful value. It took the French Revolution itself to destroy the baneful influence of the Farmers General, and in the confusion of the eventful months of 1789 the whole situation became chaotic. Yet Jefferson's mission was not a personal failure. He had represented his country creditably and had looked to its interests as diligently and intelligently as possible under the circumstances. Dr. Franklin himself could probably have done no better.[34]

A Revolution in France and a Constitution for America

Jefferson's presence in France during the beginning years of the French Revolution immediately suggests dramatic possibilities: that the philosopher of the American Revolution would be the guiding light for the revolutionaries of France; or, conversely, that Jefferson's own philosophical tenets might be revised on the basis of his observations in France. In fact, neither generalization is applicable. It is true that he was keenly interested in and sympathetic to the revolutionary change which he saw developing. At times he was barely able to restrain himself from going beyond the proprieties demanded by his diplomatic position, particularly when Lafayette and his group of young liberals of the nobility were involved. But Jefferson was preeminently a realist, and he recognized that the conditions which gave rise to the French Revolution were quite different from those which had caused the American conflict with England. The author of the Declaration of Independence who had denounced George III in such vehement language looked upon the monarchy of France as a stabilizing influence in the transition to a more liberal government. The leap from the absolutism of Louis XVI to the kind of republicanism which had been created in America was far too broad. In 1787 he cautioned Lafayette, "Keeping the good model of your neighboring country [England] before your eyes, you may yet get on step by step towards a good constitution." This was not because his ideas about monarchy had changed but because he feared that Lafayette's "Patriots" would press too hard and the result would be a blood bath of civil war from which no good would come. As late as the summer of 1789 he reported to John Jay, the secretary for foreign affairs, "The fate of the nation depends on the conduct of the king and his ministers. Were they to side openly with the Commons the revolution would be completed without a convulsion, by the establishment of a constitution, tolerably free, and in which the distinction of Noble and Commoner would be suppressed." But he was not very hopeful. "The Noblesse . . . are absolutely out of their senses. They are so furious they can scarcely debate at all." [35]

He was especially enthusiastic about the struggle for personal liberty, and he went so far as to draw up a "Charter of Rights" which he submitted to Lafayette as a proposed basis for settlement with the King. This was the closest that he came to violating his diplomatic position. He was much pleased with the Declaration of the Rights of Man, for it contained the idea which was at the core of his thinking: "Men are born and remain free and equal in rights; social distinctions may be based only upon general usefulness." [36]

As these momentous events occurred in France, "the example of changing a constitution by assembling the wise men of the state, instead of assembling armies," was taking place in the United States. Jefferson was impatient to know the results of the Constitutional Convention, and as soon as he received a copy, about the second week in November, 1787, he fired off half-a-dozen letters in which he complained that "there are things in it which stagger all my dispositions to subscribe to what such an assembly has proposed;" and again, "their President seems a bad edition of a Polish King." [37] Jefferson had been absent from the United States for more than three years. In a later letter Madison, in describing the situation at the time of the convention, made a particularly acute observation on the basic problem of representative government which tries to strike a balance between individual liberty and an orderly and secure society:

> It has been remarked that there is a tendency in all Governments to an augmentation of power at the expense of liberty. But the remark as usually understood does not appear to me to be well founded. Power when it has attained a certain degree of energy and independence goes on generally to further degrees. But when below that degree, the direct tendency is to further degrees of relaxation, until the abuses of liberty beget a sudden transition to an undue degree of power. . . . In the latter sense only is it in my opinion applicable to the Governments in America. It is a melancholy reflection that liberty should be equally exposed to danger whether the Government have too much or too little power, and that the line which divides these extremes should be so inaccurately defined by experience. [38]

What Madison was saying here was that there is great danger that a powerful government may easily develop into a tyranny, as had been the case of the monarchies of Europe.

But there was also the danger that too little power might result in so much disorder that the people would welcome "a sudden transition"—to a dictatorship perhaps—simply because they wanted an orderly society. Madison could have had no knowledge of the rise of Hitler and Mussolini to power in the confusion and disorder of Germany and Italy after World War I, but he understood the problem.

In another long and typically analytical letter of October 24, 1787, the Father of the Constitution patiently explained each of the basic features of the new government. By the time Jefferson received it in December, he had become more objective. He was nevertheless, he said, much disturbed by the absence of a bill of rights and the failure to limit the succession of the president. Jefferson was always reluctant to advocate a system which could not be easily changed by popular will, and in this he differed sharply from Hamilton's conception of a permanent and far-reaching "public good." It was in this context that Jefferson observed that the earth belonged to the living and that "every constitution then, and every law, naturally expires at the end of 19 years." He had observed that monarchs were usually the great obstacles to change, and he thought he saw in the presidency the kind of danger he had observed in George III and Louis XVI. Like many people at home who had similar fears, Jefferson was reassured by the prospect that his long-time friend Washington seemed to be the obvious choice for the presidency. This did not, however, keep him from insisting to Washington himself that "I was much an enemy to monarchy before I came to Europe. I am ten thousand times more so since I have seen what they are." [39]

The absence of a bill of rights struck Jefferson as the most serious shortcoming, and he was mollified only when he was assured that amendments to this effect would undoubtedly be added to the Constitution. As to the relationship between the federal government and the states, he had become convinced that the situation "had rendered this consolidation necessary, that is to say, had called for a federal government which could walk upon its own legs, without leaning for support on the State legislatures." He remained wary of any system which granted too much power. "I own I am not a friend to a very energetic government. It is always oppressive." Alexander Hamilton might take note. But, in the final analysis, who was Jefferson to quarrel with the result? "After all, it is my principle that the will of the majority should always prevail," and he still had unshakable confidence in the people, for "on their good sense we may rely with the most security for the preservation of a due degree of liberty." [40]

In the fall of 1788 Jefferson had written his superior John Jay for permission to take a leave of absence from his post. Patsy and Polly, the younger daughter who had joined him in 1787, must be returned home, and he needed to look after his business affairs. Monticello and his other farms had not produced as well as he had expected, and he was still hagridden by John Wayles' old debt. William Short would remain as chargé although Jefferson advised him not to make a permanent career of diplomacy. The Jefferson entourage which departed from Le Havre on October 29, 1789, consisted not only of the family and its baggage, but boxes of books for Madison and Franklin, hampers of wine for Washington and Jay, a marble pedestal for the bust of Lafayette which would stand in the state capitol, and a shepherd dog for Monticello. Still many personal belongings were left behind in Paris, for Jefferson fully expected to return to his diplomatic post as soon as he had attended to his business in Virginia. [41]

He brought back with him the satisfaction of a job well done—"I feel a degree of familiarity with the duties of my present office"—and a conviction that his homeland was

vastly superior to the Old World. He never lost the affection
for his friends in Paris, and he never forgot the richness of
his experience. "So ask the travelled inhabitant of any nation,
In what country on earth would you rather live?—Certainly
in my own, where are all my friends, my relations, and the
earliest & sweetest affections and recollections of my life.
Which would be your second choice? France." [42]

IX The Hamiltonian System[*]

HAVING CREATED A NEW CONSTITUTION, the Founding Fathers now found it necessary to convert the blueprint into a working model. The most important single man in this operation was George Washington, who seems to have been genuinely reluctant to accept the presidency but who, as always, was easily led to the call of duty. He was elected unanimously to the presidency in 1788. His importance lay not only in the character of the man but in the unique position which he held. Congress might meet and adjourn, the courts might sit and rise, but the President was and is a full-time employee of the nation. His is the administrative force which drives the engine of government, and he is the embodiment of the authority implicit in the phrase "government of the United States." Washington might seek a peaceful retreat at Mount Vernon, but any day might produce a crisis which required his decision or his presence at the capital. In our own day, the President may be officially "on vacation," but he has in his entourage a system of communications which can put

---

[*] For this chapter see especially Noble E. Cunningham, *The Jeffersonian Republicans: The Formation of Party Organization, 1789–1801,* and William Nisbet Chambers, *Political Parties in the New Nation.* Hereafter cited respectively as Cunningham, *Jeffersonian Republicans,* and Chambers, *Political Parties.*

him in instant touch with any part of the nation or the world. As commander in chief of the army, Washington had been conscious of the fact that high office imposes limitations on the capacity of the individual, and he had learned the value of delegating authority. Congress obliged by translating the rather vague injunctions of the Constitution into the creation of executive departments similar to those found in both American and some European governments. Of the four departments, State, Treasury, War, and Attorney-General, by far the most important in 1789 was the Treasury.

The Secretary of the Treasury

The most logical man for the position of financial minister was Robert Morris, and Washington offered him the post. But Morris declined. Like many prominent men of his day, Morris regarded government position as a thankless job to be performed only out of regard for one's duty. Having held such office under the Confederation Congress and received little thanks and a good deal of opprobrium, "The Financier" declined. He recommended Hamilton, whose bold genius and rare energy had aroused Morris' respect. Washington heartily agreed.[1]

Hamilton welcomed the invitation. He had refused the urgings of his friends to run for the Senate or to try to unseat Governor George Clinton. Whether he knew that Morris would recommend him or not, he had hoped for the appointment for "it is the situation in which I can do most good." Nor did the choice occasion any surprise. He was *"perhaps best qualified* for that *species of business,"* wrote Madison to Jefferson, "and *on that account would be prefered by those who know him personally."* On September 12, 1789, the Senate confirmed the appointment.[2]

Hamilton was almost thirty-five years old. He was not tall,

but his erect bearing and slender build, combined with his fashionable dress, gave him an appearance which in his day was called "elegance" and today would be called "presence." He was convivial and charming, particularly with ladies, and his wit and infectiousness undoubtedly brightened many social occasions. He could be equally persuasive in public debate or in private conversation. Yet there was about him an arrogance which bordered on conceit and an iron determination which was coupled with a streak of ruthlessness.

The task before him would tax all of his considerable talent and energy. The financial situation was by far the most serious problem confronting the nation, and its immediate solution was vital to the success of the new administration. Within two weeks of his appointment, the House of Representatives asked him for a report on the means for "support of the public credit." Hamilton was ready with his report on January 9 and informed Congress that he was prepared to deliver it. Members of the House objected to a personal appearance, and it was decided to accept a written report. What was a minor point at the time established a precedent: Cabinet officers neither presented their proposals nor defended their actions in Congress.[3]

Taken point by point, Hamilton's report was neither original in concept nor innovative. What left Congressmen gasping was its sweeping comprehensiveness and its audacity. Hamilton's first proposal was to pay the bonded public debt of the United States at par (i.e., the face value of government bonds). How was a nation which owed $50,000,000 to pay this debt? Hamilton recommended a new issue of thirty-year bonds at six percent interest.[4] Why should holders of worthless Confederation bonds, particularly European bankers, be willing to trade them for the new issue? Simply because the new government inspired confidence, as Jefferson had found out in his transactions with the Dutch toward the end of his mission. The new Constitution had conferred upon Congress the power to tax, and Congress had already in the summer of 1789 enacted tariff duties on imports and tonnage duties on shipping entering American ports.[5] The assurance of an income, the audacity and boldness of the young Secretary, the return of prosperity after the depression of the 1780's—all these things inspired confidence, which Hamilton had earlier observed was the key to the success of any fiscal policy. It was this public confidence that resulted in the sale of the entire bond issue within a few weeks of its being put on the market.

Hamilton's proposal did not gain universal acceptance. James Madison raised an objection in the House of Representatives, not to the payment of the debt, but to the question of who should be paid. It was well known that domestic Confederation bonds were bought up by speculators, particularly after the first news of Hamilton's proposals was made public. Madison believed that the original purchasers of the bonds, those who had wagered their fortunes on the success of the new nation, should have their faith rewarded. He painted a touching picture of the needy, the widows, the orphans, and the veterans who had been forced to succumb to the rapacious speculators who sometimes purchased bonds for as little as fifteen cents on the dollar. He proposed that present holders of the bonds be paid the current market value and original holders receive the remaining difference.[6]

Hamilton countered by pointing out that this would involve the hopeless problem of tracking down the legal claims of original bondholders. Furthermore, Hamilton wished the new bonds to be freely transferable, thus providing a kind of circulating medium which would make up for the shortage of hard money. He emphasized the need for an immediate settlement in order to reassure foreign creditors of the stability and good faith of the new government. In the first test of his program, Hamilton won a decisive victory. Madison's proposal for discrimination in favor of original bond holders was voted down thirty-six to thirteen. In short order Congress approved the plan for funding the national debt as Hamilton had proposed it.[7]

But the victory was short-lived. Hamilton's next proposal was even more daring and aroused more serious opposition. He proposed that the national government assume the debts which the states had incurred during the War of Independence. His argument was that the states had incurred these debts in a national cause and that the burden was one which the national government should assume.[8] This aroused opposition, and not solely on the ground of the activity of speculators which the funding of the national debt had provoked. Representatives from those states which had paid a substantial part of their debt were aroused over the prospect that their less conscientious brethren would be rewarded. Why should Virginia and Georgia be taxed to pay off Massachusetts and Rhode Island?[9] No part of Hamilton's financial system aroused such heated argument or provoked such abusive language as the bill for assumption.

The Secretary of State

Jefferson arrived in New York on March 21, 1790. He had allowed himself only three months at Monticello, where he had sadly noted the deterioration of his lands and been able only to give hopeful instructions to his friend Nicholas Lewis, who had managed his affairs for several years. Some of the time had been taken up with Martha's marriage to Thomas Mann Randolph, Jr., the son of an old friend and neighbor.[10]

Jefferson was forty-seven years old. He was still loose-jointed and slender, inclined to appear awkward and, according to the acidulous Senator William Maclay, was both stiff and relaxed in his manner.[11] Familiar as he had recently been with the manners of the Court at Versailles and the salon of Madame Helvétius, he was certainly not ill at ease at the receptions held by President Washington, but he probably did not enjoy their stiff formality. Yet he was genuinely fond of Washington, and it was in large part out of this friendship that he had consented to come to New York.

The duties of his position as Secretary of State embraced not only the conduct of foreign affairs but also the safekeeping of public records, handling commissions of federal officers, and publishing the laws. Jefferson's departmental budget, including his salary of $3,500 per year, was $8,000. He therefore limited his staff to five persons—two chief clerks, two assistant clerks, and a translator. Most of the staff was kept busy with the "home office" functions, so Jefferson did most of the "foreign office" himself, utilizing only the services of a chief clerk to assist in his correspondence. Like the other cabinet officers, he was responsible directly and only to the President through whom all department correspondence was passed as a means of keeping him informed.[12]

Hamilton's Treasury Department was different in several respects. Washington's confidence in the abilities of his former aide and his relative ignorance of the intricacies of finance led him to allow Hamilton more leeway in his operations. Also, by law, the treasury head was obliged to furnish Congress with information on request and to report periodically on the state of public finances. Thus Hamilton had greater freedom from the President and a more direct relationship with Congress than the other department heads. Also his duties entailed a much larger staff, and by the time Jefferson arrived in New York his young colleague had already assembled a staff of over forty people.[13]

The debate on the assumption bill was in full swing when Jefferson began his duties. It may be supposed that his later statement that he was largely ignorant of the full implications of the question was essentially correct, not on account of any lack of ability to comprehend its intricacies, but because he was busy. He was six months behind the rest of the administration in getting his department organized. He found on his desk a request from Congress for a standard system of weights and measures. (In his reply he advocated a decimal system which Congress never approved.) He discovered that his department had been saddled with the duty of granting patents. This proved to be an enormously time-consuming job, since the scientific Virginian needed to satisfy himself that the new devices would do what their inventors claimed they would. In the midst of all this, he was felled by one of those excruciating headaches which seemed to come and go without warning. Illness of a much more serious nature struck the President. Washington contracted pneumonia, and the whole nation held its breath while "he was pronounced by two of the three physicians present to be in the act of death." But within ten days the rugged Virginian was back in his office, and people sighed with relief. "It proves how much depends on his life," said Jefferson.[14]

During this period of hectic confusion, Jefferson was often in the company of his trusted friend Madison, and he occasionally visited Vice-President Adams and his family. From both he no doubt heard about the assumption bill but probably did not give it his close attention because it was essentially outside his realm of responsibility, and he had many matters of his own to attend to.

Madison led the opposition to Hamilton's plan for assuming the state debts, not so much because he thought it unjust for the national government to pay the states' costs for the war, but because Hamilton proposed that the accounts be paid as they stood in 1790. Thus Virginia, which had retired a great part of her debt, would be paid very little compared with Massachusetts and South Carolina which had retired almost none of theirs. Instead, Madison proposed that the states be reimbursed for the full amount of their war debts whether they had been paid by the state or not. In the middle of April, 1790, the bill came to a vote in the House and was defeated thirty-one to twenty-nine.[15]

Hamilton and his cohorts in Congress had no intention of giving up the battle. But by the middle of June the Secretary was becoming desperate. There was now talk that those who had backed the funding of the national debt would withdraw their support unless the assumption bill was passed. There were even darker hints that the whole public credit system was the "sine qua non of a continuance of the Union." At this point, Hamilton decided to appeal to Jefferson.

He intercepted his colleague in front of the presidential mansion on Broadway, probably on June 16 or 17. It was a measure of his agitation that the usually dapper Hamilton was not only "sombre, haggard, & dejected" but that his clothes were "uncouth & neglected." He implored Jefferson to use his influence to break the deadlock since "the Administration & it's success was a common concern." [16] Jefferson protested that he was not familiar with the details of the bill, since it did not concern him. However, he undoubtedly was influenced by the fact that this was an administration measure and he owed Washington—and therefore Hamilton—his support. Like Madison, he favored the establishment of the public credit "for the sake of the union, and to save us from the greatest of all calamities, the total extinction of our credit in Europe." [17]

He therefore proposed that Hamilton join him and Madison for dinner for "a friendly discussion of the subject." From this conference came an agreement on Madison's part that he would withdraw his active opposition to the assumption bill in return for a compromise. Two Virginia representatives

were to be persuaded, presumably by Jefferson, to support
the bill, and "since the pill would be a bitter one," they were
to be assured that the national capital would be permanently
located on the Potomac. The Pennsylvania delegation could
be similarly persuaded by Hamilton with the assurance that
the government would be located in Philadelphia until the
new capital city was ready for occupancy.[18]

The residence bill passed on July 9. The bill for the assumption of state debts was amended to provide some compensation for the complaining states and passed on July 26. It was
the first and greatest victory for the Hamiltonian system.[19]

Jefferson's account of this episode, probably written three
years later, closes with the observation that "it enabled
Hamilton so to strengthen himself by corrupt services to
many that he could afterwards carry his bank scheme . . .
in fact it was a principal ground on which was reared up that
speculating phalanx in & out of Congress which has since
been able to give laws to change the political complexion of
the Government of the United States." [20] At the time that
Hamilton's program was enacted, however, both Jefferson
and Madison were fully convinced of the necessity of establishing the credit of the new government. Madison, who was
the leader of the opposition to both funding and assumption,
based his objections on the injustices which he found in the
operation of the system and which he thought could be reme-
died. In the summer of 1790 neither he nor Jefferson was
thinking in terms of an organized opposition to Hamilton and
his program. By 1793 when Jefferson recounted the episode,
the Hamiltonians were firmly in the saddle, and Jefferson was
enmeshed in the bewildering antics of Citizen Genet and the
entanglements of the French alliance.[21] Thus the tone of re-
crimination and self-justification.

Yet Hamilton's success was marred by the feverish activities of speculators in both federal and state bonds. William

Maclay, the suspicious and sharp-tongued senator from Pennsylvania, remarked of Hamilton's report that "a committee of speculators in certificates could not have formed it more for their advantage." He was sure that information was being leaked from the Treasury and that "the business . . . will . . . damn the character of Hamilton as a minister forever." Maclay's suspicions were well-founded. Robert Morris, Thomas Fitzsimmons, and Jeremiah Wadsworth, all members of Congress, were deeply involved. But the most notorious offender was William Duer, whom Hamilton had appointed Assistant Secretary of the Treasury. There seems to be no doubt that Duer used his position not only to line his own pockets but to pass inside information to friends. By the end of March he found it wise to resign, and his speculative schemes eventually landed him in jail.[22]

Inevitably Hamilton became the target for gossip that gave dark hints of his corruption. Yet such charges were never seriously believed by responsible men, and certainly not by Jefferson and Madison. It was a time of trial and error in small matters as well as large, and public officials had not yet fully learned that, as Hamilton himself said, *"Suspicion is ever eagle eyed, And the most innocent things are apt to be misinterpreted."* [23]

As Congress neared adjournment Washington remarked, "By having Mr. Jefferson at the Head of the Department of State, Mr. Jay of the Judiciary, Hamilton of the Treasury and Knox of that of War, I feel myself supported by able Coadjutors, who harmonize extremely well together." [24]

The Bank of the United States

When Congress came back into session in December, 1790, Hamilton was ready to present it with what he regarded as the capstone of his financial system. He believed that the nation's economy must be stimulated by making credit available and by increasing and stabilizing the flow of currency. There was very little specie and no paper money in circulation in 1790. There were some notes issued by the few state banks which existed but these did little to meet the nation's needs.

Hamilton proposed that Congress charter a Bank of the United States. The Bank would be capitalized, partly by government securities and partly from the sale of stock, at $10,-000,000, and was to issue its own notes as circulating currency. It would make loans both to private citizens and to the government. It would also be the depository of government funds and would act as fiscal agent for the government. Five of its twenty-five directors would be appointed by the President, and twenty percent of its stock would be held by the government. But this was to be a private bank, with the public owning seventy-five percent of the stock and with the twenty directors being elected by the stockholders.[25]

The Bank bill passed both houses of Congress by comfortable majorities, and by the middle of February, 1791, it had reached the President's desk. Madison had again opposed Hamilton in Congress, and although his efforts had been to no avail, he had raised the question of constitutionality with sufficient urgency to bring forth an objection from Attorney-General Randolph. Washington, of course, had great respect for Madison's judgment. An argument put forward by the Father of the Constitution was not to be taken lightly.[26] If Madison believed that the Bank bill went beyond the limits of power set by the Constitution, the President must hear the case. As was his invariable custom, he called on Jefferson and Hamilton for opinions, and it was clear that he was not concerned about the merits of the Bank but about its legality.

Jefferson rested his (and Madison's) case on what is generally referred to as the "strict construction" view of the Constitution. "It was intended to lace them [Congress] up straitly within the enumerated powers, and those without which . . . these powers could be carried into effect." [27] He readily admitted that the proposed bank would facilitate the fiscal operations of the government, but it was by no means necessary. This led him to the "implied powers" clause of the Constitution, which he realized would be Hamilton's principal justification. Congress was here granted the power to pass laws which were "necessary and proper for carrying into effect the foregoing powers, and all other powers vested by this Constitution in the Government of the United States." [28] As Jefferson construed this, Hamilton's proposal was not "proper" but merely convenient, and "it does not follow from this superior conveniency, that there exists anywhere a power to establish such a bank; or that the world may not go on very well without it." [29]

To anyone familiar with Hamilton's concept of energetic government, his opinion was predictable. A national banking system had been generating in his mind since his correspondence with Robert Morris more than a decade past.[30] If the Bank of North America could be chartered under the Articles of Confederation, Hamilton was not prepared to concede that the Constitution conferred any less power. The Bank's function as a government depository, as an agent for the collection of taxes, as a stabilizing influence (through its notes of issue) in currency regulation—surely this made it "proper." Hamilton insisted that a *"general Principle* is *inherent* in the very *definition* of Government . . . that every power vested in a Government is in its nature sovereign, and includes, by *force* of the *term,* a right to employ all the *means* requisite . . . to the attainment of the ends of such power." [31] As he expected, Washington agreed with him and signed the bill.

Implicit in the argument between Jefferson and Hamilton was a differing concept of the purpose of constitutional government. For Jefferson, a constitution was a means of placing limitations on the power of government so that it could not "take possession of a boundless field of power." To interpret it broadly, as Hamilton suggested, would "reduce the whole instrument to a single phrase, that of instituting a Congress with power to do whatever would be for the good of the United States; and, as they [Congress] would be the sole judges of the good or evil, it would also give them the power to do whatever evil they please." [32]

Hamilton believed that government should be a positive and energetic force

> in advancement of the public good. This . . . does not depend on the particular form of a government or on the particular demarcation of the boundaries of its powers, but on the nature and objects of government itself. The means by which national exigencies are to be provided for, national inconveniences obviated, national prosperity promoted, are of such an infinite variety, extent and complexity, that there must, of necessity, be great latitude of discretion in the selection & application of those means. Hence . . . the necessity & propriety of exercising the authorities entrusted to a government on principles of liberal construction. [33]

The Bank of the United States was the capstone of Hamilton's plan to use the public debt to create a flexible system of money and credit. The parts were presented to Congress in separate bills and each provoked individual debate centering on a variety of issues. Argument swirled around constitutional questions, speculators, and state fiscal responsibility. Yet the genius of the system could be appreciated only when viewed as a whole—a view which none of Hamilton's opponents and few of his friends understood.

The new securities which were issued to redeem Confederation and state bonds paid regular interest and would therefore maintain a stable price on the public market. To further insure this, Hamilton created a sinking fund administered by an executive committee of government officers who could enter the market and trade in government securities, thereby maintaining the price level. Holders of these securities had several attractive alternatives. They could sell their bonds on the open market at an assured level; they could pass them as a medium of exchange in some private transactions; they could certainly use them as security for loans.

There was still another alternative. In selling stock for its $10,000,000 capitalization the Bank of the United States accepted government securities for seventy-five per cent of the purchase price. The Bank would then circulate its own notes as loans to private citizens. Since these notes were acceptable for the payment of taxes and other obligations owed to the government (the Bank was its fiscal agent) their circulation at par was assured.

The Bank would also have what amounted to regulatory influence on new state banks (i.e., private banks chartered in the states. There were only three of these in 1790 but twenty-nine by 1800). With Bank notes circulating at par, state banks would also have to maintain sound note issues to stay competitive. Moreover, in times of financial crisis the Bank of the United States, with its great capital resources, stood ready to extend credit to state banks to prevent their collapse.

In this way Hamilton realized his scheme for using the public debt to create a flexible currency and a flow of credit for an economy which was acutely wanting in both. At the same time there was provided a degree of control which he hoped would curb the worst excesses of speculation and irresponsible banking. This fiscal structure was the essence of his belief in government as the generating force for the "advancement of the public good."

It was to be almost a year later that Hamilton presented his Report on Manufactures which set forth additional measures for governmental promotion of the national interest. In his view the greatest economic weakness of the United States was its lack of industrial development. The promotion of manufacturing was designed to achieve a balanced economy and to lessen the dependence of the United States upon the importation of manufactured goods from abroad. To this end Hamilton's report, presented to Congress on December 5, 1791, recommended a number of measures: a protective tariff, which would give the domestic manufacturer a price advantage over his foreign rival—and also add to government revenues; government bounties to encourage industrial production; encouragement to inventors; the building of roads and canals; government inspection to insure a high quality of industrial goods.[34] Like so many of Hamilton's ideas, the scope of his grand design was probably its undoing. To the student of twentieth-century economics such proposals seem to be very modest measures of governmental aid to business. But to many congressmen in 1791, they seem to be the embodiment of the leviathan state. Adam Smith, the prophet of the economic gospel of the Enlightenment, preached the doctrine of laissez faire which insisted that man-made laws only interfered with and disrupted the economic laws of nature. It was no accident that Smith's *The Wealth of Nations* was published in 1776.

To Jefferson, Hamilton's new America wore a different aspect. In the *Notes on Virginia* he had written, "Corruption of morals . . . is the mark set on those, who . . . depend for [subsistence] on casualties and caprice of customers. Dependence begets subservience and venality, suffocates the germ of virtue, and prepares fit tools for the designs of ambition. . . . While we have land to labour then, let us never wish to see our citizens occupied at the work-bench, or twirling a distaff." [35] It should also be noted that Hamilton was asking for the support of industry from a legislative body whose constituents were overwhelmingly agricultural. To have expected them to subscribe to his program was to deny his own belief in self-interest as the main spring of human conduct. It was not surprising that Congress tabled his proposals and that very little ever came of them in his time.

Taken as a whole, the Hamiltonian system was an attempt to use the powers of government to stimulate, promote, and even to transform the American economy. But of equal importance were the political implications. Hamilton had never abandoned his belief that a public debt could be a "cement of our union." He rightly predicted that after the riot of speculation in state and Confederation bonds subsided the large majority of the holders of government securities would be that body of substantial citizens whom Hamilton thought of as the rich, the wise, and the able. He might well have echoed the sentiment which he voiced in the dark days of 1780: "The only plan . . . is one that will make it the immediate interest of the moneyed men to cooperate with government in its support." [36] In redeeming the national debt at par, Hamilton made it profitable for these security holders to endorse Hamilton's program in particular and the new government in general. By his assumption bill he severed the tie of state indebtedness which might have bound these same or similar groups to a loyalty to the states.

In order to retire the debt Hamilton proposed not only tariff and tonnage duties on foreign commerce but also taxes on liquor, houses, horses, and carriages. Here the federal government was entering an area of concurrent powers, that is, an area in which the states also exercised authority. Thus advocates of states' rights might have made a stand against the expansion of federal power which was implicit in Hamilton's whole system. But the ground was cut from under them by the fact that the state debts had been assumed by the national government. How could the states, in good conscience, deny the power to raise funds necessary to pay these debts?

By the end of 1792 Hamilton's financial measures had not only attracted support for the national government but had given rise to a group of men who looked to him for leadership and were becoming known as the Federalists. Despite the fact that these men did not yet think or act as a political party, it was apparent that their policies would not go unchallenged.

The Opposition Takes Shape

Almost from the outset the greatest obstacle to Hamilton's measures was James Madison. This came as a surprise and disappointment. "When I accepted the Office . . ." Hamilton was to write later, "it was under a full persuasion, that from the similarity of thinking, conspiring with personal goodwill, I should have the firm support of Mr. Madison. . . . Aware . . . of the powers of Mr. Madison, I do not believe I should have accepted under a different supposition." [37] Nor was Madison, as noted above, opposed to the basic premises of the Secretary's plan for establishing the public credit. It was the apparent injustice of Hamilton's methods coupled with the jobbing and wildcat speculation in securities that aroused the little Virginian's ire.

There was ample evidence that Madison's fears were justified. Besides the resignation of Duer, there were criticisms that Hamilton had let drop hints and suggestions which had resulted in wild fluctuations in the price of Bank stock. Rufus King wrote anxiously to Hamilton that "at the present juncture, the most unfair advantage may be made of your remarks." [38]

Although no suspicion of evidence has ever been found to impeach Hamilton's honesty, he betrayed a lack of circumspection in other ways. He transferred government funds to

William Seton, the president of the Bank of New York, so that Seton could stabilize the price of Bank stock. Hamilton also allowed him to delay the transfer of government deposits to the Bank of the United States branch in New York until the financial crisis of the summer of 1791 had passed. He justified his action on the ground that he had saved the city from financial panic and curbed speculation in Bank of the United States stock.

Hamilton also became a major figure in a corporation called the Society for Useful Manufactures. This was a corporation chartered in New Jersey which, according to the promotional literature, was to engage in the manufacture of paper, cotton textiles, carpets, shoes, and stockings. Among Hamilton's friends in this venture were Elias Boudinot, Robert Troup, Henry Knox, and Philip Livingston. The group also included, unfortunately, William Duer, who was elected chairman of the board, or "governor." Despite Hamilton's doubts about Duer's behavior as a Treasury official, he seems not to have lost faith in his ability as an entrepreneur. At Hamilton's suggestion, the S.U.M. decided to limit its activities to cotton textiles and paper. The town of Paterson, New Jersey, was laid out under the supervision of Major Pierre L'Enfant, who later designed the national capital.

Although it began in a flurry of land purchases, orders for machinery, and the hiring of technical experts, the Society was soon in trouble. Its stock subscriptions failed to live up to expectations, and the financial gymnastics of "Governor" Duer led to a tangle of accounts that was never successfully unravelled. Hamilton's efforts to save the company led to accusations that he was using his influence as secretary of the treasury for private gain. By the summer of 1792 the Society faced a deluge of unpaid bills and the further embarrassment of the fact that its governor was in jail. Duer's multiplicity of financial manipulations had finally caught up with him,

and his failure contributed not only to the decline of the
S.U.M. but to the financial panic which shook New York in
the fall of 1792. Hamilton's hope of demonstrating his faith
in the industrial future of the United States had gone glim-
mering by 1796.[39]

As if this were not enough, Hamilton suffered his first
serious political setback in this summer of 1791. Since the
ratification of the Constitution in New York, the combination
of Schuylers and Livingstons had held George Clinton and
his forces at bay. But the appointment of John Jay instead
of Robert R. Livingston to the position of Chief Justice of
the Supreme Court and the election of Rufus King to the
Senate had embittered the Livingstons, who felt that they had
not been properly considered in the division of the spoils. A
new Livingston-Clinton coalition elected Aaron Burr, a distinguished young lawyer with a brilliant war record, to the
United States Senate, thereby ousting General Schuyler. In
the gubernatorial campaign of 1792, Governor Clinton won
the election for the governorship, and the Hamiltonians were
temporarily removed from control of the state.[40]

In the meantime opposition was developing in the capital.
Hamilton still retained the confidence of President Washington, but he was coming into increasingly sharp conflict with
the Secretary of State over new questions of foreign policy.
These will be dealt with in subsequent chapters, but it should
be borne in mind that these issues soon overshadowed domestic matters in polarizing opinion and crystallizing the "factions" into the nation's first political parties. Jefferson became
increasingly restive during the summer of 1791 as he watched
"the rage of getting rich in a day." [41] He was kept fully
informed in events of Congress by Madison and by young
James Monroe who had been elected to the Senate from
Virginia.

Jefferson and Madison took a vacation trip that summer

through upstate New York and New England. There is no evidence that it was other than a leisurely excursion during which the two friends enjoyed the magnificent scenery of the Adirondacks, Lake Champlain, and the Berkshire hills. They undoubtedly talked of many things, and they may have laid plans to combat the Hamiltonian press and organize the opposition. But from their reports, their most strenuous activities seem to have been botanizing, hunting, and fishing.[42]

Upon his return to Philadelphia late in June, Jefferson discovered that he had been dragged willy-nilly into a newspaper controversy involving Vice-President John Adams. A series of articles had been appearing in the capital press signed "Publicola" which staunchly defended Hamilton and the administration policies. The author was thought to be Adams. (It was, in fact, "Our John," the Vice-President's son.) Jefferson had earlier received a pamphlet, *The Rights of Man,* written by Thomas Paine, defending the cause of the French Revolution. Jefferson had passed it along to an acquaintance with a note expressing his gratification that something was being said in print "against the political heresies which had sprung up among us." The note appeared as a comment on a reprint edition of Paine's pamphlet issued in Philadelphia and aroused "Publicola" to a furious denunciation of Jefferson. The upshot was that, as Jefferson wrote to John Adams, he was "thunderstruck" to find "our names thrown on the public stage as public antagonists." [43]

The episode was trivial, but it began a gradual estrangement between these two old friends which their political rivalry made complete during the next decade and did not end until after Jefferson had retired from the presidency. The incident also hardened a resolve often repeated in subsequent years: "From a very early period of my life, I had laid it down as a rule of conduct, never to write a word for the public papers." [44]

Jefferson and Madison began to intensify efforts already
begun to provide a means of answering the Federalists in the
press. John Fenno, editor of the *Gazette of the United States,*
was the recipient of government largesse because he was the
official printer of Treasury notices. Something was needed to
counteract Fenno's "disseminating the doctrines of monarchy, aristocracy, & the exclusion of the influence of the people." The two Virginians had been trying to enlist Philip
Freneau, sometime sea captain and poet of the Revolution,
who had been working for the New York *Daily Advertiser* but
who was determined to retire to the wilderness of New Jersey.
After much persuasion he was induced to come to Philadelphia by Jefferson's promise of a position as translator at
the State Department. The fact that the salary was $250 a
year may have accounted for his reluctance. Jefferson and
Madison solicited subscriptions in Maryland and Virginia as
well as in Philadelphia. In October, 1791, Freneau's *National
Gazette* began publication, and the opponents of Hamilton
finally had a partisan spokesman. Jefferson and Madison understood the power of the press fully as well as Hamilton.[45]

There was no doubt that Hamilton was stung by the appearance of the *Gazette,* and it was not long before he discovered that the Secretary of State was its benefactor. Fenno's
Gazette of the United States was soon bombarding the Secretary of State with a series of attacks by "An American,"
"Amicus," and "Catullus"—all pseudonyms for Hamilton—
which accused Jefferson of being "opposed to the Constitution" and of being "Caesar rejecting the trappings, but tena-
ciously grasping the substance of imperial domination." [46] He
was answered by Madison writing as "Aristides," and "Mer-
cator" Freneau. Jefferson did not participate in these exchanges, but he did attempt to vindicate himself with the
President. But his statement when Freneau was appointed as
translator that "I cannot recollect whether it was at that time,

or afterwards, that I was told that he had a thought of setting up a newspaper," was hardly candid in view of the persistence with which he and Madison had cajoled Freneau.[47]

At about the time he launched his attack on Jefferson, on May 26, 1792, Hamilton noted that " 'Mr. Madison cooperating with Mr. Jefferson is at the head of a faction decidedly hostile to me and my administration,' . . . it was evident . . . that he [Madison] was the prompter of Mr. Giles & others, who were the open instruments of the opposition." [48] Hamilton thus acknowledged the appearance of an organized opposition to his policies. By coincidence, three days before, Jefferson wrote to Washington, "The republican party, who wish to preserve the government in it's [sic] present form, are fewer in number. . . . The only hope of safety hangs now on the numerous representatives which is to come forward the ensuing year." [49]

It was not long before Hamilton found himself under a sharp attack by "Mr. Giles," who was William Branch Giles, a bellicose Virginia colleague of Madison's in the House of Representatives. At the next session of Congress which convened in December, 1792, they determined to launch an investigation of the Treasury and its free-wheeling Secretary. As the opening gambit Giles introduced a resolution late in January calling for reports of the balances of the government with the Bank of the United States, the sinking fund operations, and an accounting of government funds which were to have been applied on the foreign and domestic debt. It appeared to be a shrewd move, since the Secretary would be hard-pressed to make a complete accounting in the five or six weeks before Congress adjourned. Even if he did complete his report Madison and Giles were sure that a careful examination would reveal that Hamilton had played fast and loose with government funds.

If the Virginians hoped to embarrass Hamilton by imposing an extraordinary load on his energy they mistook their man. Within two weeks a series of reports came pouring from the Treasury. These were scrutinized by the hostile Congressmen and what they found seemed to indicate, not fraud, but mismanagement, technical violations of the law, and disregard for Congressional authority. The most serious charge involved two loans authorized by Congress, one for $12,-000,000 which was to be applied to the foreign debt, and another for $2,000,000 which was to be used for domestic purposes. Hamilton had simply lumped the two sums together and applied them at his discretion. This was certainly a technical violation of the law.

Seizing upon this and other seeming irregularities Giles introduced a series of resolutions charging Hamilton with violating the law and Presidential instructions, and with what today would be called contempt of Congress. This was going too far for most of the representatives. The resolutions were voted down by overwhelming majorities and the attackers retreated in confusion.[50]

Hamilton's opponents had undoubtedly pressed too hard. Although Giles' attack was designed primarily to discredit the Secretary the basis of the inquiry was perfectly legitimate. Hamilton had characteristically conducted the business of the Treasury with a degree of latitude and discretionary judgement which made him appear contemptuous of Congress. Had the resolutions simply insisted on stricter accountability and compliance with the wishes of the legislative branch they might have received more support.

Precisely what part Jefferson played in this episode is difficult to say. Undoubtedly he knew what Giles and Madison intended but it is doubtful if he either instigated it or helped plan the opening moves. Up to this point the center of opposition to Hamilton and his policies was in Congress where Madison, the acknowledged leader and master strategist scarcely needed advice. As the attack was pressed Jefferson lent his secret support and helped to frame the Giles resolutions, although he tried to give the appearance of remaining aloof from congressional matters.

The vindication of Hamilton discomfited the Virginia coterie and gave the Secretary of the Treasury and his supporters a resounding triumph. In the aftermath they levelled an accusing finger at Jefferson as the secret instigator of the plot, "cautious and sly, wrapped up in impenetrable silence and mystery." They might have done better to leave Jefferson in the obscurity which he professed to seek. James Madison "is become a desperate party leader," noted the Federalist Fisher Ames, thereby indicating that the diffident Virginian was regarded as the principal enemy. By insisting that Jefferson was the real villain of Giles' assault the Hamiltonians may have helped to propel into leadership willy-nilly the man who, next to Washington, was the greatest hero of the Revolution.[51]

But perhaps the most significant development was the fact that by the spring of 1793 the contest for power was being waged by more than "a corrupt squadron . . . at the command of the Treasury" on the one hand, and the "Antifederal fleet" commanded by "Commodore Pendulum." Hamilton in a rare flash of political insight, noted, "The spirit of party has grown to maturity sooner in this country than perhaps was to have been counted on." Despite continued condemnation of "faction" and "partisanship" from all quarters, the two-party system was beginning to take shape.[52]

Republicans and Federalists

During most of Washington's first administration, political leaders insistently and loudly denied that political parties existed and that should they arise it would be the knell of the union. Jefferson wrote in 1789 at the close of his mission to France, "If I could not go to heaven but with a party, I would not go there at all." John Adams thought party spirit "destroyed all sense and understanding, all equity and humanity, all memory and regard to truth." Hamilton told the New York ratifying convention, "We are attempting by this constitution to abolish factions, and to unite all parties for the general welfare." [53] Washington, who was determined to be President of the whole nation, insistently refused to identify himself with either party, and at times seems to have persuaded himself that those who opposed his policies were factional obstructionists and perhaps subversive.

Of them all, James Madison refused to indulge in wishful thinking. In *Federalist*, No. 10 he wrote with cold realism, "the latent causes of faction are . . . sown in the nature of man" and that only tyranny could suppress political parties. It was Madison who, late in 1792, caught a glimpse of the true role of a party system, "that of making one party a check on the other, so far as the existence of parties cannot be prevented, nor their views accommodated." [54] He did not quite arrive at the final conclusion, that a program proposed by one party and modified by the opposition of another results in a truly national policy.

By the summer of 1792 a number of developments could be observed. Party lines were taking shape on the basis of what was happening in Philadelphia rather than in the individual states. Candidates for office, whether chosen by popular election or by the legislature, were still selected more on the basis of their local prestige, their family connection, or their war record. There was little connection between the Federalists and Anti-Federalists that were forming in 1792 and the parties of the same name that had debated the question of ratification in 1788. [55] But it is interesting to note that several members of Congress were unseated that year because of positions that they had taken on national issues. Thus while a new candidate might run on his local reputation, candidates for reelection found that they had to defend their voting record in Congress.

Although lists of candidates referred to as "tickets" appeared in many states, these were often drawn up by individuals and printed in the newspapers. Such tickets were not the result of party caucuses or other nominating processes. In Pennsylvania, for example, two tickets appeared, one designated "Federalist" and the other "Anti-Federalist," but the names of seven candidates appeared on both lists. The most recognizable party techniques, such as caucuses and committees of correspondence, were to be seen in New York, but in the bitter gubernatorial fight of that year party labels meant less than whether a man's name was Livingston, Clinton, or Van Rensselaer.[56]

Basically then, the center of the nascent parties was in Philadelphia. In Congress during the session of 1791–92, there were seventeen members of the House of Representatives who voted with Madison two-thirds of the time on principal issues. Another group of twelve to fifteen just as consistently voted for the issues identified with Hamilton. In a House of sixty-five members, this meant that over half had no discernible loyalties, and it would have been difficult to ascribe to them anything that could have been called party discipline.[57] Yet there was a core of members who opposed, either from principle or self-interest, the Hamiltonian fiscal program as embodied in the funding system and the Bank. This group, with additions, later displayed a pro-French bias on questions of foreign policy. They began to call themselves "republicans" in the spring of 1792. The supporters of Hamilton, who became pro-British on foreign policy issues, referred to themselves as "federalists" or "Federalists" and called their opponents "Anti-Federalists" or simply—and one suspects contemptuously—"antis."

Political parties in American history generally have certain discernible features. Usually there is a recognizable leadership, men of considerable achievement who command respect and whose opinions and advice are listened to. In 1792 both parties possessed this leadership at the national level but not at the state and local level where such leaders were essential.

Next, parties have to have an organizational structure which can perform functions necessary to the parties' success. There must be conventions and caucuses to prevent duplication of candidacies and to reach agreements on issues and tactics. There must be come kind of communications network so that interstate and even intrastate coordination may be achieved. In 1793, under the impact of the conflict between England and France, many French sympathizers formed Democratic Societies modelled on the Jacobin Clubs in France. Although they might have formed a nucleus for a network of Republican organizations, they never did. They frequently espoused the Republican cause and supported Republican candidates, and they bombarded the press with propaganda. But they had no cohesion; they never nominated any candidates of their own; and most of them died out in the heat generated by the controversy over Jay's Treaty.[58]

A party should also be capable of attracting a wide following, not merely through the attraction of its ideology and its leaders, but by a pluralism which can enlist special cliques and special interest groups by catering to their particular interests, allowing them a share of political favors, and assuring them in various ways that their particular needs will best be served in the long run by loyalty to that party. For example, organized labor in the first third of the twentieth century consistently voted with the Democratic party. Although the stated policy of labor leaders was to refrain from permanent allegiance with any major party, it became clear to them that their interests were better protected, year in and year out, by the Democrats, and labor just as consistently gave that party its vote. In 1792 neither party had the means or the will to attract such groups.

Finally, a party must have an ideological symbolism which is glamorous enough and broad enough to attract a wide range of followers. Both the Federalists and the Republicans seemed to satisfy this requirement in 1792. But as the years passed, it appeared that the Republican program became increasingly wider in its appeal while the base of the Federalists became narrower and more restricted. There were many other factors which led to the ultimate downfall of the Federalists, but it is suggested that if this was not the major cause it was surely the most noticeable symptom.[59]

Some idea of the workings of this element may be seen in the Whiskey Rebellion, which took place in 1794. The excise tax on whiskey was particularly distressing to the farmers of western Pennsylvania and Maryland—not because they drank more whiskey, but because it was more profitable to market a crop as one wagonload of whiskey than ten wagonloads of corn. (Land transportation was, and is, the most expensive way to move goods to market.) The farmers felt that they were being discriminated against, and they carried their resentment to the point of "rebellion." Revenue officers were beaten, an inspector's house was burned, and armed bands terrorized the western counties.

Hamilton saw this as a direct challenge to the authority of the national government. Washington agreed, and 12,000 militia were called out to deal with the rebels. Hamilton accompanied the troops. The awesome authority of the government of the United States marched into western Pennsylvania in late September, 1795. Although there was no pitched battle, arrests were made and several leaders were brought to trial.[60] It was an impressive demonstration of the fact that the new government could and would enforce the law. "Without vigor everywhere, our tranquility is likely to be of very short duration, and the next storm will be infinitely worse than the present one," observed Hamilton.[61]

There was another side to the story. The army campaigned for a month and never met an enemy. This was at least in part due to the activities of Governor Mifflin and a young Swiss-American Congressman from western Pennsylvania named Albert Gallatin, who persuaded most of the rebels to go home peacefully. Jefferson reported, "The information of our militia, returned from Westward is uniform, that tho the people there let them pass quietly, they were the object of their laughter, not of their fear." There were also reports that the militiamen themselves had done a considerable amount of thieving and in some localities "did not leave a plate, a spoon, a glass or a knife." The Secretary of the Treasury may have impressed the westerners with his authority but "their detestation of the excise law is universal, and had now associated to it a detestation of the government." [62]

By 1796 the party lines had solidified sufficiently to justify the acceptance of the fact that a two-party system had come into existence. President Washington announced his intention of retiring, and for the first time the nation had a contest for the presidency. At the state level party organization was still haphazard, and swarms of candidates were still announced for every state and federal office available. But in many instances Federalist and Republican tickets, decided on by caucuses held at the state capitals, pointed the way to those who had preference for a party. The mails were packed with letters of party leaders who advised each other on candidates and strategy.[63]

At the national level there were clear signs of interstate coordination and party discipline, and it was becoming increasingly difficult for congressmen to maintain an independent position.[64] In the summer of 1796 the attempt by the

House of Representatives to block Jay's Treaty had crystal-lized opinion to the point where Madison was able to make a count of votes and predict a result. The fact that he was wide of the mark only emphasized that, then as now, party discipline can crack under severe pressure, particularly if it comes from the President.

The two presidential candidates, Jefferson and Adams, were universally accepted as party choices although there was wide disagreement as to the choice for Vice-President. In most states, presidential electors were compelled to declare the candidates for whom they intended to vote, and it was quite clear that a vote for Adams was a vote against atheism and the French terror—and that a vote for Jefferson was a vote against Britain and monarchism.[65] The Constitution pro-vided that each elector should cast two votes for two different candidates. The candidate receiving the highest vote was to be declared president and the one with the next highest was named vice-president. Despite the confusion which this created, party discipline was preserved to a remarkable de-gree. Adams received seventy-one electoral votes and Jeffer-son fifty-nine. This made a total of 130 electoral votes from 138 electors for the two men recognized as the standard-bearers of their parties.[66]

This discipline also produced an embarassing situation. John Adams, the leader of the Federalists, became President, and Jefferson, the Republican, became Vice-President.

For Jefferson it meant a return to public life. He had re-signed from the Cabinet at the end of 1793, and a year later Hamilton had also resigned. The rift between them which had begun over Hamilton's financial program had sharpened and deepened with successive crises in foreign policy. It now becomes necessary to trace these challenges to the national security and their domination of the political life of the country.

X The French Menace[*]

"THE TWO PARTIES GUARANTEE mutually from the present time and forever, against all other powers, to wit, the united states to his Christian majesty the present Possessions of the Crown of france in America . . . and his most Christian Majesty guarantees on his part to the united states, their liberty, Sovereignty, and Independence absolute, and unlimited. . . ." [1]

In the dark days of the War of Independence these words had signaled the entrance of France as an ally in the struggle against Great Britain. A grateful America acknowledged its indebtedness to France for its very existence as a nation. The friendship born of the alliance had continued through the postwar years. When the French revolutionists overthrew the monarchy in 1789 people in the United States enthusiastically applauded this fresh triumph of democracy.

But the great powers of Europe felt that the Revolution menaced the security of Europe, and France soon found itself beset by enemies. What was more natural than that it should seek help from its former ally, a sister republic also born in revolution? General Washington, intimate friend of La-

---

* For this chapter see especially Alexander DeConde, *Entangling Alliances: Politics and Diplomacy Under George Washington.* Hereafter cited as DeConde, *Entangling Alliances.*

fayette, was President, and Jefferson had just been summoned from Paris to direct the foreign policy of the United States. Surely a grateful America would honor the spirit as well as the words of the alliance of 1778.

A Meeting at Mount Vernon

Another man, even the President of the United States, might have been embarrassed. In the midst of preparations for his return from Mount Vernon to the capital, Washington found himself the host of two distinguished guests. One was the British minister to the United States, George Hammond. The other was the Secretary of State, who was on his way from Monticello to Philadelphia to resume his official duties and whose pro-French proclivities were scarcely palatable to Mr. Hammond. Yet the situation seems not to have ruffled the awesome dignity or the impeccable hospitality of the President. In fact, Jefferson's brief visit was doubly welcome on this first day of October, 1792, for it was evident that there were matters to be discussed which would not admit of delay.

Ironically, both Jefferson and Washington had set for themselves the task of persuading the other to remain in office. The former had intended this to be the last leave-taking from his beloved Monticello, but he hoped to dissuade Washington from his stated intention of retiring at the end of a single term. Yet Jefferson was smarting under the virulence of recent newspaper attacks by Alexander Hamilton, and he was reluctant to give the impression that he was being driven from his post by the Secretary of the Treasury. And the President was giving an attentive ear to the swelling popular demand that he serve a second term.

The two old friends had a long discussion in the morning hours of October 1. Jefferson detected a note of hesitation in Washington's response to his urgings to reconsider his retirement. He therefore pressed his argument, pointing out that people of both the North and the South were fearful for the future of the country and that Washington was "the only man in the U.S. who possessed the confidence of the whole." [2]

This brought a rejoinder from his host expressing concern over the quarrel between Jefferson and Hamilton. Although he had realized that there were wide differences between the two on matters of policy, Washington had only recently become aware of the personal dislike which had developed between the two members of his official family whom he most respected and who would be the most difficult to replace. Jefferson, he realized, was fully convinced of Hamilton's monarchism, and he attempted to quiet these fears. He hinted that he would find it difficult if not impossible to continue as chief executive if he were deprived of his adviser in foreign affairs. A call to breakfast ended the conversation. Shortly afterward the Secretary resumed his journey, hopeful that he had convinced the President of the necessity of a second term but still determined in his own decision to retire.

Hamilton had been no less importunate than Jefferson in urging Washington to serve another term. He had even offered his own resignation if such action would restore harmony to the administration.[4] To members of Congress and other governmental officials who gathered in Philadelphia, it appeared that Jefferson was determined to resign and that Hamilton seemed to be saying he must prevail or also resign. On the question of a second term, the President maintained a massive silence. Congress listened with tense expectancy to his message of November 6, hoping for some clue as to his intentions.[5] It listened in vain. As the time approached for electors to cast their votes, Washington could not bring himself either to announce his retirement or make known his availability for reelection.

This atmosphere of uncertainty was dispelled by two

events. As it had done in 1789, the electoral college chose Washington as President despite the fact that he refused to announce his candidacy. And in Europe, the French Revolution entered a new phase as France became involved in a war with two allies of absolutism, Prussia and Austria. Jefferson postponed his return to Virginia.

Nootka Sound: A Prelude

Jefferson had come back to America in the belief that he was on leave from his diplomatic post in Paris. When he disembarked at Norfolk in November, 1789, he discovered that President Washington had already secured Senate approval of his name as Secretary of State. Jefferson modestly protested "my inequality to it" but was probably closer to expressing his true feelings when he spoke of "gloomy forebodings from the criticisms and censures of a public . . . misinformed and misled." Washington replied, "I know of no person who, in my judgement, could better execute the duties of it than yourself," and so Jefferson accepted. He thus came to his position fresh from the French nation in the midst of revolution. As American minister in Paris, he had witnessed the triumph of the philosophy of the Enlightenment, the fall of the Bastille, and the successful establishment of the constitutional monarchy. Jefferson's obvious sympathy, and indeed his near collaboration with the revolutionaries, was scarcely consistent with the neutral attitude to be expected of a foreign minister. But when his advice was sought not only by his old friend Lafayette but by Duport, Barnave, and other notables, the philosopher of the American Revolution could not suppress his intense interest.[6]

His enthusiasm was therefore considerably dashed when he returned to New York and became part of the social circle which surrounded the presidential "court." "I cannot describe the wonder and mortification with which the table conversations filled me. . . . A preference of kingly over republican government was evidently the sentiment. . . . I found myself for the most part the only advocate on the Republican side of the Question." [7] The shock of finding Britain so warmly admired and France, former ally and recently freed from absolutism, feared and hated made Jefferson gravely apprehensive for the cause of republicanism in America. His suspicions of "monocrats" became at times almost paranoiac, and he was convinced to the end of his days that only the exertions of himself and his friends had prevented the Hamiltonians from establishing a monarchy and institutions modeled after Great Britain.

The new Secretary did not allow these forebodings to mislead him into the delusion that American policy implied unremitting adherence to France or deliberate affront to Britain. Jefferson clearly saw that great care must be taken to keep the United States from becoming involved in the growing complexities of the European power struggle. This required subtle maneuver and skillful adaptation to changing conditions.

Jefferson indicated this disposition for indirection in the near-crisis which developed as a result of the clash between Britain and Spain in the Pacific Northwest in 1790. Spain had forcibly ousted British traders and captured a British vessel which had intruded into the Spanish domain at Nootka Sound. Great Britain reacted strongly by presenting the Spanish government with an ultimatum, and it appeared for the moment that the tensions of Europe might erupt into a war in North America.[8]

At this juncture Major George Beckwith, an unofficial emissary of the British government in Canada, approached Alexander Hamilton with a proposal that the United States give permission for the passage of British troops through the

Northwest Territory to attack Spanish Louisiana. Hamilton communicated the request to the President without consultation with the Secretary of State, a breach of protocol which was matched by the failure of the President to notify Jefferson that the Beckwith-Hamilton conversations were going on. When Jefferson later discovered this interference, he was understandably incensed.[9]

He was, then, unaware of the fact that Beckwith's request had already been made when Washington summoned the cabinet to discuss American strategy. He posed the presumably hypothetical question concerning the passage of troops through United States territory. Hamilton's position appears to have been that the United States should be a gracious host to the British. Jefferson proposed that the United States should make no answer at all. Since the request was not official (Beckwith had no formal diplomatic status), it should not be recognized. More important, if the British took silence to mean consent and violated United States sovereignty, the situation "will leave us free to pass over it without dishonor or make it the handle for a quarrel." [10] As it happened, Spain retreated in the face of British determination, so Jefferson's policy was not put to the test.

This was one of the earliest occasions in which Hamilton displayed his penchant for meddling in the affairs of the State Department, and the occasions became more frequent and increasingly irksome to Jefferson. Equally irritating was the fact that the President seemed indifferent to Hamilton's intrusions, yet scarcely ever did the former consult with Jefferson or indeed any other member of the cabinet concerning the plans and programs of the Secretary of the Treasury.

The episode displayed two facets of Jefferson's thinking as Secretary of State. The first was his realization that the United States was a second-rate power and should avoid any posture which might force it into an untenable position. If

the United States had refused the British request and the
refusal had been ignored, there would have been no alternative save a humiliating acquiescence, since America was in
no position to start another war with Great Britain.

It also displayed Jefferson's inclination toward indirection
and evasiveness where foreign affairs were concerned. While
these may not be admirable traits in most areas of human
relations, they were essential to the success of diplomacy,
particularly that of weak nations like the United States in
1790 which had no power base from which to operate and
little or no leverage which it could exert. To Jefferson, it
appeared that the best course was that which offered the
widest choices.

The Neutrality Proclamation

The French Revolution had been watched with interest in
the United States, and as it progressed there was general
sympathy toward what appeared to be a repetition of the
American experiment. Even many Federalists, if they did not
display the same enthusiasm as the Jeffersonians, were not
overtly hostile. But by the fall of 1792 reaction to the sensational news from the Continent was more positive and divisive. The Tuileries had been stormed, the monarchy overthrown, and the Year One of the Republic of France
proclaimed. French troops had checked what appeared to be
an irresistible Prussian offensive at Valmy, and the Prussian
army was in full retreat. A "French frenzy" swept the land
as Americans celebrated this double victory over tyranny.
The new republic assumed heroic stature—a champion of the
struggle of oppressed peoples against the monarchism of
Europe. French songs rang out in the taverns; the tricolor
cockade, symbol of the Revolution, was prominently displayed; and republicanism became more popular than ever.

Banquets and brawls, feasts and fights marked the fact that by the end of 1792 the French Revolution had become a major factor in American politics.[11]

But the enthusiasm was not by any means unanimous. Wrote Alexander Hamilton:

> When I contemplate the horrid and systematic massacres of the 2d. & 3d. of September—When I observe that a Marat and a Robespierre, the notorious prompters of those bloody scenes—sit triumphantly in the [constitutional] Convention and take a conspicuous part in its measures—that an attempt to bring the assassins to justice has been . . . abandoned—When I see an unfortunate Prince [King Louis XVI], . . . brought . . . to the block,—without substantial proof of guilt . . . When I see the sword of fanaticism extended to force a political creed upon citizens who were invited to submit to the arms of France as harbingers of Liberty . . . I acknowledge, that I am glad, to believe, there is no real resemblance between what was the cause of America & what is the cause of France—that the difference is no less great than that between Liberty & Licentiousness.[12]

If the French Revolution had become an undeniable factor in 1792, by the spring of 1793 "the sensations it has produced here and the indications of them in the public papers have shown that the form our own government was to take depended much more on the events in France than anybody had before imagined." So Jefferson wrote to his son-in-law Thomas Mann Randolph, and the forebodings which he expressed were prompted by the almost certain conviction that England would soon be involved in the conflict.[13] Confirmation came when slow-sailing ships from France arrived early in April bearing the news that the royal family had been executed and that England had indeed entered the war.

The United States was thus drawn into the maelstrom of

European politics. On the one hand, there was the American obligation to France under the Treaty of 1778 by which the two nations had agreed that if either went to war the other would come to her aid. Yet, if in honoring these commitments the United States incurred the wrath of Great Britain, the results would be disastrous. Even if war were avoided, commercial retaliation by Great Britain, America's largest customer, would wreck Hamilton's financial plan. The country was just beginning to recover from a depression, and any disruption of her commerce would be disastrous.

Washington hurried from Mount Vernon to Philadelphia to consult the cabinet. The basic policy of the United States was clear to all. It must, at any cost, avoid becoming actively involved in the war. But how was this to be done without antagonizing either the old enemy, Britain, or an old friend, France? It was this delicate question which the President presented to his advisers when he arrived at the capital in mid-April, 1793. To his cabinet, Washington submitted a list of questions, asking for a detailed opinion on the attitude to be taken by the United States. On April 19 the members met with the President.

Washington raised the first and most basic question: Should a declaration of neutrality be issued? Hamilton was ready with an answer. An immediate proclamation was necessary, he said, and he buttressed his answer with arguments which he had previously sent to the President in the form of facts and opinions relating to the agreement with France in 1778.[14] The degree to which he delved into the problem probably reminded the President of Jefferson's complaints of Hamilton's interference. Had Washington known of the extent of Hamilton's meddling and of his close relationship with the British minister George Hammond, he might have been even more distressed. Hammond had written to his chief Lord Grenville in London, "He [Hamilton] shall exert his influence to defeat any proposition on the part of France . . . [which] would depart from the observance of as strict a neutrality as is compatible with America's present engagements." [15]

Jefferson disagreed with Hamilton. He argued that although the United States certainly should avoid involvement in the war it should use its position for whatever bargaining power it was worth; "to hold back a declaration of neutrality was worth something to the powers at war." Finally, concessions were made on both sides. Jefferson acquiesced in the President's judgement that some statement of policy was necessary, but he won assent on two points. The first was that the word "neutrality" should be avoided; the second, that the statement was not to be binding on Congress. Thus, the proclamation was reduced from a declaration of position by the United States to a statement of policy issued by the President. Jefferson thereby maintained his aim of leaving open as many choices as possible for determining future policy.[16]

The next question raised for the cabinet's consideration was whether or not the newly appointed minister from the French Republic should be received. Here Jefferson was adamant. Failure to receive the new representative would be insulting and could not fail to provoke French hostility. Hamilton gave way with good grace.

But the third problem brought on another squall of conflicting views. Should the United States receive the new minister with or without qualification? Behind this rather innocuous question lay the larger question of whether or not the United States intended to honor the Treaty of 1778. Again, Hamilton was ready with an array of facts and argument, the burden of which was that the treaty had been concluded with the government of Louis XVI and that the destruction of that

government by the revolutionaries had simultaneously destroyed any obligation on the part of the United States. Knox,
as usual, amiably agreed with Hamilton.

The Secretary of State was as firm as he was brief. The
treaty had been concluded with the French nation, not with
the monarch. As long as the French nation existed, the obligation existed. Attorney-General Randolph agreed with Jefferson. The asperity of the discussion led the President to call
a halt to the meeting. He asked the cabinet to meet three days
later to confirm the wording of the proclamation. Jefferson
and Hamilton were requested to submit written opinions on
the question of the treaty.[17]

The proclamation, drawn up by Randolph, was approved
and proclaimed on April 22. It stated that "the duty and
interest of the United States require that they should with
sincerity and good faith adopt a course of conduct friendly
and impartial toward the belligerent Powers." It went on to
"exhort and warn citizens of the United States carefully to
avoid all acts and proceedings whatsoever which may in any
manner tend to contravene such disposition." [18] Despite Jefferson's painstaking efforts to avoid the word, it was soon
universally referred to as the "Proclamation of Neutrality."

Several days later the President reviewed the opinions submitted by Jefferson and Hamilton regarding the Treaty of
1778. Jefferson's reiteration of his position was convincing.
The United States was clearly obligated under the law of
nations to honor the alliance. Specifically, this required that
the United States open her ports to French warships and
privateers and to undertake to defend the French West Indies
against attack. Jefferson acknowledged that this latter commitment held some danger, but, at least for the present, such
danger seemed remote.[19] The way was thus paved for the
reception of the new minister whose arrival in Philadelphia
was expected daily.

Citizen Genet

Edmond Charles Genet was the third of a procession of bizarre ministers which France had chosen to represent her in the United States. His predecessor was Colonel Jean Baptiste de Ternant, a capable and personable man who was nonetheless neglected by his own government and whose loyalty was questionable in the eyes of the government of the French Republic. His successful attempts to get American aid to suppress the Haitian revolt against French rule on the Caribbean island of Saint Domingue in 1792 had further compromised his position when the monarchy fell and the republican government came to power.[20] The situation in Saint Domingue became extremely complicated, as a three-cornered struggle developed between the planter aristocrats, the Jacobins who wished to establish the authority of the new Republic, and the Haitian revolutionaries who were fighting for independence. It is an interesting commentary on the American character that, regardless of their politics, Americans opened their hearts—and their pocketbooks—to the pitiful stream of refugees who poured into the United States from the bloody holocaust of the Haitian revolt. Many Federalists felt increasing antipathy for France and were dismayed at what, in their simplistic view, they regarded as an intrusion of the French terror into the Western Hemisphere.[21]

Into this storm of pro-French enthusiasm and anti-French hatred and fear strode "Citizen" Genet to replace Ternant as the Republic's minister. His mission was to enlist the aid of the United States and to remind her forcibly of her obligations under the Alliance of 1778.

Genet came to America with a background of experience which was impressive. Both he and his father had served the Old Regime and, although he was only thirty years old, Genet had already held diplomatic posts in Prussia, Austria, and Russia. His expulsion from the court of Catherine II because of his ardent and freely expressed sympathy for the American Revolution commended him to the Girondist rulers in Paris. His charm and zeal combined with his experience appeared to make him an ideal person for the American mission.[22]

Genet was instructed to secure the close cooperation of the United States although not to the extent of getting her involved as a belligerent. A neutral United States, free to trade with France and the French West Indies, was preferable to an open ally who could be easily throttled by British sea power. Infinitely more advantage could be gained by securing American cooperation and support for French naval activity, particularly the use of its ports as bases for French warships and privateers and for the disposal of captured enemy prizes and cargo. Genet was also instructed to explore the possibility of promoting a filibustering expedition against Spanish Louisiana, utilizing the restless energies of George Rogers Clark and other frontiersmen.[23]

Genet arrived in Charleston, South Carolina, early in April, 1793. He was given an enthusiastic welcome, and the adulation of the Charlestonians convinced him that the Americans were thoroughly committed to France and her cause. To test this impression thoroughly—or perhaps because of the tempting prospect of basking in more public admiration—Genet decided to travel to Philadelphia by land. His first impression seemed to be confirmed. As he passed from town to town on his leisurely way north, people by the hundreds turned out to cheer. Genet probably misinterpreted as partisan enthusiasm what was the plain curiosity and hospitality of rural America. But his reception in Philadelphia thrity-eight days after he had landed in Charleston outdid in its exuberence anything he had experienced before. He may be pardoned for believing Francophobes were virtually nonexistent in America.[24] He was therefore understandably shocked and indignant when he learned that President Washington had issued a proclamation of neutrality which announced a "policy friendly and impartial toward the belligerent powers." Did this mean that the United States did not intend to honor its obligations?

Genet's reception by the President had an almost royal atmosphere. The blue-eyed Frenchman's flamboyant personality was cloaked by a courtly dignity acquired at Vienna and St. Petersburg, and Washington was characteristically formidable and cold. Genet took the measure of the man he must either dissuade or circumvent if his mission was to succeed.[25]

A few hours later Genet was the honored guest at Oeller's Hotel. The first public house to be called a "hotel," its sumptuous atmosphere and elegant cuisine made it the finest hostelry in Philadelphia. Now its huge banquet hall and music gallery echoed toasts to "la Liberté" and the stirring strains of the "Marseillaise."[26] Such a glittering fete, typical of the adulation the young Frenchman received continuously during his first weeks in the national capital, more and more convinced him that "the true Republicans triumph, but *le vieux Washington* [old Washington] . . . cannot forgive me for my success."[27]

The Trials of Neutrality

In the beginning Genet found some encouragement from the friendliness of the Secretary of State. Jefferson thought well of him and noted that "he offers everything and asks for nothing."[28] Before the summer was over this opinion was vastly changed, and he was writing to Monroe, "His conduct is indefensible by the most furious Jacobin. I only wish our countrymen may distinguish between him and his government."[29] Few foreign ministers have gotten themselves into as much difficulty in as short a time as Citizen Genet.

Events rapidly moved to a climax. They were triggered by a note from George Hammond protesting what appeared to be the government's acquiescence to violations of American neutrality. Specifically, the British minister pointed to the capture of the British merchantman *Grange* by a French privateer in Delaware Bay—that is, in American territorial waters. He also noted that American citizens were being recruited for service aboard French warships. Although he did not deny the right of the United States to open her ports to French ships of war, he protested as unneutral the fitting out and arming of privateers. Such vessels, sailing out of Charleston, had captured another merchantman, the *Little Sarah*, which was now lying at anchor at Philadelphia itself. Hammond demanded that the two ships be restored and that American enlistments in the service of France be halted.[30]

Washington, as usual, asked for opinions from the members of the cabinet. The basic question involved an interpretation of the Treaty of 1778 as set against the proclamation of neutrality. Did opening American ports to the French imply permission to outfit privateers and send them to sea against the enemies of France? Should vessels captured by such privateers be restored to their owners? Was a citizen of the United States free to enlist in the service of a foreign power? [31]

The case of the *Grange* was clear-cut. She had been taken within the territorial waters of the United States and must be restored. On the other two questions, however, the usual Knox-Hamilton versus Jefferson-Randolph split occurred. Hamilton insisted that the *Little Sarah* be restored and that enlistments be stopped. Jefferson took the position that although it was clearly a violation of neutrality, the privateers who had taken the *Little Sarah* had been allowed to sail and that once they were at sea, the United States government had no control over them.

The President's decision was essentially a compromise. He

agreed with Jefferson concerning the *Little Sarah,* although the privateers who had brought her to Philadelphia were denied sanctuary and ordered to clear the port. In the matter of American enlistments, two men, John Singletary and Gideon Henfield, had been arrested. Let them be tried for violation of the neutral status of the United States, and let the outcome determine American policy.[32] Henfield and Singletary were subsequently acquitted in federal court, but the presiding judge made it clear that this did not thereby make their actions lawful. French consuls and other diplomatic officials were warned to cease their recruiting activities.[33]

Shortly afterward, at the end of May, the Secretary of State received from Citizen Genet a series of proposals. They revealed that France had no desire for active American participation in the war nor did she press for the defense of the West Indies. What Genet did want was for the United States to "provide sustenance and stores necessary for the armies, fleets and colonies of the French Republic." This could be accomplished by paying the balance of the American debt to France at once and allowing the minister to use these funds for the purchase of supplies. He also proposed a renewal of the Treaty of 1778 which would, he said, "establish, in a true family pact, that is, in a national compact, the liberty and fraternal basis, on which she wishes to see raised the commercial and political system of the two people." [34] Such phrases as "true family pact" rang a warning bell even in Jefferson's sympathetic ear. This was the kind of entanglement which must be avoided at all costs. Yet, as Jefferson noted, "an injured friend is the bitterest of foes." [35] He stalled Genet by pointing out that any new treaty would have to have Senate approval, and since Congress would not convene until the fall, discussion could be postponed. The proposals never were discussed again, for Genet and the administration were soon embroiled in such controversy that negotiation became impossible.

The *Little Sarah*

The French minister's reply to the cabinet decisions relating to recruitment and privateers read like a declaration of war on President Washington and his administration. He demanded that the President respond to the voice of the people and renounce "the cowardly abandonment of . . . friends in the moment when danger menaces them." [36] Genet was again misreading the signs. "I am doing everything in my power to moderate the impetuosity of his movements," wrote Jefferson to James Monroe, "and to destroy the dangerous opinion which has been excited in him, that the people of the U.S. will disavow the acts from the Executive to Congress, and from both to the people." [37] His patience with Genet was wearing thin, though he still clung to his belief that United States interests could best be served by a pro-French policy.

Genet's assumption that popular opinion supported France was not without some foundation. Had not crowds cheered when Henfield and Singletary were acquitted and derisively "re-enlisted" in the service of France? [38] Had not the *National Gazette* and its editor, Freneau, admonished: "Let not the buzzing of the aristocratic few and their contemptible minions of speculators, tories and British emissaries be mistaken for the exalted and generous voice of the American people." [39] As his policies met with increasing opposition, even from the sympathetic Secretary of State, Genêt's arrogance and impetuosity increased.

The explosion was not long in coming. The spark was provided by the same *Little Sarah* which had been captured by French privateers and which now lay in the harbor at Philadelphia. At the end of the first week of July, Jefferson received a report from Governor Thomas Mifflin that the ship, now rechristened *Petite Democrate,* had been refitted as a privateer, and the word was that she was about to sail.[40]

Jefferson hurried from his country residence outside to the city. He found that Mifflin had sent his assistant Alexander J. Dallas to try to dissuade Genet from allowing the privateer to sail. Dallas had been greeted by a storm of angry denunciations, in the course of which Genet had threatened to "appeal from the President to the people." [41] Alarmed and angry, the Secretary sought out the French minister. He was met by another harangue to which he listened with remarkable patience. He then insisted on assurances that the *Petite Democrate* would not sail, at least until the President returned to the capital from Mount Vernon. Genet replied that the ship was not ready to sail although she might drop down river to a new anchorage. Taking this to mean that there would be no departure without the government's permission, Jefferson nevertheless decided that the matter was sufficiently critical to notify the other members of the cabinet. Since Randolph was absent from Philadelphia, he met with Knox and Hamilton. The latter vehemently insisted that the *Petite Democrate* be detained, by force if necessary. Jefferson demurred for several reasons. He hesitated to take such action without the concurrence of the President. Washington would arrive shortly, and he had Genet's assurance that the ship was not ready to sail. Jefferson had, in fact, sent an order to this effect.[42] More to the point, if shots were exchanged this might create an irreparable crisis, particularly in view of the fact that a force of twenty French ships was reported moving north from the Caribbean.[43]

As the cabinet awaited the President's arrival, the French privateer dropped down the river to Chester, beyond reach of detention. Washington returned to the capital on July 11 and summoned his cabinet the next day.

It was obvious that his patience was exhausted. The question of what was to be done about the corsair was not important, for she was beyond reach and, in fact, impudently put to sea two days later. Much more urgent was the need for a statement of policy which reconciled neutrality with the French treaty. Of only slightly less importance was the question of dealing with the intolerable behavior of Citizen Genet.

The Downfall of Genet

Hamilton had, meanwhile, launched a furious attack on the Republicans and, by implication, Jefferson and his policies. In a series of newspaper articles written under the pseudonyms "Pacificus" and "No Jacobin," he caustically observed that France had aided America in the War of Independence solely to advance the interests of Louis XVI. He continued, "The preachers of gratitude are not ashamed to brand Louis XVI as a tyrant, La Fayette as a traitor." [44]

In more moderate language he replied to a request from the President for suggestions on a statement of American policy. His written reply, along with that of the Secretary of State, furnished Washington with the answers he needed. The President must have marveled at how brilliantly these two could assist him as long as they were kept out of each other's presence. [45] Rules prohibiting any belligerent from outfitting vessels of war or recruiting American citizens were agreed upon at a cabinet meeting on August 4. [46]

In the meantime the cabinet was also dealing with the fate of Citizen Genet. In a series of meetings, his blatantly undiplomatic conduct was reviewed, including "forcing that appeal to the public & risking the disgust which I had so wished would have been avoided . . . the mass of the Republican interest has no hesitation to disapprove this meddling by a foreigner." [47] Jefferson was at last completely disillusioned by the Frenchman.

It was the manner of Genet's going that created the dissension. Hamilton insisted that his recall must be demanded and that full details of his indiscretions and insulting behavior be made public. Knox wanted to suspend his diplomatic powers at once. But the Secretary of State dissented vigorously. Genet's dismissal, he protested, must be handled so that the French government would realize that the United States' animosity was directed at the minister but not the country he represented. Public disclosure of Genet's conduct would only intensify public divisiveness which the crisis had aroused and create the impression that the President was "the head of a party instead of a nation." Moreover, Genet might be provoked into some greater indiscretions. Let a detailed account of his misbehavior, along with supporting documents, be submitted to the French government so that it could initiate the recall of its minister. He presented to the cabinet a delicately worded statement which was careful to make the distinction between the man and the country which he represented.[48] Although it was not known at the time, the government which had dispatched Genet to the United States had been overthrown, and the Jacobins under Robespierre had seized control. Genet soon discovered that the new government "must not, we cannot recognize in America any legitimate authority other than that of the President and Congress. . . . Dazzled by a false popularity, you have alienated the one man [Washington] who must be our mouthpiece of the American people." [49]

Incredibly, Genet maintained a bolder front than ever. He insisted that he be allowed to address Congress, since "it is . . . for the representatives of the American People, not for a single man [Washington] to exhibit against me an act of accusation, if I have merited it." [50] Not until official notification came in the person of his replacement, M. Joseph Fauchet, was it fully borne upon Citizen Genet that the French government wanted not only his recall but his head. Abjectly, he asked the President for asylum and Washington granted it.[51]

Despite Jefferson's protests, Genet's conduct was thoroughly aired to the public. The decision had scarcely been taken to recall him before Hamilton had written the details, including Genet's threat to appeal over the head of the President to Rufus King and John Jay. From these two ardent Federalists and from "No Jacobin" himself,[52] the word soon spread, and public sentiment swung abruptly to the support of the President, "the living idol which the Americans have set up for themselves," as one contemporary remarked sarcastically.[53] The Secretary of State and the party which he led suffered by the inference. Jefferson notified the President that he intended to resign. Only the earnest persuasion of Washington led him to remain until the end of the year.[54]

Hamilton had also written a letter of resignation to take effect at the end of the current session of Congress.[55] Washington was understandably upset. He complained that he had undertaken four years of additional duty from which he could not resign, only to find himself abandoned by his principal advisers.[56]

For the moment, the question of Hamilton's resignation became academic. The dreaded yellow fever struck the capital in epidemic proportions, and the Secretary of the Treasury and his wife were both victims. Dr. Benjamin Rush, dean of American medicine, exerted himself heroically in applying what he referred to as the "new methods" to counteract the dread disease. These consisted of strong purges induced by calomel and jalap, a vegetable diet, exercise, and cleanliness. Hamilton would have none of this. Dr. Edward Stevens was summoned from New York and recommended rest, frequent baths, a full diet, and occasional dosages of Madeira wine. Purges and bloodletting were avoided to preserve the patient's strength. Under this "West Indian" treatment of Dr. Stevens the Hamilton family soon recovered.[57] Ostensibly because of a threatened Congressional investigation of the Treasury, he postponed his decision to retire. A more probable reason was the growing crisis in Anglo-American relations, which for a time created tensions equal to those caused by Citizen Genet.

Citizen Genet was neither the first nor the last foreign representative who failed to understand the peculiar American character. To him, as to others, it was totally incomprehensible that Americans could vilify and denounce their leaders, including the President himself, yet turn upon a foreigner who echoed these sentiments and denounce his "interference . . . upon any pretense what ever, in the dissensions of fellow-citizens." [58] Yet Genet was no fool. His education, culture, and experience were remarkable for a young man barely turned thirty. Much of his trouble came from his brashness and impulsiveness, much of it from bad advice by Americans who were more interested in partisan politics than in the welfare of either France or the United States. Had he listened more carefully to Jefferson's tactful remonstrances, he might have been more successful in his mission. As it was, Genet had seriously damaged the alliance that he had come to strengthen and partially discredited the Republican party whose support was so vital to the success of French diplomacy.

The whole episode had been a lesson in the shaping of foreign policy. Jefferson deplored, not so much the measures which had been taken, as the manner of their implementation. The proclamation of neutrality and the rules for governing belligerents had been issued without consultation or consent of Congress. To Jefferson this appeared to be excessive exercise of executive authority. Yet President Washington, with no precedent to guide him, had judged that critical situations must be met with swift and decisive action. As President, he was charged with the conduct of dealing with rapidly changing diplomatic situations, and in such emergencies he felt that the executive should not remain passive. Thus, on the two occasions of the neutrality question and the crisis created by the *Little Sarah,* he had rejected Jefferson's suggestion that Congress be called into special session and had acted on his own authority.

The Secretary of the Treasury had irritated Jefferson beyond tolerance with his interference. Yet the State Department was the one branch whose activities could not be conducted separately from the others. The Justice, Treasury, and War Departments were more or less sufficient unto themselves. But diplomacy involved all. Randolph's opinion had to be sought on judicial questions, such as the handling of Henfield and Singletary and the application of international law to belligerents and neutrals. The French alliance had far-reaching commercial implications which would vitally affect the financial structure of the nation. And over all there hung the threat of war, which was to be avoided, but which the United States must be prepared to meet.

The clashes between Jefferson and Hamilton grew out of more than the abrasiveness of their personalities. These two were emerging as the leaders of increasingly delineated political parties. For Hamilton the French Revolution was a prime example of the anarchy which resulted from the unbridled rule of the masses and made the word "democracy" an obscenity. Jefferson deplored the excesses of the Reign of Terror, but he regarded this as part of the price of revolution. He did not deny that people in the mass would rule unwisely, but he believed that a broad democratic base was the only assurance against tyranny. Hamilton saw revolutionary France as an evil force which would wreck the social order of Europe. Jefferson believed that it was the harbinger of a future Europe which would be finally free of the tyranny of absolutism.

For the moment it was obvious that the Federalists were in the ascendency and that their views controlled the administration. Yet certainly it was the brilliant statesmanship of both Hamilton and Jefferson that carried the United States successfully through its first major crisis in diplomacy. Although relations with France were wrecked, England was convinced that a pro-French neutrality was no longer basic to American policy, and this fact greatly facilitated the solution to a diplomatic crisis with Great Britain.

XI The British Menace*

IT WAS EVIDENT that the war in Europe was developing into a titanic struggle for survival. France had undertaken a crusade against aristocracy and monarchy. "We must annihilate the enemies of the Republic at home and abroad, or else we shall perish," trumpeted Robespierre.[1] Great Britain and her partners in the First Coalition had at first treated the fledgling republic with contempt, thinking that the Jacobin rabble would collapse in the face of a determined opponent. By the end of 1793 Britain had come to the grim conclusion stated earlier by Edmund Burke that the French Revolution constituted "a great crisis, not of the affairs of France alone, but of all Europe, perhaps more than Europe."[2] Contempt had given way to a desperate determination that nothing must stand in the way of the destruction of this threat to western civilization.

Jefferson Retires

This time Jefferson meant it. "I am going to Virginia . . . to be liberated from the hated occupations of politics and to remain in the bosom of my family, my farm and my books."[3] He had grown discouraged with the disaster which had be-

* For this chapter see especially Bemis, *Jay's Treaty.*

212

fallen his French policy and Hamilton's domination of the President. The only hopeful sign was the increasing opposition to Hamilton's policies in the House of Representatives where Madison's skillful hand applied constant pressure on Hamilton, first by demanding retaliatory measures against Britain, then asking for an accounting of the use of government funds.

Jefferson's valedictory consisted of two documents. The first was a note to British Minister George Hammond, a reminder that there were still old grievances for which Britain must account. Contrary to the terms of the Treaty of 1783, British garrisons had still not evacuated American forts along the northern frontier, and "we have been intercepted entirely from the commerce of furs with the Indian nations" by British meddling and interference. The confiscation of property by enemy troops during the war, the unsettled boundaries in the northeast, and uncollected debts of English creditors were problems which still vexed relations between the two nations after twenty years.[4]

More important was the report on the current state of commercial relations which the retiring secretary prepared for Congress on December 16, 1793. More than half of the report was devoted to a meticulous breakdown of American trade with other nations. Jefferson noted that three-fourths of all imports were from Great Britain and about one-half of all exports went to her. This exhaustive review was for the purpose of establishing a basic tenet: "Free commerce and navigation are not to be given in exchange for restrictions and vexations. . . . Our navigation involves still higher considerations. As a branch of industry, it is valuable, but as a resource of defense, essential." What Jefferson expounded on was the use of economic coercion which he had first observed when boycotts had been employed against the Stamp Act. He proposed that the United States give privilege for privilege and penalty for penalty. "It is not to the moderation and justice of others we are to trust for fair and equal access to markets with our productions . . . but to our means of independence, and the firm will to use them." [5]

Jefferson's policy was also based on a principle of international law which had been set forth in the "Plan of 1776" and incorporated into the first American commercial treaties with France, the Netherlands, and Sweden. The "Plan of 1776" was based on the assumption that "free ships make free goods;" that is, cargoes not materials of war which were shipped to belligerent nations aboard neutral vessels were neutral.

This was a grand concept. It was not only directed toward providing legal protection for "small navy" powers but was particularly adapted to the situation of the United States. With the major powers of Europe engaged in their titanic struggle, Americans could make tremendous profits as the only major suppliers to both sides. In fact, during the wars of the French Revolution and Napoleon, American commerce enjoyed phenomenal growth. Despite constant harassment and restriction by both France and England, the United States twenty years later had become a maritime power second only to Great Britain. [6]

Jefferson hoped that Congress would use his report as the basis for retaliatory legislation, but he did not wait to see the results. On January 5 he packed the last of his belongings and set out for Virginia "where I hope to spend the remainder of my days in occupations infinitely more pleasing than those to which I have sacrificed 18 years of the prime of my life." [7]

The Mistress of the Seas

The pressure on Hamilton did not ease with Jefferson's departure. Public opinion was becoming increasingly intolerant of British policy. England had left no doubt that she intended to employ her maritime power against neutrals as well as belligerents. By an Order in Council of June, 1793, she declared the coast of France under blockade and, by declaring grain contraband, announced her intention of starving the enemy into submission. Hamilton protested indignantly to Hammond that this was "harsh and unprecedented." He also challenged the legality of the "paper blockade" by which England seized ships anywhere on the high seas and condemned them on such flimsy evidence as log entries, invoices, or even the nature of their cargo. A seizure was legal, Hamilton contended, only if the vessel were apprehended as it actually entered or left the blockaded zone.[8]

The full fury of American public opinion was unleashed against Britain in November, 1793, when the ministry invoked the "Rule of 1756." Issued initially during the Seven Years' War, it declared that vessels could not trade in time of war where they were not allowed to trade in time of peace. Britain was thus declaring illegal American trade with the French West Indies which had been opened to the United States after the war began and French ships no longer had easy access to them. But this was not all. The ministry kept the November decree a secret until British raiders had descended on the Caribbean and captured 250 fat American merchantmen.[9]

James Madison, the Republican leader in the House, launched the counterattack early in January, 1794, before a highly indignant audience. Jefferson's report gave him the cue for recommending additional duties on goods and ships from countries with which the United States had no commercial treaties and lowering duties for treaty nations. He also proposed retaliation in kind against those nations, notably Britain, who violated American rights on the high seas.[10]

Hamilton watched with dismay as the fruits of Genet's debacle began to disappear. News was soon coming in of American shipping losses in the Caribbean. The press had gotten a copy of a speech by Lord Dorchester, governor-general of Canada, urging the Indians to resist American settlers in the Northwest. All the while the debate on Madison's resolutions raged in the House. Hamilton primed William L. Smith of South Carolina to try to stem the torrent. Smith derided the "philippic on the . . . persecuting policy of Great Britain." Retaliation against Great Britain would lead to war and this would surely ruin the United States.[11] Charge and countercharge filled the air. Federalists were said to be taking British gold, and Republicans were accused of political expediency.

The delay which Hamilton and his friends worked for did no good. Anti-British feeling increased, and there were demands for even sterner measures than Madison had advocated. Hamilton was driven to denounce the Orders in Council as "atrocious," and urged the President to increase the army and construct coastal fortifications against the possibility of war.[12] Similar defense proposals were made by Federalists in both houses of Congress. Scare tactics, Jefferson scoffed at Monticello. It was "not that the monocrats & paper men in Congress want war; but they want armies and debts." [13]

Congress passed Madison's proposal for discriminatory duties against England, but it went even further. Late in March it approved a thirty-day embargo, and when this expired it was renewed for another thirty days. In vain George Hammond pointed to an instruction which he had received relaxing the severity of the restrictions on the West Indian trade interdicted by the November Order.[14] Congress was in a killing mood. Most alarming to Hamilton was a proposal to sequester debts owed by Americans to British creditors.

This was a threat to private property, and Hamilton saw in it the kind of belligerence which might provoke British temper beyond the breaking point.

The situation was getting out of hand. Republicans raged furiously against England. Provocation of an Indian war, refusal to abandon forts in American soil, piracy on the high seas—the Federalists were hard pressed to defend against such charges. Hamilton was baffled by a British policy which he found "inexplicably mysterious and afflicted with strong tokens of deep-rooted hatred." [15] Madison and Jefferson were also alarmed. "I hope some means will turn up of reconciling our faith & honor with peace," Jefferson wrote to John Adams. "I confess to you I have seen enough of one war and never wish to see another." [16]

Jefferson and Madison had worked painfully through the crisis with Genet and France to gain support for stern measures against Great Britain. Now it was obvious that with the unwitting connivance of Britain they had done their work too well. Madison's original proposals for commercial retaliation were forgotten as hawkish Republicans and defense-minded Federalists prepared for a war which neither Hamilton nor Jefferson and Madison wanted.

A group of Federalist Senators decided to take the play away from Congress and put it in the hands of the President. During the second week of March, 1794, they proposed to Washington that a special envoy be sent to England and recommended Hamilton for the position. Whatever Hamilton's qualifications as an envoy, Washington was wise enough to realize that he was not acceptable. The special mission was a political move, and Hamilton was too close to the political storm center. Similar considerations eliminated Jefferson or Madison, names urged by Republican leaders. [17] The man finally chosen was John Jay, Chief Justice of the United States Supreme Court.

John Jay's Mission

Jay was a New Yorker who had served his country well
for many years. He had been a member of the Continental
Congress until 1777, when he resigned to become chairman
of the committee which drew up the state constitution of New
York and to serve as the state's first chief justice. The next
year, he was back in Congress as its president. He served as
minister to Spain and as peace commissioner in Paris at the
end of the war. When he was chosen as the Secretary of
Foreign Affairs for the new nation in 1784, he was not yet
forty years old. Three years later he helped Hamilton and
Madison write the Federalist papers and was appointed by
President Washington to head the Supreme Court.

By background, then, Jay seemed the ideal choice for the
mission to England. But to many Republicans, he was only
slightly less repugnant than Hamilton. Not only was he a
staunch Federalist and anglophile, but it was still remembered that in 1786 he had tried to bargain away American
navigation rights to the Mississippi in exchange for commercial concessions to Spain. Southerners and westerners did not
trust him.[18]

Jay's mission was political as well as diplomatic. A settlement with Britain offered a way out for the beleaguered Federalists. A war or even a commercial imbroglio would not
only sink their political fortunes but scuttle the Hamiltonian
economic structure. It was not surprising, therefore, that
Jay's mission was managed from first to last by Alexander
Hamilton. Although there is no clear evidence that Hamilton
originated the idea of negotiating with England, he suggested
Jay's appointment,[19] wrote his instructions, maneuvered to
assure a favorable reception for him in London, and later
battled for Congressional approval of the treaty.

Upon other occasions President Washington had attempted to implement the "advice and consent" role of the Senate in foreign negotiations. He had been careful to get its approbation for special appointments and its approval of diplomatic instructions, although he had been rebuffed on one occasion when he actually went to the Senate chamber to get its "advice." But Republican outrage at Jay's appointment —one critic thought it the occasion for Washington's impeachment [20]—made any bipartisan approach hopeless. Senator Rufus King thought that because of "the difficulty of passing particular instructions in the Senate, it seems to me to be most suitable that the Pr. shd. instruct." [21] This view had been shared by Jefferson who was also conscious of the need for secrecy. On another occasion, a year earlier, he had said, "We all [the cabinet] thought if the Senate should be consulted & consequently apprised of our line, it would become known to Hammond, & we should lose all chance of saving anything." [22] It was thus decided that the executive should instruct Jay without Senate consultation or approval. Although Republicans demanded that the President "inform the Senate of the whole business," they were voted down.[23] This early precedent established by Washington considerably reduced the role of the upper house in the control of foreign policy.

Edmund Randolph, the former Attorney-General, had succeeded Jefferson as Secretary of State. He was temporizing by nature and was the only Republican left in the cabinet. He lacked the confidence of the President, who asked Hamilton to make suggestions for Jay's instructions. The Secretary of the Treasury prepared four major documents for Jay's guidance, not one of which was addressed to the Secretary of State.[24]

These lengthy and somewhat contradictory instructions were almost entirely in the form of recommendations and gave Jay unusually wide discretion. He was to stand firm on

only three points. By implication he was to insist on the
evacuation of the northern forts. Hamilton also enjoined him
to insist upon the opening of the British West Indies to
American trade and to agree to nothing which might impair
any treaty obligations to France. Otherwise Jay was to work
for British acceptance of the principle "free ships make free
goods," relaxation of the Rule of 1756 and indemnification
for goods and vessels seized "unlawfully," boundary settle-
ments in the northeast and northwest, mutual responsibility
for curbing Indian hostilities, settlement of the question of
American debts to English creditors, and agreement on other
minor matters still unsettled since 1783. It was no easy mission upon which the Chief Justice embarked early in May.[25]

Prior to Jay's departure, George Hammond had dutifully
attempted to draw from his friend Hamilton the nature of
Jay's instructions. In the course of the conversation, the British minister had alluded to the fact that his country and the
United States might both have to "suffer some inconven-
iences" when "the dearest interests of society were involved."
Hamilton bristled. He turned on Hammond and replied that
"however the Government and people of Great Britain might
be united against France, he [Hamilton] doubted not that
when the wrongs to which the American commerce had suffered were known in Britain, a very powerful party might be
raised in the nation in favor of this country." Hammond was
taken by surprise. He expressed "my astonishment at his
indulging in a belief which, however it had been entertained
by the demagogues in the House of Representatives and by
uninformed masses of the American community, I should
never have ascribed to him." [26] Like Genet before him, Hammond simply could not understand how men like Jefferson
and Hamilton could take such a thoroughly American point
of view.

The Treaty

Jay's task was indeed a formidable one. He was, after all, the representative of a second-rate power attempting to wring concessions from the British Empire. To be successful, Jay would have to have a considerable amount of diplomatic leverage. In fact, he had very little, and he failed to use what he did have. This was in part due to the indiscretion of Hamilton.

In the early part of 1794 England's fortunes had declined. The First Coalition was falling apart, and one of her partners, Spain, was about to go over to the enemy. Although Britain was still victorious at sea, French armies were winning sweeping victories on the Continent. Most important for American policy, the Baltic states were reviving the League of Armed Neutrality in an effort to apply commercial pressure on Great Britain and had invited the United States to join them.

The question was discussed by the cabinet early in July. All agreed that, as Hamilton put it, "the entanglements of a treaty with them might be found very inconvenient. The United States had better stand upon their own ground." [27] But there was no reason why Jay should not conceal American intentions and run a bluff on his English adversary. Poker, after all, was an American invention, and he had been instructed to "sound those [Danish and Swedish] ministers upon the probability of an alliance." [28] Had Jay chosen this line of action, he would have found that Hamilton had tipped his hand. After the President's decision Hamilton had promptly informed Hammond, and by the end of September Lord Grenville, the British Foreign Secretary, had "this very acceptable" news in his hands. It was obvious that the possibility of such a coalition disturbed Grenville, for he urged that Hammond "still attend to this subject, and you should renew it from time to time in conversation with those [Hamilton] whom you have reason to think well disposed." [29]

Had Hamilton's incredible performance occurred in the middle of the twentieth century, the uproar would have ruined him. Fortunately his indiscretion was not discovered, and the phrase "security risk" had not yet been coined. His behavior can only be explained by his consuming desire to remove all obstacles from the path of negotiation and his naive belief in British good faith and good will. The results of Jay's mission shattered his illusions.

Jay himself seemed unaware of the degree to which he was at a disadvantage.[30] His adversary, Lord Grenville, although only thirty-five years old, was one of the most astute diplomats in Europe. He recognized and played upon the petty faults of the American envoy—his vanity, his love of important society—in short, Grenville concluded that "Mr. Jay's weak side is Mr. Jay." [31] Yet to say that his personal foibles were responsible for the outcome of Jay's negotiations is to leave out of account the essential weakness of his position.

Grenville had already decided to abandon the northern posts. He hoped to be able to continue the British control of the fur trade by a reciprocal agreement permitting British and American traders to operate freely on both sides of the border and by continued British domination of the Indians.[32] This last ambition, unknown to Jay and Grenville, was being destroyed by General "Mad Anthony" Wayne who had decisively defeated the Indians at the Battle of Fallen Timbers on August 20, 1794. The next year most of the Ohio tribes made their submission to the United States in the Treaty of Greenville. Jay and Grenville could reach no agreement on the disputed boundaries and decided to refer these questions to a mixed commission. A similar commission was to decide the question of American debts.

The negotiations dragged on for almost five months. By

the end of that time Jay had conceded much and gotten little in return. American trade was admitted to the British West Indies but only in vessels of less than seventy tons burden, and the United States agreed not to export a list of products which competed with British West Indian exports. Britain also agreed to pay indemnity for the seizures which had occurred under the November 6 (1793) Order in Council, but she did not renounce the Rule of 1756. By default Jay abandoned the American demands of "free ships make free goods," the illegality of paper blockades, and a restricted definition of contraband.[33] These were principles which the United States had obligated herself to uphold in her treaty with France. Thus, while Article XXV of Jay's Treaty contained a provision that "Nothing in this treaty contained shall . . . be construed or operate contrary to former and existing Public Treaties with other Sovereigns or States," [34] it would be difficult to maintain that Jay had not compromised one of his instructions. Viewed as a whole the treaty scuttled the agreement with France, and within two years France virtually repudiated the Treaty of 1778.

Jay's Treaty, formally known as the Treaty of London, was signed November 19, 1794. The American envoy wrote wearily to Hamilton, "My task is done. . . . If this treaty fails, I dispair of another. . . . I shall stay here till spring; indeed I shall want repairs before I am quite fit for any voyage." [35]

The Great Debate

"YES, Sir, you have bitched it; you have indeed put your foot in it Mr. Jay—for shame, Sir,—." [36] Such was the typical Republican outburst against the treaty when its contents became known to the public. The history of the United States has seldom recorded an issue which so thoroughly aroused public opinion. Washington believed it was the greatest crisis of his administration, and indeed his lofty reputation was seriously damaged in the controversy.[37]

Jay's Treaty arrived in Philadelphia in March, 1795. Washington was so disappointed in the contents that he immediately blanketed it in secrecy. This in itself aroused suspicions. "I suspect," observed Madison in one of his regular reports to Jefferson, "that Jay has been betrayed by his anxiety to couple us with England, and to avoid returning with his finger in his mouth. . . . It is apparent that those most likely to be in the secret of the affair do not assume an air of triumph." [38] But perhaps the most disappointed was Hamilton, for politically and diplomatically, it was his treaty. He had retired from the Treasury Department at the end of January, 1795, but, unlike Jefferson, he remained close to the political arena. "When the treaty arrived, it was not without full deliberation and some hesitation, that I resolved to support it." [39]

The President delayed calling the Senate into special session until June, and even then he tried to preserve secrecy, requesting a pledge of silence from its members. After eight days of strenuous debate the Senate approved the treaty by the exact vote necessary, twenty to ten. However, its approval was contingent upon the rejection of Article XII which provided for the restrictive West Indian trade. Washington still hesitated to sign. Jefferson later remarked that he "was the only honest man who assented to it," and it was obvious that the President was struggling to reconcile his good judgement with necessity." [40]

At this point the inevitable happened. A copy of the treaty was leaked to Benjamin Franklin Bache, the vituperative editor of the *Aurora,* who promptly gave it wide circulation.[41] The attempt at secrecy had failed, and "Sir John Jay" became the most hated man in America. The Republicans "with hell in their hearts and faction on their tongues" blasted away at "that d____'d Arch Traitor J____n J____y;" the Senate, which had succumbed to *"British gold;"* Washington, who "now defies the whole Sovereign [people] who made him what he is—and can unmake him again." Hamilton attempted to address a mass meeting called to debate the treaty in New York and was shouted down.[42]

Washington was stunned by the volume and the violence of the Republican attack. On July 15 he left the capital for Mount Vernon, ostensibly for relaxation, but more likely to escape the storm which had broken around his sensitive ears. There was also news that Britain was again seizing American provision ships bound for France. Washington's departure from the capital may well have given Mr. Hammond some uneasy moments; Secretary of State Randolph had urged the President to withhold his signature from the treaty until some assurances of good faith were forthcoming from the British ministry.[43]

By mid-August Washington had changed his mind, and the principal factor was Randolph himself, although the evil genius was George Hammond. The British had captured a French ship carrying dispatches of Fauchet, the French minister in the United States. One of these seemed to imply that Randolph had conspired with the Frenchman to use bribery to create civil disorder during the Whiskey Rebellion. Hammond received the captured documents late in July, 1795, and turned them over to Oliver Wolcott, Jr., Hamilton's successor as Secretary of the Treasury. Wolcott promptly notified the President who hastened back to Philadelphia. Tormented by the abuse of the Republicans, Washington was ready to believe the worst, and Randolph's defense of the President's charge was bumbling.[44] Jefferson knew Randolph. He remarked sadly, "Whether his conduct is to be ascribed to a superior view of things, an adherence to right without regard

to party, as he pretends, or to an anxiety to trim between
both, those who know his character and capacity will decide." [45] Randolph resigned, and Washington signed the
treaty. To what extent he felt that in so doing he was forestall-
ing the insidious effects of "French influence" is difficult to
judge. But it is certain that Randolph was the victim of a
political war, shot down by men who viewed his opposition
to their principles as something close to treason.

Washington had a difficult time finding a replacement.
Rufus King preferred an appointment to the Court of St.
James rather than the position of Secretary of State. Thomas
Johnson of Maryland, Patrick Henry, and Charles Cotesworth Pinckney all refused to risk their reputations. When
the President wearily sought Hamilton's advice, the latter
could only lament that some mediocre person would have to
be persuaded. [46] Washington's choice was his Secretary of
War, Timothy Pickering, a diehard New England Federalist.
James McHenry of Maryland replaced Pickering. The cabinet was now purged of any opposition, but at a price. John
Adams, himself a bulwark of Federalism, noted grimly: "The
offices are once more full. But how differently filled than
when Jefferson, Hamilton, Jay &c, were here!" [47]

"Camillus"

Even before Washington approved the Jay Treaty, he had
detected a change in the current of public opinion, and he
thought he knew the reason. "I have seen with pleasure that
a writer in one of the New York papers under the signature
of Camillus, has promised . . . to defend the treaty," he
wrote to Hamilton. "To judge of this work from the first
number, which I have seen, I augur well of the performance;
and shall expect to see the subject handled in a clear, distinct
and satisfactory manner." [48] Hamilton had committed him-

self to the cause of Jay's Treaty which he was convinced was
the cause of peace. It boded ill for the opposition when
Hamilton decided to take his pen to war, and Jefferson so
warned Madison. "Hamilton is really a colossus to the anti-
republican party. Without numbers, he is a host within himself. They have got themselves into a defile, where they might
be finished; but . . . his talents & indefatigableness [will]
extricate them. . . . Thus it is that Hamilton, Jay &c, in the
boldest act they ever ventured on to undermine the government, have the address to screen themselves. . . . A bolder
party-stroke was never struck." [49]

Hamilton's technique was of an excellence to be expected
from a veteran of many newspaper wars. He first accused his
opponents of political motives. It was not really the treaty
which they wished to discredit but John Jay, a potential
candidate to succeed Washington. But more important, "it
was absurdly asserted . . . that Mr. Jay was to . . . dictate
to Great Britain the terms of an unconditional submission." [50]
Diplomacy was not that simple. "A very powerful state may
frequently hazard a high and haughty tone with good policy;
but a weak state can scarcely ever do it without imprudence.
The last is yet our character. . . . We should scrupulously
abstain from whatever may be construed into reprisals, till
after the employment of all amicable means has reduced it
to a certainty that there is no alternative. . . . This is a
consideration of the greatest weight to determine us to exert
all our prudence . . . to keep out of war as long as it shall
be possible." [51]

In this situation, it was absurd to charge that Jay had
relinquished the traditional rights of a neutral. They had been
taken away from America already by nations at war.

> The United States could not have insisted upon it . . .
> and in point of policy it would have been madness in

them to go to war. . . . It is not for young and weak nations to attempt to enforce novelties or pretensions of equivocal validity. . . . In the midst of a war, like that in which Great Britain was engaged, it were preposterous to have expected that she would have acceded to a new rule, which, under the circumstances of her great maritime superiority, would have operated so much more conveniently to her enemy than to herself. And it would have been no less absurd to have made her accession to that rule the *sine qua non* of an arrangement. . . . *The game was not worth the candle.*[52]

In short, critics of the treaty opposed it for not obtaining what was unobtainable at the outset. They should be grateful, said "Camillus," that so much had been conceded. Most important was the fact that a treaty—any treaty—had been agreed to. "To precipitate nothing, to gain time by negotiations, was to leave the country in a situation to profit by events which might turn up, tending to restrain a spirit of hostility to Great Britain, and dispose her to reasonable accomodation."[53] Nations about to go to war do not make treaties with one another.

Nor did "Camillus" neglect the call to national pride, combined with a little judicious mudslinging. "Our country never appeared so august and respectable as in the position which it assumed upon this occasion. Europe was struck with the dignified moderation of our conduct; and the character of our government and nation acquired a new elevation."[54] On the other hand, "there will always exist among us men irreconcilable to our present national Constitution. . . . Such men will watch, with lynx's eyes, for opportunities of discrediting the proceedings of the government, and will display a hostile and malignant zeal . . . to favor their enterprises."[55]

"Camillus" was one of Hamilton's great performances. He did not like the treaty, but he recognized that the negotiation and the result were basically his responsibility. The essays—22 pieces totalling more than 65,000 words—were political masterpieces and went far toward recovering the political fortunes of the Federalists.

The Price of Peace

The Republicans were not done. The Father of the Constitution did not miss the fact that all money bills must originate in the House of Representatives, and here the Republicans had a majority. Madison and his colleagues were determined to force the issue of the treaty again when it became necessary to appropriate funds to implement it. On March 2, 1796, the preliminary step was taken, in the form of a motion by Edward Livingston of New York, to request that the President lay before the House Jay's instructions and correspondence. The motion was passed and once more Washington was on the spot.[56] Despite "Camillus" and other defenders of the treaty, public opinion against England still smouldered. The situation was not helped by the news of continued seizures of American ships in the West Indies; "the British ministry are as great fools or as great rascals as our Jacobins," [57] lamented Hamilton.

Submission of the treaty papers "will do no credit to the administration," he advised Washington. They had been hastily drawn, "in general a crude mess," and would indeed show that Jay had violated his instructions. It would also reveal, for example, that it was Hamilton who had suggested the seventy-ton limitation on American vessels trading with the British West Indies. (Why not "in canoes?" said Madison.) [58]

Washington, "from the fullest conviction in my own mind . . . resolved to *resist the principle* wch. was evidently intended." [59] In a government based on the principle of separation of powers, the executive was not responsible to the legis-

lature and might therefore withhold information and papers.
Thus the President established another important precedent
in governmental procedure. He also chose this moment to
submit to the Senate a treaty with Spain concluded by
Thomas Pinckney which opened the mouth of the Mississippi
to American trade and acknowledged the United States'
claim to the thirty-first parallel as the northern boundary of
Spanish Florida.[60] It was a brilliant triumph of American
diplomacy, and the President obviously hoped that its
popularity would take some of the wind out of Republican
sails. .

For a time it appeared that the House Republicans would
succeed in their strategy to block Jay's Treaty. Madison reported that the rejection would pass by twenty votes. But as
the crisis approached, the majority melted away, and the
treaty was saved by a single vote.[61] Whether it was the moving
oratory of Fisher Ames on the last day of the debate—a
performance that held the House spellbound for hours—or
whether it was as Madison thought, "the exertions of the
Aristocracy, Anglicism and Mercantilism," [62] the Federalists
had a narrow squeak. Jefferson was convinced that "nothing
can support them but the Colossus of the President's merits
with the people," [63] and doubtless the weight of Washington's
enormous prestige was the crucial factor.

Thus ended the most bitter and desperate political struggle
which the nation had witnessed since 1789. The beginning
of the European war in 1793 had propelled the United States
into an unavoidable diplomatic conflict with the great powers. If neutrality was the key to official policy there had been
almost no one who was neutral in opinion. Men in high places
and low had been charged with treason, bribery, drunkenness,
adultery, and malfeasance in office. Reputations had been
blasted and old friendships wrecked. John Rutledge of South

Carolina, a member of the Supreme Court since 1789, had been nominated by the President to succeed Jay as Chief Justice. Although a staunch Federalist, Rutledge had denounced Jay's Treaty. Rumors were immediately circulated that he was a drunkard and insane. Washington did not lift a finger to defend him, and the Senate refused to confirm him.[64]

The most compelling argument used by the Federalists was fear—fear of a war with Great Britain, fear of civil disorder of which the Whiskey Rebellion and rumors of western conspiracies seemed to give evidence. Yet Hamilton, like Jefferson in the French crisis, allowed his prejudices to blind him to reality. If there were to be a war, the United States would have to start it. England was far too preoccupied with the shifting fortunes of war and alliances to contemplate seriously a major military effort against the United States. Two decades later it was the United States who declared war, and its temerity did not seriously endanger its security until Napoleon had been defeated and England's military resources were free for a major campaign in America.

What Hamilton failed to see was that the basic issue was not just to preserve peace with England but with France as well. Though Jay's Treaty finally won acceptance, it was at the cost of virtually destroying the friendship of France. In short, Hamilton's belief that the failure of the treaty meant war with England had little foundation. The Republican claim that its implementation meant war with France was almost justified in the event.

What other course was open? Since the United States was Britain's best customer, the obvious answer seemed to be commercial reprisals. This was the theme of the Republican opposition, and particularly of Madison, who recognized that concession was more easily obtained by diplomatic pressure. Jefferson had expressed the same view in observing that when "particular nations grasp at undue shares [of commerce] . . . defensive and protecting measures become necessary." [65]

"Camillus" had disagreed. "To begin with reprisals is to meet on the ground of war, and put the other party in a condition not to be able to recede without humiliation." [66] Yet on the eve of Jay's departure for England, Hamilton had sent him a last minute supplementary instruction which contained the following observation: "The great political and commercial considerations which ought to influence the conduct of Great Britain toward this country are familiar to you. . . . This country, in a commercial sense is more important to Great Britain than any other. . . . How unwise then in Great Britain, to suffer such a state of affairs to remain exposed to the hazard of constant interruption and derangement." [67] To use this situation to pressure Britain into greater concessions might have resulted in more serious depredations on American commerce; it might even have created a serious situation in the nation's economic and financial structure. But Britain would not have gone to war with the United States.

XII The Alien and Sedition Acts

WHEN HAMILTON RETIRED from the Treasury at the end of January, 1795, he had no intention of abandoning his role as "mayor of the palace." Washington sought his advice with almost as much regularity as if he were still a member of the Cabinet, and Hamilton urged the President not to "have any scruples about commanding me." [1] As noted above, he not only defended Jay's Treaty in the newspaper war as "Camillus" but advised both Washington and the Federalist Congressmen in the struggle to secure its acceptance. He directed a steady flow of instructions to his successor Wolcott and complained bitterly when Congressional actions did not conform to Hamiltonian orthodoxy. Obviously there were times when Hamilton believed that without his master touch at the controls the engine of state would wreck itself.

The Farewell Address

A year later Washington was also ready to retire. The President was sixty-four years old in 1796, and he was discovering, as his successors would discover, that the presidential office exacted a fearful physical and mental strain. To an English visitor he appeared "considerably older" than his age would indicate and "the innumerable vexations he has met with . . . have very sensibly impaired the vigour of his consti-

233

tution and given him an aged appearance." [2] The monumental calm was more often broken by bursts of temper, and it was obvious that he was easily moved to indignation at the "indecent" invective of some of his critics. The father of his country was not tolerant of filial impiety. [3]

In the summer of 1796 Washington decided to announce his intention not to stand for reelection. He sent to Hamilton a draft of an address which had been prepared by Madison in 1792 when Washington had first contemplated retirement. Hamilton made revisions and extensive additions and also brought in John Jay for consultation. There were several exchanges of correspondence between Philadelphia and New York. The final draft was thus the work of several hands, but the ideas were Washington's, approved and embellished by Hamilton. [4]

No doubt Washington was disturbed by the highly charged atmosphere generated by the Jay Treaty and the Whiskey Rebellion. The first admonition of the Farewell Address [5] was an appeal for national unity. "The name of American, which belongs to you in your national capacity, must always exalt the just pride of patriotism more than any other appellation." He warned against the divisive tendencies of sectionalism and noted that the Constitution, "adopted upon full investigation and mature deliberation," was designed to reconcile conflicting regional interests.

Respect for its authority was fundamental to the exercise of liberty. "The basis of our political systems is the right of the people to make and alter their constitutions of government. But the constitution which at any time exists till changed by an explicit and authentic act of the whole people is sacredly obligatory upon all. The very idea of the power and right of the people to establish government presupposed the duty of every individual to obey the established government."

Yet Washington deplored the existence of political parties which, ironically, he had done so much to create. He refused to believe that "parties in free countries are useful checks upon the administration of government and serve to keep alive the spirit of liberty." Instead, he insisted that "the spirit of party" was dangerous. "It agitates the community with illfounded jealousies and false alarms . . . [and] foments occasionally riot and insurrection. It opens the door to foreign influence and corruption. . . . Thus the policy and the will of one country become the policy and will of another."

The last part of the Address was the most enduring. He warned against "permanent inveterate antipathies against particular nations and passionate attachment for others," and he concluded with the much-quoted injunction: "It is our true policy to steer clear of permanent alliances with any portion of the foreign world." The frequency with which this and other fragments have been lifted from the context of the Address to buttress the policy of isolation indicates an ignorance of both Washington's and Hamilton's ideas and the times in which they were set forth. The President could not ignore the fact that the United States had a permanent alliance with France, and he noted that "so far as we already have formed engagements let them be fulfilled with perfect good faith." Moreover, "Harmony, liberal intercourse with all nations are recommended by policy, humanity and interest." In short, Washington and Hamilton were aware of the fact that the United States existed in a place called the world.

The Address was in many ways a curious document. The President wanted it to constitute an enduring credo by which future Americans would be guided. But it was written only a few months after the furious debate over Jay's Treaty, the most serious challenge to his leadership since he had taken office. Although he was deeply hurt by the stinging criticism of the opposition, it never occurred to Washington that he might be wrong. His attitude toward Britain, he was convinced, displayed "an equal and impartial hand" while the friends of France were "its tools and dupes [who] usurp the applause and confidence of the people to surrender their interests." Thus, however Washington might have attempted a detached and lofty approach, his partisanship showed through.[6]

Hamilton frankly regarded the Address as a campaign document. "The proper period now for your declaration seems to be *Two months* before the time for the Meeting of the Electors." Madison saw it not only as a political document but as a deliberate attempt to alienate France. He wrote Monroe that "it was not easy to suppose his mind wrought up to the tone that could dictate . . . some parts of the performance." [7] Jefferson noted ruefully, "Such is the popularity of the President that the people will support him in whatever he will do or will not do, without appealing to their feelings toward him." [8]

The French minister Pierre Auguste Adet was sure that Hamilton's fine hand lay behind "the lies it contains, the insolent tone which governs it, the immorality which characterizes it." He sent a copy of the Address to Paris and commented that, together with Washington's recall of the American minister James Monroe, it put an end to Franco-American friendship.[9]

Monroe in Paris

The most frustrated man in the international crisis of 1795–96 was James Monroe. This Republican stalwart and close friend of Jefferson had been named to succeed Gouverneur Morris, whose open sympathy with Great Britain had so offended the French government. The President hoped that the appointment of a prominent Republican would soothe French feelings and allay their alarm over the Jay mission to England.

Monroe had little experience to guide him. His observations of Genet in America and Morris in France and his own sympathies seemed to indicate the need for a frank and friendly attitude. Upon his arrival in Paris in August of 1794, two months after Jay had reached England, he addressed a florid speech to the National Convention and presented it with an American flag. He was, in turn, enthusiastically welcomed by the President and the flag was ordered hung in the assembly hall beside the tricolour.

It was an auspicious beginning, but the news of his exhibition of "sweetest fraternity" angered Federalists at home and vastly annoyed Jay in England.[10] Yet Monroe justified his behavior because Franco-American relations were stretched to the breaking point. He had been instructed to reassure the French that Jay's mission in no way compromised the alliance and to assert that *"in case of war, with any nation on earth, we shall consider France as our first and natural ally."*[11] By the end of 1794 Monroe could point to the fact that France had agreed to restore treaty rights to American ships in French ports and had reaffirmed the principle that free ships made free goods.

Monroe had also followed his instructions to give reassurance to the French government during Jay's negotiations in London. Then news reached Paris early in January, 1795, that a treaty had been signed. Monroe was in a dilemma. The French government was insistent on knowing its terms and Secretary of State Randolph had repeatedly assured him that Jay was "positively forbidden to weaken the engagements between this country and France."[12] Monroe therefore notified the Paris government that he would transmit the contents of Jay's Treaty "as soon as I shall be informed."[13] But, as noted above, Washington had decided not to reveal the terms of the treaty until the Senate convened in June. For six months Monroe repeated his assurances and insisted that if the treaty injured France the Senate would not approve it. It was not surprising that the French became increasingly suspicious and distrustful and Monroe indignant at Secretary of State Randolph's silent treatment.

In late August the contents of the treaty reached Paris along with the news of Senate confirmation. The French felt that their suspicions were amply justified, and Monroe could only predict hopefully that Washington would not sign it.[14] By November it was known that the President had not only signed the treaty but had dismissed Randolph, the only Republican in the cabinet.

As the summer of 1796 ended with the failure of the House of Representatives to block the treaty, the American position had deteriorated beyond repair. The French government announced that the Franco-American Alliance had "ceased to exist" and that its minister would be recalled. Monroe's outrage at his treatment by Pickering led him to criticize the administration in several letters which found their way into print and which openly expressed the hope that the Republicans would win the presidency in 1796.[15] Although this unusual diplomacy may have eased tension in Paris, his apostasy infuriated the Federalists. Hamilton joined the chorus which demanded that Monroe be recalled, but his reasons were not entirely partisan. "This state of things [with France] is extremely serious," he wrote to Wolcott. "The government must play a skilful card, or all is lost. . . . To this end a person must be sent in place of Monroe."[16]

The person sent was Charles Cotesworth Pinckney. The French regarded Monroe's recall as an affront dictated by political considerations and refused to receive his successor or to listen to his communications from the American government. Frustrated to the end, a hapless Monroe came home in the spring of 1797.

A School For Scandal

A perverse provision of the Constitution had placed John Adams in the presidency and Jefferson in the office of vice–president. The President-elect observed: "We labored together in high friendship in Congress in 1776 and have lived and acted together very frequently since that time. His Talent and Information I know very well, and have ever believed in his honour, Integrity and love of Country, and his friends." [17]

It might have been a great collaboration, but Jefferson shied away. "My letters inform me that mr. A speaks of me with great friendship, and with satisfaction in the prospect of administering the government in concurrence with me," he wrote to Madison. "I never felt a diminuation of confidence in his integrity, and retained a solid affection for him." But, he continued, "I cannot . . . wish to see the scenes of 93. revived as to myself, & to descend daily into the arena like a gladiator, to suffer martyrdom in every conflict. As to duty, the Constitution will know me only as a member of the legislative body." [18] He might have added that the Federalists would soon know him as the leader of a movement for "a revolution of opinion" in the country.

For Hamilton, Washington's retirement meant that the principle public support of his policies had been removed. As he later wrote on the occasion of Washington's death, "Perhaps no man in this community has equal cause with myself to deplore the loss. . . . he was an *Aegis very essential to me.* " [19] He did not deceive himself that he could manipulate John Adams, whose "discernment and independence forbid all hope of influencing the decisions of the Executive." [20] He had no doubt that his advice would not be welcome. Yet the President unwittingly left Hamilton's lines open. Adams' veneration for Washington led him to retain all of the members of the cabinet. Of these only Attorney-General Charles Lee, appointed in 1795, was not slavishly devoted to Hamilton. Wolcott, Pickering, and McHenry continually sought his advice and followed it faithfully.

Jefferson and Hamilton were each the target for the scandalmongers in the summer of 1797. If either had wanted to top the best seller lists with his personal memoirs, each could have done so with ease.

The source of Jefferson's embarrassment was a letter which he had written to an old friend, Phillip Mazzei. Mazzei was an Italian radical who came to the United States just before the Revolution, had visited Jefferson at Monticello, and had then made his home in Albemarle for several years. The master of Monticello had been as fascinated by his neighbor's Italian farming methods as by his philosophy. Although Mazzei returned to Italy, Jefferson continued to correspond with his old friend.

In the summer of 1796, following the controversy over Jay's Treaty, Jefferson wrote Mazzei a long letter in which he gave vent to his wrath over "an Anglican monarchical, & aristocratical party . . . whose object is to draw over us the substance, as they have already done the forms, of the British government." He then went on to denounce "men who were Samsons in the field & Solomons in the council, but who have had their heads shorn by the harlot England." [21] The latter reference was obviously to Washington.

Mazzei translated the letter into Italian and passed it to the local press. From there it was picked up by the Paris *Moniteur* and finally, three translations and a year later, it appeared in the Federalist *Minerva*.[22] With Washington in honored retirement, Americans were not inclined to brook criticism of their first authentic hero—and by a foreigner, at that. The Federalist press heaped excoriations on the Vice-President, and Jefferson maintained an uncomfortable silence. His keenest regret was that Washington was deeply offended and never spoke to him during the two years which remained of Washington's life.

The furor over Mazzei had not completely subsided when a much more sensational storm broke around Hamilton. Six years before, the sophisticated Secretary of the Treasury had incredibly fallen victim to one of the oldest con games in the world.

James Reynolds was a petty swindler who possessed a larcenous heart and a beautiful wife. Maria Reynolds appeared in Hamilton's New York office one day in 1791 and gave a magnificent performance in the role of a wife wronged and betrayed. When Hamilton took the lure, she set the hook. Husband James duly appeared, acted out his indignation, and was mollified by a "loan" of $1000. It was more than a year and several more such loans to Reynolds before Hamilton's infatuation cooled sufficiently to make him suspicious. But as a prominent figure in a highly sensitive position in government, he found that escape was difficult. The situation reached a climax when Reynolds was jailed attempting to recover the government claim of a dead Revolutionary soldier who turned out to be very much alive. Reynolds did not intend to languish in jail and appealed to Hamilton to intervene in his behalf. But Hamilton had had enough. He refused to help even when Reynolds threatened to disclose "evidence" of malfeasance by the Secretary of the Treasury.

With his bluff called, Reynolds "exposed" Hamilton's misconduct to Congressmen James Monroe, Frederick Muhlenberg, and Abraham Venable. These gentlemen would have been highly pleased to destroy Hamilton's carefully laid financial system, but when they confronted him with the charges, the Secretary convinced them that he had only been guilty of private indiscretions. His accusers agreed to keep silent, and there the matter might have rested.

The man who revealed Hamilton's secret was John Beckley, the scandalmongering Republican who was the clerk of the House of Representatives. At the time of the Reynolds affair, Beckley's secretary had transcribed some of the documents used by Monroe and his fellow Congressmen. In 1797 the Federalists were finally joined by enough Republicans to oust Beckley from his Congressional post. The vindictive ex-clerk revealed the story to James Callender, a newspaper editor who was noted for his scurrilous journalism even among the many notable practioners of the 1790's. Callender published *A History of the United States for the Year 1796* in which the whole affair, including the charges of Hamilton's dishonesty in office, was spread before the public.

Hamilton at first attempted to obtain vindication of his official conduct by securing affadavits from Muhlenberg, Venable, and Monroe. Muhlenberg and Venable replied promptly and convincingly, but Monroe was silent. Hamilton vehemently demanded that Monroe speak, and for a time it appeared that the situation would be resolved by pistols at the traditional ten paces. Cooler councils prevailed, but although Monroe did not affirm the charge against Hamilton, he refused to deny it. Much against the advice of his friends Hamilton decided to reveal the whole sordid affair, and in 1797 he published *Observations of Certain Documents contained in the History of the United States for the Year 1796.* It is perhaps as much a tribute to Hamilton as to his wife Elizabeth that their marriage survived the episode. It undoubtedly ruined whatever ambition Hamilton may have had for elective office.[23]

The whole atmosphere of villification and insult, of which these episodes were a part, distressed Jefferson. "The passions are too high at present, to be cooled in our day," he wrote an old friend. "You and I have formerly seen warm debates and high political passions. But gentlemen of different politics would then speak to each other, & separate the business of the Senate from that of society. It is not so now. Men who have been intimate all their lives, cross the street to avoid meeting, & turn their heads another way, lest they be obliged to touch their hats. This may do for young men with whom passion is an enjoyment. But it is afflicting to peaceable minds." [24]

The Failure of a Mission

President Adams called his department heads together to consider the deterioration of Franco-American relations. The situation had reached a critical point. The spectacular campaigns of a brilliant young general named Napoleon Bonaparte had led to the French conquest of Italy and had knocked Austria out of the war. Emboldened by these successes, the Directory struck hard at England by barring its merchandise from the Continent and declaring that all ships laden with British goods were subject to seizure. The French were soon pillaging American commerce, and by the summer of 1797 over three hundred ships flying the American flag had been taken by privateers, most of whom operated from Caribbean bases. [25]

Adams was therefore in a belligerent mood, and so were the members of the cabinet. But Adams' belligerence was tempered by a determination to avoid an open rupture with France by negotiating through a special diplomatic mission. The department heads were more inclined to join with Federalist Congressmen who were demanding war with France as vehemently as the Republicans had demanded war with England three years before. But Hamilton remained consistent and clear-sighted. "To be in rupture with France united with England . . . as is possible, would be a most unwelcome situation. . . ." he wrote firmly to Wolcott. "We ought to do everything to avoid a rupture . . . and to keep in view, as a primary object, union at home. No measure can tend more to this, than an extraordinary mission." If this were accompanied by strong defense measures the situation might be saved.[26] If Adams was surprised by the sudden change of his cabinet's opinion he did not guess the reason.

In May, 1797, Adams called a special session of Congress in which the Federalists as a party claimed control of both houses of Congress for the first time. The President outlined the nature of the crisis and advocated increases in the armed forces, convoys, and the arming of merchant ships.[27] William L. Smith, the Hamiltonian spokesman in the House, introduced a series of resolutions embodying these suggestions. He was vigorously opposed by William Branch Giles of Virginia, who pointed out that convoying and arming merchant ships would surely provoke a war. Gallatin argued that the enormous cost of these measures would not be worth the dubious benefits. Between Federalist war hawks in the Senate and the Republican opposition in the House, the President's program was reduced to shreds. Only the three frigates already under construction were to be completed, and the Federalists agreed to drop the proposal for arming merchant ships in return for an authorization for convoys.[28]

Jefferson, presiding in the Senate, was pessimistic. He was unhappy about "the spirit which is driving us on here, & beyond the water" and deplored the belligerent atmosphere in Philadelphia. "War is not the best engine for us to resort to, nature has given us one *in our commerce,* which, if properly managed, will be a better instrument for obliging the interested nations of Europe to treat us with justice." With the news of the failure of the Bank of England and the general distress of Britain he thought that "it would certainly be better for us to rub through this year" and hope that the restoration of peace would follow shortly.[29] Unlike many Republicans he neither desired nor expected a successful French invasion of England. "The subjugation of England would indeed be a general calamity. But happily it is impossible. Should it end in her being republicanized, I know not on what principle a true republican of our country could lament it. . . . I do not indeed wish to see any nation have a form of government forced upon them; but if it is to be done, I should rejoice at it's being a freer one." [30]

Meanwhile, Hamilton was having a difficult time with the belligerent members of Adams' cabinet. To Pickering he insisted that a special mission "appeared to me to be indispensable." He shrewdly proposed that either Jefferson or Madison be named along with C. C. Pinckney and a third member "on whom perfect reliance could be placed." The presence of either of the two Republican leaders would make the mission acceptable to France, and if they refused to serve, "they will put themselves in the wrong; for on so great an emergency they cannot justifiably decline. . . . The refusal, too . . . would furnish a reply to the Jacobin clamor." To objections to his plan, he pointed out that too belligerent a tone would lay the Federalists open to exactly the same sort of accusations of warmongering which they had leveled at the Republicans in 1794. But, in any event, "I repeat it with extreme solicitude—another mission is absolutely indispensable." [31]

Although Adams decided to send the mission, he was not knowingly following Hamilton's urgings. His attitude was that "the Creole" was a private citizen, and he neither sought nor heeded his advice. With his cabinet advisers it was otherwise. The commission was composed of John Marshall and C. C. Pinckney, two staunch Federalists, and Elbridge Gerry, a Republican and a Massachusetts friend of the

President. The three envoys sailed for France in the fall of 1797.

Upon their arrival they found that the Directory had been purged of its moderate members. The new ministers were not only hostile toward the United States but much more interested in lining their own pockets than they were in the fortunes of France. For months the three Americans were kept cooling their heels while unofficial emissaries insisted upon payment of a *douceur,* or gratuity, to Talleyrand, the minister of foreign affairs, and the assurance of a loan from the United States. These, insisted the Frenchmen, were indispensable conditions to the opening of negotiations. Such a proposition was not unusual in the course of European diplomatic negotiations, and the American envoys expressed no particular indignation except at the size of the amounts which were demanded ($250,000 for Talleyrand and a loan of about $13,-000,000). It was in exasperation and impatience that Pinckney finally exclaimed to the importunate French, "It is ño; no; not a sixpence!" This was as close as he ever came to "Millions for defense and not one cent for tribute!" the later rendition of his words by a Federalist orator.[32]

After months of fruitless waiting and unofficial exchanges with Talleyrand, Marshall and Pinckney left Paris to return to the United States in April, 1798. Gerry, defying his instructions, remained in the hope of salvaging something. It was his own belief that he had succeeded. By the time he sailed, in October, 1798, the Directory had ordered French raiders to cease their depredations and Talleyrand was making strenuous efforts to renew negotiations. But these were the result of an upheaval and near overthrow of the Directory, and of Talleyrand's realization that he had overreached himself with the United States. He was still trying to redress his error when the Directory succumbed to Napoleon's coup d'etat in 1799.[33]

"Dangers Real or Pretended . . ."

The dispatches from the French mission reached the President in the first week in March, 1798. Many of them were in code, but even before they were deciphered Adams knew that they were highly explosive. He consulted with his cabinet, and they in turn consulted with Hamilton. Secretary of State Pickering's belligerent frame of mind had to be restrained. Hamilton advised "leaving still the door to accommodations open, and not proceeding to a final rupture" while at the same time taking "vigorous and comprehensive measures of defence." [34]

With the full contents of the dispatches before him, John Adams' ire was thoroughly aroused. He set about drafting a message to Congress which clearly invited a declaration of war. But on cooler reflection, he decided simply to announce a state of limited hostilities. He then submitted a list of measures for defense: coastal fortifications; increased manufacture of arms; arming of merchant ships; and, last but not least, legislation for the raising of necessary revenue.

At this point Jefferson and his followers committed a grave blunder. The message, said Jefferson, was "insane" and others joined in charging the President with sabre rattling. [35] They then resorted to the tactics of former days by demanding that the correspondence of the envoys be submitted to Congress. The President complied. The dispatches contained every word of the transactions except for the removal of some profanity and the substitution of the letters X, Y, and Z for the names of the French negotiators.

The Republicans were appalled. In the confusion, Jefferson noted bitterly, some literally beat a retreat from the capital. The triumphant Federalists rammed through an unprecedented resolution to publish the papers, and overnight the sinister Messieurs X, Y, and Z were notorious throughout the country.[36] There was now no stopping the Federalist juggernaut. Bills were passed for harbor fortifications, a national militia, increase in the regular army, use of the navy for convoying, authorization for privateering, tripling the number of naval vessels—disorganized and demoralized Republicans were helpless to stem the torrent.

A wave of revulsion for France and Frenchmen swept the country. True Americans were urged to wear the black cockade, and theatre audiences hissed the playing of "Ça Ira" and the "Marseillaise." "Yankee Doodle" and the "President's March" were now the favorites. A young man named Joseph Hopkinson composed some new lyrics for the "March," and the President's wife, the redoubtable Abigail, was present at the theatre when Gilbert Fox sang the first public performance of "Hail, Columbia." [37] Early in May the President proclaimed a day of fasting and prayer in the capital, but "black cockade" demonstrators clashed with defiant Republicans wearing the red cockade. The solemn day ended as Adams ordered a chest of arms sent to his residence and guards were mounted at his door.[38]

It was not long before there were undercurrents of something more sinister than war talk and patriotic demonstrations. An early manifestation was an exchange of remarks in the House of Representatives when Francis Dana of Massachusetts and John Allen of Connecticut made slurring references to Gallatin, whose heavily accented speech marked him as a "foreigner." By the middle of April suggestions were being made that only native-born Americans be allowed to hold office or even to vote. Although many Republicans were either absent or remained silent, the gallant Swiss-American maintained his lonely fight against the opposition, his words reasonable, his logic impeccable.[39] Said Madison from his retirement in Virginia, "Perhaps it is a universal truth that the loss of liberty at home is to be charged to provisions against dangers real or pretended from abroad." [40]

As the war fever tightened its hold on the country, the Federalists took measures not only for defense against France but against "its partisans among ourselves, who aid and abet their measures." [41] During June and July Congress passed four acts which were designed as measures for internal security. The first was the Naturalization Act which increased the residence requirements for citizenship from five to fourteen years.

Congress also passed two Alien Acts. Essentially these gave the President control over aliens during wartime. At his discretion, he might order the arrest, imprisonment, or deportation of foreign residents whom he considered dangerous to the security of the country. The act was to lapse automatically in 1802. It was worthy of note that John Adams, although he could and did become completely exasperated with both the French and the Republicans, never allowed his temper to control his judgement. He refused to use the sweeping powers as he might have, and the only positive order he seems to have issued was for the arrest of an avowed French agent who was never apprehended.

The Sedition Act was the capstone of the Federalist attempt to suppress the opposition. It declared that any person who was convicted of writing or publishing anything which tended to "defame the government, or [bring] either house of the . . . Congress, or the . . . President, or either of them, into contempt or disrepute" might be imprisoned for as much as two years and fined $1000.

A close reading of these laws reveals that they were not particularly oppressive.[42] Congress restored the five-year residence requirement in 1802. And surely the nation had to find some means of controlling foreigners who might engage in subversion in wartime. As for the Sedition Act, it simply applied the common law of libel to critics of officers of the national government. Indeed, the "intent" provision and the specification that the truth of libels could be used as a defense made it more liberal than many state laws.

If the founding fathers were somewhat thin-skinned, it was because young America had not yet learned that politics was a rough-and-tumble brawl and only those with thick hides need apply. Nor had it learned in this, its first serious threat from a foreign foe, that, as Jefferson remarked, "A little patience, and we shall see the reign of witches pass over, their spells dissolved, and the people recovering their true sight, restoring their government to its true principles." [43] It is much less understandable that after 175 years America still occasionally tolerates the "reign of witches."

A Reign of Terror?

It was not the laws themselves, then, but the threat behind them that added to the smell of fear in the nation. Thousands of French emigrés prepared to leave the country. Most of them had come to the United States for sanctuary against the terror of revolutionary France or Saint Domingue. Nevertheless, they feared reprisals simply because they were foreign. [44]

It was the Sedition Act which thoroughly aroused the Republicans. Jefferson reported to Madison that the act was "so palpably in the teeth of the Constitution as to shew that they [the Federalists] mean to pay no respect to it." [45] John Taylor of Caroline, who had had nothing good to say about the Constitution since it was first proposed in 1787, wrote to Jefferson suggesting that the time had come to dissolve the union. He proposed that Virginia and North Carolina be joined to create a separate republic. Despite his concern Jefferson was not inclined to such a drastic step. He replied that "in every free and deliberating society, there must, from the nature of man, be opposite parties, and violent dissensions and discords; and one of these, for the most part, must prevail over the other for a longer or shorter time. . . . But if on a temporary superiority of the one party, the other is to resort to a scission of the Union, no federal government can ever exist." He then wryly pointed out the *reductio ad absurdum:* "Seeing, therefore, that an association of men who will not quarrel with one another is a thing which never yet existed, from the greatest confederacy of nations down to a town meeting or a vestry; seeing that we must have somebody to quarrel with, I had rather keep our New England associates for that purpose." [46]

Yet Jefferson was thoroughly alarmed at the partisanship with which the Sedition Act was enforced and the vindictiveness with which Republican newspaper editors were harried. Many more were brought to trial under state libel laws than under the Sedition Act, but this was small comfort when a federal judge like Samuel Chase refused to allow any but Federalists to sit on a jury. In another case Chase rebuked the distinguished defense counsel John Nicholas as being "irregular . . . subversive . . . [and] calculated to deceive the people." This was during the trial of the infamous James Callender which later became a *cause célèbre.*[47] Other more respected editors, such as Thomas Cooper, Benjamin Bache, and Anthony Howell, were indicted under state or federal laws.

Nor were arrests confined only to editors and public figures. In New Jersey Luther Baldwin, town drunkard and *bon vivant,* was taking his ease in the village tavern with a group of convivial companions when John Adams passed through. When the cannon on the green began booming a presidential salute, one imbiber observed, "There goes the President and they are shooting at his arse." Said Baldwin belligerently, "I do not care if they fired *through* his arse." To which the tavern keeper indignantly exclaimed, "That is sedition!" and had Baldwin arrested. He was fined $100 in a New Jersey court.

Altogether about two dozen persons were brought to trial in federal court, most of them editors, of whom about half were convicted. Many more were convicted in state courts, but fines and prison terms were not particularly severe.[48]

At the time of the passage of the Sedition Act, Hamilton favored it. He expressed concern lest the government "establish a tyranny," but he seemed satisfied with the act as passed by Congress.[49] His lawyer's mind particularly approved the provision that juries decide the question of the truth or falseness of the alleged libel. As far as the larger issue was concerned, Hamilton viewed the Alien and Sedition Acts, and perhaps even more stringent laws, as necessary for the order and security of the nation. He welcomed the implication that the Sedition Act seemed to extend the jurisdiction of federal courts into the area of common law since this increased the power of the federal government at the expense of the states. When he became commander of the army, he announced his readiness to use federal troops in Virginia where "the leaders . . . who possess completely all the powers of local government, are resolved to possess those of the national, by the most dangerous combinations." [50] It never occurred to Hamilton that the country's liberty might be endangered by an excessive zeal for order. His only concern was that the storm of protest might strengthen the Republican opposition.

His fears were justified.

The Virginia and Kentucky Resolutions

In the fall of 1798 Jefferson quit the Senate and returned to Monticello. The question raised by the Alien and Sedition

Acts was far more serious than the passage of bad laws. What recourse was there when the federal government enacted and enforced laws which were clearly in violation of the Constitution? The question took on added significance because the issue involved the curbing of freedom of speech and thus establishing that "tyranny over the mind of man" which Jefferson regarded as fatal to liberty.

Was the only alternative the fragmentation of the union which John Taylor had suggested? Jefferson thought he had another answer but he needed the constitutional genius of his friend James Madison. The two were agreed that the authorship of the forthcoming protest must be kept secret so there exist only sketchy records of the correspondence and conversations which took place. They decided that the protests should be presented publicly as resolutions of state legislatures. John Breckinridge was entrusted with this task in Kentucky and John Taylor of Caroline introduced the resolutions in the Virginia legislature.[51]

Jefferson's reasoning began with the assumption that the Constitution was a compact agreed to by the states. In this compact the states had agreed to grant certain powers to the central government and these powers, along with certain prohibitions, were set forth in the compact, that is, the Constitution. Those powers not granted to the federal government were reserved to the states. In other words, Jefferson viewed the Constitution as a contractual agreement between the states and the central government that they had created.

In the event that the federal government went beyond the limits specified by the Constitution, then the states must intervene to prevent intrusion upon the area of power reserved to them. Although the question involved the dividing line between federal and state power, or "states' rights," the more crucial question was one of "state sovereignty"; that is, who was to be the final arbiter of whether or not the federal government had trespassed on state authority? In other words, it was necessary not only to determine *where* the line between federal and state power lay but to decide *who* was to make the final determination.

Jefferson concluded that since the states had granted the powers to the central government, since they had, indeed, created it, obviously theirs was the final judgment. Madison himself had pointed out in *The Federalist* that the states could be relied upon to prevent federal usurpation, and even Hamilton had noted that the "state governments will, in all possible contingencies, afford complete security against invasions of the public liberty by the national authority." [52]

Jefferson's Kentucky Resolutions stated that "the government created by this compact [the Constitution] was not made the exclusive or final judge of the extent of the powers delegated to itself." The resolution therefore declared the acts "altogether void and of no force." Did Kentucky and Virginia then propose to nullify the acts of the federal government? Jefferson and Madison drew back from such an extreme doctrine. Kentucky directed the governor to "call on its co-States for an expression of their sentiments" while Virginia "doth solomnly appeal to the like disposition of the other states in the confidence that they will concur . . . that the acts aforesaid are unconstitutional." [53]

The response to the Virginia and Kentucky Resolutions was discouraging. Not a single state gave its approval to the doctrine which it contained. Nevertheless Jefferson and Madison were determined to pursue the question. Madison postponed his plans for retirement and was reelected to the Virginia General Assembly.

Jefferson decided that a bolder approach was necessary. In the spring of 1799 he proposed to Madison another set of Kentucky Resolutions which would assert that while "not at all disposed to make every measure of error or wrong a cause of scission," nevertheless "to sever ourselves from that union we so much value, rather than give up the rights of self government . . . in which alone we see liberty, safety and happiness." He concluded his letter to Madison, "These things I sketch hastily . . . wishing you to consider on them or what else is best to be done." [54] To Jefferson the union did not have an absolute value, and its preservation could not be viewed as an end in itself. Its function was to preserve liberty, and if it became ruthlessly suppressive then, as the lesser of two evils, the compact of states must come to an end.

Nowhere is the interaction of two great intellects more clearly revealed than in the aftermath of this radical statement. In a visit to Monticello in August, 1799, Madison calmed his friend and softened the language of the proposal. He may have reminded Jefferson that there was a more obvious solution to the present dilemma—a victory in the election of 1800. At any rate he succeeded in moderating Jefferson's outline for the new resolutions and removed the threat of nullification. Thus Jefferson's determined campaign against repressive federal legislation was made effective by Madison's refinement and moderation. The Kentucky Resolutions of 1799 professed an "attachment to the Union" and a "solemn protest" against the laws which violated the Constitution. [55]

The Virginia and Kentucky Resolutions were often read— and frequently misread—in future years as support for a plethora of theories and doctrines. The most notable was the parallel drawn between the ideas they contained and the nullification doctrine of John C. Calhoun. Certainly Calhoun's premise of the union as a compact of states drew on Jefferson's similar concept. But Jefferson and Madison never visualized a doctrine in which a single state could nullify an act of Congress; rather they foresaw action by the "co-states."

Moreover Madison doubted that state legislatures could

act in a sovereign capacity. They were only the agents of the people and therefore had no more sanction of power than Congress. As John Marshall pointed out some years later in *McCulloch* v. *Maryland,* when the Constitution was proposed the state legislatures had turned the question of its acceptance over to the ratifying conventions and had thus removed themselves from any part in the decision.

But most important was the fact that Jefferson was opposing the suppression of dissent. His goal was progressive, and he was fighting against a kind of conservatism which advocated a "passive obedience under the newfangled names of *confidence* and *responsibility.*"[56] He would never have used the doctrines of 1798 to support the institution of slavery.

XIII The Election

of 1800

THOMAS JEFFERSON APPRAISED the state of the nation in the summer of 1798. "The most long-sighted politician could not, seven years ago, have imagined that the people of this wide extended country could have been enveloped in such delusion, and made so much afraid of themselves and their power, as to surrender it spontaneously to those who are maneuvering them into a form of government, the principal branches of which may be beyond their control." [1]

He was not alone in his pessimistic view of the future. Alexander Hamilton was equally sure that the republic was in peril although the danger was from a different source. He wrote to Washington that "the powerful faction [Republicans] which has for years opposed the government . . . are ready to *new model* our constitution under the *influence* or *coercion* of France. . . . This would be in substance . . . to make this country a province of France." [2]

The War Drum

The trouble was that in young America the leaders and the led had not learned how to tolerate opposition. Each party was certain that it was right and equally certain that victory for its opponents would be the death knell of the nation.

An emotional and biased press contributed to the confusion. Republican newspapers envisaged a return to monarchy under a British tyrant if Hamilton and his minions prevailed. Federalist editors related in blood-curdling detail the ghastly fate of true Americans if the "Jacobins" and the archfiend Jefferson ever seized political power. The press was virtually the only regular medium through which national and international news could reach the public. Editors were not so foolish as to believe that circulation could be increased by a reputation for accurate reporting. In fact, many were subsidized directly or indirectly by patrons whose avowed purpose was to maintain a channel through which to propagate political gospel to the faithful. Thus one had only to say, *"Argus, Minerva, Aurora,"* and it readily translated as "Republican, Federalist, Republican."

Except in the large cities few areas had more than one newspaper. Where two or more existed, they were sure to represent opposing parties. The public was then treated to an exchange of billingsgate between rival editors in which "liar," "hypocrite," and "scoundrel" were among the mildest epithets. These were no remote executives in paneled offices but hot-eyed, ink-stained partisans whose blasts of insult and innuendo did not spare even the President of the United States.[3]

It was not surprising, then, that Americans tended to react emotionally. The people in general refused to forget the vital role played by France in the War of Independence. They were sympathetic to the French Republic because it represented a struggle against the oppression of monarchy. To be sure, the capture of American ships and incidents like the XYZ affair could temporarily shift public opinion, but just as surely the British could be counted on "to produce a countercurrent . . . to plunder and oppress . . . and they will make the worst possible impression."[4]

Yet, as Hamilton pointed out time and again, the economic

interest of the nation was overwhelmingly invested in Great Britain. Trade with the Empire amounted to five or six times that of trade with France.[5] Thus merchants and businessmen who were involved in commerce wanted to avoid the disruption of a British war. Such a disruption would also cut deeply into the tariff and other revenues from foreign trade and upset the structure of government finance which Hamilton had so carefully built. It was obvious, much as Americans hated to admit it, that one of the major factors in the security of the United States was the British navy. France and Spain had a difficult time supporting their own New World colonies against British marauders in time of war. For the United States there was little to fear from the continent of Europe as long as England dominated the Atlantic.

The detached observer might wonder, then, what the United States had to gain by going to war with either France or England. If war was indeed "the ultimate weapon of diplomacy," what objectives could be attained by a declaration of war? Perhaps some degree of safety for United States shipping in the Western Atlantic but surely not a successful challenge to British or even French sea power. Just as surely, America could not lend sufficient military power as an ally to either England or France to enhance its own security.

There were of course vociferous and eloquent "appeals to the pride, the patriotism, and the honor of the nation!" [6] And there was muted talk and covert intrigue about the conquest of Louisiana and the Floridas. But this was hardly consistent with a war for the defense and preservation of the nation. C. C. Pinckney, the rejected American envoy in Paris, reported that war was apparently the only language that the French understood.[7] The havoc created by French privateers among American ships in the Caribbean seemed to support this view. George Cabot, New Englander and die-hard Federalist, thought that "we have much more to fear from peace than war," not only because of the threat from France but because a war "would also extinguish the hopes of internal foes." [8]

Spurred on by the "war whoop" faction, Congress in the summer of 1798 authorized an increase in the regular army to 10,000 men, with additions of 50,000 troops for the "Provisional Army" and 80,000 militia to be called out in the event that war was declared. It also created a Department of the Navy and formally established a Marine Corps under naval jurisdiction. Merchantmen were allowed to arm themselves for defense, privateers were to be commissioned, and the navy was authorized to take armed French ships.[9] Yet, imbued as he was with the martial spirit, John Adams refused to take the fatal step of asking Congress for a declaration of war. Extreme Federalists canvassed the situation and decided not to risk a vote without the President's endorsement.[10] This was as close as Congress ever came to a declaration of war without the invitation of the chief executive. It appeared at the time to make little difference since it was daily expected that France would declare war on the United States.

The President and the General

There was no doubt about who would command the new army. On July 2, 1798, the President sent Washington's name to the Senate for confirmation without consulting either his cabinet or Washington himself. More perplexing was the question of the subordinate generals. The commander in chief did not wish to be "called into the field until the army is in a situation to require my presence." [11] Indeed, his age and health might preclude Washington from exercising active command at all. The real operational command would obviously fall to the ranking major general who would also have the title of inspector-general.

Adams conferred with his cabinet. His intention was to name Henry Knox, wartime artillery commander under Washington and former Secretary of War, as the senior major general. Both Knox and Charles Cotesworth Pinckney, whom the President wished to place next in rank, had been generals during the War of Independence. By personal preference and by precedence Adams rated them above ex-Colonel Hamilton. The triumvirate of Pickering, Wolcott, and McHenry, however, unanimously and vehemently urged that Hamilton be named the senior general under Washington. Adams was thunderstruck. He wanted no part of an army which would for all practical purposes be commanded by Hamilton. His decision was firm: Knox would rank first Pinckney second, and Hamilton third.[12]

The commander in chief would not have it so. Washington was somewhat miffed that the President had not previously consulted him, and his acceptance of the appointment was conditional upon his being allowed to name his subordinates. He at first notified Pickering that Pinckney was his choice for second in command. This created consternation in the Hamiltonian ranks. Pickering urged Hamilton's case to Washington, and Secretary of War McHenry hurried to Mount Vernon to deliver the General's commission and to add a personal exhortation. He returned triumphantly to Philadelphia with Washington's official acceptance and his recommendation for the order of major generals: Hamilton, Pinckney, and Knox.[13]

Adams had gone to Quincy in mid-July to attend a seriously ill Abigail. When he learned late in August that his appointments had been challenged, he wrote McHenry a stern letter reminding him who was President and reiterating his original choice of generals. A month later he received a letter from Washington which was as inexplicable as it was infuriating. Washington insisted that his own wishes be hon-

ored as a condition of his service.[14] The President must give
way to the general.

Adams confessed defeat. He was aware that Washington's
resignation would have political repercussions which might
shatter the divided counsels of his administration. But Hamilton had his way at a price. John Adams was thoroughly
aroused. His reply to Washington contained a rebuke which
was no less stinging because it was veiled. If "controversies
[over command] should arise, they of course will be submitted to you as Commander-in-chief, and if, after all, anyone
should . . . appeal to me from the judgement of the Commander-in-chief, I was determined to confirm that judgement; because . . . there is no doubt to be made, that by the
present Constitution of the United States, the President has
authority to determine the rank of officers." [15]

The rift between Hamilton and the President was now
complete. John Adams would never forget that he had been
"compelled . . . to promote . . . the most restless, impatient,
artful, indefatigible, and unprincipled intriguer in the United
States, if not in the world." [16] Hamilton had challenged executive authority with even greater flagrance than he had
denounced in Jefferson six years before. He had achieved his
coveted command of the army—which never fired a shot in
anger.

The Inspector-General

The wrangle over the army command lasted until October
of 1798, and the real work of organizing the army did not
begin until November. Washington came to Philadelphia
and, with Hamilton and Pinckney, began the work of select-
ing senior officers from the deluge of applications which came
to army headquarters. This selection board was careful to
screen out all Republicans for, in the opinion of the com-

mander in chief, "you could as soon scrub a blackamore white, as to change the principles of a profest Democrat." [17] The refusal of a commission to New York Republican Senator Aaron Burr, whose war record was certainly as distinguished as Hamilton's, lent credence to the Republican charge that the Federalists intended to use the army to "overawe public sentiment." [18]

With the completion of the selection of officers, Washington returned to Mount Vernon leaving to Hamilton the enormous task of recruitment, organization, and training. The acting commander undertook his duties with his customary energy and enthusiasm. It was the kind of assignment which brought out the best of Hamilton's talents. His keen, incisive mind went to the heart of every problem; yet no detail was overlooked. His furious energy turned out reports and orders at an astounding rate. A meticulous and sweeping Act for the Better Organization for the Troops was passed by Congress in almost the exact form in which Hamilton had submitted it, and many of its provisions were surprisingly modern.[19]

He attempted to transmit his own urgency to subordinates and superiors alike. Poor James McHenry, who had done so much to secure the command for Hamilton, squirmed under the sting of his whip. The Secretary of War seemed dazed by demands for arms and uniforms, a service of supply, plans for harbor fortifications—"I proposed to the Secretary to change the buttons [on the uniforms of a western regiment]. It has not been done." Indeed, McHenry may have wondered who was subordinate to whom. "Believe me the service everywhere is suffering for the want of proper organization," Hamilton admonished him sharply. "It is one thing for business to drag on —another for it to go well." [20]

Hamilton's grasp of military affairs was extraordinary. He pressed for the establishment of a permanent military academy to train officers. He drew up plans for the classification of militia according to age and marital status so that "the first class, consisting of all unmarried men from 18 to 25" be called to duty first and "none of a higher number to be called until all of a preceding lower number have . . . served their tour." Students "in universities, colleges and academies, and of divinity, law, and medicine" were exempted.[21] He pointed out that "it is essential the Executive should have half a million of secret-service money" and recommended the organization of an army medical department "the right fashioning of which I feel myself more than ordinarily competent." [22]

But few of these far-reaching proposals went beyond the desk of the Secretary of War. Hamilton wrote in despair to Washington that "if the Secretary's energies for execution were equal to his good dispositions, the public service under his care would prosper. . . . It is only to be regretted that there can be no reliance that the future progress will be more satisfactory than in the past." [23]

Meantime, by the beginning of 1799, the problem of recruiting was becoming acute. The decline of the "black cockade fever," the continuing rumors that France did not intend to declare war, the taxes imposed by Congress to pay for increased military costs—all these dampened considerably the martial fervor of the previous year. It was difficult to recruit an army when it appeared that there would be nothing to fight. Hamilton half-hopefully thought he saw the embers of a revolt in Virginia where the legislature had protested the Alien and Sedition Acts, but it came to nothing.

In February there was a flare-up in Pennsylvania. Germans in the western part of the state refused to pay the real estate tax levied by the federal government. When several farmers were jailed, Jacob Fries, a Bucks County resident, led a party of armed men to their rescue. Hamilton urged McHenry to suppress the insurrection vigorously and offered to send additional troops to properly "awe the disaffected." [24] Remembering the fiasco of the Whiskey Rebellion, Hamilton did not rush to the scene himself. It was just as well for the insurrectionists were as illusory as the Whiskey Boys. Fries was arrested and eventually tried in the court of the hanging judge himself, Samuel Chase, who sentenced him to the gallows. John Adams, in an act of mercy which disgusted the extreme Federalists, gave Fries a last-minute reprieve.[25]

Hamilton had labored long and hard to build the fledgling army, and he was determined to use it. If France would not accommodate, there might be other opportunities. "France is not to be considered as separate from her ally. Tempting objects will be within our grasp." [26] These objects were Spanish Louisiana and the Floridas which the United States had eyed covetously for many years. Not only would they round out the American empire, but possession of them would forestall well-known French ambitions to re-establish New France in America. (These ambitions were eventually to result in the cession of Spanish Louisiana to France in 1800.)

But Hamilton's vision did not stop here. "If universal empire is still to be the pursuit of France, what can tend to defeat the purpose better than to detach South America from Spain, which is only the channel through which the riches of *Mexico* and *Peru* are conveyed to France?" [27] He undoubtedly was thinking of the schemes of the Venezuelan soldier of fortune, Francisco Miranda, who had broached the idea of Latin American independence to Hamilton soon after the War of Independence.

In 1798 Miranda was still searching for support for his plan, and he had found a sympathetic listener in William Pitt, the British prime minister.[28] Although Hamilton wrote Miranda off as an impractical dreamer, he was not inclined to dismiss the government of Great Britain. He immediately projected a plan whereby the United States army under his command could cooperate with British naval forces and thus consumate the liberation of Latin America. This would reduce Spain's power in the Western Hemisphere to a nullity and free Latin American commerce from the restrictions of Spanish mercantilism. It would also insure to the United States "the advantage of keeping the key to the western country." [29] For this purpose, early in 1799, he summoned to Philadelphia the commander of the army in the southwest, the ubiquitous General James Wilkinson, for "a more full examination of the affairs of the Western scene, and to the concerting of ulterior arrangements." [30]

But Hamilton's road to glory was never laid. Lord Grenville viewed the Latin American enterprise as a British project. Any Americans involved would be commanded by an admiral of His Majesty's Navy. Furthermore General Washington effectively scotched the idea when he disapproved of Wilkinson's (Hamilton's) suggestion that troops be sent to Natchez, a possible staging point for an advance beyond the Mississippi. He felt that such a move would "excite, in the Spaniards, distrust and jealousy of our pacific disposition: would cause an augmentation of force on their part . . . until the *thing* which was *intended* to be *avoided* would . . . be produced, i.e., hostility." [31]

This undoubtedly reflected the policy of John Adams, who was completely unenthusiastic about western adventures and who refused to give up his hopes for a settlement with France. As the summer of 1798 waned, the President became increasingly optimistic over reports from Elbridge Gerry, from William Vans Murray at the Hague, and from his son John Quincy Adams in Berlin. These convinced him that he should make one more attempt to wage peace instead of war.[32]

Adams Chooses Peace

It was apparent by the beginning of 1799 that almost the entire Federalist program rested on the premise of a war with

France. The prosecutions under the Alien and Sedition Acts were justified on the assumption that "there shall be a declared war." Although the Virginia and Kentucky Resolutions represented a more extreme position than most of the opponents of the acts were willing to take, there was no doubt that there was a reaction against the antics of federal judges like Iredell and Chase. The house and property taxes passed by Congress to pay for the mounting military budget aroused increasing popular discontent. The President himself remarked that the public "have submitted with more patience than any people ever did to the burden of taxes . . . but their patience will not last always." [33]

But it was the army which rankled—the army upon which Hamilton had wagered so much of his own and his party's future. Even Washington noted that "zeal and enthusiasm are evaporated. . . . and if this idle and dissipated season is spent in inactivity, none but the riff-raff of the country" could be recruited. The public reacted as it usually does to an idle army, "loungers who live upon the public . . . under the pretext of protecting them from a foreign yoke." [34]

Only the navy seemed to have lived up to expectations. It was almost a year before the hard work of the new Secretary of the Navy, Benjamin Stoddert, began to pay off. Late in 1798 four American squadrons appeared in the Caribbean. The two most powerful of these contained some illustrious names. The first consisted of the frigates *Constitution* and *United States* plus eight smaller vessels, Commodore John Barry commanding. The thirty-eight gun *Constellation* carried the flag of the second squadron commander, Thomas Truxton, and was accompanied by four smaller vessels.

Their mission was to blockade French bases in the West Indies, harry French ships of war, and protect American merchantmen. Truxton scored the first victory for the United States when he captured the French frigate *L'Insurgente* in February, 1799. The best testimony to the effectiveness of the navy was the fact that insurance rates dropped to one-half of their former level by the middle of 1799. Just a year after his initial victory, Truxton defeated *La Vengeance,* fifty-four guns, in a slam–bang, five–hour battle. This was the last naval action of the quasi-war with France.[35]

The effectiveness of the navy not only impressed Europeans in general but deprived France of its most effective weapon against the United States—depredations on American shipping in the western Atlantic. The Directory had already regretted its high-handed treatment of the XYZ envoys and was now seeking to negotiate. By the early part of 1799 Adams was convinced that France was sincere. Not only were there the unofficial reports of Gerry, but of Dr. George Logan, a self-appointed emissary who had gone to France on his own and talked with Tallyrand. The Federalists vehemently denounced both men, and Logan's strange odyssey provoked the passage of the Logan Act which forbade private individuals from attempting to make representations to a foreign power.[36]

But Adams listened to Gerry, his old friend, and accorded Dr. Logan a respectful hearing. Even Rufus King, the staunch Federalist who was the American minister in London, reported to Pickering, "You will have no war!" although it is doubtful that the war-hawk secretary passed this to Adams.[37] Most impressive to Adams' mind were dispatches from William Vans Murray at the Hague. Murray had talked with Louis André Pichon, Talleyrand's personal representative, and had received both written and verbal assurances that the XYZ affair would not be repeated.[38]

On February 18, 1799, without consulting his cabinet, Adams suddenly sent Murray's name to the Senate as minister plenipotentiary to the French Republic. Jefferson, presiding in the Senate, read the President's message and admitted that he could not conceal his astonishment. But the "war-whoop" group was sent into shock. Jefferson noted that "they are gravelled and divided; some are for opposing it and others do not know what to do. . . . It silences all arguments against the sincerity of France and renders desperate every further effort towards war." [39]

"Desperate" was the word. Some Federalists had perhaps not fully realized how completely they were committed to war. "Mad," "ruinous," and "degrading" were some of the words used to describe the President's policy.[40] But John Jay, John Marshall, and, most important, Washington backed the effort to avoid "the horrors and calamities of war." [41] Attorney-General Lee and Secretary of the Navy Stoddert also supported Adams. The Federalists were painfully learning a political lesson: public opinion can be raised to a fever pitch by something like the XYZ affair; but the public is human, and high emotion cannot be sustained for long.

Perhaps Hamilton recognized this. He certainly did not at this time attempt to move Adams from his determination. Instead he approved the strategy of Pickering and Theodore Sedgewick to divert the President from his purpose. Hamilton suggested that two members be added to the mission, and this was urged upon the President by a committee of senators headed by Sedgewick. Adams reluctantly agreed and appointed Chief Justice Oliver Ellsworth and William R. Davie of North Carolina. It was hoped that these two would offset any rash action by the "feeble, credulous" Murray.[42]

The Hamiltonians also hoped to thwart the President by delay. Ellsworth and Davie were not optimistic about the success of their mission and were in no hurry to depart. Adams unwittingly cooperated by going home to Abigail for most of the summer. News from Europe of French reverses on several fronts raised hopes that some turn of events would make negotiations impossible. John Adams calmly directed the government from his ailing wife's bedside in Quincy.

Although the President was not wanted in the capital, his absence was also exasperating. General Hamilton noted impatiently that "if the chief is too desultory, his ministry ought to be more united and steady. . . . And if there was everywhere a disposition . . . to concert a rational plan I would cheerfully come to Philadelphia and assist in it. . . . Break this subject to our friend Pickering . . . send for me and I will come." [43] These were bold words, bolder perhaps than Hamilton intended. If it were a coup he was hinting at, it met with no response. More likely it was the impatient spirit that chafed at inaction and sought vainly to infuse the cabinet with some of his driving energy.

Adams was finally shaken from his lethargy. Conciliatory dispatches arrived from the Directory, and Lee and Stoddert urged him to return to the capital before Pickering sabotaged the mission. In the middle of September Stoddert warned that "artful designing men might make such use of your absence from the seat of government." [44] In October the President returned to Trenton, where the administration had moved to escape one of the yellow fever epidemics that periodically swept Philadelphia.

Hamilton now realized that the envoys were indeed to be sent. He made a last effort to save the situation. He left army headquarters in New York and came to Trenton on October 16. He spent several hours with the President using all the persuasion at his command to change Adams' course. [45] He might better have tried to move Plymouth Rock. As a last resort Hamilton went to Ellsworth and tried to get his refusal to embark on the mission. The Chief Justice had no liking for his assignment, but he would not back out of his commitment to the President. Now Hamilton's only hope was that the mission would fail. [46]

By the end of the year, even though the envoys had not reached Paris, war with France was becoming increasingly unlikely. The whole country mourned the passing of General Washington, who died on December 14, 1799. Hamilton knew that Adams would never appoint him to the supreme command. Within six months the army was disbanded.

It was the end of the dream.

"The Spirit of 1776 Is Not Dead"

By December, 1799, when Jefferson arrived in Philadelphia to preside over the Senate, the cloud which had hung over the Republican cause was beginning to lift. Republicans were beginning to come out of hiding and rally to his leadership. There was no doubt that Jefferson would be their candidate in the next presidential election and that he and the other Republican leaders were building a solid base of support, north and south.

The key state in the north was New York where Aaron Burr's astute management was winning control of New York City and thus of the state legislature. Since he had run very respectably as a presidential candidate in 1796, the canny Senator had demonstrated his mastery of the complexities produced in New York politics by the clannish factions of Livingstons, Schuylers, and Clintons. He arrived in Philadelphia early in January, 1800, to confer with Jefferson and to cement the Virginia–New York alliance. By changing the election laws, Burr proposed to have presidential electors chosen by the legislature, which he was confident would be won by the Republicans in the coming election. The implication was that this coup would earn him the position as Jefferson's running mate when the Republican caucus was held later in the spring. Jefferson obviously had some qualms about this undemocratic procedure. But, as in other cases, he justified the means in order "to see this government brought back to its republican principles." [47]

The Constitutional silence on the method of choosing electors meant that the founding fathers had in this, as in other
cases, left the matter to the states. They, in turn, had adopted
a variety of methods. In some instances electors were chosen
by the legislatures, in others by popular election in each
congressional district. There was an increasing tendency toward the present-day system of state-wide tickets consisting
of a slate of electors pledged to specific candidates, thus giving the party winning a majority vote the entire electoral vote
of the state. Jefferson noted that in such a system "the
minority is entirely unrepresented." [48] By 1800 party leaders
had lost some of their early innocence. Republicans and Federalists alike chose the system most likely to win the greatest
number of electors regardless of whether the system was
"democratic" in principle.

In Virginia, for example, there were always certain congressional districts which invariably returned a Federalist
majority. But with Jefferson as the presidential candidate, it
was obvious that a statewide election for a general ticket
would give him all of the state's electoral votes. Jefferson
therefore approved the plan of Madison and Taylor to change
the election law so as to insure this result.[49]

In New York Burr was as good as his word, but the victory
was a narrow one. Hamilton typically wanted a group of
legislators from New York City who would be easily controlled, and so the Federalist candidates were a colorless lot
of sycophants. Taking careful note of this lack-luster group,
Burr induced his most politically potent friends to run for
the lowly office of state assemblyman. The Federalists found
themselves opposed by such glamorous figures as former
Governor George Clinton, war hero General Horatio Gates,
former Postmaster General Samuel Osgood, and a member
of the great patroon family, Brockholst Livingston. Hamilton

awoke to the peril too late. In vain he toured the polling places on election day, a martial figure mounted on a splendid white stallion. But the disciplined Republican committee and its ward chiefs had arranged for voters to qualify and urged the people to the polls with an efficiency which would have won the admiration of a twentieth century committee chairman.[50]

The national party leader had also done his work well. From Jefferson's pen flowed a steady stream of letters to state leaders from New England to Georgia. Jefferson may not have been familiar with the phrase "grass roots," but he understood the principle. He communicated not only with the Gerrys and the Madisons and the Pinckneys but with men who were unknown in national politics but potent in the states. Which of these was not flattered by a letter from the author of the Declaration of Independence reminding him that "the spirit of 1776 is not dead. It is only slumbering"?[51]

In state after state, Republicans demonstrated not only an increasing popular strength, but the skill to control it. By comparison the Federalists were bumbling. In Pennsylvania the radical Thomas McKean, chief justice of the state, won the governorship, but the attempt to have electors chosen on a general ticket was thwarted by the Federalists in the state senate. Even in Adams own state of Massachusetts, George Cabot barely won the gubernatorial election from Elbridge Gerry.

As the Federalist editor of the Hartford *Courant* put it ruefully, the Republicans had developed a talent for "a certain number of sounds, thrown into the form of regular and well connected sentences, which they can on all occasions utter with the utmost facility and volubility. In these sentences, the words—British Influence—Standing Army—Direct Taxes—Funding System— . . . Aristocracy—and

Washington's Grave Stones, are ever and anon distinctly heard." [52]

The political pot was beginning to boil.

The Federalist House Divided

The increasing signs of Republican resurgence failed to unify the Federalists. On the contrary, the political crisis brought their wracking internal dissensions to the surface. What induced the President to tolerate the obvious disloyalty of the members of his cabinet for so long is a puzzle, for John Adams was not a patient man. By the spring of 1800 he had decided that it was time to purge the Hamiltonian influence and be master of his own house. In April he requested the resignation of McHenry and Pickering. The former protested his dismissal but complied with the President's request. The sour and resentful Secretary of State refused to resign, intimating his lofty contempt for his superior. John Adams swung the ax and Pickering was out. John Marshall was appointed in his place, and Samuel Dexter of Virginia became Secretary of War. Wolcott escaped, perhaps because Adams was not aware of the extent of his collaboration with Hamilton, perhaps because he did not want to lose an able administrator. [53]

The last controlling links to "the frantic old man" were severed, and the feud between Hamilton and the President exploded—with disastrous results. The occasion was the charge made by Adams, in defense of his decision to negotiate with France, that he was being opposed by a "British faction" headed by Hamilton. When Hamilton demanded an explanation from the President, his answer was a cold silence. [54]

Hamilton was determined not to abandon his role as kingmaker. If Adams could not be controlled, he must be destroyed. Hamilton therefore urged Wolcott and the discredited Pickering to comb their departmental files for whatever might be damaging to Adams.[55] He then drew up a fantastic document titled *The Public Conduct and Character of John Adams, Esq., President of the United States.* Its purpose was to discredit Adams tenure of the presidency and thus disqualify him as the party's candidate. He reviewed Adams' four years in office and charged him with "disgusting egotism, distempered jealousy, and ungovernable indiscretion" in the conduct of affairs. He impugned the blackest and meanest motives to Adams' every action and showed that only his, Hamilton's, restraining influence had saved the Republic.

He left no doubt that Charles Cotesworth Pinckney was the nation's only salvation. Adams was totally unfit. Yet this amazing document closed with the admonition, "To refrain from a decided opposition to Mr. Adams' re-election has been reluctantly sanctioned by my judgement; which has been not a little perplexed between the unqualified conviction of his unfitness for the station contemplated, and a sense of the great importance of cultivating harmony among the supporters of the government." [56]

The *Public Conduct* should be considered in the light of Hamilton's intended use of it. He had the piece printed but distributed it privately to a few key Federalist leaders as part of his plan to displace Adams with Pinckney. The final admonition to support Adams was perhaps a half-hearted plea for party unity.

Why Hamilton thought he could keep such political dynamite confidential is a mystery. By October, thanks probably to the devious talents of Colonel Burr, a copy was purloined from the printer, and it was soon in the hands of Republican editors throughout the country. William Duane of the *Aurora* printed it as a pamphlet and delightedly distributed it in the capital.[57] No conceivable political artifice of the Republicans could have done more damage to the Federalists. Yet Hamilton and the other extreme Federalists persisted. Confidential conferences and private meetings were held by party leaders to promote Pinckney's candidacy—as if a secret plot could be somehow conveyed to the public.

The Federalists had previously nominated Adams and Pinckney in a caucus held in early May. The key to Hamilton's plan was the Constitutional provision, unchanged since 1796, by which the electors cast two votes for two different candidates, with the highest vote determining the President and the second highest determining the Vice-President. If New England supported Adams and Pinckney equally, the South Carolina electors could no doubt be induced to throw away a few Adams votes and allow their native son to secure the majority.[58]

This plan assumed a great deal. It hardly seemed likely that Jefferson and Burr would stand quietly by and allow Adams and Pinckney to decide the election between them. It was true that Jefferson's unorthodox views on religion had led to a savage attack which charged that, with such a President, God would be dead in the United States. But Americans simply could not be brought to believe that a Republican victory would bring about a revolution which would see the horror of the French terror repeated and magnified. When Federalists predicted that the mild Virginian would march his enemies by the score to the gibbet or would lead a howling mob bent on massacre and rapine, the public imagination boggled. Such propaganda might have served in 1798, but by 1800 it had worn thin.

The spectre of a nation beset by a French army of invasion seemed equally incredible with the army disbanded and diplomats negotiating in Paris. The Federalists might have salvaged something by foreswearing their war policy and lauding President Adams as the savior of the nation. Yet the sharpest attacks on the French mission came from Hamilton and his follow conspirators. Their desperate efforts to discredit Adams blinded them to the fact that they were digging their own grave.

It remained for James McHenry to see the situation with the clearest vision. "Have our party shown that they possess the necessary skill and courage to deserve to be continued to govern? What have they done? . . . They write private letters. To whom? To each other, but they do nothing to give proper direction to the public mind." He was convinced that their "cunning, paltry, indecisive, backdoor conduct" would wreck the Federalist party.[59] But who could be expected to heed a discredited ex-Secretary of War? Certainly not Alexander Hamilton.

Republican Victory

As the summer of 1800 drew to a close the campaign in the various states intensified. Although the leadership of the Federalist party was torn with dissension, it should not be supposed that this paralyzed the lesser ranks at the state and local levels. The Federalists enjoyed the advantage of having been the party in power for as long as parties could have been said to have existed. Although it may not have been fully appreciated at the time, Adams had a distinct advantage as the incumbent, and Washington had set the precedent for an eight-year presidential tenure.

Certainly Adams was confident of victory. Yet he longed for news from Paris and a vindication of his policy. He knew that Napoleon had overthrown the bankrupt Directory but that the envoys had been received nonetheless. What he did not know was that Napoleon was anxious to stabilize both France and Europe. He was preoccupied with large questions, but he did not neglect the Americans. Although the negotiations dragged on into weeks and then into months, the envoys found themselves treated with courtesy, and their arguments and proposals received the respectful attention of the French foreign ministry. The foreign secretary was the ubiquitous Talleyrand, a man whose talent for survival was altogether remarkable in an era when public men were notoriously short-lived.

By the end of the summer of 1800 a working basis for negotiations had been reached, and on September 13 a convention was signed. It provided for arbitration of indemnities, mutual restoration of property seized by either party, cessation of privateering, and a "most favored nation" agreement. For whatever it might be worth, France recognized the American principle that free ships made free goods. Most important was the fact that the convention effected the cancellation of the obligations of the Treaty of 1778. Although each nation had previously done this unilaterally, each had acted in anger at the other's alleged violations. Now it was done bilaterally in a spirit of mutual amicability. The actual terms of the convention (the word "treaty" was carefully avoided) were somewhat vague, and subsequent stipulations by both the United States Senate and Napoleon rendered them even more ambiguous. But the good will with which the negotiations were conducted and the mutual expressions of friendship and cordiality which accompanied the signing of the articles left no doubt that the undeclared war with France had ended.[60]

The news from Paris arrived too late to avert the defeat of the Federalists. Jefferson and his lieutenants had done their work too well. The key to the election was South Carolina where electors were not chosen until December 2. Up to this point New England had voted solidly for Adams and Pinckney and the South almost as solidly for Jefferson and Burr. In fact, before the South Carolina returns were in Jefferson seemed doomed to defeat, for surely South Carolina would cast its vote for its favorite son Charles Cotesworth Pinckney. Ironically, it was Pinckney's cousin, also named Charles Pinckney, who lead—or maneuvered—the Republicans to victory. This Jeffersonian stalwart, in an intricate and delicate game whose details are still not completely known, delivered all eight of South Carolina's electors to Jefferson and Burr.[61]

In the final total Jefferson and Burr received seventy-three votes apiece, Adams and Pinckney sixty-five and sixty-four respectively.[62]

The Would-Be Usurper

"The Person having the greatest Number of Votes," reads Article II of the Constitution, "shall be President, if such Number be a Majority of the whole Number of Electors appointed; and if there be more than one who have such Majority, and have an equal Number of Votes, the House of Representatives shall immediately chuse by Ballot one of them for President." [63]

The shattered Federalists had suddenly been granted an opportunity to retrieve something from the disaster of their defeat. With Jefferson and Burr receiving seventy-three votes each as a result of the disciplined balloting of the Republican electors, the Sixth Congress would decide who was to be the new chief executive. The Federalists' opportunity lay in the chance that they could prevent Jefferson from becoming President by supporting Burr. This Congress had been elected in 1798, and the Federalists had won a majority in the House. They hoped that Burr was the cynical opportunist that Hamilton had always thought him to be, and they confidently expected that if they could elect him he would be properly grateful.

The possibility had first suggested itself in mid-December,

when returns from the various states gradually trickled into the capital and the electoral votes were counted and recounted. It was noted that there was no scattering of votes as there had been in 1796 when no less than forty-eight ballots had been cast for candidates other than the four recognized as the party nominees. In 1800 only one elector, a Federalist, threw away a vote (for John Jay), and this was simply in order to put Adams ahead of Pinckney.

It appeared, however, that the Federalist hopes were doomed, for on December 16 Burr wrote to General Samuel Smith, a Republican leader in Baltimore, that although it was "highly improbable that I shall have an equal number of votes with Mr. Jefferson . . . if such should be the result . . . I should utterly disclaim all competition." [64]

Two weeks later, when the vote from South Carolina had produced a final result, Burr's repudiation was not so positive. General Smith received another letter which was redolent with double talk. One presumptuous fellow had, according to Burr, "asked me whether, if I were chosen President, I would engage to resign—The suggestion was unreasonable, unnecessary and impertinent, and I therefore made no reply. If I had made any I would have told that as at present advised, I would not." But a few lines further on, "I presume however that before this time you are satisfied that no such event is or ever was to be apprehended by those who laugh at your absurd claims—" [65]

There now began a delicate game of bluff and parry. Early in January Smith wrote apprehensively to Burr of a new development. David Ogden, a New York Federalist, had appeared in the new national capital at Washington professing to be in Burr's confidence and had attempted to persuade the Republican members from his state to vote for Burr. On January 16 Burr replied soothingly that he had "said nothing to contravene my letter of the 16 ult. but to enter into details would take reams of paper and years of time." [66]

General Smith's fears were not without some foundation. James A. Bayard, Delaware's single representative in the House and a Federalist, wrote to Hamilton on January 7, "By persons friendly to Mr. Burr it is distinctly understood that he is willing to consider the Federalists as his friends." [67] Smith went to Trenton to meet with Burr and get further reassurance. What Smith heard was far from reassuring. Burr's position was now "that if they [the House of Representatives] could not get Mr. Jefferson they could take him." [68]

It was a complex situation. Republicans could not attack Burr, for he was technically their own nominee for the presidency. Nor could Burr solicit votes from members of his own party in order to work for the defeat of Jefferson. To gain his objective Burr's best—indeed, his only—strategy was that given him by Maryland Federalist Robert Goodloe Harper: "I advise you to take no step by which the choice of the House can be impeded or embarrassed. Keep the game perfectly in your hands, but do not answer this letter, or any other that may be written to you by a Federalist man, nor write to any of that party." [69] This was precisely the course which Burr followed.

The House began balloting on February 11, 1800. Fifty-five members voted for Burr against fifty-one for Jefferson. But the Republicans were rescued by the Constitutional provision which required that in choosing the President the House should vote by states. Thus the result of the first ballot was eight states for Jefferson, six for Burr and two, Vermont and Maryland, divided. [70]

In thirty-four subsequent ballots lasting until February 17 the results remained the same. Republicans made it evident that they did not intend to change a vote if the balloting continued until Judgement Day. During all this, of course, Burr needed only to have announced that he would resign in Jefferson's favor if he were elected, and the Federalist game would have ended. But Burr was silent.

To Alexander Hamilton the thought of Burr as President was appalling. "If there be a man in the world I ought to hate, it is Jefferson. . . . But the public good must be paramount to every private consideration." [71] He flooded the capital with exhortations to his Federalist friends. Burr was, he said, a man of "inordinate ambition," "corrupt expedients" and "unprincipled selfishness." "He is the most unfit and most dangerous man in the community;" "decidedly profligate;" "deficient in honesty." [72] Yet Hamilton failed to influence a single vote of the Federalist congressmen.

James Bayard finally broke the deadlock. Fearful that a continuation of the stalemate might bring about serious consequences, he caucused the Federalists from Vermont, Maryland, and South Carolina. He had received assurances, he told them, that Jefferson did not intend radical reforms or revolutionary purges of federal officers. He himself intended to vote blank. If the others would do the same they would be spared the ignominy of voting for Jefferson, yet allow the deadlock to be broken. [73] When the thirty-sixth ballot was taken, Jefferson was declared President by a vote of ten states to four.

In this moment of Republican triumph perhaps Hamilton had the last word. " 'Tis not to the chapter of accidents that we ought to trust the government, peace and happiness of our country." [74]

XIV Jefferson in Power

In 1811 JEFFERSON reported a conversation which he had with John Adams in the spring of 1800. Shortly after the Republican victory in New York City, which many felt presaged a Republican victory, he paid a call on the President to discuss some matters of business. " 'Well, I understand that you are to beat me in this contest, . . .' " was Adams' greeting. " 'Mr. Adams,' " replied Jefferson, " 'this is no personal contest between you and me. Two systems of principles on the subject of government divide our fellow citizens into two parties. With one of these you concur, and I with the other. . . . Were we both to die to-day, to-morrow two other names would be in the place of ours, without any change in the motion of the machinery.' "

" 'I believe you are right . . .' " was Adams' reply, " 'that we are but passive instruments, and should not suffer this matter to affect our personal dispositions.' " [1]

But the estrangement between the two men lasted for another decade, and when Jefferson delivered his inaugural address on March 4, 1801, John Adams was on the road home to Quincy.

The Big Change

"We have called, by different names, brethren of the same principle. We are all republicans: we are all federalists." [2] The words spoken by the tall, slender man standing in the half-finished capitol building were heard by only a few of the almost one thousand people who had gathered to witness the inauguration of the third President.[3]

"If there be any among us who wish to dissolve this union, or to change its republican form, let them stand undisturbed, as monuments of the safety with which error of opinion may be tolerated where reason is left free to combat it." These ringing words are a timeless injunction against intolerance and suppression of dissent. Yet Jefferson spoke, as he so often did, not only to the future, but to the time and place in which he found himself. He certainly did not mean that the Federalists and Republicans who had fought each other so bitterly in the recent elections were "brethren of the same principle." What he hoped to accomplish was to allay the acrimony and partisanship of the campaign, to convince the nation that peaceful change in government was not only possible but normal. In victory he did not want to inflame the temper of the opposition, but to cool it. He was offering amnesty to the enemy, for he was still not convinced of either the desirability or the inevitability of permanent political parties. Less than a month before, he had expressed the hope that "the distinction will soon be lost, . . . that the body of the nation, . . . will rejoin the republicans, leaving only those who were pure monarchists and who will be too few to form a sect." The conciliatory tone was a veiled invitation to "obliterate the traces of party and consolidate the nation." [4]

The inaugural address also reassured those who feared that "this government, the world's best hope may, by possibility, want energy to preserve itself." Could the mild and tolerant system which Jefferson advocated maintain an orderly and secure society? "I believe this . . . the strongest government on earth. I believe it the only one where every man, at the call of the law, would fly to the standard of the law; and would meet invasions of the public order, as his own personal concern." If this were not so, then the American experiment would fail. He suggested the dark alternative. "Some times it is said that Man cannot be trusted with the government of himself.—Can he then be trusted with the government of others? Or have we found angels in the form of kings to govern him?—Let History answer this question."

The remainder of the address contained further reassurances: "a wise & frugal government, which shall restrain men from injuring one another, shall leave them otherwise free to regulate their own pursuits;" "the support of the State governments in all their rights," but virtually in the same breath, "the preservation of the General government, in it's whole constitutional vigor;" friendship and commerce with all nations, "entangling alliances with none."

So the message as a whole was a warning that the tactics had changed but the goals were much the same. That, at least, was how it struck Alexander Hamilton. He noted that in using the phrase "in the *full tide* of *successful* experiment," (Hamilton's emphasis) Jefferson had, by implication, endorsed "that administration . . . hitherto in the hands of the Federalists." He was sure that "the new President will not lend himself to dangerous innovations, but in essential points will tread in the steps of his predecessors." On the whole, Hamilton thought that the address deserved "a public declaration of our approbation of its contents." [5]

Republicans throughout the country were somewhat more enthusiastic about their victory. Cannon were fired, festivals and banquets were held, songs were composed, and the number of toasts that were drunk was infinite. Celebrations sometimes began several days before March 4 and continued for several days afterwards. In Richmond sixteen-gun salutes —one for every state in the union—were fired at dawn, noon, and sunset. In New York a disgruntled Federalist com-

plained, "Drunken frolicks is the order of the day," and in
Philadelphia Republicans roared out fourteen stanzas of the
new song, "Jefferson and Liberty." It was indeed a clean
sweep, for never before had the nation made a complete
political change of President, cabinet, and Congress.[6]

The President's advisors were soon announced and created
little surprise. The appointment of Madison as Secretary of
State was dictated by his eminent qualifications for the post,
but also by Jefferson's need to have his closest friend and most
trusted advisor at his side. Albert Gallatin, for years the
acknowledged financial wizard of the Republicans, was appointed to the Treasury. Henry Dearborn, a Republican stalwart from Massachusetts and a war veteran, was appointed
Secretary of War. Levi Lincoln, another Massachusetts
Republican, became Attorney-General. The Navy Department went begging since campaign promises of strict economy made it evident that the navy would be a poor relation.
Samuel Smith, prominent merchant and Congressman from
Baltimore, was persuaded to become Acting Secretary, and
it was his brother Robert, an admiralty lawyer, who received
the permanent appointment in July, 1801.

The President and his official family comprised a congenial
group which nonetheless conducted its affairs with a formality which seems quaintly alien to the twentieth century. A
brief note from the Secretary of State to the President, even
though it was delivered only a few hundred yards away,
gravely presented the secretary's compliments, and the President's return memorandum would close with "assurances of
my constant esteem and respect." Madison and Gallatin were
constantly in and out of Jefferson's office, and full meetings
of the cabinet, although sometimes spirited, usually ended in
a general meeting of minds. Jefferson never forgot the squab-
bles with Hamilton in Washington's cabinet, and he was
determined that no similar situation should arise in his own.

Yet there was no doubt about who was in command. He arranged for all significant papers to be routed through his office, and he showed the same meticulous attention to administrative matters that always characterized his public and private affairs.[7]

But could this harmonious relationship be extended throughout the entire administrative system? Exclusive of postmasters and military appointments, the President was responsible for the appointment of something over three hundred civil servants.[8] Neither Washington nor Adams had ever knowingly appointed any but Federalists to government positions. In an era when these officials had no tenure of office and when no special skills were required, the new administration faced the multitudinous problems of patronage. Although the phrase "spoils system" had not yet been coined, there were many of the party faithful who claimed the victor's privilege, or so it seemed to the President.

Jefferson discovered—as every President since him has learned—that the problem was virtually insoluble. If he accommodated the defeated party by retaining Federalists in office, a storm of protest rose from Republicans who wanted position and influence. If he made sweeping dismissals, then what of his offers of reconciliation to the Federalists? Were not war veterans entitled to consideration? Should an efficient and conscientious man be dismissed from his post because of the way he had voted? Would dismissals for inefficiency be recognized as such or be taken as thinly disguised partisanship?[9] Typically, Jefferson attempted to establish rules by which appointments and dismissals could be judged, but he soon found it difficult to follow them. In the Federalist stronghold of Connecticut, "a general sweep seems to be called for on principles of justice and policy." But in Delaware the President refused to remove Federalist Allen McLane from the position of collector. McLane had a particularly distinguished war record, and there was ample evidence that he was competent. Despite strong pressure from the state's Republican leader Caesar Rodney and despite the fact that McLane's retention was blamed for Federalist gains in the elections of 1802 and 1804, the President was adamant. McLane was still at his post at the end of Jefferson's second term.[10]

In 1801 Jefferson attempted to formulate a policy based on removals "on delinquency, on oppression, on intolerance, on incompetence, on ante-revolutionary adherence to our enemies." But he was ruefully aware of the political problem. "If a due participation of office is a matter of right, how are vacancies to be obtained? Those by death are few; by resignation, none."[11]

By 1803 he had modified his policy to the degree of "waiting till accidental vacancies should furnish opportunity of giving to republicans their *due proportion* of office. To this we have steadily adhered. Many vacancies have been made by death and resignation, many by removal for malversation [incompetence] in office and for open, active and virulent abuse . . . in opposition to the order of things established by the will of the nation." Jefferson was not sure how much political activity should be engaged in by Republicans holding government office, but he left no doubt that he would not tolerate partisan Federalists.[12]

Jefferson's patronage policy was one of the best examples of the dilemma of a man of good will and morality when face to face with the realities of political life. In trying to steer a middle course, he eventually wound up by deciding individual cases on their merits, political or otherwise. In the end he satisfied neither the Republicans who cried for the spoils nor the Federalists who were convinced of his vindictiveness. He probably did not satisfy even himself.

Republican Reforms

Presidents Washington and Adams had presented their programs to Congress in person, and Congress had accepted this as an invitation to make a formal reply. Jefferson had never liked making speeches, and he was not very good at it. Perhaps for this reason he decided to send a written message to Congress. Or perhaps it was to avoid "the bloody conflict to which the making an answer would have committed them. They consequently were able to set into real business at once." [13]

The message to the Seventh Congress pointed the way to the principle reforms which the new administration wished to undertake.[14] The most important of these was in fiscal policy which was designed not only to implement the inaugural promises of "economy in public expenses" and "honest paiment of our debts," but to reap the political benefits inherent in a balanced budget and lower taxes. Such a financial miracle was the work of the new Secretary of the Treasury. Gallatin, after innumerable conferences with the President, had outlined a plan which had as one of its primary objectives the payment of the national debt which amounted to $83,-000,000. This would entail an annual appropriation of $7,-300,000 for the next sixteen years. Furthermore, Jefferson insisted that all internal taxes be repealed, including that symbol of Hamiltonian Federalism—the despised whiskey tax. Although this would also eliminate the salaries of a number of collectors, it would reduce the government's income to less than $10,000,000.[15]

Hamilton seized upon Jefferson's message as a point of departure for a full-scale attack on the new administration. In a series of newspaper articles he caustically analyzed the President's program. He professed to be astonished at Gal-

latin's economics. Such proposals indicated, he said, "a deficiency of intellect, and . . . an ignorance of our financial
arrangements, greater than could have been suspected . . .
[or] the culpable desire of gaining or securing popularity."
Jefferson retorted, "Bitter men are not pleased with the suppression of taxes . . . they ascribe it to a desire of popularity.
But every honest man will suppose honest acts to flow from
honest principles, & the rogues may rail without intermis-
sion." [16] Nevertheless, Jefferson did have fewer patronage
headaches, and what could be more popular than the disap-
pearance of tax collectors?

Government expenses would have to be drastically reduced
since annual operating expenses had not been less than $3,-
000,000 since 1793. In recent years this would have been
barely enough for normal expenses of the armed forces. It was
just here that Gallatin expected to produce the greatest sav-
ings. The army was to be reduced to 3,000 men, sufficient,
it was hoped, to garrison a frontier which stretched from the
Straits of Mackinac to Natchez. The navy also felt the blows
of Gallatin's economy ax as it cut twenty-five of the thirty-
four captains from the active list and laid up seven frigates.
Total expenses for the entire federal establishment were thus
reduced to $2,300,000. [17]

Hamilton especially condemned the cuts in defense appropriations. There were not only the omnipresent threats from
Europe and the frontier but the immediate danger from the
Barbary states. *"Can the proposed abolition take effect without
impairing the PUBLIC FAITH?"* [18]

In fact, the Bey of Tripoli had declared war on the United
States during the summer of 1801, at the very moment when
Commodore Dale was on his way to the Mediterranean in
command of a punitive naval expedition. Jefferson's indignation at the insolence of Barbary blackmail was tempered by
his reluctance to engage in an expensive and long range polic-

ing operation. Secretary of the Navy Robert Smith urged that the "war" be prosecuted and won the President's approval over the spirited objections of Gallatin. Thanks to a group of young and enthusiastic naval officers, notably those commanded by Commodore Edward Preble, Tripoli was brought to terms in 1805. It was another ten years before the pirate states of North Africa finally ceased their depredations on Mediterranean commerce, but it is perhaps worth noting that the United States was the only maritime power that defied them.[19]

Despite this flurry of naval activity—and unusual expense—Jefferson and Gallatin did cut defense appropriations drastically. This policy assumed that the United States would remain at peace, and, whatever else may be said of Jeffersonian foreign policy, it achieved this goal until 1812. Since ninety percent of the government's income came from imposts, the phenomenal growth of American commerce during the Napoleonic Wars more than made up for any unforeseen expenditures. Only during the year of the embargo did the treasury fail to record a surplus until the outbreak of the War of 1812.[20]

Jefferson's message to Congress plainly invited reform in the federal courts by hinting at his desire to have the Judiciary Act of 1801 repealed. This measure, passed by the "lame duck" session of the Sixth Congress, had created nineteen new federal courts. In the last days, and even the last hours of his administration, John Adams had appointed judges, federal attorneys, and marshals to fill the positions thus created. To a man they had been Federalists. Jefferson was infuriated. "This outrage on decency," he wrote to Henry Knox, "should not have its effect. . . . I consider the nominations as nullities." [21]

This stirred Hamilton to vehement condemnation. "In the rage for change," he charged, "or under the stimulus of a deep-rooted animosity against the former administration, or for the sake of gaining popular favor . . . even our judiciary system has not passed unassailed." He was not far from the mark. Unlike administrative officials, judges held their appointments for life, so the prospect of ousting them was somewhat remote. But the new courts authorized during the last gasp of the Adams administration had not yet begun to function, and Jefferson was determined that they never would. The "midnight appointments," Jefferson declared several years later, "were from among my most ardent political enemies, from whom no faithful co-operation could ever be expected." [22]

The repeal passed Congress early in March, 1802. The new Chief Justice, John Marshall, a Virginia cousin of Jefferson's but a Federalist who had also been a last minute Adams appointment, moved to block the administration. William Marbury, who had been appointed to one of the judgeships created by the Judiciary Act of 1801, asked the Supreme Court for a writ of mandamus requiring the delivery of his commission. Since Marbury was only a justice of the peace for the District of Columbia, his case could easily have been dismissed for lack of jurisdiction, which was the essence of the final decision. But Marshall set a date for a hearing on the spring calendar of the 1803 session of the Supreme Court.[23]

The famous case of *Marbury* v. *Madison,* then, was more important at the time for its political implications than as a landmark in constitutional history. Marshall used the occasion to lecture the President on his failure to deliver, through the Secretary of State, the commission to which he claimed Marbury was entitled. Jefferson, he implied, had clearly broken the law. He pointed out, however, that the writ which Marbury sought, although authorized under the Judiciary Act of 1789, would require a judicial order to the executive branch of the government, clearly a violation of the Constitutional principle of separation of powers. "A law repugnant to the constitution is void, and . . . courts, as well as other departments, are bound by that instrument." With this as a point of departure, Marshall laid the foundation for judicial review, arguing from premises set forth by Alexander Hamilton more than a decade before.[24] But these implications were largely ignored in 1803, and the case was seen primarily as a political jab by the Federalist Chief Justice at the Republican President. Jefferson later remarked that Marshall's "twistifications in the case of Marbury . . . shew how dextrously he can reconcile the law to his personal biases."[25]

It should be understood that until 1803, and indeed for some years thereafter, the Supreme Court did not command the prestige and influence which has since made it comparable in power to the other two branches of the federal government. Since 1789 it had heard only sixty cases, and none had created a great deal of controversy. The Court had been of little importance in shaping national policy, and its justices were best known—or notorious—in their capacity as circuit judges in the trials stemming from the Sedition Act. Nor did John Marshall ever again in his thirty-three years on the bench attempt to declare an act of Congress unconstitutional.[26] Like so many events in this early period, *Marbury* v. *Madison* was significant because of what subsequent history made of it.

Jefferson was not done with the judiciary, which he felt had "braved the spirit and will of the nation, after the nation has manifested its will by a complete reform in every branch depending on them."[27] He did not set out to purge the federal courts, but he seems to have had his eye on some of its most partisan members. Yet after the initial moves, he did not display his customary persistence, possibly because he recognized that further action was futile, but more probably because other important matters claimed his attention.

The most obvious cause for action involved Judge John

Pickering of New Hampshire. A Federalist merchant charged with smuggling was prosecuted in Pickering's court by the Republican federal attorney in what appeared to be a fairly open and shut case. Judge Pickering, who was suspected of being insane and was obviously intoxicated during the trial, ruled against the government and profanely denied an appeal. Upon being informed of the situation, Secretary of the Treasury Gallatin hinted that Pickering should be persuaded to resign. The judge belligerently refused, and the President then turned the matter over to Congress.

Poor, sick Pickering thus became a political bone of contention between bitter Federalists who wanted to block a Republican appointment to Pickering's place and rancorous Republicans seemingly bent on a purge. In the spring of 1803 the House of Representatives voted impeachment, and at the Senate trial the judge was found guilty. Although not convicted of "high crimes and misdemeanors" as strict Constitutional law required, the verdict provided a way out of an unfortunate situation for which there was no real legal remedy.[28]

The decision in the Pickering case came three weeks before Marshall's opinion in *Marbury* v. *Madison,* and some attributed his rebuke to Jefferson as a reaction. In any event, the Republicans now struck at one of their most inveterate enemies, Samuel Chase, associate justice of the Supreme Court. The impeachment proceeding was managed by John Randolph of Roanoke, the brilliant, razor-tongued Virginian who was the administration floor leader in the House of Representatives but whose performance had been rather erratic. Under his leadership, the House in January, 1804, voted impeachment on eight counts, all of them stemming from Chase's high-handed conduct of sedition trials. The most serious charge was his behavior in the trial of James Callender, the notorious newspaper editor, in which Chase's instructions to the jury had been a polemic against Jefferson, democratic government, and the constitutions of Maryland and Virginia.[29]

The trial, held in February, 1805, was one of the most dramatic episodes of the decade. Vice-President Aaron Burr supervised the decoration of the Senate chamber in red and green draperies and had extra galleries installed for the overflow crowd. Randolph, as chief prosecutor, indulged in such abusive invective as the Senate had never heard before—and seldom heard afterward, except from Randolph himself. A brilliant and impassioned defense was conducted by a battery of defense counsels which included Luther Martin, Charles Lee, Philip Barton Key, and Chase himself. Randolph's intemperate language undoubtedly alienated many Republican Senators, and some were doubtful about a political attack on the judicial branch. The closest vote on any charge was nineteen to fifteen for conviction,[30] four votes short of the necessary two-thirds.

This somewhat sour and disappointing episode nevertheless held implications for the future. Chase's acquittal had been a near thing, and henceforth judges would be more circumspect in venturing into the muddy waters of partisan politics. But his acquittal also made it clear that there were difficulties in attempting to check the judiciary through impeachment. Six Republicans had voted "not guilty" on every count against Chase. In future years Congress might seek other ways to limit the power of the federal courts but seldom by making an individual judge its target.

Louisiana: Jefferson as Machiavelli

When Jefferson first confronted the problem of the French in the Mississippi west, he might well have asked, what was Louisiana? Jefferson himself could not say even after he had dispatched Lewis and Clark all the way to the Pacific ocean. The *voyageurs* of New France had by 1776 explored the northern wilderness all the way to the Shining Mountains (the snow-capped Rockies). La Salle had been attempting to fasten the linchpin of Louisiana when he explored the lower Mississippi and the Arkansas in 1682 and named the region for the "Sun King" Louis XIV. Both the French and the Spanish considered New Orleans its capital city although technically it was on the eastern bank of the Mississippi. Prior to the Seven Years' War the pioneers of New France had penetrated the heartland of the Great Plains as far south as the Platte, and the Spanish had sent expeditions as far north as the upper Arkansas, but the two frontiers had never met. Some maps of the middle eighteenth century placed the "L" of Louisiana on the South Saskatchewan River and the final "a" squarely on Mobile Bay.

When France was evicted from North America by the Treaty of Paris of 1763 which ended the Seven Years' War, Spain acquired title to French possessions west of the Mississippi and New Orleans; there was then no need to take up the troublesome question of the western boundary of Louisiana. Britain received Florida by the same treaty and created two colonies, East and West Florida (which gave rise to the term "the Floridas" to describe all the territory eastward from New Orleans). By the Treaty of Paris of 1783 the Floridas were returned to Spain.

The western and southern frontier of the United States created a number of problems, and Jefferson was familiar with most of them through first hand knowledge and experience. He was not particularly concerned about the Spanish presence in the Old Southwest so far as it posed any threat to American security. When the United States had demanded the thirty-first parallel as the boundary of West Florida from the Chattahoochee to the Mississippi, Spain had acquiesced in the Treaty of San Lorenzo (1795).

Of more serious importance was Spanish possession of the entire littoral of the Gulf of Mexico and thus of the mouth of every river which drained the western country. The Mississippi and its tributaries, in particular, were vital to the land west of the Appalachians, and the "men of the western waters" were restive over Spanish control of their trade. Their aggressive, expansionist spirit had spawned seccessionist and filibustering conspiracies of which at least one was serious enough to result in the expulsion of William Blount of Tennessee from the United States Senate in 1797. Spain had agreed at San Lorenzo to allow Americans to trade through New Orleans, a not altogether satisfactory arrangement, but one which the United States was prepared to accept for the time being. But the Mississippi, New Orleans, Louisiana, and the Floridas constituted an explosive package which required delicate handling.

Much has been made of the fortuitous circumstances which dropped Louisiana in Jefferson's lap like the proverbial gift from the gods. Such circumstances usually attend great diplomatic victories. Jefferson and his colleagues worked long and hard to ascertain some things, guess shrewdly at others, and devise a cunning and successful diplomacy. The gods relinquished their gift only with greatest reluctance and, one may suppose, with a good deal of admiration.

The first suggestion that a crisis was developing came from Rufus King, the American minister in London. King was a Federalist appointed by Washington, but Jefferson was convinced that he would serve his country capably regardless of the party in power. His judgement proved to be eminently correct. Less than a month after the President had taken office, King warned that the longstanding French project for taking Louisiana back from Spain had "in all probability since been executed." [31] He was right. Spain had concluded that to hold Louisiana between the jaws of the United States and Canada was beyond her power. By the Treaty of San

Ildefonso (1800) she had decided to gratify Napoleon's ambitions for the renaissance of New France in exchange for advancing her own interests in Italy and the Mediterranean. That document, incidentally, defined Louisiana simply as the region "with the same boundaries which it presently has in the hands of Spain, and which it had at the time that France possessed it." [32]

At about the same time, word reached Washington that Toussaint L'Ouverture, the revolutionary leader in Santo Domingo who had been defying the French government for more than a decade, was about to proclaim an independent republic. Since Santo Domingo was at the heart of Napoleon's colonization scheme, France could not fail to react, and this was soon confirmed. The French chargé in Washington, Louis Pichon, asked the President informally if American supplies would be available should an expeditionary force be sent to retake the island. Jefferson was awaiting French ratification of the Convention of 1800 which had been delayed because of disagreement over some of its terms. Anxious not to ruffle French feelings, he answered Pichon that "nothing would be easier than to furnish your army and fleet . . . and reduce Toussaint to starvation." A year later, when Marshal Leclerc, Napoleon's brother-in-law, led his forces against Santo Domingo, the United States gave him no cooperation at all. Pichon remonstrated with Secretary Madison and received a lecture on the obligations of nations under international law. He went to see Jefferson and got another lecture on the unfriendly attitude of the French government toward the United States over the last ten years. [33] The episode was typical of Jeffersonian indirection and deviousness in matters of diplomacy. In 1801 France needed to be conciliated; in 1802 the objective was to make the French reconquest of Haiti as difficult as possible. The fate of L'Ouverture was immaterial, for Jefferson had no fear of the proximity of the

Black Republic to southern slaveholders. "The possibility that these exiles might stimulate & conduct vindicative or predatory descents on our coasts, & facilitate concert with their brethren . . . here, looks to a state of things . . . not probable on a contemplation of our relative strength." [34] The objective was the security of the United States, and since it was a second rate power, Jefferson intended to substitute cunning and guile for fleets and armies. Not that he was above using the *threat* of force as soon became apparent.

When the ominous rumors reached Washington that it would be Napoleon rather than Spain on the Mississippi, Jefferson had already decided to appoint Chancellor Robert Livingston of New York for the delicate position as American minister in Paris. Livingston was deaf and did not speak French well (but read it easily), and he was inclined to be impatient and irascible. Talleyrand found his egotism easy to bruise with irony and sarcasm. But he was dogged and persistent, and he faithfully executed both the letter and the spirit of his instructions. If he lacked brilliance and imagination, there was plenty of both in Washington.

His departure was delayed until the late summer of 1801, that is, until the Convention of 1800 was ratified by Napoleon. He was instructed to find out explicitly the status of Louisiana and New Orleans; and if they had been acquired by France, he was to explore the possibility of securing territory in the Floridas, particularly the area immediately to the eastward of the mouth of the Mississippi. He was also to get assurances that France would honor the terms of the Treaty of San Lorenzo. [35]

By the early fall of 1801 King, in London, had definite news of a truce between France and England to be formally concluded at Amiens the following March. By November he had secured documentation which confirmed the cession of Louisiana. King was sure that Napoleon intended to reconquer Santo Domingo but was uncertain about plans for the occupation of Louisiana.[36] By the New Year all this information had been received in Washington, and Jefferson and Madison had some basis for planning.

They were aware that little could be done until the Peace of Amiens was finally concluded, but some groundwork could be laid. Jefferson intimated to Pichon that French occupation of Louisiana would have grave effects on relations with the United States. A renewal of the European war might find the country strongly sympathetic to England. The British chargé in Washington, Edward Thornton, found the President positively loquacious on the subject of Louisiana. French ambitions on the Mississippi would no doubt lead to an entirely new approach to Anglo-American relations. All these informal remarks were duly reported by the two ministers to their superiors, as Jefferson intended. But both the Frenchman and the Englishman found the Secretary of State difficult to approach and extremely reticent and vague on such matters. This was also intended, for Madison spoke for official American policy.[37]

The full import of Jefferson's strategy was contained in a private letter to Livingston written on April 18, 1802. The letter was delivered by Du Pont de Nemours, the French physiocrat whom Jefferson had met in Paris and who had come to the United States in 1800. Although he was now an American resident, Du Pont had many important friends in France, and his visit to Paris in 1802 was for political as well as business reasons. Jefferson invited his friend to read the instructions to Livingston before he delivered it, hoping that Du Pont would impress French officialdom with the seriousness of American intentions.[38]

To Livingston, Jefferson explained that the cession of Louisiana constituted "a new epoch in our political course."

The long-standing friendship between the United States and France was now threatened by Napoleon's New World ambitions.

> There is on the globe one single spot, the possessor of which is our natural and habitual enemy. It is New Orleans, through which the produce of three-eighths of our territory must pass to market. . . . France placing herself in that door assumes to us the attitude of defiance. Spain might have retained it quietly for years. . . . Not so can it ever be in the hands of France. . . . The day that France takes possession of N. Orleans fixes the sentence which is to restrain her forever within her low water mark. . . . From that moment we must marry ourselves to the British fleet and nation. We must turn all our attentions to a maritime force, for which our resources place us on very high grounds: and having formed and cemented together a power which may render reenforcement of her settlements here impossible to France, make the first cannon, which shall be fired in Europe the signal for tearing up any settlement she may have made. . . . France will have held possession of New Orleans during the interval of a peace, long or short, at the end of which it will be wrested from her.[39]

Was this powerfully threatening language real, or was it a colossal bluff? Was Jefferson really serious about an alliance, "cemented together" with Britain? Hamilton could have told him that such an alliance would not be necessary since Britain would oppose Napoleon's expansion in the Western Hemisphere in any case. The best appraisal of the instruction is that Jefferson wanted Livingston—and Du Pont—to make it abundantly clear to Napoleon that if he overcame the difficulties of Santo Domingo and of the logistical problems inherent in an expedition to the Mississippi, he still faced a threat from the United States. And Jefferson wanted this threat to sound as formidable as possible.

Louisiana: "A Noble Bargain . . ."

With Jefferson's private letter and Madison's similar if more circumspect formal instructions to guide him, Livingston began to press his case on Talleyrand, the French minister of foreign affairs. In August he prepared a memorandum setting forth the arguments against French occupation of Louisiana. The threat of an alliance with England was veiled, but he left no doubt that New Orleans and the Floridas were vital to the United States and that unless they were in American hands France could expect only hostility from his government. So far, Madison and Jefferson had not considered any territory west of the Mississippi. Talleyrand promised to consider the proposal and pass it to Napoleon, but it was apparent to Livingston that the First Consul was oblivious to advice. Livingston was not hopeful.[40]

Yet on September 1, 1802, he wrote a letter to Madison that was altogether remarkable in its shrewd predictions. He reported that the expedition which was to occupy Louisiana was being organized in Holland, but he doubted that it would ever sail. News of the capture of L'Ouverture and Leclerc's success in subjugating Santo Domingo had reached Paris, but Livingston believed that "their islands call for much more than France can ever furnish." He thought that the Peace of Amiens would be of short duration and that the war in Europe would soon be renewed. "I am persuaded that the whole will end in a relinquishment of the country [Louisiana], and the transfer of the capital to the United States." [41] Livingston may have been indulging in wishful thinking, but he was right on every count.

Unable to get any satisfaction from Talleyrand, Livingston finally decided to try to get to Napoleon through his brother Joseph Bonaparte. Several months before, Rufus King had suggested from London that the proper approach to the First

Consul was money, "actual money and a great deal of it." [42] This may have been the genesis of the unique practice introduced by the United States of settling territorial disputes by purchase. It ultimately became a standard American diplomatic procedure. Livingston's overture to Joseph Bonaparte at first got an encouraging reception, and the latter even suggested that the United States accept Louisiana instead of Florida. But this path also proved to be a dead end. [43]

Meantime Jefferson was applying pressure of another kind on Pichon. The French chargé found the President "very reserved and cold" and noted that France was becoming increasingly unpopular in America. On the other hand, Thornton found that he had easy access to the President. Jefferson talked freely about Louisiana with the young Englishman and did not hesitate to express his distaste for France and Napoleon. None of this was official, of course. Simply remarks passed in casual conversation—"I leave all details of business to their official channel," said Jefferson in a letter to Livingston. By the fall of 1802 the reports which Talleyrand received from Pichon argued forcefully that French colonial policy was not only doomed but was extremely provocative so far as Franco-American relations were concerned. It was driving the United States into the arms of Great Britain and was creating a belligerent restiveness in the western country which boded ill for the future of New France. [44]

The full implications of the west as a factor in this diplomatic game were revealed in November, 1802, when news reached the President that the Spanish intendant in New Orleans had closed the port to American trade in violation of the Treaty of San Lorenzo. (Although it had been almost two years since the Treaty of San Ildefonso, Spain had not yet transferred the government of Louisiana to France.) The closing of New Orleans had repercussions of far-reaching

significance, but the Spanish motive seems to have been simply retaliation against American abuses of trading privileges.[45]

Jefferson was deeply concerned, but outwardly he appeared
to take little notice of the Spanish breach of diplomatic good
faith. In his message to Congress on December 15 he apparently saw no cause for alarm since he thought "no change
. . . necessary in our military establishment." Louisiana was
dismissed in an innocuous statement of five lines.[46] But he was
well aware not only of western discontent but of the political
capital which the Federalists could make of the situation.
Hamilton denounced the "last *lullaby* message" and "the
pretty scheme of substituting economy to taxation." As for
the west, "I have always held," said Hamilton, "that the *unity
of our empire* and the best interests of our nation require that
we shall annex to the United States all the territory east of
the Mississippi, New Orleans included." His solution was
typically Hamiltonian: "Of course I infer that, in an emergency like the present, energy is wisdom." [47] The goal was
the same, but the tactics were different.

Jefferson was not so complacent as his message to Congress
indicated. He was aware that the Federalists were desperately
looking for an issue upon which they could revive their political fortunes. They might "force us into a war if possible, in
order to derange our finances, or . . . to attach the western
country to them, as their best friends, and thus get again into
power." [48] He was not concerned about the Spanish. The
Marqués de Casa Yrujo, the Spanish minister in Washington,
was almost pathetic in his vehement denunciations of his
government's policy, and he immediately set about reversing
the intendant's proclamation.[49] Jefferson's course was to pla-
cate the westerners, cut the ground from under the Federalists, and exploit the situation to influence events in Paris.

Early in January, 1803, the President asked Congress for

a special appropriation of $2,000,000 "to defray any expenses which may be incurred in relation to the intercourse between the United States and foreign nations." This vague language concealed a more specific proposal which was explained to a secret session of Congress. Jefferson also appointed James Monroe as special envoy to assist Livingston.[50] Monroe, recently retired as governor of Virginia, had a reputation as a defender of western interests which dated back to 1786, when he had opposed the Jay-Gardoqui agreement.

These actions appeared to calm the agitators at home. When Federalist Senator James Ross of Pittsburgh introduced a resolution in mid-February to call out 50,000 militia to "repel and punish the indignity put upon the nation," he was voted down. (Livingston was at pains to bring the Ross resolution to the attention of the French government, although he innocently professed not to know whether it had passed.) Monroe embarked for Europe on March 9 under instructions to purchase New Orleans and the Floridas "or as much thereof as the actual proprietor can be prevailed on to part with." [51]

Even as Jefferson made these arrangements, the circumstances which Livingston had predicted in the fall of 1802 began to crystalize. Early in January, 1803, Napoleon heard of the death of Leclerc, victim of that deadly ally of the Haitian revolutionists—yellow fever. A week later, while at dinner with Madame Bonaparte and a group of his ministers, the moody First Consul suddenly and savagely burst out, "Damn sugar, damn coffee, damn colonies." [52] In March, at a reception given by Madame Bonaparte, he was deliberately rude to Lord Whitworth, the British ambassador, threatening that, *"I must either have* [British-occupied] *Malta or war."* The Peace of Amiens was obviously in danger of disintegration. The French expeditionary force originally destined for Louisiana, which had been locked in the winter ice at Dunkirk, was now regarded as a threat to England, and the British fleet was watching it closely and warily. So Santo Domingo was unconquered, the Louisiana expedition immobilized, and peace in Europe precarious. In late March there came another warning to Talleyrand from Pichon: "The [Louisiana] crisis grows greater every day, and we cannot push it into the distant future." [53]

On April 10 Napoleon summoned his minister of finance Françoise Barbé-Marbois and peremptorily announced that he intended to cede Louisiana to the United States. "I renounce it with the greatest regret; to attempt obstinately to retain it would be folly. I direct you to negotiate this affair. Do not even wait for the arrival of Mr. Monroe." [54]

Robert Livingston was almost unhinged. For almost a year he had vainly cajoled and threatened and had received evasion and insult from Talleyrand, Joseph Bonaparte, and Napoleon. When Talleyrand casually suggested on April 11 that all of Louisiana was for sale, "I told him no; that our wishes extended only to New Orleans and the Floridas." [55] This indeed was the instruction which Madison had issued to both Livingston and Monroe. By the time Monroe arrived two days later Livingston had recovered. After less than three weeks of haggling over the price, $15,000,000, and other details, the two Americans concluded the momentous purchase on April 30, 1803. [56]

What had Livingston and Monroe bought? In their haste to conclude the negotiations before the temperamental First Consul changed his mind, they decided to repeat the vague wording of the Treaty of San Ildefonso. Certainly this meant New Orleans. Just as certainly it did not mean the Floridas, at least not to Livingston. In following his instructions to gain "a Cession . . . of New Orleans and of West and East Florida," he had pressed the Spanish government to declare whether the Floridas were included in the cession of San

Ildefonso. He had been assured that they were not. Now he pressed Talleyrand, but the Frenchman would only indulge in a final irony. "I do not know. . . . You have made a noble bargain for yourselves, and I suppose you will make the most of it." [57]

The news arrived in Washington in time for the President's annual open house commemorating the Fourth of July. On New Year's Day, 1802, Jefferson had received an enormous cheese from the farmers of the Berkshire Hills in Massachusetts. Four and a half feet across, fifteen inches thick and weighing 1,235 pounds, it had been deposited in the unfinished East Room. Now, eighteen months later, the President decided that the glorious news from Paris was the proper occasion for serving it to his guests. The Republicans thought it delicious, but the Federalists pronounced it wretched. [58]

The Course of Empire

In his first message to Congress Jefferson had stressed the desirability of limiting the powers of the national government. He had also made a point of deferring to "the legislative judgement" in contrast to the executive tyranny which the Republicans had criticized during the Federalist regime. Now, with the rich prize of Louisiana in his grasp, he was vastly troubled. "The general government has no powers but such as the constitution has given it; and it has not given it a power of holding foreign territory, & still less of incorporating it into the Union." [59] He therefore believed that a constitutional amendment was necessary, and he even prepared a proposal for submission to Congress.

News from Paris sharpened his dilemma. Monroe urged the President to take immediate action on the treaty. "If the thing were to do over again, it could not be obtained, & . . . if we give the least opening, they will declare the treaty void."

Jefferson may well have envied Hamilton his philosophy of
energetic government which did not hesitate to act for the
public good. There were not many occasions in which Jefferson indulged in the kind of "twistification" which he condemned in others, but this was one of them. "When an instrument [Constitution] admits two constructions, the one safe,
the other dangerous, the one precise, the other indefinite, I
prefer that which is safe & precise. . . . Our peculiar security
is in possession of a written Constitution. Let us not make
it a blank paper by construction." [60]

Yet he had already done so. A week before writing this
dissertation on strict construction, he had advised Attorney-
General Levi Lincoln that "the less that is said about any
constitutional difficulty, the better; and . . . it will be desirable for Congress to do what is necessary, *in silence.*" [61] Congress complied, and the enabling act was approved October
21, 1803.

His justification, of course, was that the acquisition of
Louisiana was of such tremendous benefit to the nation that
Congress, "casting behind them metaphysical subtleties, and
risking themselves like faithful servants, must ratify & pay
for it . . . doing for them [the people] unauthorized what we
know they would have done for themselves." [62] Jefferson's
philosphical conscience did not bother him as much as it
would have if he had been subverting the popular will. His
dream of a western empire was shared by his countrymen.

He had never been beyond the Shenandoah, but he had a
continental vision. His "empire for liberty" had suddenly
acquired wide horizons. The carping Federalists still insisted
that a republican system could not govern so vast a land, but
this did not distrub him. He had always viewed government,
republican or otherwise, as a means by which men could be
free. If there were to be "the formation of a new confederacy,
embracing all the waters of the Mississippi, on both sides of

it . . . if their happiness should depend on it so strongly," was such a prospect so dreadful that his generation should condemn it? "The future inhabitants of the Atlantic and Mississippi States will be our sons. . . . We think we see their happiness in their Union, & we wish it. . . . God bless them both, & keep them in union, if it be for their good, but separate them, if it be better." [63]

He could not see the great domain of Louisiana for himself, but he was determined that others should see it for him. In January, 1803, he sent a confidential message to Congress asking for an appropriation of $2,500 for an expedition to explore the Missouri "to the Western Ocean." Obviously the Congress must have good and sufficient reasons and Jefferson supplied them: "The country on that river is inhabited by numerous tribes, who furnish great supplies of furs and peltry to the trade of another nation." [64]

But to young Captain Meriwether Lewis, his private secretary whom he had chosen to head the expedition, he outlined a much more expansive project. He wanted reports on the Indian tribes: names, numbers, language, tradition, monuments, occupations, agriculture, hunting, war, morality, religion. This was only the beginning. "Other objects worthy of notice" will be soil, animals of the country, "remains & accounts of any which may be deemed rare or extinct;" minerals, weather, "the dates at which particular plants put forth or lose their flowers," birds, reptiles, insects. "Your observations are to be taken with great pains & accuracy, to be entered distinctly, & intelligibly for others as well as yourself." [65] Heaven help Meriwether Lewis if he brought back his reports and Jefferson could not read them!

Lewis and his co-captain William Clark prepared their expedition in the summer of 1803. They witnessed the brief and unimpressive flag-raising ceremony in St. Louis which made Louisiana an American territory and in May, 1804, set off on their western journey. They spent the first winter in the Dakotas with the Mandan Indians and then disappeared into the endless wilderness of the upper Missouri. It was twenty-eight months before they returned.

A more prosaic and more difficult project for the President was the government of New Orleans and its neighborhood. The United States had never before attempted to assimilate a region already inhabited by Europeans. Spanish and French tradition was buttressed by a system of law based on the old Spanish colonial system. The government of New Orleans was vested in the autocratic and aristocratic *cabildo*, a combination executive directory and supreme court. The slave-holding aristocracy of sugar planters was venal and corrupt, and religious bigotry and lack of education were hallmarks of the upper as well as the lower classes.

Jefferson had been given the authority to direct the government of the territory until Congress could formulate a comprehensive plan. He appointed W. C. C. Claiborne as acting governor, and the President at first intended to install a system modeled on the Northwest Ordinance of 1787. But ignorance and ineptitude combined with the recalcitrance of the entrenched Creoles soon made the situation chaotic. Yet the President was determined to adhere to the principles of representative government on the American model and the treatment of the inhabitants as American citizens. He insisted that the foreign slave trade be abolished, but he did not try to abolish slavery itself, although he briefly considered the idea.

However, his first attempt to deal with the problem was an act introduced by his friend Senator John C. Breckinridge of Kentucky and passed in March, 1804. This provided for an "assembly of notables" appointed by the President to assist the governor. Judges were also appointed. The slave trade was prohibited, and Spanish land grants after 1800 were annulled. The plan was certainly not representative government, and the roar of protest from Louisiana was voiced not only by the Creoles but by American malcontents. Edward Livingston, the discredited former federal attorney from New York, and Daniel Clark, the former American consul in New Orleans, were in the forefront of the protesters who invoked the language of the Revolution to denounce the tyranny and despotism of the federal government.

Jefferson never intended the first phase of government to be more than a transitional stage, but the discontent and confusion moved him to ask Congress for an act which provided for a representative assembly based on white manhood suffrage. As expected, the legislature was dominated by the "old inhabitants" who, although they chanted the litany of self-government, were really concerned about the prohibition on the slave trade. Claiborne finally found partial solutions in a tolerant policy toward smuggling and acquiescence in a Roman law code. Although these measures were hardly in what would be called the republican tradition, they represented Jefferson's pragmatic approach to a unique and difficult problem. Foreign territory became American when Louisiana became a state in 1812, and Jefferson gratified his hope of adding "new brethren to partake of the blessings of freedom and self-government." [66]

"Good patriots must at all events please the people." [67] Alexander Hamilton's comment on Jefferson's first message to Congress, stripped of its sarcasm, might have constituted a valid appraisal of the first term. Sarcasm was about the only weapon left to the Federalists, whose strength in Congress had diminished to only 39 of 142 Representatives and 9 of 34 Senators. [68]

In the process Jefferson had become a very powerful chief executive, one of the most powerful in American history until the twentieth century. Congress had enacted every one of his major requests and had passed only a few minor measures of which he did not approve. This resulted from the very fact that Jefferson avoided as much as possible the appearance of imposing presidential leadership on Congress and on the country. He resorted instead to as many indirect devices as possible in order to implement his program.

These were both formal and informal. His use of patronage and his attempt to diminish the power of the judiciary have been noted. Instead of dominating Congress by the force of formal persuasion, he used skillful colleagues to manage his proposals. John C. Breckinridge of Kentucky in the Senate and Randolph of Roanoke in the House proved to be capable lieutenants, although by 1804 Randolph was beginning to show more of that irascible independence which finally led him to break with the President. In addition to this liason with Congress, Jefferson made himself easily accessible to everyone including Congressmen. This was partly the result of his own gregarious nature and his memories of the dreadful boredom of the receptions and levees given by Washington and Adams. It was also because at the small informal dinners at the presidential residence he could drop a hint or an explanation which would soothe or persuade doubting legislators. Diplomats, administrative officials, and others who casually came and went enabled him to keep his finger on the pulse of public affairs almost as much as the official business routine which he had established.[69]

Jefferson never lost sight of the importance of the press. He continued to be the target of outrageous personal attacks by the most extreme of the embittered Federalists, and his sensitive nature recoiled at "the brutal hackings & hewings of these heroes of Billingsgate." One marvels at his forbearance in refusing to use his power and prestige to retaliate, but he never abandoned his fundamental belief that "the only security of all is in a free press." [70]

In 1800 he persuaded young Samuel Harrison Smith to come to Washington and publish a newspaper. Although he expected it to be Republican in sympathy, he also wanted a paper with a national circulation. Smith's *National Intelligencer* soon established a reputation for moderation and excellence which made it one of the most respected newspapers of the early nineteenth century.[71]

Jefferson discovered that as President he was not only the head of the nation but the head of his party, and he recognized its importance as a source of power. He used this leadership sparingly, for he realized that a political party was a fragile thing and that one of the reasons for the decline of the Federalists was their lack of flexibility. He sensed, too, the delicate interrelationship of local and national issues and had "long since made up my mind on the propriety of the general government's [party's] taking no side in state quarrels."[72]

By the end of his first administration, then, Jefferson wielded a vast amount of power, a considerable portion of which was the "executive influence" which he had often criticized in Washington's administration, though Jefferson's was of a different kind. He also discovered that he could not entirely undo the work of his predecessors. He told Gallatin in 1802 that "the monopoly of a single bank is certainly an evil," but he found that the Secretary of the Treasury was a staunch defender of the Bank of the United States so he grudgingly acquiesced in its continued operation.[73] Finally, he had found that the doctrine of constitutional strict construction was much handier when he had been a critic of the party in power than when the roles were reversed and he was called upon to deal with the crises of national policy.

Alexander Hamilton might well have invoked the irony of

his remark on Jefferson's message to Congress in 1801. "He furnishes frequent opportunities of arraying him against himself—of combating his opinions at one period by his opinions at another." [74] But by the end of Jefferson's first term, Hamilton was dead.

XV A Giant Passes

THE VICTORY OF Jefferson and the Republicans left Hamilton in a political void. That election had shown that John Adams had the largest political following among the Federalist leaders. It was soon evident that he was retiring, and it was hardly to be expected that his adherents would accept Hamilton's leadership after his sweeping denunciation of the man from Massachusetts. At the other end of the political spectrum were such bitter diehards as Timothy Pickering and Fisher Ames, who saw in defeat the end of the world—or at least of the American union. The younger Federalists, like Harrison Gray Otis and John Eager Howard, on which a new foundation might be built, had scarcely distinguished themselves by supporting Burr in the disputed election of 1801.

Perhaps most galling of all was the fact that when Jefferson said, "We are all republicans, we are all federalists," he seemed to mean it. Albert Gallatin's ideas of fiscal responsibility were embodied in a balanced budget and a sinking fund to pay the national debt. The Bank of the United States found itself as respectable among the Republicans as in the heydey of Federalism. In a rare mood of despondency Hamilton resolved to "withdraw from the scene. Every day proves to me more and more, that this American world was not made for me." [1]

Retirement to Private Life

For the first time since he had been a student at King's, Hamilton felt freed of public affairs and ready to devote his time and energies to his personal affairs. He had always maintained his reputation as a practicing lawyer, and he was not long in re-establishing a large and profitable clientele. He was also prepared to spend more time with Eliza and the children. "Experience more and more convinces me that true happiness is only to be found in the bosom of one's own family," he wrote in 1800.

A few months later, in the fall of 1801, Hamilton's hopes for a tranquil life received a devastating blow. His oldest son Philip, a handsome, attractive lad recently graduated from Columbia, was killed in a duel. The quarrel grew out of a Fourth of July speech made by George Eacker in which Federalists in general, but not Philip's father in particular, were savagely attacked. Since the exchange of insults between Eacker and young Hamilton did not take place until November, it was a senseless tragedy in every respect. "Never did I see a man so completely overwhelmed with grief as Hamilton has been," reported his friend Robert Troup.[2]

He worked out his despair in a busy law practice and in the building of a country estate. In 1800 Hamilton had bought about thirty acres on a hilltop overlooking the Hudson where it sweeps by the Jersey Palisades. Here he built a large country residence which he called "The Grange." He was soon busy with an extensive flower garden, "wild roses around the outside of the . . . garden with laurel at foot"; grass for the surrounding meadows; melons from seeds solicited from his friend C. C. Pinckney in South Carolina—"a garden, you know, is a very useful refuge of a disappointed politician," he observed. If he intended to adopt the role of the country gentleman, it was evident that Hamilton had not abandoned city life. His law office on Wall Street required constant attention, and he maintained a residence in the city.[3]

All this was expensive, and Hamilton hoped to acquire financial security through investments as well as his law practice. Although he had always been the prophet of commerce and manufacturing, he knew that the quickest way to an American fortune was in land speculation. He organized several such ventures and acquired extensive holdings in western New York, borrowing heavily from the Merchants Bank of New York, which he helped to found in 1803. He estimated his assets at $75,000 in 1804, a considerable sum for that time, but his untimely death came before the profits from his investments could be realized.[4]

Most of Hamilton's time was taken up with his law practice, and he was soon back in the public eye in a case involving the libel of President Jefferson himself. In this instance he appeared as counsel for the alleged perpetrator of the libel and as a champion of freedom of the press. If Hamilton saw any irony in the situation he left no record of it.

The defendant was Harry Croswell, the editor of an obscure upstate weekly called *The Wasp*. His allegation was that Jefferson had paid James Callender, of poison-pen fame, to call President Washington "a traitor, a robber, a purger"; venerable John Adams, so the charge read, had been characterized as "a hoary-headed incendiary." [5] Hamilton did not appear at Croswell's first trial, in which the editor was found guilty. The case was heard on appeal in February, 1804, before the Supreme Court of New York, and it was at this point that Hamilton was invited to join the defense. The justices of the court were Morgan Lewis, Smith Thompson, James Kent, and Brockholst Livingston, certainly a distinguished group and evenly divided in their political associations.

The final summation for the defense was Hamilton's last

important public appearance. He was faced with the same problem that had troubled legal waters for almost three-quarters of a century. In 1732 another Hamilton named Andrew had defended John Peter Zenger against a charge of libel in what had then been the colony of New York. He had contended that, contrary to common law precedent, the truth or falseness of the alleged libel constituted a legal defense and that such a question should be decided by the jury. As noted above, this interpretation had gained acceptance in federal courts and in many state courts but not in New York. It was to this point that Hamilton made his argument.

"The liberty of the press," he said, "consists in the right to publish with impunity truth, with good motives, for justifiable ends, though reflecting on government, magistracy, or individuals." He noted that in so doing the press had a responsibility not to use "the weapon of truth wantonly; . . . for the purpose of disturbing the peace of families; . . . for relating that which does not appertain to official conduct." But he warned particularly of the necessity of truth as a defense against libel when public officials were involved. Since government controls the judicial process there is danger that its officials will become entrenched in office and establish a despotism. "To watch the progress of such endeavors is the office of a free press—to give us early alarm, and put us on our guard against the encroachments of power."

It was a ringing defense of freedom of the press which was somewhat tainted by the fact that Jefferson was the target of the libel and that Federalist fortunes were low. Yet there is no reason to doubt that Hamilton was sincere in his belief that the press constituted a fundamental safeguard of liberty and that the degree of its restraint should rest in the hands of the jury, "a changeable body of men chosen by the people." [6]

The panel of judges voted along straight party lines, two

for acquittal and two for conviction, so Hamilton lost his case. But his associate William Van Ness guided a bill through the legislature three years later which incorporated Hamilton's argument into the law of New York State. For once, Hamilton lost a battle but won the war.

Moribund Federalism

One reason that Hamilton had an interest in the Croswell case was because the New York *Evening Post* had also printed Callender's article. Hamilton had been the principal founder of the paper and was closely associated with its editor, although the attack on Jefferson appears to have been published without his knowledge.

The Federalist press had declined alarmingly since the election of 1800. William Cobbett had returned to England, and John Fenno had died in 1798. That stalwart of Federalism, Noah Webster, seemed to have deserted the cause in disgust. "Some unworthy intrigues of the federalists," he said, "and their overbearing, persecuting spirit, which devoted every man to execration, who will not be as violent as themselves, have greatly disgusted many men of the party who have no wish but to see their country prosperous & happy." Such sentiments may have been admirably honest, but they did not attract Federalist subscribers.[7]

No one understood the power of the press or used it more effectively than Hamilton. Perhaps he also understood that a new and more temperate breed of journalist, like Samuel Harrison Smith, was replacing the shrill malevolence of Duane and Cobbett. Hamilton chose William Coleman, an able and moderate New Englander, to edit the *Evening Post,* and its first issue appeared on November 16, 1801. Thereafter, Hamilton frequently dictated pieces to Coleman which the latter transcribed in shorthand. The *Post* thus became the voice through which Hamilton attempted to rally the cause of Federalism.[8]

Yet the prospect was not bright. "Hamilton is supremely disgusted with the state of our political affairs," observed Troup. "He has already said and still maintains the opinion that Jefferson and his party had not the talents or virtue sufficient to administer the government well." Hard on the heels of Jefferson's election had come another resounding defeat in New York. George Clinton, though advanced in years, not only was again elected governor of New York, but the Republicans carried New York City. Hamilton stumped the polling places on election day and was dumbfounded when he was greeted with cries of "Thief—traitor—rascal—villain." [9]

At first there was the hope that the Republican party would "menace our country with all the horrors of revolutionary frenzy," thus paving the way for the Federalists to return to power as the saviors of the nation. But Hamilton was confounded by the fact that Jefferson apparently "will not lend himself to dangerous innovations, but in essential points will tread in the footsteps of his predecessors." In fact, the great threat was that the Federalists would be absorbed into the Republican party and disappear without a trace. John Quincy Adams referred to Federalism in 1802 as "a carcass seven years in its grave," and five years later he himself abandoned it.[10]

As Hamilton surveyed the disorder and confusion of the situation, he decided that he must once more appeal to that good sense of the people which he had so often derided. It must be pointed out to them that only the wise and the good could save the country from ruin. He therefore proposed to take a leaf or two from the Republican handbook on politics and organize political societies. The basis of their appeal would be two powerful forces: constitutionalism and religion.

He hoped to muster the clergy against Jefferson's deism and at the same time appeal to the Constitution (Hamiltonian edition) as the safeguard against the menace of a Republican reign of terror.

He therefore proposed the organization of the Christian Democratic Societies which would disseminate information, "promote the election of *fit* men," manage societies for the relief of immigrants, and promote "institutions of a charitable and useful nature in the management of Federalists." [11] It was a weird scheme and wholly impractical from its inception. The clergy, particularly in New England, was already the stronghold of Federalism, and it had been no match for the Republican tide, except perhaps in Boston. Nor could the prospect of a reign of terror be conjured up in a country as peaceful and prosperous as the United States in 1802. Prosperity at home and peace in Europe were not entirely the work of the Republicans, but in the lexicon of American politics they got the credit. Hamilton's political balloon was scarcely launched before it collapsed.

The Essex Junto

Discouraged as Hamilton was by the seeming invincibility of the Jeffersonians, he was not overcome by the gloom and despair of diehards like Pickering, Tracy, Hillhouse, and Griswold. These men saw no salvation in the American union. The only hope appeared to be to shut themselves off from "the men who now rule us with their measures. . . . The coward wretch at the head . . . like a Parisian revolutionary monster, prating about humanity, could feel an infernal pleasure in the utter distruction of his opponents." With Louisiana added to the nation New England was beginning to shrink geographically as well as politically. History knows these men as the "Essex Junto," and they began to dream strange dreams of a northern confederacy with New England joined by New York and perhaps New Jersey. Moreover, they calculated that they would find a leader—or a pawn—in the person of Aaron Burr, whose pliability they had recognized as early as 1801. It was reported that at a gathering of Federalists in New York to commemorate Washington's birthday "a strange *apparition*, which was taken for the Vice-President, appeared . . . and toasted 'the union of all honest men.' " [12]

Burr's curious and questionable behavior during the disputed election had made his own party distrustful of him. His letters to the President and other members of the administration recommending persons for political appointments had gone unanswered. He was soon painfully aware that in the national councils of the party he was persona non grata. He therefore decided to recover his political fortunes by becoming a candidate for governor of New York.

This fitted in precisely with the plans of the "Junto." If Burr became governor, "were New York detached (as under his administration it would be) from the Virginia influence, the whole Union should be benefited. Jefferson would then be forced to observe some caution and forbearance in his measures. And if a *separation* should be deemed proper, five New England States, New York and New Jersey would naturally be united." [13]

But the plan immediately ran into difficulties. The New York Republican leaders were suspicious of Burr and nominated Morgan Lewis, chief justice of the state supreme court. It was also obvious that the two outstanding Federalist leaders Rufus King and Alexander Hamilton would have nothing to do with any scheme which threatened disunion. Hamilton, in fact, made it clear to a gathering of Federalist leaders as early as February, 1804, that he would actively oppose Burr, whom he considered "a man of irregular and insatiable ambition."

It is doubtful if Burr could have won, with or without Hamilton's opposition. The Republicans had carried the state in 1801, and they were immeasurably stronger after the brilliant successes of Jefferson's first administration. Only a few of Burr's Republican friends joined the Federalists in his support. Lewis won handily, polling a majority of three to two over Burr. The scheme of the "Essex Junto," which was never supported by more than a small conclave of dissidents, collapsed.[14]

But the intensity of feeling generated by the election led to fatal and tragic consequences. Two letters had appeared in the Albany *Register* in April, 1804, in which the writer quoted Hamilton as saying that Burr was "a dangerous man, and one who ought not to be trusted." The author of the letters also added that he could "detail . . . a still more despicable opinion which General Hamilton has expressed of Mr. Burr." Other newspapers had subsequently printed the letters.[15]

On June 18, 1804, a few days after the election, Burr wrote to Hamilton demanding "a prompt, unqualified acknowledgement or denial" of the implied insults. Hamilton replied in a long and rambling note that the language and circumstances were vague and that he "could not, without manifest impropriety, make the avowal or disavowal which you seem to think necessary." Burr persisted, saying that Hamilton's reply was evasive. There ensued an involved exchange which took the form of letters and conversations between the two men and their representatives. It would appear that Burr was spoiling for a fight but that Hamilton could have apologized with good grace, since he later admitted that he "may have been influenced by misconstruction or misinformation. It is also my ardent wish that I may have been more mistaken than I think I have been." On June 27 Burr challenged Hamilton to a duel. Hamilton accepted, and July 11 was set as the date.[16]

There have been many explanations as to why Hamilton accepted the challenge and why he then determined to throw away his first fire. It has been argued that Hamilton had acquired a deep religious conviction, and that this, coupled with a conviction that he had wronged Burr, determined him not to "shed the blood of a fellow creature in a private combat forbidden by law." To this may be added the despondency and frustration which he felt at the disaster which had befallen his party and his own political career. He certainly was painfully conscious of the blow which his death would deal to his wife and children, but there remained perhaps the most important of his considerations. "The ability to be in future useful, whether in resisting mischief or effecting good, in those crises of our public affairs which seem likely to happen, would probably be inseparable from a conformity with public prejudice in this particular." [17]

Possibly not until a day or two preceding the meeting did the struggle in his tortured mind come to some final justification and decision. Yet his manner was so astonishingly composed that he completed an orderly arrangement of his business affairs, drew up his will, and attended religious services with his family on July 10. Eliza received no hint that he was about to fight a duel, much less that "I have resolved . . . to reserve and throw away my first fire, and I have thoughts even of reserving my second fire, and thus giving a double opportunity to Col. Burr to pause and reflect."

In the early hours of the morning of July 11 Aaron Burr neither paused nor reflected. He fired on the word and Hamilton fell, mortally wounded. After thirty-one hours of severe and agonizing pain, he died in the early afternoon of July 12, 1804. [18]

In the spring of 1804, in a letter to an unknown acquaintance, Hamilton wrote:

Arraign not the dispensations of Providence, they must be founded in wisdom and goodness; and when they do not suit us, it must be because there is some fault in ourselves which deserves chastisement; or because there is a kind of intent, to correct in us some vice or failing, of which, perhaps, we may not be conscious; or because the general plan requires that we should suffer partial ill.

In this situation it is our duty to cultivate resignation, and even humility, bearing in mind, in the language of the poet, "that it was pride which lost the blest abodes." [19]

XVI Commercial Warfare*

THE ELECTION OF 1804 was gratifying in several ways. The Republicans in Washington for the first time utilized the caucus as a device for indicating the party's nominees for president and vice-president. Their choice of Jefferson to head the ticket was a foregone conclusion. Just as obviously, Aaron Burr was now virtually ostracized from the party, not only because of his questionable conduct in the disputed election of 1801, but because of allegations since made by Burr that Jefferson had made a bargain with the Federalists to secure their votes. The caucus met in February, 1804, and chose Burr's ancient rival in New York, George Clinton, as the vice-presidential nominee. It was thus painfully clear to the retiring Vice-President that he was persona non grata in the Republican party. Whatever popularity he might have subsequently retained vanished in the explosion of the shot which had killed Hamilton.[1]

The ratification of the Twelfth Amendment in September, 1804, providing a separate electoral vote for president and vice-president, removed any possibility of the sort of embarrassment which had resulted in the last two elections.[2]

* For this chapter see especially Bradford Perkins, *Prologue to War: England and the United States, 1805–1812*. Hereafter cited as Perkins, *Prologue to War*.

The electoral vote, 162 for Jefferson and 14 for C. C. Pinckney, was indicative not only of the President's enormous popularity but of the disaster which had overtaken the Federalist party in national politics. The Congressional elections left only 25 Federalists in the House and 7 in the Senate.[3]

Jefferson's second inaugural address was a mirror of the serenity of the victors. He enumerated the accomplishments of the past administration: reduction of taxes and public offices; continued retirement of the national debt; the purchase of Louisiana; the effort "to cultivate the friendship of all nations." He modestly refused to "arrogate to myself the merit of the measures," but insisted that credit should go to the "reflecting character of our citizens," and "the zeal and wisdom" of the representatives which they had elected to "lay the foundations of public happiness."[4]

But the apparent confidence which this message reflected was short-lived. One of the strongest unifying forces of any political party is the opposition. No one understood better than Jefferson that with the decline of the Federalists "we must expect division . . . as soon as the Republicans shall be so strong as to fear no other enemy."[5]

Complications and Conspiracies

"Manifest destiny" is a phrase that belongs to a later period of American history, but Thomas Jefferson may well have embodied its earlier spirit. Throughout his life his imagination was fired by the frontier expansion of the United States, and there was no project which he pursued with more persistence when he was President. But his attempt to claim the Floridas provoked charges that he was devious and secretive and that he failed to take Congress into his confidence.

This was in part because Jefferson, despite his frequent strictures against executive power, believed that "the transaction of business with foreign nations is Executive altogether." [6] Moreover he had always recognized that diplomacy was a delicate and hazardous game in which strategy must be masked and intentions concealed. It is one of the curious facets of Jefferson's character that despite his open and honest manner he could engage in diplomatic *realpolitick* with consumate skill.

Jefferson always professed to believe that the Louisiana cession certainly included West Florida (the region south of the 31st parallel and west of the Apalachicola River). Since the diplomatic game dictates that one always claims more than one is likely to get in the final bargain, Jefferson and Madison also at various times put forward claims to East Florida (most of the present state) and Texas. The claim to the Floridas was more than mere acquistiveness. Though less important than New Orleans, possession of the Florida gulf coast by Spain blocked the river outlets of the entire Mississippi Territory (the present states of Alabama and Mississippi). Early in 1804 Congress enacted an administrative revenue bill which established a revenue district for "Mobile," and this, along with American territorial claims presented in Madrid by the American Minister Charles Pinckney aroused the Spanish government to indignant protest. The Spanish minister in Washington, Yrujo, protested the usurpation of Spanish territorial rights implied in the Mobile Act. Madison soothed him by insisting the United States merely wanted to control shipping which entered the United States by way of the Mobile river and that the control would be exercised on the American side of the boundary at Fort Stoddert. [7]

Nevertheless, it seems certain that Jefferson and Madison were not altogether displeased at the Spanish reaction. The implied threat was not so much of belligerent action by the United States government but the expansion of truculent American frontiersmen who might be difficult to restrain from taking what they considered to be theirs by "natural right."

Monroe, who was in England, was ordered to Madrid early in 1804 to assist Pinckney. He travelled by way of Paris to see if perhaps the good offices of Napoleon could be obtained to persuade the Spanish into a more amenable attitude. Monroe found only hostility in Paris, and his mission to Spain was a failure, as Jefferson expected that it would be.[8] For the next year Jefferson and Madison pursued a policy of alternate bluster and conciliation. "We want nothing of hers, . . ." the President wrote to Monroe's successor, James Bowdoin, "But she has met our advances with jealousy, secret malice and ill-faith." It was up to Spain to "decide whether our relations with her are to be sincerely friendly, or permanently hostile."[9] Actually, Jefferson was waiting for the same kind of fortuitous circumstances which had yielded up Louisiana. He thought he saw an opportunity with the renewal of the European war and the British naval victory at Trafalgar in 1805, followed by the matching victory of Napoleon at Austerlitz. With the balance thus struck, Jefferson thought that both powers would be anxious to curry favor with the United States. Napoleon might be induced to further American plans for acquiring Florida by exerting pressure on Spain. For once, Jefferson's judgement was completely awry.

In the first message to the Ninth Congress in December, 1805, the President followed his strategy of bluff and guile. His public message was a mildly belligerent castigation of Spanish offenses, with references to obstructed commerce, "our citizens . . . seized and their property plundered," and orders to troops "to protect our citizens." A few days later he sent a secret message in which he requested an appropriation of $2,000,000 for foreign negotiations.[10] The message was referred to John Randolph's House Ways and Means Committee. Randolph, the administration leader in the House during the first term, was already irritated at what he regarded as Jefferson's abandonment of the strict construction Republicanism of 1798. He had also denounced the role of the administration in the Yazoo land frauds.

This bizarre episode involved an enormous land grant in the Mississippi Territory which the Georgia legislature had made to the Yazoo Land Company in 1795. The corruption and bribery among the legislators had been so blatant that a newly elected legislature had repealed the cession. But the Yazoo Company had already made a number of bona fide sales to honest buyers. Madison and Gallatin had been appointed as commissioners to settle the tangled affair and had arranged a compromise compensation to the supposedly innocent victims in 1803. Randolph, ignoring the fact that no settlement could have been made with justice to all concerned, savagely attacked Madison and Gallatin as having condoned a fraud and successfully blocked the passage of the compromise.[11]

Randolph now professed having found in the Florida negotiation confirmation of his worst fears. Despite a confidential explanation from Madison and a plea for cooperation, Randolph charged publicly that the President intended to bribe Napoleon who in turn would blackmail Spain into ceding Florida. Having delivered his denunciation, Randolph then stalled Congressional action by simply leaving town. Without a chairman the Ways and Means Committee could not meet. Finally Barnabas Bidwell, a freshman Representative from Massachusetts of whom Jefferson had already taken note as a successor to Randolph, introduced the appropriation bill, and it passed by a solid majority of seventy-six to fifty-four. It was approved by the Senate in February, 1806.[12] The showdown with the administration was a decisive defeat for Randolph and ended his party leadership. He had already alienated most of Washington with his insults and invective, and it is doubtful that his tempestous spirit could ever have been tamed to the role of an obedient lieutenant.

Jefferson had misjudged the situation in Europe, and his Florida scheme went up in smoke when the collapse of the Third Coalition made Napoleon supreme on the European continent. The Emperor refused to aid the United States by coercing Spain, and within a year his Continental System had cast a pall over Franco-American friendship. Jefferson was by this time deeply involved in commercial warfare with Britain. So the Florida failure, the first important one thus far in Jefferson's presidency, showed him to be fallible, but Randolph became increasingly lonely in his apostasy. Local schisms were beginning to wrack some Republican party organizations in the states, but Jefferson held steadily to his hands-off policy, and his prestige and the control of his administration over national policy were only slightly impaired by the Florida fiasco.[13] An attack of another sort came from the frontier and pitted Jefferson against old enemies.

Aaron Burr, like many another discredited politician, decided to seek his fortune in the West. Exactly what he planned remains a mystery to all save Burr himself, and even he may have kept his schemes so fluid that he could resort to whatever fitted the circumstance. To the Spanish minister Yrujo, he held out the promise of detaching New Orleans and the Southwest and restoring them to Spain. To the British minister Anthony Merry, he offered an independent confederacy friendly to England. To Edward Livingston and Daniel Clark in New Orleans, it was to be a filibustering expedition against Texas and Mexico, a triumphant conquest which Jef-

ferson and Madison were too timid to take.[14] The author of
the Burr Conspiracy was not a very good conspirator. He
talked too much.

The key figure in Burr's scheme was General James Wilkinson. Here was a real conspirator. Although he had been
receiving money from the Spanish government for almost
twenty years for "services rendered," he had retained the
confidence of Washington and Adams, had risen to the rank
of brigadier general, and had recently been appointed governor of the Louisiana Territory by President Jefferson. He
would subsequently survive two government investigations
and become senior general of the United States Army. The
only crisis to which he was unequal was facing the enemy in
combat. Two biographies have traced his career and their
titles are a fitting historical epitaph: *The Tarnished Warrior*
and *The Finished Scoundrel.*[15]

Burr had conferred with Wilkinson in the spring of 1805,
when the former had gone west to lay the groundwork for
his schemes. Now, in the summer of 1806, Burr had recruited
the services—and money—of one Harmon Blennerhassett, a
wealthy expatriate Irishman who owned an island in the Ohio
River just below Wheeling. Here Burr intended to embark
with the nucleus of an armed force and move downriver
toward New Orleans, recruiting as he went. Wilkinson was
now commanding government troops guarding the Spanish
frontier on the Sabine river, an ideally strategic spot from
which he could deal with any contingency which might
arise.[16]

Reports of a western conspiracy had been filtering into
Washington since early summer, and even the newspapers
had picked up garbled stories. By the time Burr made his
move early in November, reports from reliable sources had
thoroughly alarmed the President, but he reacted cau-
tiously.[17] He was justifiably confident that western loyalty to

the union would render Burr impotent. He was also being careful not to move until the conspirator had committed himself to the extent that his conviction for treason would be certain.

The slippery Wilkinson now decided that it was time for him to make his play. Correctly estimating that Burr's scheme would collapse, he sent a dispatch to Washington warning of the plot—and so transformed himself from conspirator to savior of the republic. He marched to New Orleans and arrested a number of people thought to be Burr's henchmen. Jefferson received Wilkinson's dispatch on November 25 and immediately issued a proclamation denouncing the "criminal conspiracy" and ordering the authorities to take proper action. By the time Burr reached Natchez early in February, 1807, the game was up. After a futile attempt to escape into the Mississippi Territory, he was arrested.[18]

Burr was taken to Richmond for trial since the "overt act" of embarking with a body of armed men had occurred in Virginia (now West Virginia). Jefferson displayed an uncharacteristic vindictiveness in his eagerness to see Burr convicted. He furnished documents and instructions to the prosecuting attorney, George Hay, and publicly expressed his belief that Burr was guilty. Whether this grew out of his desire to get rid of this nemesis once and for all or whether he felt that as President he was justified in dealing harshly with the threat of treason, his hopes were thwarted.

Chief Justice John Marshall, presiding judge for the Richmond circuit, made it clear from the outset that he had not softened his attitude toward Jefferson and the Republican administration. He even assented to the issuance of a subpoena ordering the President to testify. Jefferson coldly refused and cited Marshall's own dictum on the principle of separation of powers which forbade the judiciary to control the executive. However, he did submit documents to the court which had been subpoenaed as evidence by Burr's defense counsel. But the Chief Justice, whether intentionally or not, rendered a signal service to the history of American jurisprudence. He narrowly construed the definition of treason, ruling out all evidence except that which bore on the specific "overt act" at Blennerhassett's Island.[19] He thus virtually eliminated the charge of treason as a means of suppressing political opposition, a practice which had been common in England during the seventeenth and eighteenth centuries.

Under the restrictions of the Chief Justice, the testimony of the prosecution's star witness Wilkinson and others on the periphery of the plot was worthless, and Burr's acquittal assured. It was perhaps as well that it was left to history rather than to a partisan President to render the final verdict on Aaron Burr.

The Quarrel with England

It may seem strange to present day students that the diplomats of the early nineteenth century spent so much time arguing questions of international law and attached so much importance to both legal and moral issues. It is possibly farfetched to say that the philosophy of the Enlightenment, with its emphasis on natural rights based on the law of nature, could have an impact on the diplomacy of two great powers locked, as they believed, in a struggle for survival. But legality counted for something in the wars of the French Revolution and Napoleon. In England the various ministries had to maintain political support if they were to remain in power, and they often defended their policies on the basis of international law. Britain and Napoleon may have treated American diplomats with condescension and even insult, but neither was unaware of the dominant American position in the Western Hemisphere or of the importance of American shipping.

The United States constantly appealed to "the law of nations" because the moral position suited its situation. There were two reasons for this. The United States was a second-rate power, and its was obvious that its naval strength could not be developed to the point of protecting American commerce. International law was therefore one of the few weapons of diplomacy available. Also the United States had, by virtue of its geography, free security, and it could therefore afford to assume the stance of morality. Its commerce might be plundered and its ports virtually blockaded, but its national existence could not be threatened, as Britain had already discovered in 1783 and was to discover again in 1814. The fact remained that since the United States chose to play the game of international law both Britain and France paid more than lip service to it in order to influence American policy. When *HMS Leander* fired upon an American ship and killed one of her crew and later when the *USS Chesapeake* was fired on, Britain offered apologies and at least went through the motions of reprimanding the responsible naval commanders.

The situation in which the United States found itself when the Peace of Amiens came to an end in 1803 was a familiar one to both Jefferson and Madison. The United States was once more the most important neutral carrier of goods to both belligerents, and each alternately sought to suppress American trade with its enemy and utilize American shipping to its advantage. In the case of England, however, the practice of impressing American seamen into the royal navy was an issue which far outweighed all others, and it continued to be the great obstacle to any possible Anglo-American *rapprochement*.

England justified impressment on the ground that thousands of men from her chronically short-handed navy were deserting to American merchant ships and even to the American navy. This was undoubtedly true for, as the great mutinies of 1797 had demonstrated, British sailors would go to any lengths to escape the living hell of the royal navy. Probably over 6,000 of them found refuge aboard American vessels. They were eagerly signed on by American captains whose crews were also frequently shorthanded. The American merchant marine in 1805 had doubled in size since 1793, and the value of its imports was four times as great.[20]

The British government also insisted that its citizens had no right to expatriation—that is, "once a subject always a subject." Jefferson denied this, saying that "they cannot take from a citizen his natural right of divesting himself of the character of a citizen by expatriation."[21] With no physical distinctions to go by, it was difficult to establish bona fide citizenship, especially on the deck of a merchant vessel before a hard-eyed British boarding officer. It was understandable that a captain of His Majesty's Navy would not be too particular if his ship lacked hands—and the British navy always lacked hands. The number of American seamen who found themselves serving involuntarily under the Union Jack was approximately the same as the number of British deserters—about six or seven thousand.[22]

The fact that this violation of American rights involved the freedom of individuals rather than the loss of ships or cargoes gave it an emotional quality that damned Britain in America as did no other issue. In the halls of Congress, in the newspapers, on the political stump, one had only to mention "the barbarous THEFTS OF AMERICAN CITIZENS" to be sure of a thoroughly aroused audience.[23]

With the renewal of the war, Britain also revived the Rule of 1756 which prohibited neutral trade in time of war where it had not been permitted in time of peace. This struck hard at American trade with the French and Spanish West Indies, which was particularly valuable to Middle Atlantic and southern ports. Merchants in these areas provided flour, wheat, corn, and lumber to the sugar islands and exported West Indian products to Europe. This was not permitted by the French mercantile system in time of peace. When war broke out, the homelands found it difficult to supply their islands, especially after Trafalgar, so they removed restrictions on colonial trade. Until 1805, Britain permitted the West Indian trade under the Admiralty Court decision of 1800 in the case of the *Polly,* which permitted re-export if the goods were first landed in an American port and paid a duty. This is known as the doctrine of "broken voyage." In 1805, however, the court reversed this decision in the case of the *Essex.* Here the burden was put on the shipper to show that his cargo was intended for permanent landing in the United States. The *Essex* decision revived the full force of the Rule of 1756.[24]

Madison and Jefferson also had difficulties with the American principle that "free ships make free goods." As in the 1790's the United States made no headway in gaining acceptance of this doctrine by Great Britain. The French government, which had accorded it some recognition in the past, also refused to accept it. Napoleon decided to play the game of commercial warfare with his Continental System, which was designed to exclude British trade from Europe and establish economic self-sufficiency throughout his domain.

By the time Jefferson began his second term, it was evident that the two great antagonists were engaged in a fight to the finish. As the struggle became more and more desperate, each became less considerate of the amenities of international law and neutral rights. Senator Samuel Smith was led to remark in 1806, "The law of nations is with us, the law of power is against us." [25]

The Monroe-Pinkney Treaty

James Monroe, having shuttled back and forth among London, Paris, and Madrid, finally came to rest as the American minister in London. He reported to Madison in January, 1806, that the new coalition ministry headed by Charles James Fox seemed·to be more inclined to Anglo-American friendship than that of his predecessor William Pitt, who had died the previous year.[26] Fox ordered the recall of Anthony Merry, the British minister in Washington, and the little capital heaved a sigh of relief officially and unofficially. Mr. Merry had not been able to adjust himself to republican manners nor to Jeffersonian informality. His formidable wife had been vastly offended when the President failed to escort her into the dining room when they were invited to dinner. Jefferson subsequently announced that he recognized no rank or precedent on such occasions and that his guests proceeded on the principle of "pell mell" and "next to the door." Washington society immediately dubbed the minister "Toujours Gai" and snubbed his wife. David Erskine, who replaced him, found Washington's easy social ways to his liking, and the feeling was mutual.[27]

Fox was in the difficult position of trying to ease Anglo-American tension and at the same time mollify the followers of Pitt who advocated a hard line. Here, in fact, was illustrated the two opposing English points of view. The Pittites (unlike Pitt himself) represented the traditionalists who clung to the old principles of the Navigation Acts. They believed that if American commerce profited it was bound to be at the expense of Britain. "The English hate us because they think our prosperity filched from theirs," said Jefferson.[28] But there were other Englishmen who represented the rising manufacturing interests and advocated a more modern approach. Unfortunately they did not yet have political power, but they believed that the profits to American merchants would be spent in the purchase of English manufactures. "Indeed," said Lord Holland, a spokesman for the Fox ministry, "the more powerful and wealthy they become, the better it would be for this country . . . and increased riches would only give them increased means of consumption." [29]

In an effort to please everyone, including the United States, the Fox ministry issued an Order in Council of April, 1806, which declared the coast of Europe under blockade from Brest to the Elbe. This answered the hard liners. As a gesture to the United States the minstry indicated that enforcement would be limited to the French ports on the English Channel and that the *Essex* rule would not be applied to American shipping outside this sensitive area. In effect, the ministry was saying that Americans could re-export West Indian goods to Europe if they avoided the Channel ports.[30] Whether this would have paved the way for better understanding, Jefferson was not fully convinced of England's good faith. Its good intention, if any, was virtually nullified by the *Leander* episode in April, 1806. An American seaman was killed accidentally when the British vessel fired a shot intended to warn an American merchantman to heave to. Since it occurred in American territorial waters, public opinion was thoroughly aroused and the President ordered British vessels out of New York Harbor and demanded the court martial of the *Leander*'s commander.[31] Fox complied on his deathbed, and with his passing went the last real hope of an amicable settlement with England.

Meanwhile Jefferson had decided to arm the administration with some diplomatic leverage. He indicated in January, 1806, that Congress should enact legislation which would apply restrictions on British imports. Barnabas Bidwell, the fledgeling administration leader in the House, fumbled, and Jefferson seemed unwilling to supply the needed direction.

Finally Senator Samuel Smith of Maryland took the initiative
and introduced a non-importation bill calling for restrictions
on a selected list of British manufactured goods. Both the
degree of restriction and the effective date of enforcement
were left to the President. The bill had stormy passage in the
House. Randolph railed at it as a "milk-and-water bill, a dose
of chicken broth." A substitute bill by Andrew Gregg of
Pennsylvania which would have excluded all British imports
was suppressed with difficulty. Finally a version of Smith's
bill was enacted in March, but the Maryland senator was not
through.[32]

General Smith headed a delegation which called on Jefferson and recommended an extraordinary mission to England.
The senators forcefully reminded him of "the responsibility
which failure to obtain redress would throw on . . . both [the
Senate and the President]." Jefferson found it necessary "to
yield my own opinion to the general sense of the national
council, and," he added sardonically, "it really produced a
jubilee among them." [33]

This would involve sending a special envoy to assist
Monroe. Jefferson was afraid that Monroe would consider
this an implied rebuke of his services, and indeed he did. As
to the appointment of the envoy, Jefferson selected William
Pinkney, a Maryland Federalist, and this offended Senator
Smith who probably wanted the appointment himself.[34]
Pinkney sailed at the end of May, 1806, with instructions to
seek to establish the American position on all points of dis-
pute: free ships made free goods; blockades, to be legal, must
be enforced at the point of violation; American territorial
waters must be respected. There were two indispensable conditions to a settlement. The practice of impressment on the
high seas must cease, and some satisfactory arrangement
would have to be made concerning the American re-export
of West Indian goods to Europe.[35]

The instructions dismayed Monroe. He went so far as to question whether Jefferson and Madison were trying to ruin his political reputation. It was obvious to him that England would pay little heed to the "chicken broth" threat of the Non-Importation Act.[36] It was an ill omen for the mission that Charles Fox became fatally ill just as Pinkney arrived. The negotiations dragged on, delayed by the confusion caused by Fox's death in mid-September. Finally, on the last day of 1806, a treaty was signed.

Monroe and Pinkney had abandoned the administration view on impressment, and the issue was not mentioned in the treaty. Instead they accepted a note in which the British government promised "the observance of greatest caution in the impressing of British seamen." So far as the Rule of 1756 was concerned, the re-export trade would be allowed if goods were landed in the United States and a two per cent duty paid. To complicate the situation, in November Napoleon had issued his Berlin Decree declaring the British Isles to be under blockade. Monroe and Pinkney were given to understand that Britain expected the United States "to do what they ought to do" in resisting the French decree. The treaty also pledged the United States to refrain from any commercial retaliation against Great Britain for ten years. There were minor restrictions on the trade with India, and nothing was said about trade with the British West Indies.[37]

The arrival of the treaty in the United States had repercussions which were political as well as diplomatic. Jefferson was deeply disappointed, for it meant that not only had the threat of non-importation been ineffective but that Monroe had failed in his mission. "The British commisrs appear to have screwed every article as far as it would bear, to have taken everything and yielded nothing." Senator Smith, invited by Madison to comment, saw an intent on the part of Britain, not simply to defeat Napoleon, but to cripple or destroy

American trade as an end in itself. The treaty, he said, "would completely prostrate our trade at the feet of G. B. . . . . . We ought to risque every consequence that can possibly result to us, even war, rather than . . . binding ourselves to such an instrument." [38]

Jefferson decided that the treaty should not even be submitted for Senate consideration. This was bound to have a political effect, as Senator Smith noted: "What a responsibility he takes! By sending it back he disgraces his ministers and *Monroe is one*. . . . 'Why was it refused?' Jealousy of Monroe and unreasonable antipathy by Jefferson and Madison to Great Britain!—this will be said and this will be believed. And Monroe will be brought forward, new parties will arise, and those adverse politically will be brought together by interest. . . . Monroe will be called a martyr but the martyr will be the President." [39]

Jefferson wrote to Monroe that he was inclined to "let the negotiation take a friendly nap." He had one of his fearful headaches, and this always sapped his energy. He decided not to invoke the Non-Importation Act, believing that, "one or the other may be disposed to yield the points which divide us." As he had frequently done before, he was counting on "time, the most precious of all things to us." [40]

Jefferson's "Dambargo"

Admiral Sir George Berkeley, commander of His Majesty's naval forces in American waters, was an angry man. Reports had reached him at Halifax in the late spring of 1807 that four seamen had deserted from *HMS Melampus*, anchored off Norfolk in the Chesapeake Bay. The probable reason for the admiral's rage was not so much the desertions but the impudence of the deserters. They had gotten ashore in the captain's gig. They had brazenly enlisted in the crew of the *USS Chesapeake*. They had then strutted openly through the streets of Norfolk in their American uniforms insulting and taunting British officers whom they met. Commodore James Barron, the American commander, refused to deliver them up to the British even though he knew they were deserters, and the British knew that he knew. (They did not know that Barron believed the men were Americans who had been impressed.)

A general order went out from Halifax: when the *Chesapeake* could be found outside American waters the deserters were to be recovered. The occasion came on June 22. The *Chesapeake,* fresh from overhaul, put to sea bound for the Mediterranean, her decks littered with gear and her guns unserviceable. *HMS Leopard* followed from her anchorage in Lynnhaven Bay. The ships reached international waters and the British commander demanded that the *Chesapeake* heave to for search. When Barron refused, the *Leopard* opened fire and nearly blew the *Chesapeake* out of the water. Barron was forced to strike his colors and submit to the removal of the four deserters.[41] The execution of Berkeley's order had resulted in an act of war against a vessel of the United States Navy.

The nation roared defiance. Said Senator Wilson Cary Nicholas of Virginia, "I would instantly employ force to avenge the injury. . . . I would not ask; I would take satisfaction." The citizens of Amelia County, Virginia, resolved to "consider the attack on the Frigate *Chesapeake,* as the commencement of a war on the United States by the British Government." [42] According to Louis Turreau, the French minister in Washington, Jefferson angrily declared, "If the English do not give us the satisfaction we demand, we shall take Canada . . . and when, together with Canada, we shall have the Floridas, we shall no longer have any difficulties with our neighbors." But the President did not call Congress into special session. He cooled the flaming temper of the country in order to give England "an opportunity to disavow & make reparations." He would leave to Congress the choice of what measures were to be taken. "In the meantime we shall make all preparations which time will permit, so as to be ready for any alternative." [43]

This last was an obvious reference to military preparedness. Jefferson was painfully conscious of the weakness of American defense forces. His military policy was based on several factors. He shared the general dislike and fear of most Americans for a large army. In the world of his time such military forces, he felt, were incompatible with democratic government. He had been alarmed at the militaristic pretensions of Hamilton and the Federalists during the undeclared war with France, and in his first message to Congress he had said that "it is not conceived needful or safe that a standing army should be kept up in time of peace." [44] Moreover, he detested war, believing it to be both immoral and wasteful, and he was convinced that the security and welfare of the nation could be maintained by skillful diplomacy.

He was not unaware of the necessity for military security. In 1805 he had drawn up a detailed militia bill (which Congress never considered) providing for classification by age groups of all adult males fit for military service. The youngest men, those between the ages of 19 and 26, would be required to train "one whole day each month." These would provide a force for an immediate emergency until the rest of the nation's manpower could be mobilized. [45] As for the navy, his famous gunboats represented a compromise. They were designed primarily for inshore defense, providing a mobility which would, he thought, be superior to fixed and expensive shore fortifications. He asked for funds to build 300 gunboats, but niggardly congressional appropriations had provided for slightly more than half this number by the time he left office. [46]

As for the fleet, he took a realistic view that it should only be strong enough "to keep the Barbary States in order." It was manifestly impossible to try to attain parity with Great Britain, "that gulph which has swallowed, not only minor navies, but even those of the great second rate powers of the sea." [47] The flaw in his reasoning was his failure to realize that gunboats were useful only if used in conjunction with frigates and fortifications. Yet if his severest critics, then and later, had had their way, the United States would have built vast and expensive armadas for wars that never came.

During the summer and fall, then, Jefferson bided his time, hoping that Monroe might use Britian's embarrassment over the *Chesapeake* incident to gain a diplomatic advantage. Monroe was instructed not only to secure an apology and reparations for the *Chesapeake* but to insist on British abandonment of the right of impressment.[48] Britain did disavow the act and gave reparations for the firing on the *Chesapeake,* but not until years later. In the fall of 1807 it was evident that England was not cowed by war-like emanations from the United States. Not only did Britain reaffirm its right of impressment, but news filtered in that a new Order in Council (November, 1807) was about to be passed which forbade all neutral trade with ports under Napoleon's control unless the trade passed through England.[49] Compliance with this, of course, would subject the neutral vessel to French seizure since calling at an English port would violate the Berlin Decree. Napoleon tightened his system even more by the Milan decree of December, 1807, which declared that any vessel which complied with British orders or submitted to British search would be treated as an enemy.[50]

The cordon was now complete. An American vessel bound for England was subject to seizure by the French; if she were bound for the Continent, she could be seized by the British. When Congress convened in the fall of 1807, Jefferson was prepared to go the limit in commercial warfare. On December 18 he asked Congress to enact an embargo closing American ports to all trade with foreign nations. The bill went through the Senate in a single afternoon. In the House Republican dissension clogged the administration's machinery, but Randolph was reduced to futile hectoring and tearful pleading, and the Federalists were impotent. On December 22 Jefferson signed the bill.[51]

The embargo represented economic warfare on a scale never before conceived. Up to this time an embargo was usually for the purpose of getting merchant ships off the high seas as a preliminary to a declaration of war. Jefferson intended to use it to coerce England and, to a lesser extent, France into respecting American rights. But during the ensuing months it became evident that Jefferson and Madison had overestimated the effect of the embargo as a coercive weapon. This was in part due to the fact that although it did have an impact in England—and a far greater one in the British West Indies—the political system of England was less responsive to popular will than in the United States. Limited suffrage and the "rotten borough" system made it virtually impossible for the lower classes to express their feelings at election time. Merchants and planters interested in the British West Indian trade had lost much of their former influence and were likewise impotent.[52]

Although Jefferson and Madison were ostensibly using the embargo to protect American sailors and ships, their real aim was, of course, to coerce England into concession. Nobody doubted this, and some enraged Federalists charged that Jefferson was being paid by Napoleon to aid him against England. George W. Campbell, Jeffersonian Congressman from Tennessee, almost killed Federalist Barent Gardinier of New York in a duel, but the critics were not silenced. The opposition of New England merchants was especially vocal and violent. Since their trade was directed primarily to the British Isles, they had suffered less from British depredations on their commerce. The merchants of the Middle Atlantic and southern ports, except for the tobacco interests, traded extensively with the West Indies and re-exported their goods to the Continent. These merchants therefore stood to benefit much more both from the administration's professed purpose, to keep American ships and sailors safely in port, and from the coercive effects which would hopefully force the relaxation of British restrictions. They therefore supported the embargo, and their support was far more effective than the outcries of the Federalist press—and subsequent historians—would indicate.[53] When Congress reconvened a year later in the fall of 1808, Senator James Hillhouse, a Massachusetts Federalist, introduced a resolution to repeal the embargo. Senator Smith, a wealthy Baltimore merchant, led the defense of the embargo, and Hillhouse's resolution was smothered by a vote of twenty-five to six.[54]

Nevertheless, with elections in the offing, the political pressure was beginning to be felt, not only from merchants, but from farmers whose export crops were going to waste. Secretary of the Treasury Gallatin complained of increasing violations and asked Jefferson for more stringent means of enforcement. The President himself was disgusted with "the frauds of unprincipled individuals who . . . are enriching themselves on the sacrifices of their honester fellow citizens." [55] His message to Congress in November urged continuation of the embargo. It also recommended increased measures for strengthening the military and naval forces should it become necessary "to repel a powerful enemy." [56]

But there was no denying that the country faced an economic depression and that there was rising discontent and impatience. The strident tone of the Boston *Repertory* was not altogether beside the point:

Our ships all in motion,
Once whitened the ocean,
      They sail'd and return'd with a *cargo*.
Now, doom'd to decay
They have fallen a prey
      To Jefferson, worms, and Embargo.

There were eleven more verses.[57]

The Embargo: Success or Failure?

Monroe had come home in December, 1807, to find that he was a central figure in a mild campaign to challenge the presidential claims of Madison, who was Jefferson's choice to succeed him as president. The machinery of the caucus had been so successful as a means of choosing candidates in 1800 and 1804 that Republican leaders used it again to indicate the party nominees for 1808. The cracks and fissures which had been developing in the party structure in the states led some Republican leaders to urge Jefferson to serve a third term. It was evident, however, that the President was determined to retire.

Jefferson had known of Monroe's discontent over his situation in London and had offered to appoint him governor of Louisiana, "the 2nd office in the U.S. in importance." Monroe had refused, and after the repudiation of the Monroe-Pinkney treaty, he had become something of the martyr that General Smith had predicted. At least he seemed a good rallying point for Randolph and his followers. George Clinton was also the focal point for some northern Republican malcontents. Many of the Federalists, desperate for some means to escape oblivion, seemed willing to support a Republican schism.[58]

The real flaw in the schemes of the dissidents was their lack of agreement on a standard bearer. Monroe's strength was in Virginia, where a "rump" Republican caucus in Richmond nominated him in late January, 1808. But the southerners had only contempt for Clinton, and the New Yorker's supporters were less than enthusiastic about Monroe. Also, although neither one made strenuous efforts to disavow his candidacy, each refused to challenge Madison openly. The Congressional caucus nominated Madison at a meeting in Washington on January 23 and cut the ground from under Clinton by again endorsing him for vice-president.[59]

By the fall of 1808 Madison's election was assured, but Republicans were feeling the political pinch of dissatisfaction with the embargo. In the Congressional elections the Federalists doubled their seats in the House of Representatives although they would still be badly outnumbered, forty-eight to ninety-four. In the states, besides making expected gains in New England, the Federalists won control of both houses of the New York legislature and the lower house in Maryland.[60] The Congress which convened in the fall of 1808 had been elected two years previously, and so Jefferson still apparently maintained firm control of the national legislature. But he and the Secretary of State, now president-elect, had no new policies to propose. Indeed, it appeared that executive leadership was sadly wanting as Jefferson declared in his annual message of November 8, 1808, that "it will rest with the wisdom of Congress to decide on the course best adapted to such a state of things." He may have felt a reluctance to institute any new policy because "I think it is fair to leave to those who are to act on them, the decisions they prefer, being . . . myself but a spectator." He thought that there were three alternatives: continuation of the embargo; a resort to war, or at least warlike measures, such as the authorization of privateering; finally, "submission and tribute & wonderful to tell the last will not want advocates." [61] Madison was perhaps just as unwilling to act until he was constitutionally authorized to do so.

Yet Congress was still responsive to the will of the executive. Gallatin, determined to enforce the embargo to the limit, advocated stringent measures. At his request the President asked that customs officials be authorized to search and seize any time anywhere under general warrants and that the armed forces be authorized for enforcement. The necessary legislation was enacted by Congress in January, 1809, by resounding majorities. Rarely had such sweeping executive powers had been granted. The Federalists were enraged. The Baltimore *Federal Republican* thundered that "a law which is to be enforced at the point of a bayonet will bring on a struggle which will terminate in the overthrow of the government." [62]

Somewhat more serious were defiant rallies, town meetings, and legislative resolutions in New England. To Jefferson this was no more than a loud echo of the Essex Junto which he believed "had found their expectation desperate of inducing the people there to either separation or forcible opposition." [63] But he failed to transmit his confidence to Congress. By the end of January the members "in a kind of panic" voted to end the embargo on March 4, the day of Jefferson's retirement.

It was a stunning defeat for the President. The panic was ascribed by the Republican members to fear of New England disunion. More likely it was the realization that the embargo was shattering many a carefully constructed political fence outside New England. A little over a year later Jefferson still could not conceal his anger at the spinelessness of the "lame duck" Tenth Congress. "I ascribe all this," he said, "to one pseudo-Republican, [Joseph] Story. He came on . . . and staid only a few days, long enough however to get complete hold of [Ezekiel] Bacon, who giving into his representations became panick struck, & communicated his panick to his colleagues & they to a majority of the sound members of Congress." [64]

The specific measure which Congress had been debating was a bill sponsored by Wilson Cary Nicholas to extend the embargo until June 1. A special session had already been voted for May, and Congress would then decide what further measures would be taken—presumably, belligerent. After the panic, all thoughts of war-like measures vanished, and March 4 was set as the date for repeal. In place of the embargo, Congress passed the Non-Intercourse Act which continued the restrictions on trade with England and France only. The President was authorized to resume trade with either nation if that nation repealed its restrictions on American trade.[65]

Thus ended the great experiment. Never before or since did the United States resort to such extreme economic coercion, and perhaps never did a president ask his people for greater forebearance and sacrifice in time of peace. Yet Jefferson came closer to success than perhaps even he realized.

At the time that Congress reconvened in the fall of 1808 the British minister, young David Erskine, sent his government a series of alarming reports. Conversations with members of the cabinet, he said, including Gallatin, Secretary of the Navy Robert Smith, and Madison, indicated that the repeal of the embargo would be accompanied by a declaration of war.[66] George Canning, the foreign secretary, was under considerable pressure from the opposition in Parliament, partly because his policy was endangering peace with the United States. On the basis of Erskine's reports Canning issued him new instructions dated January 23, 1809.

These fresh instructions offered the repeal of the Orders in Council of January and November, 1807. The condition was that the United States repeal its embargo on trade with England while continuing to prohibit trade with France.[67] In short, Erskine was authorized to accept virtually what Congress subsequently enacted. In the first weeks of the Madison administration Erskine concluded an agreement with Robert

Smith, the new Secretary of State, which reopened trade with England and secured a "gentlemen's agreement" on impressments.[68] The agreement was repudiated by Canning in May, 1809, after he learned of the repeal of the embargo. Would his actions have been different if the embargo had still been in effect? There were those who thought so.[69] William Pinkney, the American minister in London, wrote to Madison in August, 1809, that Canning's rejection of the Erskine Agreement was due to the "Inability to persevere in a System which was on the point of accomplishing all its Purposes." [70] And Samuel Smith declared in 1810 that the embargo was repealed "at the very moment when Great Britain, smarting under its effects, was modifying her Orders in Council; and she would have done us complete justice but for the wavering, indecisive conduct that she saw we were pursuing." [71] Jefferson himself thought that "we could coerce her [England] to justice by peaceable means, and the embargo . . . would have coerced her, had it been honestly executed." [72]

"Never did a prisoner, released from his chains, feel such relief as I shall on shaking off the shackles of power." If Jefferson felt deep disappointment over the failure of his great experiment, he concealed it in the relief of leaving office "with the most consoling proofs of public approbation." [73]

The second term had been as disappointing as the first had been gratifying. From the Florida debacle to the back-handed reproof which Congress delivered in fixing the date of his retirement as the last day of the embargo, there had been little sense of accomplishment. Ironically the last failure had been sustained despite the fact that he had stretched executive authority to the limit and brought down on his head maledictions which condemned him for betraying the principles of republicanism.

His disappointments were as much the result of unfortunate circumstances over which he had little control as his earlier successes had turned on good fortune. But there was a failure of leadership as well. It is again ironic that this flaw developed from pursuing what had at first been a successful technique. He had avoided using the immense weight of his personal popularity and prestige, particularly in the crisis of the embargo. Congress had faltered partly because it had lacked decisive direction from the President. Much of the popular criticism of his policy was because he himself did not clarify his motives. He and Madison were inclined to explain issues in terms of legalisms and points of international and moral law. He could not bring himself to rally the nation behind a declaration of economic warfare against imperious Britian and the tyrant Napoleon. Hamilton, in similar circumstances, would have wielded his pen like a fiery sword, calling up the patriotism and courage of the citizenry. He would have imposed his will upon subordinates with inflexible purpose and ruthlessly overridden the opposition.

Jefferson did not lack courage. It was simply that he shrank from waging war in the political cockpit. He tolerated the outrageous behavior of Randolph, and he offered Louisiana to a sulking Monroe. These men had been his friends, and he did not have enough iron in his gentle soul even to offend much less to destroy them. If he had, he would not have been Thomas Jefferson.

His old companion Madison invited him to ride with him to the capitol for the inauguration but "I wished not to divide with him the honors of the day." But he was in the audience for Madison's inaugural and attended the ball given in honor of the new president.[74] A week later, on a raw blustering March day, he left Washington for the Little Mountain and home.

XVII The Sage of Monticello

IT WOULD BE A mistake to suppose that because of Jefferson's failure in his last battle with England he left public office in disgrace, pursued by the maledictions of the people. Undoubtedly the embargo was unpopular and undoubtedly many men of both parties were happy that he was gone from Washington. So he left under something of a cloud, but his chosen successor was safely seated in office. Perhaps the Federalists had not been reduced to "malcontents and monarchists," but the election returns seemed to show that his earlier hope that Federalists would be converted to Republicanism had been realized to a considerable degree.

Americans are always prone to forget rather quickly the errors of their leaders. They have always respected a president who has retired and frequently have exhibited a remarkable affection for some who were mediocre or even downright failures. If Jefferson's popularity was diminished upon his retirement, it soon became evident that he was regarded as a hero of the people. Albemarle was hardly the crossroads of the United States, yet in the seventeen years which were left of his life, thousands of people found their way to the village of Charlottesville and climbed the steep winding road to Monticello. The list of names—Lafayette, the Marquis de Chastellux, Benjamin Latrobe, George Ticknor, the Abbe Correa—read like an assembly of the world's notables. But

354

there were the others, the people who were not at all distinguished, who came to look with awe at the man who personified the spirit of freedom and remained to admire his monument to the Enlightenment—Monticello.

Monticello

Jefferson selected the site of his home in 1767, began building it in 1769, and settled on the final plan for it in 1772. It will be remembered that when he brought Martha there as a bride his "home" consisted of a single room which was eventually the south pavilion. Jefferson decided on the architectural design only after the kind of careful study which he brought to any project which he undertook. The style was that of the Roman country villa, which was so much admired by the Italian Renaissance master Andrea Palladio. Yet Jefferson's was not slavish imitation, and he consciously sought to combine the beauty of classical design with the approved standards of architecture and at the same time adapt it to its surroundings. He chose the hilltop site in disregard of prevailing practice because it offered an extensive view of the countryside. The gardens avoided the formal European style because they were surrounded by woods and fields. The design of the building demonstrated its author's grasp of the details of architectural design, but it clearly showed that Jefferson planned it for its basic function as a country residence and farmhouse. In fact, Jefferson almost never referred to Monticello as an "estate" or "seat" but simply as "my farm." [1]

To say that he "built" Monticello is to use that word in almost its literal sense. At the beginning there was a naillery and a brick kiln as well as the usual smithy and carpenter shop. Jefferson, the scientist of the Enlightenment, was also an inveterate mechanic. He furnished Monticello with such innovations as double-sashed windows, which are today called storm windows; a dumb waiter, which led to the wine cellar; and an eight-day clock which had cannon balls for weights. All of his plans for Monticello were never entirely finished, but the building in its present design was completed in the 1790's after he resigned as Secretary of State.[2] It was with him a lifelong task, not just of ornamentation, but of workmanship.

All his life, too, Jefferson expressed his enthusiasm for farming, but he was not a successful farmer. His long absences from his lands and his extravagance, whether in Philadelphia, Paris, or Washington, may well have kept him from becoming a wealthy man. When he came home in 1809, he was determined to live modestly, but his family now included Martha and Thomas Mann Randolph and eleven grandchildren. He had not the heart nor the inclination to turn away the hordes of guests who descended on him, and it was not unusual for fifty of them to gather at the hospitable board of the venerable ex-President.[3]

He had also inherited a large debt from the estate of his father-in-law John Wayles, which he never fully discharged because of problems relating to currency inflation. During the Panic of 1819 his close friend Wilson Cary Nicholas defaulted on notes amounting to $20,000 on which Jefferson was the endorser.[4] So during the whole period of his retirement he was hagridden with debt, and it cast a long shadow over what would otherwise have been the happiest period of his life.

His freedom from public affairs allowed him to devote more time to his lands, and he considered himself a farmer by profession. He owned approximately 200 slaves and 10,-000 acres of land, most of it divided between Albemarle and Poplar Forest in Bedford County. However, he rarely had an income of more than $6,000 to $7,000 a year. He was, of course, a firm believer in the application of science to farming and was insatiable in his desire to learn the latest ideas in crop rotation, fertilization, and farm equipment. He was one of the earliest practitioners of contour plowing and constantly experimented with new crops. Yet the pernicious system of slave labor and the steady deterioration of Virginia farm land was already beginning to take its toll, and even a modern scientific farmer like Jefferson had indifferent success.[5]

He had much to occupy his time. He received over a thousand letters a year, many of them from well wishers but many more which asked for information or advice about science, politics, philosophy, or farming. These he attempted to answer himself. "My mornings are devoted to correspondence. From breakfast to dinner, I am in my shops, my gardens, or on horseback among my farms; from dinner to dark, I give to society and recreation with my neighbors and friends; and from candle light to early bed time, I read."[6]

Of his six children only two daughters survived childhood. Mary, the younger, married John Wayles Eppes, but she died toward the end of Jefferson's first administration. One of her children lived at Monticello. Martha Randolph was a tower of strength to her father as she had always been, and she managed the large household. She was Jefferson's daughter, not pretty, tall, and "loosely made," but charming, gracious, and intelligent. So the patriarch grew old in the midst of his farm and family. His health was excellent for a man of his years. He used spectacles only for night reading, and he rode horseback until shortly before his death.[7] He was distrustful of both medicines and doctors; three of the latter, he said, always attracted buzzards.

The Passing of the Revolutionary Generation

Jefferson's refusal to "share the honors of the day" at Madison's inauguration was a portent of his determination to withdraw completely from the affairs of state. He was conscious of the fact that Madison had been regarded as sort of a junior partner, and he wanted his friend to be President in his own right. Inevitably there were rumors, which were without foundation, that control wires led from Monticello to Washington, but the correspondence between the new President and his predecessor was more infrequent than at any time in the past. The Madisons usually made their annual summer visit as had been their custom for some years, and it is certain that conversation between these two companions of more than three decades ranged over political topics. But Jefferson seldom gave his advice, and Madison almost never sought it. Jefferson was particularly scrupulous in avoiding, even in private correspondence, opinions which might seem critical of his successor. To those who sought his help in securing appointments to public office, he sent a printed circular in which he firmly declined "to interpose . . . in any application whatever." [8]

He watched with obvious anxiety the course of events leading to the War of 1812. Madison's administration was not a happy one, and his cabinet was soon disrupted by a quarrel between Robert Smith, the new Secretary of State, and Gallatin. When Smith resigned Monroe took his place, and this reunion of his two Virginia friends was gratifying. Yet neither the President nor Congress seemed capable of formulating an effective policy. The Non-Intercourse Act was followed in 1810 by Macon's Bill No. 2, which only inspired Napoleon to wily trickery and England to stubborn defiance. Jefferson watched with growing apprehension as the nation became infected with war fever. "When, indeed, peace shall become more losing than war," he wrote in 1811, "[the people] may owe it to their interests what those Quixotes are clamoring for on false estimates of honor." [9]

Once the United States committed itself Jefferson became

a patriotic supporter of the war. "Against such a banditti, war had become less ruinous than peace," he declared. He temporarily forgot his strictures against offering advice, although he was careful to maintain a deferential air. After the failure of the projected invasion of Canada in 1812 "Hull will of course be shot for cowardice & treachery. And will not Van Renslaer be broke for cowardice and incapacity?" [10]

The war rekindled Jefferson's unfulfilled dreams for rounding out his "empire for liberty." He had never given up his hope of acquiring Florida, and he thought the war opened the prospect of the conquest of Canada and "the final expulsion of England from the American continent."

Though these aspirations were not realized, he believed that the United States might at last be freed from the tangle of European polity. "The European nations constitute a separate division of the globe; their localities make them part of a distinct system. . . . America has a hemisphere to itself." The nation had finally achieved true independence, and he foresaw the eventual rise of the United States to world power. "Not in our time but at not a distant one, we may shake a rod over the heads of all, which may make the stoutest of them tremble. But I hope our wisdom grows with our power and teaches us, that the less we use power, the greater it will be." [11]

In a sense the nation had completed its independence. A new nationalism was sweeping the land which manifested itself in several ways. If the United States had not achieved the status of a great power, it was certainly the great power of the Western Hemisphere, and other nations acknowledged it. Great Britain acquiesced in American claims to the Oregon country and looked the other way when Andrew Jackson executed two British subjects in the course of his unauthorized invasion of Spanish Florida in 1817. When the United States bullied the tottering Spanish empire into ceding

Florida and drew the boundaries of Jefferson's Louisiana at the Continental Divide, it did so with impunity. Jefferson observed all this with benevolent approval and allowed his imagination to go even further. The Adams-Oñis Treaty, he said, "has had the valuable effect of strengthening our title to the Techas [Texas]. . . . This province . . . the Floridas and possibly Cuba will join us." [12]

Other manifestations of nationalism alarmed him. The expansion of federal authority implicit in the sweeping decisions of the Supreme Court, over which his old nemesis, Chief Justice John Marshall presided, revived Jefferson's fears of the subversion of state powers. Marshall and the former Federalists, "finding that monarchy is a desperate wish . . . rally to the point which they think next best, a consolidated government. . . . Hence new Republicans in Congress, preaching doctrines of the Old Federalists, and the new nicknames of Ultras and Radicals." But he ruefully reminded himself that the Revolutionary generation was being supplanted by a new era. "If I am right, you will approve; . . . if wrong, commiserate them as the dreams of a Superannuate." [13]

He nevertheless still felt capable of altering his views and refused to surrender completely to the dogmatism of old age. In particular Jefferson realized that the agrarian society which he had praised in the *Notes on Virginia* belonged to an earlier day when peace and friendship existed among the nations of the world and allowed free exchange of goods. The experience of recent years, the embargo and the war itself, had shown "that there exists both profligacy and power enough to exclude us from the field of interchange with other nations. . . . We must now place the manufacturer by the side of the agriculturalist. . . . Experience has taught me that manufactures are now as necessary to our independence as to our comfort." What had not changed was his belief that "no one axiom can be laid down as wise and expedient for all times and circumstances." [14] The earth still belonged to the living.

As Jefferson approached his eightieth birthday, two events perceptibly altered his characteristic cheerfulness and optimism over the progress of his country. The Panic of 1819 struck at a particularly unfortunate time. His farm lands seemed finally to be on the point of recovery as the result of careful cultivation and fertilizing when the panic and the depression which followed drove the prices of his crops down to a pittance. He was heavily in debt to the Bank of the United States in Richmond and the Bank of Virginia, and when they both sharply curtailed credit, he was able to avert bankruptcy only by further borrowing. He bitterly assigned the cause of his distress to "the enormous abuses of the banking system." He had never shared Madison's and Gallatin's approval of Hamilton's Bank of the United States. "We have been truly sowing the wind, and are now reaping the whirlwind," he lamented. [15]

Far more ominous for the future was the storm over the expansion of slavery. Missouri asked for admission to the union in 1819, and when it was proposed that slavery be prohibited in the new state as a condition of admission, Congress erupted in the first full-fledged debate on the question of which Jefferson said, "I consider it at once the knell of the Union." The settlement known as the Missouri Compromise, in his view, solved nothing. "Justice is in one scale, and self-preservation in the other," he said, and he recognized the fateful consequences because it was one with which he had struggled since the day almost half a century ago when he had declared his belief that all men were created equal. [16]

In the end he retreated with Randolph of Roanoke and John Taylor of Caroline to the dusty labyrinth of state sovereignty. He publicly acknowledged his authorship of the Kentucky Resolutions, and when John Quincy Adams delivered his boldly nationalistic message to Congress in 1825, Jefferson drafted a "solemn Declaration and Protest" for the Virginia General Assembly.[17] Although it was not published until after his death, it played its part in the evolution of a party and a doctrine which was sadly out of character for the philosopher of the enlightenment and the apostle of liberty.

The Peculiar Institution

Slavery was something with which Jefferson was never able to come to terms. It had so many ramifications that it was almost impossible to isolate as a scientific or economic or social or political question. It was a subject which intruded into his life as a philosopher and as a statesman, as a person with a warm attachment to people and as a scientist who, while he believed in an orderly world of natural law, realized that man's knowledge of it was incomplete.

The *Notes on Virginia* had contained his first attempt to present a comprehensive view of both the scientist and the philosopher. There was no question about the moral judgement of the philosopher. "Can the liberties of a nation be thought secure when we have removed their only firm basis, a conviction in the minds of the people that these liberties are of the gift of God? That they are not to be violated but with his wrath? I tremble for my country when I reflect that God is just and that his justice will not sleep forever. . . . The Almighty has no attribute which can take side with us in this contest." [18]

The scientist was beset by serious doubts and contradictions. "I advance it as a suspicion only, that the blacks, whether originally a distinct race, or made distinct by time and circumstances, are inferior to the whites in endowments of both body and mind. It is not against experience to suppose that different species of the same genes, or varieties of the same species, may possess different qualifications." So, in a very tentative way, Jefferson arrived at the conclusion of biological inferiority which most of his contemporaries accepted with firm conviction. He believed that blacks were "in reason much inferior," but he was careful to note that it was necessary to "make great allowance for the differences of condition, of education, of conversation, of the sphere in which they move." [19]

There was no doubt in his mind about the necessity for an eventual solution. His efforts to mitigate its effects in the laws of Virginia and the western ordinance have already been noted. The twenty-year Constitutional ban on legislation affecting the slave trade expired during his second administration, and he had promptly recommended, and Congress passed, a law prohibiting the importation of slaves. [20] That little was done to enforce the prohibition may be partly attributed to the fact that his last months in office were overshadowed by the chaotic events of the commercial war with England.

Famous as he was, Jefferson's views on slavery were widely read and provoked a great deal of comment and controversy. He was criticized almost as severely by opponents of slavery as by its defenders. He characteristically ignored most of this although he must have been outraged by attacks such as that of James Callander and others who circulated the allegation that he was guilty of sexual relations with the slave girl Sally Hemings. [21] But he was genuinely interested in whatever seemed to be contradictions of his ideas. Benjamin Banneker, a Negro mathematician and astronomer, first came to Jefferson's attention when Banneker was appointed to the commission to survey the federal district iñ 1791, an appointment made through the Secretary of State. Later Banneker published an almanac, a copy of which Jefferson sent to his friend the Marquis de Condorcet. Jefferson expressed the hope that Banneker was an example of the fact that "the want of talents in them [Negroes] is merely the effect of their degraded condition, and not proceeding from any difference in the structure of the parts on which intellect depends." [22]

After his retirement Jefferson continued to express his concern over slavery. Beyond his recognition of the conflict between the existence of slavery—Jefferson himself owned over 200—and his natural rights philosophy, he found himself in the dilemma which he had long recognized. "Deep rooted prejudices entertained by the whites, ten thousand recollections, by the blacks, of the injuries they have sustained; new provocations; the real distinctions which nature has made; and many other circumstances will . . . produce convulsions which will probably never end but in the extermination the one or the other race." [23] He recognized two infinitely difficult problems inherent in universal emancipation: the fact that the slaves would be "as incapable as children of taking care of themselves" and the impossibility, as he thought, of the two races living peaceably together. Jefferson concluded that the only solution was gradual emancipation and deportation of the black population either to Santo Domingo or Africa. But he did not think this or any solution would come in the immediate future.[24]

He regretted that the Revolutionary generation had not "sympathized with oppression wherever found, and proved their love of liberty beyond their own share of it." He himself felt that he had done all he could do. When his aid was solicited in the various causes for emancipation by people like the historian Jared Sparks or the young feminist and liberal Fanny Wright he excused himself "These . . . I must leave to another generation. . . . and I pray to heaven for their success." [25]

Mr. Jefferson's University

The principal task to which Jefferson addressed himself in his retirement was the reform of Virginia's educational system. His belief that education was an essential ingredient of a free society was a theme reiterated at every stage of his long career. One of his earliest disappointments was the failure of his native state to adopt his general education bill of 1778. As the War of 1812 drew to a close, he determined to devote his energies to the promotion of his plans. Before he was done he had utilized every weapon in his considerable arsenal: his talent for meticulous planning; his enormous political and personal prestige; his political cunning; his talents as engineer and architect. It may well have been that he shied away from participation in any emancipation schemes because he felt that it would deprive him of public support for the fulfillment of his educational program. The former he did not believe was possible in the immediate future, certainly not in the years left to him. The latter he thought he might be able to realize. In this he was also doomed to diappointment, for his plan included a system of general education "to enable every man to judge for himself what will secure or endanger his freedom." [26] Virginia was perhaps less inclined to accept his comprehensive system of local "ward" and district schools than in 1778. He did, however, manage to bring to fruition his plan to establish a state university.

After his earlier failure to renovate William and Mary he had tried in 1806 to arouse interest in a national university, but Congress was unresponsive. Now, in 1814, he proposed a new state university to be the capstone of his educational system. Georgia, North Carolina, South Carolina, and Tennessee had already established state institutions although some were still in the planning stage. Except for William and

Mary, the only "higher education" available was in the small private academies which, as Jefferson remarked to John Adams, gave their students "just taste enough of learning to be alienated from industrious pursuits, and not enough to do service in the ranks of science." [27]

The state university which Jefferson planned grew out of one such academy which was planned by his neighbors. Invited to serve on the board of Albemarle Academy, he enlarged the original plan so that the charter provided for the establishment of a college designed to reach the level of a state university. Through Joseph Cabell, Albemarle's representative in the legislature, and with the sympathetic support of his friend Governor Wilson Cary Nicholas, Jefferson pushed forward a plan for a comprehensive system designed to provide education for all classes. It included tax-supported elementary schools, classical schools or "colleges" surprisingly similar to the modern community colleges, and vocational trade schools to train artisans and mechanics.[28] Unfortunately such a comprehensive plan was far beyond the limited financial support which the General Assembly was willing to grant. The bills providing for the establishment of the lower schools which were introduced in 1817 were emasculated in legislative committees so that what finally emerged was essentially the continuation of the existing system of county "charity" schools for the poor.

Cabell managed to salvage something from the wreckage. He attached a rider that appropriated the small fund available for the support of a state university to the final bill.[29] Jefferson had already selected a site just west of Charlottesville, and the cornerstone of the first building was laid in 1817 in a ceremony attended by the Board of Visitors (trustees). Rarely has a university been started under such distinguished auspices. The board included the President of the United States and his two predecessors. Two years later the General Assembly granted a charter for the University of Virginia.[30]

Jefferson the architect and engineer now went to work laying out plans for an academic community. The center of this community was the Rotunda which housed the library. Ranged on either side of "The Lawn" were rows of rooms for housing students, interspersed with "pavilions" or residences to house the professors of each of the ten colleges. The pavilions, like the Rotunda, were of classic design, each containing an individual facade modeled on famous buildings of antiquity. Additional quarters for students were constructed in the form of two "ranges" parallel to the sides of the quadrangle, which was left open at the end opposite the Rotunda.[31]

But these were only plans. Jefferson personally supervised the buildings over the next few years, always insisting that workmanship be of the highest order. Such meticulous care led to some extravagances. For instance, Italian artisans were brought to America to fashion the Ionic and Corinthian capitals for the Rotunda and the pavilions. When it was found that Virginia stone was not suitable for their intricate design, Jefferson arranged for them to be made in Italy and transported to Charlottesville.[32]

The most important aspect of the development of the new institution was the selection of a faculty. Jefferson was determined not to have the university decline into an academy of classical learning as had occurred with many colleges. He flatly refused to consider a school of divinity or the appointment of clergymen to the faculty. Pious critics at once charged that he was creating a Godless university, but he reminded them of the principles of separation of church and state and cannily suggested that religion would be included in the teaching of literature, philosophy, and moral law.[33]

His search for a faculty proved to be arduous and difficult. He persuaded Thomas Cooper, whom he considered to be the greatest scientific mind in America, to accept a position.

Eventually, however, Cooper's views on religion aroused such opposition among church leaders, particularly the Presbyterians, that Jefferson felt it necessary to withdraw his appointment.[34] It was one of the most galling compromises of his life. He had hoped to be able to find qualified professors in America, but he finally had to send his neighbor and friend Frances Walker Gilmer to recruit in Europe. Gilmer eventually found six scholars in England and Scotland, not men of such eminence as Jefferson had hoped for, but well qualified. The chair of law and philosophy was filled by George Tucker, scion of a prominent Virginia family and former member of Congress.[35]

For a man of nearly eighty his industry was amazing. He cajolled his political friends for financial aid from the legislature. He wrote anonymous articles for Thomas Ritchie's Richmond *Enquirer* appealing to the public for support, thus overcoming his life-long aversion to pamphleteering. He summoned the Board of Visitors to deal with matters of policy and planning. And almost daily he rode down from Monticello to supervise the work on the buildings and grounds. Early in 1825 he wrote, "The Professors of our University, 8. in number, are all engaged . . . and on their arrival the whole will assemble and enter their duties." About fifty students enrolled the first year and over a hundred in the second.[36]

At last the University of Virginia became a reality. Toward the end of 1825 he wrote to William Branch Giles, "I fear not to say that within twelve or fifteen years from this time, a majority of the rulers of our State will have been educated here. . . . I cannot live to see it. My joy must only be that of anticipation." [37]

The University of Virginia, more than any other, was the embodiment of the ideas and energy of one man. It was, indeed, Thomas Jefferson's university.

Just before Christmas, 1825, Jefferson wrote to his old friend and foe John Adams, replying to the latter's question whether "I should be willing to go again over the scenes of past life. I should not be unwilling, without however wishing it. And why not? I have enjoyed a greater share of health than falls to the lot of most men; and my spirits never failed me . . . and with good health and good spirits the pleasures surely outweigh the pains of life. Why not then taste them again, fat and lean together?" [38]

One of the great satisfactions of his retirement was the reconciliation with Adams brought about through the efforts of a mutual friend Dr. Benjamin Rush in 1812. The correspondence between the two heroes of the Revolution was a rich legacy for future generations. Adams was far more prolific than Jefferson and showed an eagerness to relive the events of the past. Jefferson was much more interested in discussing science and philosophy. Adams, with cantankerous geniality, recalled for Jefferson the bloody failure of the French Revolution. Jefferson twitted the Sage of Quincy with reminders of aristocratic Federalism and the Essex and Hartford men. But Jefferson generally refused to be drawn into controversy, answering Adams' bombastic denunciation of the idea of the perfectability of man with comments on Botta's *History of the American Revolution.* Both men were obviously delighted with themselves and with each other. "Mr. Jefferson and I have grown old and retired from public life," said Adams, "So we are upon our ancient terms of good w??." [39]

As 1825 drew to a close, Jefferson's health began to fail. It was as though the completion of the University drained him of his last energies and the will at last permitted the amazingly durable body to spend itself. A disease of the urinary tract struck him down in his eighty-third year. In March, 1826, he knew he had not long to live. [40]

In June he declined an invitation to go to Washington to attend the fiftieth anniversary of the Declaration of Independence. He hoped, he said, that the Fourth of July would continue to be "the signal of arousing men to burst the chains under which monkish ignorance and superstition had persuaded them to bind themselves, and to assume the blessings and security of self-government." [41] It was on that memorable day that he died, and to the north, at Quincy, John Adams also died with Jefferson's name on his lips. As he wished, Jefferson was buried on the mountain of Monticello under a plain brownstone obelisk. "Here was buried Thomas Jefferson, Author of American Independence, of the Statute of Virginia for religious freedom & Father of the University of Virginia." He had meticulously dictated that this was to be the inscription, "& not a word more." [42]

XVIII The Verdict of History

THE COINCIDENCE OF HISTORY placed Thomas Jefferson and Alexander Hamilton in the age of democratic revolution. As the United States was born and struggled for survival, their presence produced such high drama that historical objectivity has frequently suffered as a result. Biographers of Jefferson have often cast Hamilton as the arch-villain whose dark monarchic intrigues were designed solely to bring down the noble Virginian. Partisans of Hamilton saw in the bland, aristocratic Jefferson a masked Machiavelli who would destroy their hero.

Jefferson and Hamilton have attracted history students because theirs was not merely a personal quarrel nor was it simply a struggle for power—though both of these elements were involved. But there was a deeper philosophical conflict which was reflected in the positions which the two men and their followers took on key political issues during the early national period. Jefferson was concerned primarily with the liberty of the individual, Hamilton with the order and security of society—what he referred to as the "common good." This simplistic statement does not do justice to the complexities and ramifications of either man's philosophy but may be taken as a point of departure for a discussion of how the two men have been treated by various writers through two hundred years of historical study. Sources have been

371

subjected to "exhaustive study," the "final" and "definitive" words have been pronounced, and the "hard facts" adduced by successive generations.

The deaths of Jefferson and Hamilton did not end their rivalry, nor was it left solely to the historians to decide which of the two had made the greater contribution to the future of America. The controversy could be found in politicians speeches, newspaper editorials, historical novels, and writings of poets, essayists, and dramatists. The Jefferson–Jackson Day Dinner remains to this day a part of the ritual of the Democratic party, and in 1957 there was a nation-wide bicentennial celebration of Hamilton's birthday.

The Age of Jackson

The image of Jefferson dominated much of the history and the politics of the pre-Civil War period. There were obvious reasons for this. Jefferson outlived Hamilton by more than twenty years and while yet alive became the venerated "apostle of American democracy." Hamilton's Federalist party had not only fallen into oblivion but had, by its antics in the Hartford Convention, inscribed treason on its grave. The nationalism of the period following the War of 1812 produced the "American System" of Henry Clay, with its revival of the Bank of the United States, internal improvements, and the protective tariff. Alexander Hamilton reincarnated! But when the two-party system was revived in the bitter rivalry of the election of 1828, Clay's National Republicans as well as the Jacksonian Democrats both solemnly proclaimed that they were the true disciples of the "Sage of Monticello."

Indeed it appeared that the Jeffersonian heritage was a prize of the election. Jackson's triumphant Democracy extolled the virtues of the people and denounced the forces of money and privilege. To the Jacksonians, Jefferson's first inaugural address was still the touch-stone: "a wise and frugal government, which shall restrain men from injuring one another, which shall leave them otherwise free to regulate their own pursuits of industry and improvement, and shall not take from the mouth of labor the bread it has earned." [1]

But even as the people elected Jackson, his Vice-President John C. Calhoun was secretly writing South Carolina's "Exposition and Protest" to the tariff of 1828. The secrecy was necessary because Calhoun invoked the states rights doctrines of the Virginia and Kentucky Resolutions of 1798, in which Jefferson and Madison had challenged the authority of the federal government in the passage of the Alien and Sedition Acts. But such an idea might provoke a violent reaction from Old Hickory whose nationalism was no less profound because it was intuitive.

By 1832 Congress had passed another protective tariff and South Carolina had nullified it. Jackson reacted in characteristic fashion. He asked for and got Congressional authority to use armed force in South Carolina if it became necessary to enforce federal law. The break with Calhoun was complete, and the nascent rupture of the Democrats exposed. As the years passed the Southern minority was increasingly drawn to what they conceived to be the states rights doctrines of 1798 against the "tyrannical majority" (although the aging Madison denounced this as "an anomalous conceit").[2]

On the other hand, Jackson's implacable opposition to the centralization policies of Henry Clay and the Whigs was done in the name of Jeffersonian principle. The veto of the recharter of the Bank of the United States and of the Maysville Road Bill seemed the embodiment of Jefferson's admonition that "that government is best which governs least."

The Whigs were not to be outdone. They stormed against "King Andrew the First" as the symbol of monarchy which the Declaration of Independence had condemned. Daniel

Webster counted himself in the company of "the old-fash-ioned Republicans of Virginia" and William Henry Harrison, the Whig candidate for the presidency in 1840, declared, "If the Augean stables are to be cleansed, it will be necessary to go back to the principles of Thomas Jefferson." [3]

The final irony was the adoption of Jefferson by the aboli-tionists. James Birney, abolitionist candidate for the presi-dency, saw Jefferson as an early proponent of slave emancipa-tion. An abolitionist Congressman said that "Jefferson, the great and good Jefferson" taught him to hate slavery.[4] How could the author of the Declaration of Independence be un-derstood except as a champion of the democracy whose creed affirmed that "all men are created equal"? The Free-Soilers and then the new Republican party of the 1850's insisted that slavery must be banned from the territories and pointed to Jefferson as the author of the prohibition of slavery in the Ordinance of 1784. Abraham Lincoln insisted that freedom was a national problem, "that the Declaration of Independ-ence includes ALL men, black as well as white." [5]

And so America plunged down the road to civil war, caught in what Edward S. Corwin has called "the Jeffer-sonian dilemma." In the North democracy demanded equal-ity as a condition of national unity. In the South states rights decreed the denial of democracy and so brought the nation to the edge of the destruction of the union.[6]

The Ante-Bellum Historians

The Jefferson "history" can be said to begin when *The Memoirs of Thomas Jefferson* was published in 1829 by Thomas Jefferson Randolph, Jefferson's grandson and execu-tor of his estate.[7] The appearance of the papers would have excited enormous interest at any time, but the four fat volumes at once became the bible of politicians and factions. The *Memoirs* was basically impersonal and selected primarily to shed light on Jefferson's public career. It was received with much acclaim and criticism aimed at both the editor and the author. In particular, the *Anas*, a mixture of gossip and anecdote as well as a sort of running account of men and events which Jefferson compiled in his old age, aroused bitter feelings among former Federalists and their descendants. It probably was a deliberate piece of propaganda devised by Jefferson to counter-act John Marshall's *Life of Washington*, and it is a curious contradiction to Jefferson's general tendency to let criticism go unanswered.

But it was as a source of authority that the *Memoirs* proved most useful. Those who claimed the Jeffersonian legacy—which was practically everyone in public life—could find justification for their cause in the words of the Apostle of Liberty, whether they quoted from a casual expression in a personal note to family or friends or from a public address. Only three years after his death Jefferson's political sainthood seemed confirmed.

The *Memoirs* served as a principle source for the first important biography of Jefferson by George Tucker. Tucker was a lawyer, country squire, and former professor of moral philosophy at the University of Virginia. As such he had been at pains to preserve the liberal tradition of the university's founder, but the increasing conservatism of the Old Dominion, engendered by the slavery controversy, drove Tucker to Philadelphia. *The Life of Thomas Jefferson*, published in 1837, appeared at a time when few writers of history attempted to attain objectivity. More often than not their purpose was frankly to portray the epic nature of men and events, for the young nation needed heroes and historic grandeur. Yet Tucker, perhaps tempered by frequent consultation with

Madison, revealed much of the real Jefferson although one would be hard put to characterize the *Life* as "dispassionate" or written in "cool retrospect" as its author claimed.[8]

Much of Tucker's work was devoted to the story of the rise and rivalry of the Federalist and Republican parties and the two leaders Hamilton and Jefferson. He accepted Jefferson's view that Hamilton was bent on centralization and concentration of power in the executive as a prelude to the establishment of a monarchy. Jefferson emerged as a masterful politician, but also as a man of courage, ready to sacrifice popularity and prestige for principle. Most of his mistakes, according to Tucker, were the result of unbounded confidence in the people and an excessive faith in the progress of mankind.

The domination of the Jefferson image did not go unchallenged. In New England Federalism could be talked about above a whisper and the name of Hamilton still evoked enthusiastic admiration. New England writers were producing some of the best history of the republic, even though much of it was colored with a sort of "we-who-built-America" paternalism. George Gibbs, grandson of Connecticut Federalist Oliver Wolcott, in his *Memoirs . . . of George Washington and John Adams* (1846) contended that the American Revolution had merely preserved basic English liberties which had taken root in America. Jefferson had advocated radical revolution—the overthrow of existing institutions—but his insanity had been curbed by the moderating wisdom of Washington, Hamilton, and Adams.[9]

William Sullivan brought out his *Familiar Letters of Public Characters and Public Events* in 1834.[10] Sullivan reminisced on the halcyon days of righteous Federalism when Hamilton and his colleagues had given respectable stamp to politics. All this had been swallowed by a demogogic democracy nurtured by Jefferson and brought to its immoral triumph by the despotism of Andrew Jackson. The old Federalist charge that Jefferson had connived with Napoleon against England was reiterated by Theodore Dwight in his *Character of Thomas Jefferson* which appeared in 1839.[11]

The most notable general history of the United States to appear before the Civil War was written by Richard Hildreth, a Massachusetts Whig. His massive six volumes, published in 1849, were notably partisan toward the Federalists, but for its time it constituted restrained and sober history. If Hildreth were firmly Hamiltonian, he refused to indulge in character assassination. Jefferson, he said, was "a sincere and enthusiastic believer in the rights of humanity. . . . This faith on his part will ever suffice to cover a multitude of sins." But his admiration for Hamilton was unqualified. His "penetrating judgement and superior executive abilities" had led to his leadership in Washington's cabinet, "fixing all eyes upon him as the leading spirit of the government."[12]

Henry S. Randall's *Life of Thomas Jefferson* is one of the mile-stones in American biography. The three volumes which appeared in 1858 represented almost a decade of Randall's immersion in Jefferson manuscripts, pictures, garden plans of Monticello, "personal relics, and other things not to be classed." Partisan as it was, the *Life* was for almost a hundred years the point of departure for any study of Jefferson. Randall depicted the private and personal life of the Virginian as well as that of the party leader and political philosopher. The work therefore had a wide appeal, not only to the students of political history, but to those who could admire the master of Monticello, the affectionate father and the keen observer of nature. Yet Randall never wandered far from the political history of which Jefferson was the pivot, the bulwark of liberty against the machinations and intrigues of Hamilton. Like Tucker, Randall devoted a major part of his writing to the twelve years between 1789 and 1801. This was the critical period for the future of America. From the turmoil of the titanic struggle with Hamilton and the Federalists, Jefferson and his party emerged triumphant, and the nation was embarked on its serene and harmonious course.

By a supreme irony, two years after the publication of his great work, Randall invited an exchange of views on Jefferson from the great English historian Thomas Babington Macaulay, which revealed the wide diversion between British and American notions of democracy. Lord Macaulay did not approve of either equality or majority rule for which, he said, the American system provided no restraint. "I can not reckon Jefferson among the benefactors of mankind," he added, and predicted that a calamity would result from America's excessive admiration for Jeffersonian polity.[14] The year was 1860.

The Gilded Age

The Civil War revolutionized every aspect of American life. From the South where the Cotton Kingdom was gone forever and four million black Americans began their struggle for equality; to the West where teeming thousands settled more land in twenty years than had been settled since 1607; to the North with its bursting cities and giant industrial empires—wherever one looked the old order had passed. And to many minds the great struggle for the Union had buried the Jeffersonian Utopia forever. The simple agrarian society of yeoman farmers, the diffused and local democracy, the free and unrestrained individual—these were inadequate concepts for the new Leviathan. Moreover, Jefferson's states rights doctrine was the evil seed which had borne the fruit of secession. Yet the public image of Jefferson survived as the defender of the proposition of equality for all men, of "hope to the world for all future time."

The new America was Alexander Hamilton's prophecy

brought to fulfillment. The post-war nationalists lauded him
as the man who had given the new nation the centralizing
strength which had enabled it to survive the first Revolution
and the example which had preserved it through the second.
The new industrial age admired the genius who, as Webster
had earlier exclaimed, "smote the rock of the national resources and abundant streams of revenue gushed forth." [15]
The United States had become a nation diversified, self-suffi-
cient, and on its way to the leadership of the world's industrial producers. Its government aided this development with
protective tariffs, subsidies, and a benevolent policy of laissez
faire. Its statesmen preached the "gospel of wealth" which
extolled the rugged individual and the survival of the fittest.
A new aristocracy decreed the Calvinistic virtues of thrift,
hard work, and sobriety, yet it could wink knowingly at the
"robber barons" like "Jubilee Jim" Fiske and Daniel Drew.
The philosophy of pragmatism, which tested truth according
to the validity and utility of consequences, was admirably
suited to the age of science and progress.

The Democratic party of the post-war period, fighting for
its political life, clung stubbornly to the time-honored and
tested magic of the name of Jefferson. Most of these Jeffersonians were from the South and West, regions which were
as politically helpless as they had been before the war. For
William Jennings Bryan, John Sharpe Williams of Mississippi, and Tom Watson of Georgia the lexicon of politics
contained only St. Thomas and the fiery dragon Alexander
Hamilton. Bryan, who led the Democratic and Populist crusade in the campaign of 1896, admired the Sage of Monticello
extravagantly and lost no opportunity to identify himself with
"the greatest statesman our country produced." [16]

But Bryan's simple agrarianism was outdated. The challenge to the corporate power of industry was taken up by the
Progressives, and the "Square Deal" of Theodore Roosevelt

stressed the positive exercise of executive power. The style was Hamilton's, and the Rough Rider saw in himself Hamilton's "touch of the heroic, the touch of the purple, the touch of the gallant, the dashing, the picturesque." [17] Energy, vitality, positive leadership rather than Jeffersonian passiveness were the qualities that Hamilton inspired.

The romantic aspect of the Hamiltonian myth found expression in a novel *The Conqueror* published in 1902 as a result of what its author Gertrude Atherton described as a love affair with its hero. He would have "made one of the finest and wisest autocrats," she wrote, but "he accepted the situation with his inherent philosophy . . . [and] forced . . . measures in whose wisdom he implicitly believed, and which, in every instance, time has vindicated." [18]

The philosopher of the new Hamiltonian cult was Herbert Croly. The future founder of the *New Republic* magazine was disturbed because he thought Americans were falling into a sort of fatalistic optimism that accepted the inevitability of progress. In *The Promise of American Life* (1909) he urged a new dynamism of which Hamilton was the early embodiment. The Jeffersonian tradition was too vague and slipshod. Hamilton's Federalism, said Croly, "implied an active interference with the natural course of American economic and political business and its regulation and guidance in a national direction. It implied a conscious and indefatigable attempt on the part of the national leaders to promote the national welfare." [19] Roosevelt was tremendously impressed by Croly, and in announcing that he stood for the "square deal" he continued, "I stand for having . . . rules changed so as to work for a more substantial equality of opportunity and reward." [20] Thus was Hamilton's "subversion" of the Constitution converted to the New Nationalism.

The coterie of the new Hamiltonians included Senator

Henry Cabot Lodge, who had written a biography of Hamilton for John T. Morse's "American Statesmen" series and edited twelve volumes of Hamilton's *Works* (1903).[21] Another senatorial scholar, Albert Beveridge, wrote a biography of John Marshall in which it was obvious that the author shared his subject's dislike for Jefferson.[22] William Graham Sumner, the Yale economist, published a biography of Hamilton in 1890 which reflected his social Darwinism.[23] Captain Alfred T. Mahan, the great advocate of sea power excoriated Jefferson's "gun-boat" policy which had led to the humiliation of the American navy in the War of 1812.[24] Whitlaw Reid, editor of the New York *Tribune,* delivered an anti-Jefferson diatribe in a speech while he was ambassador to England which was so denunciatory that it called forth a rebuke on the floor of Congress.[25]

There was a brief Jeffersonian revival in 1912. The Democratic party, faithful custodian of the Jeffersonian symbol, took advantage of the split in the Republican party and won the presidency for Woodrow Wilson. Although his "New Freedom" was hard to distinguish from Roosevelt's "Bull Moose" platform, Wilson had no difficulty in invoking the Jeffersonian spirit. Dr. Wilson, professor of jurisprudence at Princeton University, had observed that Hamilton "hated anarchy and saw the country drifting into it. He believed that nothing short of centralized government could be relied on to check . . . it. He was for efficiency rather than for sentiment." [26] When Woodrow Wilson, as a politician, donned the Jeffersonian mantle, he was honest enough to say that the nation could not "seek to be governed by Jefferson's opinions or search among his policies for measures to suit our times." [27] Wilson's appeal for a League of Nations was as spokesman for the people of the world, the kind of dream that would have fired Jefferson's vision. The irony of history de-

creed that the dream would be shattered by Henry Cabot
Lodge, who had done so much to revive the spirit of Alexander Hamilton.

The Scientific Historians

By the end of the Civil War the writing of history had
entered a new phase. The German historians of the von
Ranke school were developing theses of history which were
"demonstrated" by "scientific" examination of evidence, usually documents and other forms of original source material.
The German scientific history and the seminar method found
its way across the Atlantic to Johns Hopkins and Harvard.
George Bancroft, John Lothrop Motley, and the German
historian von Holst, who became the chairman of the history
department at the University of Chicago, were all representative of the "new history." Beginning with George Bancroft's
ten-volume *History of the United States* (the first volume was
published in 1834, the last in 1874),[28] there was an outpouring
of multi-volume histories, most of them by New Englanders
who had inherited the Federalist tradition on which had been
grafted the postwar nationalism and anti-slavery sentiment.
Their scholarly authority gave approval to the popular
revival of Alexander Hamilton.

John Bach McMaster had begun his career as a civil engineer but soon turned to history and became the chairman of
history at the University of Pennsylvania. He published his
first volume of *The History of the United States* in 1883. The
last volume did not appear until 1913. McMaster saw in
Hamilton the firmness and authority which successfully with-
stood the Whiskey Rebels and the hysteria of the French
Revolution. "Of all the men who, in the judgement of posterity, are ranked high among the founders of the republic . . .
by far the most brilliant and versatile was Hamilton." Jeffer-

son, on the other hand, "was saturated with democracy in its worst form, and he remained to the last day of his life a servile worshipper of the people." [29]

The most distinguished historian of the late nineteenth century was Henry Adams, scion of a family which has probably influenced American history more than any other. Though his research, especially in European archives, was prodigious and his scholarly approach formidable, one modern scholar thought his *History of the United States, . . . 1801–1817* should have been subtitled "Henry Adams' Revenge." [30] Irving Brant, the twentieth-century biographer of James Madison, was led to conclude that "any resemblance between the facts which Henry Adams presents and the conclusions which he draws from them is purely coincidental." [31] This is manifestly unfair to Adams' monumental study, yet he could not bring himself to give Jefferson any unqualified praise. Commenting on Jefferson's retirement after the failure of the embargo, Adams wrote, "Throughout the twistings and windings of his course as President, he clung to this main idea [a new era of peace]; or if he seemed for a moment to forget it, he never failed to return and persist with an almost heroic obstinacy." [32]

Of the remaining general histories James Schouler's *History of the United States* (1880–1913) was more balanced. He acknowledged Hamilton's "soaring greatness" and "precocity of intellect" but criticized his "frankly avowed conviction that mankind were vicious . . . and should be ruled upon that theory." [33] Edward Channing attended the lectures of Henry Adams and Henry Cabot Lodge as a student at Harvard but refused to accept their Hamiltonian bias. In his six volume history (1905–1925) as well as in *The Jeffersonian System* (1906) he treated Jefferson in a much more sympathetic fashion than his predecessors. [34]

The first important biography of Hamilton by a historian

of the scientific school came from England. C. J. Riethmüller's *Alexander Hamilton and His Contemporaries,* published
in 1864, took the position that Hamilton's major effort to
rescue the nation was his attempt to establish a highly centralized government in the Constitutional Convention.[35] Failing this, the remainder of his career was spent in a desperate
and futile attempt to stave off the debilitating effects of Jeffersonian polity. Hamilton's son, John C. Hamilton, had published an incomplete biography of his father in 1840. Seventeen years later he began a seven volume *History of the
Republic of the United States* in which his avowed purpose
was the vindication of his father.[36] This he attempted to do
by insisting that had Hamiltonian policies been followed the
catastrophe of the Civil War would have been avoided. It was
the Jeffersonian heresy which was at the root of the tragedy.
A more scholarly treatment, John T. Morse's two volume
biography, appeared in 1876.[37] Yet Morse's nationalism left
no room for a balanced picture. Jefferson and Hamilton faced
each other in a vendetta of history in which Hamilton—or
Morse—gave no quarter.

Henry Cabot Lodge, the Boston Brahmin, actually
achieved a better balance than most even though he had no
formal training in history. He acknowledged that Hamilton
went too far in his aristocratic pretensions and was largely
responsible for the political ineptitude which wrecked the
Federalist party. Yet even in victory Jefferson could not destroy the national strength which Hamilton and Washington
had created. Lodge's lasting contribution was the twelve
volumes of Hamilton's *Works,* which is only now being superseded as the basic source for Hamilton's papers by the
definitive Columbia University edition.

In the generation following the Civil War, while Hamilton
was clearly the hero of most historians, two writers made
important contributions toward the emergence of the human

and personal Jefferson. Sarah Nicholas Randolph, his great-granddaughter, recorded *The Domestic Life of Thomas Jefferson*.[38] Her account of his personal charm and graceful manner of living gave warmth and vitality to a man whose heroic stature had hitherto seemed larger than life. This talent for portraying the human qualities of historical personages was the particular contribution of James Parton to the art of biography. Parton, like Miss Randolph, relied too much on the kind of family legend and myth that always surrounds the lives of the famous, but for his ability to make great men come alive—Jackson, Burr, and John Jacob Astor as well as Jefferson—he richly deserves the title of "Father of Modern Biography."[39]

One of the most important achievements in Jeffersonian scholarship in this period was Paul Leicester Ford's ten-volume edition of the *Writings of Thomas Jefferson* which is only now being superseded by the comprehensive *Papers* under the editorship of Julian Boyd.[40] Ford was a New Englander and most of his work had been done on Hamilton and Washington. Yet the complexities of Jefferson fascinated him. He finally concluded that Jefferson's fundamental and unfaltering struggle to preserve the freedom of the individual was the basis for his universal appeal.[41]

The Progressive Historians

In the early part of the twentieth century two of the giants of American historical literature, Charles A. Beard and Vernon L. Parrington, emerged. Beard, a Progressive and a proponent of the economic interpretation of history, first drew national attention when he wrote *The Economic Interpretation of the Constitution*.[42] Beard always strenuously denied that he was an economic determinist; in fact, he said, "I have never been able to discover an all-pervading deter-

minism in history." [43] But he viewed the members of the
Convention of 1787, not as a group of far-sighted demigods,
but as individuals, each with an economic stake and a determination to frame a government which would protect that
interest. Here, indeed, Beard thought, were men governed by
what Hamilton called "their passions"—meaning material
self-interest. In 1915 Beard followed with *The Economic Origins of Jeffersonian Democracy*. Jefferson was not a great
democrat, after all, Beard decided. He failed to destroy the
Hamiltonian system, but merely shifted the base of its leadership. "Jeffersonian Democracy simply meant the possession
of the federal government by the agrarian masses led by an
aristocracy of slave-owning planters." Jeffersonian Republicans were no more "enamored of equalitarian democracy"
than Hamilton.[44]

Beard's detachment represented a kind of historical attitude which was becoming increasingly prevalent in the "new
history" of the twentieth century—which was replacing the
"new history" of McMaster and von Holst and would inevitably be replaced by another "new history." His emphasis on
economic causation marked a departure from the partisan
approach represented by "Jefferson or Hamilton" and
"North or South." Instead historians sought overall and per-
vading themes upon which a pattern of history could be
woven. "The whole theory of the economic interpretation of
history," Beard concluded, "rests upon the concept that social progress in general is the result of the contending interests in society." [45]

This tentative approach to historical interpretation was
reflected in the work of the foremost intellectual historian of
the early twentieth century Vernon Parrington. Parrington
was fifty-six years old when he published the first volume of
Main Currents in American Thought (1927) and died before
he could complete the third and final volume. "The point of

view from which I have endeavored to evaluate the materials is liberal rather than conservative, Jeffersonian rather than Federalistic, and very likely," he admitted candidly, "I have found what I went forth to find, as others have discovered what they were seeking." [46]

While he acknowledged an indebtedness to Beard, Parrington thought that the economic interpretation did not take into account the impact of the equalitarianism of the Age of Reason upon the American Revolution. He detected a strain of liberalism that ran from Roger Williams through Franklin to Jefferson's philosophy of the Enlightenment, which prevailed over Hamilton's capitalism.

Another historian who refused to deprecate the role of ideals in the shaping of history was Carl Becker. In 1922 he wrote a tight little volume on the Declaration of Independence which, despite its brevity, is a classic study of Jefferson's most famous piece of writing. Becker here underscored his belief that the philosophy on which the Declaration was founded "preached toleration instead of persecution, good-will in place of hate, peace in place of war. It taught that beneath all local and temporary diversity, beneath the superficial traits and talents that distinguish men and nations, all men are equal in the possession of a common humanity." [47]

Albert Jay Nock, in his *Jefferson* (1926), also had a high regard for the Jeffersonian ideal, but he did not think that Jefferson was a great radical. On the contrary, he was the rare combination of a man who had the instincts and tastes of an aristocrat but who nevertheless practiced democracy. Nock thought that Jefferson was right in his emphasis on governmental decentralization because subsequent history had showed that strong government usually lent its power to the exploiter rather than to the producer. But Jefferson's real greatness lay in his study of mankind and how man could improve his world. [48]

The Golden Twenties and the Age of Roosevelt

"The business of government is business," said President Calvin Coolidge. The mood of post-war Republicanism and the Big Bull Market seemed tuned to Hamilton the nationalist, the isolationist, the capitalist or whatever else conservative America in the 1920's might wish to ascribe to him. Arthur Vandenberg, the Michigan publisher and later a distinguished Senator, wrote three books on Hamilton. Built on the theme of *If Hamilton Were Here Today* (1923) Vandenberg wrote, "If Hamilton was indispensable in 1787 . . . he is impressively required in 1923 to maintain [the nation's] scepter against the heresies of a radical and thoughtless age." [49] The conservative Democrat John W. Davis, candidate for the presidency in 1924, did not abandon the Jefferson touchstone but felt compelled to acknowledge that "without Hamilton [America] might have perished in the quagmire of false finance." [50] And the ubiquitous Nicholas Murray Butler, president of Columbia University, affirmed that "the name of Hamilton would have honored Greece in the age of Aristides." [51]

James Truslow Adams decried such patriotic myths in *The Epic of America,* and pointed out the crux of the matter: whether "a Jeffersonian democracy could survive in a Hamiltonian economy. . . . The colt has already been roped and thrown. Thereafter he would have to get used to the harness of a complex civilization." [52]

The Jeffersonian revival began in 1925 with the publication of Claude Bowers' *Jefferson and Hamilton,* a study of the decade of the 1790's which the author characterized in his subtitle as *The Struggle for Democracy in America.* [53] Franklin Roosevelt reviewed the book for the New York *Evening World* and saw in Jefferson the symbol for the revival of the liberal credo of the Democratic party. [54] Bowers himself be-

came a familiar figure on the lecture platform and delivered
a rousing keynote speech at the Democratic National Convention in 1928. The prophet was not without honor, for
Bowers was appointed ambassador to Spain in 1933.

Franklin Roosevelt, campaigning for a "new deal" in 1932,
thought the struggle between Jefferson and Hamilton had
marked "a new day" in American political life, "the day of
the individual against the system, the day in which individualism was made the great watchword of American life." [55] Of
necessity, the New Deal emphasized ends rather than means,
for it scarcely embodied the Jeffersonian dictum that "that
government is best which governs least." Nevertheless,
Democrats strove for the identity: Roosevelt, like Jefferson,
the patrician who championed the forgotten man; who fought
the monied interests; who, Jefferson-like, attacked the Supreme Court as the enemy of liberal progress. Was it not
Jefferson who said that "the earth belongs to the living"?

As had happened a hundred years before, the many-sided
Sage of Monticello could be enlisted in any cause. Republicans denounced the executive tyranny of "Franklin the
First." John D. M. Hamilton, chairman of the Republican
party, attempted to revive the Jeffersonian precepts of isolation, frugality, and abhorrence of centralization. [56] Southern
conservatives, self-styled Jeffersonian Democrats, wistfully
appealed to an agrarian utopia and local autonomy in a collection of essays titled *I'll Take My Stand*. [57] And on the far
left the Communist *New Masses* saw a link between a
proletarian revolution and the author of the Declaration of
Independence.

Sydney Kingsley had Jefferson and Hamilton confront
each other in his Broadway production of *The Patriots* in
1943. Says Hamilton, "And when you stir up the mobs,
remember—we who really own America are quite prepared
to take it back for ourselves, from your great beast, 'The

People.' " To which Jefferson replies, "And I tell you, when our people have the government securely in their hands, they will be as strong as a giant. They will sooner allow the heart to be torn out of their bodies than their freedom to be wrested from them by a Caesar." [58]

Newsman Elmer Davis had his fictional creation Godfrey D. Gloom pronounce what was presumably the final word. Gloom, "the well-known paw-paw planter and old-fashioned Jeffersonian Democrat from Amity, Indiana," had cast his first vote for James Buchanan in 1856 and had regularly attended Democratic conventions until 1936. Divine judgement in the form of an automobile had struck him down in Philadelphia in 1936 soon after he had attended the Republican Convention. His dying pronouncement was: "Jefferson has now been endorsed by both parties, and there seems as little prospect that the endorsement will ever be repudiated as that either party will ever put Jeffersonian doctrine into practice." [59]

Not so many scholarly volumes on either Jefferson or Hamilton appeared in the 1930's. Claude Bowers added another volume *Jefferson in Power* in 1936. The central theme was less a study of Jefferson than of the decline and fall of the Federalist party. After the death of Hamilton, who had already lost his position of leadership, "the most scintillating of the Congressional leaders of the party were as insects crawling on the earth, compared to Jefferson." [60]

James Truslow Adams had become more partisan since writing the *Epic of America*. Critics of the New Deal who insisted that Hamilton was needed in the crisis were answered by *The Living Jefferson*, who understood that an abundant life of material things was worthless without the personal liberties which are "essential to the happiness and dignity of human life." [61] Gilbert Chinard, a French scholar, suggested an approach to the intellectual Jefferson in *The Apostle of*

Americanism.[62] Jeffersonian Democracy ought properly to be called Americanism said Chinard. The European background of Jefferson's experience had led him to reject European civilization and to formulate a philosophy which was specifically attuned to the United States.

Finally, Marie Kimball, wife of the architect Fiske Kimball who had devoted so much energy and talent to the restoration of Monticello and to the planning of the Jefferson Memorial, published *Thomas Jefferson's Cook Book* in 1941.[63] Two years later she began a biography with *The Road to Glory.*[64] Mrs. Kimball denied the assertion of Bowers and others that Jefferson was an amalgam of an aristocratic "Tuckahoe" mother and a "cohee" frontiersman Peter Jefferson. The latter was a Tidewater gentleman whose movement to the Piedmont was the natural progression of a prosperous planter and speculator. The great democrat was the child of the Age of Reason not of the wild frontier which was, in fact, one hundred miles to the west of Albemarle.

Though the published books were comparatively few in number, the periodical literature indicated that scholars were still stimulated by Jefferson. A list of titles is indicative: Henry Bamford Parks in "Jeffersonian Democracy"; Frank Owsley, "Two Agrarian Philosophers, Jefferson and Du Pont"; Charles Beard, "Jefferson in America Now"; Dennis Brogan, "The Ghost of Thomas Jefferson"; and Dumas Malone, "Jefferson and the New Deal." [65]

Embattled protagonists of Hamilton fought to save their hero from entombment. Broadus Mitchell, a Johns Hopkins economist who was beginning a lifetime of study on Hamilton, insisted that it was Hamilton's precepts that pointed the way to the control of the complex American economy. It was precisely because individualism had led to economic anarchy that the present chaos existed.[66]

Rexford Tugwell and Joseph Dorfman, two Columbia

economists, praised Hamilton's achievements as the major
architect of governmental centralization and fiscal responsibility in mid-twentieth century. It was due to Hamilton as
much as "any other single person" that "we have a constitution at all." Hamilton believed that control of economic
power was the key to stability and that such control could
never "center in the people, in workers and small farmers,"
because they would use it irresponsibly. Only if such power
were centered in the wealthy "who would use it with deco-
rum" whould chaos be avoided.[67]

When President Roosevelt spoke at the dedication of the
Jefferson Memorial in 1943, he closed his address with the
words which are inscribed around the Memorial Room: "I
have sworn upon the altar of God eternal hostility to any
form of tyranny over the mind of man." [68] For the President,
Jefferson had become something more than a convenient
source for quotations in political speeches (although a "Jefferson file" was maintained by the White House writers). He
seldom mentioned his efforts in behalf of the Memorial or in
the restoration of Monticello. The Jefferson quotations had
become less frequent and the 1943 dedication seemed to mark
a point at which Jefferson became at last an American hero.
Agrarianism, frugality, decentralization—these were concepts of a bygone day. What America still needed and still
remembered was Jefferson's unfaltering faith in the power of
free men to determine their own destiny.

XIX Jefferson, Hamilton, and the Living Generation

In the second half of the twentieth century the people of the United States came to realize that their world had undergone a transformation. The gap which had always existed between young and old was widened by the fact that the new generation of Americans was conditioned to radical and accelerated change—change which often frightened and antagonized those who were used to a more static world of traditional concepts. At mid-century man traveled across continents and oceans at 600 miles an hour. Less than two decades later he had traveled to the moon at 25,000 miles an hour. The older generation was awe-struck and incredulous. The young bet ten to one that Mars was next and considered that they had a sure thing.

New nations emerged by the scores and traditional empires evaporated. New ethnic and cultural peoples demanded recognition, and everywhere old values and even ways of measuring them were being challenged. The phrase "an age of revolution" became trite because it was so self-evident.

Many radicals disavowed the uses of past experience, but their nihilistic attitude toward history was not shared by most. Increasing numbers of people of all viewpoints, radical,

393

liberal, conservative, and reactionary, turned to history—in the broadest use of the word—for justification of past values and future action. And in such a revolutionary period it was not surprising that an older and less epochal American Revolution should have been given an exhaustive re-examination. Jefferson and Hamilton were two of the leaders who were studied by a wide range of scholars, but virtually all of the Founding Fathers were subjected to intensive scrutiny.

The Living Hamilton

Nathan Schachner, who wrote the first full-scale biography of Hamilton in the post-war period, was a lawyer, novelist, and publisher before he turned to biography. He had previously written a life of Aaron Burr and followed his work on Hamilton with a two-volume study of Jefferson in 1951. Schachner's treatment of Hamilton was orthodox and he added little that was new, but his lively literary style did much to illuminate Hamilton's career. He thought that Hamilton's later career was marred by inflexibility which could not change with the changing times. "Stability, order, hierarchies, the rule of the rich and intelligent, power abroad and a firm hand at home, were his minimum requirements for a nation." [1]

The two hundredth anniversary of Hamilton's birth helped to inspire the proliferation of literature about him in the late 1950's. Richard B. Morris, a noted historian of the Revolution, published *Alexander Hamilton and the Founding of the Nation*, a collection of writings in which he sought to alter the picture of Hamilton as "a symbol of party, class and faction. . . . No man of his generation accomplished more to break down local barriers and sectional prejudices which had hampered the formation of a strong union." He noted Hamilton's insistence on "a government possessed with energy and initiative," one that would not "stand inert while the economy stagnated." He felt that Hamilton's failure was due "more to personality and tactics than to basic principles. . . . With some justice it has been said that Hamilton loved his country more than he did his countrymen." [2]

Louis Hacker, an economic historian, contrasted the views of Jefferson and Hamilton by suggesting that "if we believe in human freedom, the dignity of the individual and his right to dissent, the wide dispersion of political power, we recognize Jefferson's enduring contribution; and if we believe in the necessity for stable political institutions, honorable government in its relations at home and abroad, and freedom of economic enterprise as the real key to national progress, we recognize Hamilton's." Hacker thought that the great contribution of Hamilton was his matchless "management of the business of government, that rare capacity, which he possessed, of recognizing a crisis and knowing how to meet it." He lauded the Hamiltonian economic blueprint for the nation which pointed out "the direction for its future development, nay, survival." [3]

The status of the United States as a super-power in the 1950's led historians to look to the Founding Fathers for guidance in the conduct of foreign policy. A special point of contention was the question of whether diplomacy conducted on moral principles was in the American tradition or whether the thrust of that tradition was one of realistic self-interest. Hacker observed, "A Hamiltonian would be a realist in foreign affairs today as Hamilton was in the 1790s; by the same token, a Jeffersonian would be an idealist." [4]

Hans Morganthau, professor of political science, discussed the problem in the context of the 1790's and the different approaches of Jefferson and Hamilton. "It illustrates both the depth of the moralistic illusion and the original strength of the opposition to it that the issue between these two opposing conceptions of foreign policy . . . was decided in favor of the realistic position, and was formulated with unsurpassed simplicity and penetration by Alexander Hamilton." He added, "Hamilton unswervingly applied one standard: the national interest of the United States." Jefferson, by contrast, was hampered by a "dedication to abstract morality" and his "realistic touch in foreign affairs was much less sure," although Morganthau conceded that "the moral pretence yielded often . . . to the impact of national interest." [5]

This view was sharply challenged by Alfred K. Bowman in a perceptive article "Jefferson, Hamilton and American Foreign Policy." Bowman insisted "that Jefferson, not Hamilton, did 'unswervingly apply as standard the national interest of the United States.'" He pointed out that "Hamilton's concept of the national interest, in fact, was grossly in error. . . . To further his retrogressive, Hobbesian system, Hamilton consciously and cynically sought to transfer to America what Professor R. R. Palmer calls 'the vicious practice and virtuous theory' of the eighteenth-century British Constitution." [6]

In 1957 Broadus Mitchell culminated ten years of study with his first volume of *Alexander Hamilton,* which he titled *Youth to Maturity.* The second volume *The National Adventure* appeared in 1962. Mitchell summarized his estimate of Hamilton in a series of lectures at Columbia University titled *Heritage From Hamilton.*

Mitchell thought that the constant attempts to compare Jefferson and Hamilton were downright "vulgar" in making their rivalry a central theme of history. Theirs was not "a conflict of absolutes," he said, "for time entered as an ingredient. Broadly the Federalists, pitching their case on the need for order and control, were correct at the outset. They were pragmatic and serviceable in the first formative period. The progress of the democrats was necessarily delayed. . . . Then they became positive when rights could be asserted without peril to primary requirements." The attachment of Jefferson and Hamilton to the success of the United States "is not to be doubted. That they viewed this object from divergent angles was our chief political blessing." He did not gloss over Hamilton's resorts to political expediency. "This was inevitable while the country was in its infancy. His claims as an economist, which were high, have been blurred by his constant recourse to political means. This is not to be regretted. His concern was nothing less than the making of a nation." [8]

John C. Miller approached Hamilton's career as *A Portrait in Paradox.* He believed that "no American statesman has displayed more constructive imagination than did Hamilton," and "he left an imprint upon this country that time has not yet effaced." But he pointed out that Hamilton's career was full of contradictions: He had little faith in the Constitution, yet he fought for its adoption and supported it; he pitted himself against Jefferson, yet supported his election when the Federalists turned to Burr. "The supreme irony," said Miller, ". . . is that methods by which he sought to lay the economic foundations of the American union actually aggravated political sectionalism in the United States—the very eventuality he most dreaded." By the time he left the cabinet "the fissures between North and South had begun to assume menacing proportions." [9]

There have been a number of monographs which provide special insights into the complexity that was Alexander Hamilton. Clinton Rossiter studied *Alexander Hamilton and the Constitution* and concluded that Hamilton's great contribution was in his formulation of Constitutional interpretations in *The Federalist* and in his subsequent policies as Secretary of the Treasury, rather than any influence he had in the convention. [10] This idea was elaborated by Samuel J. Konefsky in *John Marshall and Alexander Hamilton: Architects of the*

Constitution. "To the extent . . . that Alexander Hamilton helped bring about its adoption and to infuse it with principles of liberal interpretation, to that extent he made the Constitution an instrument of lasting utility to Americans—all Americans, regardless of political persuasion." [11]

Julian Boyd in *Number 7* criticized Hamilton's dealings with the British ministers in the early 1790's as going "far beyond the mere act of violating his own cardinal principle of administrative unity—far indeed beyond the limits of honorable conduct." [12] Leonard White in his study of *The Federalists* pays tribute to Hamilton as a public administrator. "Alexander Hamilton was the greatest administrative genius of his generation in America and one of the greatest administrators of all time. . . . His enormous energy, his quick perceptions, his extraordinary capacity for analysis and clear expression, his willingness to take responsibility . . . conspired to make him enevitably a force in the public life of his age." [13]

Cecelia Kenyon saw him as "The Rousseau of the Right." Hamilton's flaw, she thought, was in his priorities. "Hamilton mistook the means for the end, and tipped the scale too far in the direction of national interest. In so doing he gave it ethical priority over the demands of the individual." [14] Saul Padover in *The Mind of Alexander Hamilton* felt that Hamilton erred in his assumption that man was beyond redemption, "a corrupt and selfish animal, motivated by the worst passions. . . . For how can the corrupt and the selfish be expected to rule, with any prospect of success or stability [in a system of self-government], over others who are no less corrupt and selfish?" Woodrow Wilson's verdict that Hamilton was a great man but not a great American ought to be reversed, said Padover. "In his magnificent contribution to the building of the United States, Hamilton was a very great American. That he was a great man—in the universal sense that Washington and Jefferson were great— is doubtful." [15] Jacob E. Cooke, coeditor of the Hamilton papers, felt that Hamilton was "neither probusiness nor anifarmer, but rather wished to follow whatever policy promoted national strength." The Report on Manufactures recognized the industrial lag of the United States and reflected Hamilton's belief that America would have to attain economic self-sufficiency before it could earn respect abroad. "Only then could the Revolution's promise of America be fulfilled." [16]

The Living Jefferson

Thomas Jefferson was such a prolific writer and the range of his intellect so wide that he furnished nearly inexhaustible sources of inspiration for investigation. Bernard Mayo constructed a "rounded and intimate" portrait of *Jefferson Himself* entirely from his writings. Mayo found that Jefferson, "whether speaking of politics, religion, economics, science, or education, is concerned with one great objective: the freedom and happiness of man." [17] A decade and a half later Mayo still thought the goal unchanged. "Nothing does greater injustice to him and to 'the sanctity of history' than to confuse the changing methods he used in his generation with his unchangeable democratic goals." [18]

In 1948 Dumas Malone began his monumental study of Jefferson.[19] Few biographers have matched the excellent literary quality of Malone's writing or his meticulous scholarship and balanced conclusions. If some critics thought his approach too one-sided and bland it was because Malone invited his reader to look at the whole of Jefferson's experience before rendering judgements. "If, under the pressure to which he was subjected, he had lived up to his own ideals at all points," wrote Malone in the introduction to *Jefferson the President* (1970), "he would have been more than human, and unquestionably there were times when he manifested the proneness to self-deception that is common to mortals." [20]

Nathan Schachner turned from his biography of Hamilton to a study of Jefferson which appeared in two volumes in 1951. "Without a close study of the man, his philosophy and works no proper understanding of America as it was and is today can be arrived at," said Schachner,[21] and his lively account made his work a thoroughly readable addition to Jeffersonian literature.

Merrill Peterson brought a charming style and twenty years of study to his *Thomas Jefferson and the New Nation* (1970). The result was a work impeccable in its scholarship and a delight to the general reader, scarcely "a cockboat" of Jefferson history that its author called it. Peterson thought that Jefferson's career could be understood in the context of the themes of democracy, nationality, and enlightenment.

> "By *democracy* I refer to the gradual emergence in Jefferson of a revolutionary creed of liberty, equality and popular government. By *nationality* I mean to embrace his sense of the newness of the new nation, his *amor patriae,* all his directives toward independence, cultural or political or economic. . . . *By enlightenment* I wish to emphasize Jefferson's thrust beyond nationality to the cosmopolitan fraternity of science and philosophy . . . and his participation in the eighteenth century campaign to enlist man in the cause of nature and nature in the service of mankind." [22]

The multiplicity of Jefferson's thought and activity attracted the interests of a wide variety of scholars in the second half of the twentieth century. Max Beloff, an Oxford scholar, in a little book on *Thomas Jefferson and American Democracy* pointed out what he thought was an insoluble problem in Jefferson's democratic polity. "The rights of the individual lead to majority rule; and majority rule, resting inevitably in the disregard of the rights and interests of minorities, leads back to the search for individual guarantees." [23] The philosopher Sidney Hook believed that Jefferson's writings revealed a pragmatic tone which indicated that the validity of natural rights rests on their "personal and social utility in furthering human happiness." [24]

Merrill Peterson presented a convenient *Profile* which included observations on Jefferson by a number of notable writers. Carl Becker answered the question "What Is Still Living in the Philosophy of Thomas Jefferson" by pointing out that Jefferson's methods were ill-suited to the modern world. But his belief in republican government is still accepted "from the profound conviction that it is the only form of government that is not at war with . . . those familiar rights and privileges which we regard as . . . imprescriptibly American." [25]

John Dos Passos, a novelist with a keen sense of history, suggested that the low point of Jefferson's life, his unsuccessful service as governor, brought him close to despair and disillusionment. But Jefferson was one of those rare persons who "can't shake off a feeling of responsibility for other men, the type of mind in which qualities grouped under the tag 'the parental bent' are dominant." So he refused to turn cynic or to abate his idealism.[26] Robert R. Palmer, the historian of *The Age of the Democratic Revolution,* believed that Jefferson regarded the French Revolution in the 1790's through the eyes of a "dubious democrat" but finally took the side of the revolutionaries because, despite their bloody excesses and wrongheadedness, they were the only hope in the struggle against European monarchy and aristocracy.[27]

William D. Grampp re-examined Jefferson's economic ideas and demonstrated the progression of his views from agrarianism in the Revolutionary period to "measures that were consistent with the objectives established by Hamilton, though his methods differed." [28] Julian Boyd tended to gloss over Jefferson's strict construction ideas, emphasizing rather that his "Empire for Liberty" was based on something "deeper even than an intellectual acceptance of the philosophy of self-government. . . . The salient fact . . . is that the cardinal principle of Jefferson's life was his uncompromising devotion to the Union because of its identity with human rights." [29]

Irving Brant's biography of James Madison re-examined the intimate relationship between the two great Virginians, refusing to accept for Madison the secondary role which history had so often assigned to him. Brant noted, for example, that it was Madison who took the lead in opposing the Hamiltonians in the early 1790's and Jefferson who followed.[30] Adrienne Koch pursued a similar idea in the realm of political theory and concluded that the relationship was *The Great Collaboration.* "The inescapable conclusion . . . ," she wrote, "is that the political philosophy known simply as 'Jeffersonian' is actually an amalgam of ideas, which owes very much to James Madison." [31] Daniel Boorstin brought new insight to Jefferson's scientific thought in *The Lost World of Thomas Jefferson.* Jefferson's scientific assumptions were naive in terms of twentieth century knowledge, but his natural philosophy was the precursor and guide for those who sought to make science serve as an instrument of progress and freedom.[32]

No summary of the writings about Jefferson and Hamilton would be complete without echoing the grateful praise of all scholars for the two great works of compilation now in progress. Julian Boyd and his associates at Princeton have edited eighteen volumes of the papers of Thomas Jefferson. Harold Syrett, Jacob Cooke, and their associates have published nineteen volumes of the Alexander Hamilton papers at Columbia University.

In 1960 Merrill Peterson asked the question, "Could

Americans make a patriarchal hero of Jefferson?" *The Jefferson Image in the American Mind* traced how and why this had indeed come about. "Jefferson was preeminently great," said Peterson. ". . . The successive generations of American experience testified, 'Thomas Jefferson still survives.' " [33]

By Way of Conclusion

In looking for the uses of the past we must first understand the past itself. One of the most serious difficulties in judging men like Jefferson and Hamilton is that we cannot fully project ourselves into their world and measure them by their standards and values. Why, for example, did not two men who were pledged to the welfare and happiness of mankind take a militant stand against slavery? If Jefferson were such a champion of the rights of man, how could he reconcile this with owning, buying, and selling human beings? The answer, however incredible it may sound to modern Americans, is that this was not a primary concern of men of the late eighteenth century. Perhaps it should have been, but it was not. The generation of the Enlightenment was concerned about a theory of natural law which proposed an entirely new relationship between man and his government. Locke's idea of a compact between the ruler and the ruled gained limited acceptance in the English Bill of Rights of 1689. But it was not until almost one hundred years after Locke's treatise that the Declaration of Independence successfully demonstrated that rulers could be made completely responsible to the people.

That slavery contradicted the new doctrine of equality many Americans painfully acknowledged. A rough analogy might be made to the scientist who denounces pollution of the atmosphere as deadly to the future of mankind. Why, then, does he drive his automobile to his laboratory. He might answer, "I am drawn along by the general Inconvenience of living without [it]," the words which Patrick Henry used to justify his ownership of slaves. It is this failure to understand the requirements of the past as contrasted with those of our own society which has led to the misuses of history. We too easily tend to confuse means with ends and to forget the Jeffersonian dictum that the earth belongs to the living generation. Jefferson's strict construction doctrine of 1798 has been appealed to ad infinitum and even ad nauseum as the answer to various ills of our time. But Jefferson believed that restrictions of national power would provide the best *means* by which individuals (and states) could work out their future happiness. Had either Jefferson or Hamilton lived to see the "Robber Barons" plundering the public under the banner of laissez faire and individual (i.e., corporate) rights, either might have become the author of the "Square Deal" or the "New Frontier," for the ends which they sought were not different from those of Teddy Roosevelt or John F. Kennedy.

Yet a comparison of the methods of approach of Jefferson and Hamilton is worth making, though not in the sense of the confrontation of antagonists, which Professor Mitchell called "vulgar in obscuring deeper motives." Rather it is the contribution of both to the founding of the nation. It is doubtful whether Jefferson's tentative and experimental approach would have sufficed to bring order out of the confusion of 1789. Hamilton's boldness, energy, and even rashness brought order and stability to the fundamental economic ills of the country. But his contribution was even greater, for his dynamic leadership generated a great confidence and swept aside the doubters and the carpers. We might imagine him saying, as Franklin Roosevelt said in a later national crisis, "The only thing we have to fear is fear itself." And we might note for the incidental benefit of those who make modern comparisons that Hamilton, with his deficit spending and his daring spirit of experiment, would doubtless have found a warm reception among the "Brain Trusters" of the New Deal.

The result of Hamilton's program was a concentration of power in the central government and the attraction of "the rich and well born" to his standard. Jefferson was convinced that the Hamiltonian system aimed at monarchy and he determined to stem the forces which he believed would threaten freedom. Whether or not he was justified, he was sure that the triumph of Republicanism in 1801 had returned the nation to a broad base of democracy, the "consent of the governed" which he considered so essential to good government.

Their differences of personality were perhaps more marked than their goals. Jefferson was not as retiring and diffident as some contemporary observers thought, but he did not dominate large gatherings of people. There is no record of applause during his first inaugural address, perhaps because it was not fashionable, but mostly because only a few people in the audience heard him. Hamilton, by contrast, performed brilliantly in public from his first harangue at "The Fields" to his magnificent plea for the Constitution before a hostile convention at Poughkeepsie. The House of Representatives refused him a personal appearance when he presented his first report, partly to maintain the form of separation of executive and legislative branches, but also because some members feared that his persuasive art would stampede them into precipitate action.

People who met Hamilton were impressed at once with his polished sophistication, his flashing wit, his graceful manner. But he turned off some by his arrogance and conceit. Jefferson often failed to impress those he met because of his casual dress and informal, offhand manner. But the visitor who stayed was invariably charmed by the range and depth of his conversation, his rather quiet wit, his ease and lack of pretension. Hamilton dominated any social gathering, large or small, and his gaiety was infectious. Only a few days before his duel with Burr he enlivened a Fourth of July celebration by mounting the dinner table and singing an old army song. Jefferson's Virginia background and his experience in the *haute monde* of Paris was evident in his courtly manner, but he despised large social functions and found formality insufferable.

At the age of fourteen Hamilton wrote, "my ambition is prevalent," and ambition continued throughout his career to be as compulsive as it was honorable. His dreams of military glory led him from the staff of the commander in chief of the Continental Army to a field command at Yorktown, and from leadership of the troops which quelled the Whiskey Rebels to second in command of the army which was to conquer Spanish America. Oddly enough, he scarcely ever sought elective office, never after 1789. He was immune to the kind of popularity which came from public acclaim, and he denounced Jefferson for being driven by "the culpable desire of gaining or securing popularity." Hamilton might make a passionate appeal to the people for support of his policies, but he never asked them to elect him to office.

Why this curious refusal to be the popular hero? A tentative answer is that Hamilton saw himself as Rousseau's Legislator, the man above the cheapness of personal politics, who understood what the goals and responsibilities of the nation were—what was right for the country. He did not ignore individual interests, and he sincerely desired the happiness and freedom of the people. But he did not want to be answerable to them, for he thought that they were too selfish and had too little understanding of "the public good." He was convinced that their particular interests were fused with and part of the "common interest." He was responsible for the nation, but not responsive to it; he acknowledged that republicanism was the only form of government suited to America, but he was not a republican. His destiny was the nation's destiny, his interest the nation's interest, his driving thrust for power the nation's power. When the nation rejected his party his despair and disillusionment led him to conclude, "This America was not made for me."

The phrase which is one of the most frequent in Jefferson's correspondence is "my family, my farm and my books." These represented to him the best of all possible worlds. Yet he was in public life for forty years. It would be ridiculous to suppose that he was dragged kicking and protesting from one public office to another. Yet it is difficult to find any evidence of personal ambition in all his voluminous writings. Deep satisfaction with his accomplishments, disappointment at public disapproval, acute sensitivity to criticism—all these indicate his pride. But at the end of each episode of his career, Monticello with its "family, farm and books" drew him like a magnet. In the periods of his retirement he withdrew from public affairs almost completely. Between his resignation as Secretary of State and his return to the capital as Vice-President his remoteness from the party conflict was the despair of his friends and followers.

Certainly Jefferson had, like most upper class Virginians and many other eighteenth-century Americans, a strong sense of public duty, perhaps an unusual amount of what Dos Passos called the "parental bent." Nor is there any doubt that when he entered the political arena he fought his battles with redoubtable energy and a shrewdness which his enemies called cunning and devious. He dominated in a curious way, which was consistent with both the gentleness and the strength of his personality, but totally at variance with the heroic mold of the other leaders of his time. Margaret Bayard Smith, of the Delaware Federalist Bayards and the wife of editor Samuel Harrison Smith, was completely nonplussed at her meeting with "the violent democrat, the vulgar demagogue . . . and profligate man" about whom she had heard so much. Jefferson overwhelmed her with his charm, as he did crusty old William Plumer, the senator from New Hampshire.

It was in part this personality which accounted for Jefferson's emergence as the nation's first "champion of the people." Even those who had never seen him seemed to sense his sympathetic understanding, his humanness. Total strangers came to the presidential residence in Washington and were cordially received. We can readily imagine this desire to view a national hero, but would a visiting farmer intrude on the august presence of George Washington or John Adams? Yet one such found himself at dinner talking of clover and manure with President Jefferson.

He not only understood the people, but he had a great deal of faith in them. Like Hamilton and the philosophers of the eighteenth century, he believed that few men were enlightened and that the wisdom of the people left a great deal to be desired. "What a Bedlamite is man!" he exclaimed to John Adams. But, unlike Hamilton, he believed that the people were the surest safeguards of liberty and that the remedy for their mistakes was not to take away their power but "to inform their discretion" by education.

Jefferson believed that the function of government was to provide for the safety and happiness of the people by allowing them as much freedom as possible in the pursuit of their ambitions. Where Hamilton saw government as a generating force for furthering their interests, Jefferson saw it primarily as an instrument for their protection. For his generation that government was best which governed least. Hamilton's government as a creative force for positive action in promoting the general welfare would appear to be a keener perception of its proper role in the complexities of the twentieth century.

But I think that Hamilton might not have recognized that man was not made for government—nor for corporate or labor or other structured organizations. These were made for man, and Jefferson would be the first to question whether they have not tended to submerge the individual to the point where the ends of human happiness and freedom have been lost in the confusion of the struggle for other goals—corporate profits, institutionalized welfare, augmentation of power for the sake of power itself.

I may be doing Hamilton an injustice. Basically the cleavage between Jefferson and Hamilton was as old as man's attempt to govern himself. To what degree must society be regulated so that it is orderly and secure, so that some members of the society do not injure others; and to what degree may the individual members of that society be left free to engage in their own particular pursuit of happiness? In other words, where is the nice balance between liberty and order? As between Jefferson and Hamilton there are no "either or" solutions for the twentieth century any more than there were for the eighteenth. Those who see the dangers of anarchy and disorder as threats to security would with Hamilton tip the scales in favor of more order. Those who are alarmed at institutional threats to the free individual would say with Jefferson, "I would rather be exposed to the inconvenience attending too much liberty than to those attending too small a degree of it."

Appendix I
Excerpts from Jefferson's writings

Jefferson fears the effects of industrialization in the United States (Chapter VIII).

The political economists of Europe had established it as a principle that every state should endeavour to manufacture for itself: and this principle, like many others, we transfer to America, without calculating the difference of circumstance which should often produce a difference of result. In Europe the lands are either cultivated, or locked up against the cultivator. Manufacture must therefore be resorted to of necessity not of choice, to support the surplus of their people. But we have an immensity of land courting the industry of the husbandman. Is it best then that all our citizens should be employed in its improvement, or that one half should be called off from that to exercise manufactures and handicraft arts for the other? Those who labour in the earth are the chosen people of God, if ever he had a chosen people, whose breasts he has made his peculiar deposit for substantial and genuine virtue. It is the focus in which he keeps alive that sacred fire, which otherwise might escape from the face of the earth. Corruption of morals in the mass of cultivators is a phenomenon of which no age nor nation has furnished an example. It is the mark set on those, who not looking up to heaven, to their own soil and industry, as does the husbandman, for their subsistance, depend for it on the casualties and caprice of customers. Dependance begets subservice and venality, suffocates the germ of virtue, and prepares fit tools for the designs of ambition. This, the natural progress and consequence of the arts, has sometimes perhaps been retarded by

410

accidental circumstances: but, generally speaking, the proportion which the aggregate of the other classes of citizens bears in any state to that of its husbandmen, is the proportion of its unsound to its healthy parts, and is a good-enough barometer whereby to measure its degree of corruption. While we have land to labour then, let us never wish to see our citizens occupied at a work-bench, or twirling a distaff. Carpenters, masons, smiths, are wanting in husbandry: but, for the general operations of manufacture, let our work-shops remain in Europe. It is better to carry provisions and materials to workmen there, than bring them to the provisions and materials, and with them their manners and principles. The loss by the transportation of commodities across the Atlantic will be made up in happiness and permanence of government. The mobs of great cities add just so much to the support of pure government, as sores do to the strength of the human body. It is the manners and spirit of a people which preserve a republic in vigour. A degeneracy in these is a canker which soon eats to the heart of its laws and constitution.

Jefferson, *Notes on Virginia*, ed. Peden, Query XIX, pp. 164–65.

Jefferson points out the logic of a "small navy" policy for the United States (Chapter VIII; cf., Chapter XVI).

Never was so much false arithmetic employed on any subject, as that which had been employed to persuade nations that it is their interest to go to war. Were the money which it has cost to gain, at the close of a long war, a little town, or a little territory, the right to cut wood here, or to catch fish there, expended in improving what they already possess, in making roads, opening rivers, building ports, improving the arts, and finding employment for their idle poor, it would render them much stronger, much wealthier and happier. This I hope will be our wisdom. And, perhaps, to remove as much as possible the occasions of making war, it might be better for us to abandon the ocean altogether, that being the element whereon we shall be principally exposed to jostle with other nations: to leave to others to bring what we shall want, and to carry what we can spare. This would make us invulnerable to Europe, by offering none of our property to their prize, and would turn all our citizens to the cultivation of the earth; and, I repeat it again, cultivators of the earth are the most virtuous and independent citizens. It might be time enough to seek employment for them at sea, when the land no longer offers it. But the actual habits of our countrymen attach them to commerce. They will exercise it for themselves. Wars then must sometimes be our lot; and all the wise can do, will be to avoid that half of them which would be produced by our own follies, and our own acts of injustice; and to make for the other half the best preparations we can. Of what nature should these be? A land army would be useless for offence, and not the best nor safest instrument of defence. For either of these purposes, the sea is the field on which we should meet an European enemy. On that element it is necessary we should possess some power. To aim at such a navy as the greater nations of Europe possess, would be a foolish and wicked waste of the energies of our countrymen. It would be to pull on our own heads that load of military expence, which makes the European labourer go supperless to bed, and moistens his bread with the sweat of his brows. It will be enough if we enable ourselves to prevent insults from those nations of Europe which are weak on the sea, because circumstances exist, which render even the stronger ones weak as to us. Providence has placed their richest and most defenceless possessions at our door; has obliged their most precious commerce to pass as it were in review before us. To protect this, or to assail us, a small part only of their naval force will ever be risqued across the Atlantic. The dangers to which the elements expose them here are too well known, and the greater dangers to which they would be exposed at home, were any general calamity to involve their whole fleet. They can attack us by detachment only; and it will suffice to make ourselves equal to what they may detach. Even a smaller force than they may detach will be rendered equal or superior by the quickness with which any check may be repaired with us, while losses with them will be irreparable till too late. A small naval force then is sufficient for us, and a small one is necessary.

Jefferson, *Notes on Virginia,* ed. Peden, Query XXII, pp. 174-76.

Jefferson states his reasons for approving the new Constitution, although he still has some reservations (Chapter VIII).

You say that I have been dished up to you as an antifederalist, and ask me if it be just. My opinion was never worthy enough of notice to merit citing: but since you ask it I will tell it you. I am not a Federalist, because I never submitted the whole system of my opinions to the creed of any party of men whatever in religion, in philosophy, in politics, or in any thing else where I was capable of thinking for myself. Such an addiction is the last degradation of a free and moral agent. If I could not go to heaven but with a party, I would not go there at all. Therefore I protest to you I am not of the party of federalists. But I am much farther from that of the Antifederalists. I approved from the first moment, of the great mass of what is in the new constitution, the consolidation of the government, the organisation into Executive, legislative and judiciary, the subdivision of the legislative, the happy compromise of interests between the great and little states by the different manner of voting in the different houses, the voting by persons instead of states, the qualified negative on laws given to the Executive which however I should have liked better if associated with the judiciary also as in New York, and the power of taxation. I thought at first that the latter might have been limited. A little reflection soon convinced me it ought not to be. What I disapproved from the first moment also was the want of a bill of rights to guard liberty against the legislative as well as executive branches of the government, that is to say to secure freedom in religion, freedom of the press, freedom from monopolies, freedom from unlawful imprisonment, freedom from a permanent military, and a trial by jury in all cases determinable by the laws of the land. I disapproved also the perpetual reeligibility of the President. To these points of disapprobation I adhere. My first wish was that the 9. first conventions might accept the constitution, as the means of securing to us the great mass of good it contained, and that the 4. last might reject it, as the means of obtaining amendments. But I was corrected in this wish the moment I saw the much better plan of Massachusetts and which had never occurred to me. With respect to the declaration of rights I suppose the majority of the United states are of my opinion: for I apprehend all the antifederalists, and a very respectable proportion of the federalists think that such a declaration should now be annexed. The enlightened part of Europe have given us the greatest credit for inventing this instrument of security for the rights of the people, and have been not a little surprised to see us so soon give it up. With respect to the re-eligibility of the president, I find myself differing from the majority of my countrymen, for I think there are but three states of the 11. which have desired an alteration of this. And indeed, since the thing is established, I would wish it not to be altered during the life of our great leader, whose executive talents are superior to those I believe of any man in the world, and who alone by the authority of his name and the confidence reposed in his perfect integrity, is fully qualified to put the new government so under way as to secure it against the efforts of opposition. But having derived from our error all the good there was in it I hope we shall correct it the moment we can no longer have the same person at the helm. These, my dear friend, are my sentiments, by which you will see I was right in saying I am neither federalist nor antifederalist; that I am of neither party, nor yet a trimmer between parties. These my opinions I wrote within a few hours after I had read the constitution, to one or two friends in America. I had not then read one single word printed on the subject. I never had an opinion in politics or religion which I was afraid to own. A costive reserve on these subjects might have procured me more esteem from some people, but less from myself.

To Frances Hopkinson, March 13, 1789, *Papers,* ed. Boyd, XIV 650–51.

Jefferson replies to John Taylor's proposal that Virginia and other Southern states secede to escape federal tyranny (Chapter XII).

Perhaps this party division is necessary to induce each to watch and delate to the people the proceedings of the other. But if on a temporary superiority of the one party, the other is to resort to a scission of the Union, no federal government can ever exist. If to rid ourselves of the present rule of Massachusetts and Connecticut, we break the Union, will the evil stop there? Suppose the New England States alone cut off, will our nature be changed? Are we not men still to the south of that, and with all the passions of men? Immediately, we shall see a Pennsylvania and a Virginia party arise in the residuary confederacy, and the public mind will be distracted with the same party spirit. What a game too will the one party have in their hands, by eternally threatening the other that unless they do so and so, they will join their northern neighbors. If we reduce our Union to Virginia and North Carolina, immediately the conflict will be established between the representatives of these two States, and they will end by breaking into their simple units. Seeing, therefore, that an association of men who will not quarrel with one another is a thing which never yet existed, from the greatest confederacy of nations down to a town meeting or a vestry; seeing that we must have somebody to quarrel with, I had rather keep our New England associates for that purpose, than to see our bickerings transferred to others. They are circumscribed within such narrow limits, and their population so full, that their numbers will ever be the minority, and they are marked, like the Jews, with such a perversity of character, as to constitute, from that circumstance, the natural division of our parties. A little patience, and we shall see the reign of witches pass over, their spells dissolved, and the people recovering their true sight, restoring their government to its true principles.

To John Taylor of Caroline, June 1, 1798, *Writings,* ed. Ford, VII, 264–65.

Jefferson makes a tentative suggestion for extreme measures in proposing a second series of Kentucky Resolutions (Chapter XII).

That the principles already advanced by Virginia & Kentucky are not to be yielded in silence, I presume we all agree. I should propose a declaration or Resolution by their legislatures on this plan. 1st. Answer the reasonings of such of the states as have ventured into the field of reason, & that of the Committee of Congress. Here they have given us all the advantage we could wish. Take some notice of those states who have either not answered at all, or answered without reasoning. 2. Make a firm protestation against the principle & the precedent; and a reservation of the rights resulting to us from these palpable violations of the constitutional compact by the Federal government, and the approbation or acquiescence of the several co-states; so that we may hereafter do, what we might now rightfully do, whenever repetitions of these and other violations shall make it evident that the Federal government, disregarding the limitations of the federal compact, mean to exercise powers over us to which we have never assented. 3. Express in affectionate & conciliatory language our warm attachment to union with our sister-states, and to the instrument & principles by which we are united; that we are willing to sacrifice to this every thing except those rights of self government the securing of which was the object of that compact; that not at all disposed to make every measure of error or wrong a cause of scission, we are willing to view with indulgence to wait with patience till those passions & delusions shall have passed over which the federal government have artfully & successfully excited to cover it's own abuses & to conceal it's designs; fully confident that the good sense of the American people and their attachment to those very rights which we are now vindicating will, before it shall be too late, rally with us round the true principles of our federal compact. But determined, were we to be disappointed in this, to sever ourselves from that union we so much value, rather than give up the rights of self government which we have reserved, & in which alone we see liberty, safety & happiness.

These things I sketch hastily, only as topics to be enlarged on, and wishing you to consider on them or what else is best to be done. At any rate let me hear from you by the post or before it if you can. adieu affectionately.

To James Madison, August 23, 1799, Koch, *The Great Collaboration,* pp. 197–98.

Jefferson discusses the desirability of an aristocracy based on talent and ability rather than heredity.

For I agree with you that there is a natural aristocracy among men. The grounds of this are virtue and talents. Formerly bodily powers gave place among the aristoi. But since the invention of gunpowder has armed the weak as well as the strong with missile death, bodily strength, like beauty, good humor, politeness and other accomplishments, has become but an auxiliary ground of distinction. There is also an artificial aristocracy founded on wealth and birth, without either virtue or talents; for with these it would belong to the first class. The natural aristocracy I consider as the most precious gift of nature for the instruction, the trusts, and government of society. And indeed it would have been inconsistent in creation to have formed man for the social state, and not to have provided virtue and wisdom enough to manage the concerns of the society. May we not even say that that form of government is the best which provides the most effectually for a pure selection of these natural aristoi into the offices of government? The artificial aristocracy is a mischievous ingredient in government, and provision should be made to prevent it's ascendancy. On the question, What is the best provision, you and I differ; but we differ as rational friends using the free exercise of our own reason, and mutually indulging it's errors. *You* think it best to put the Pseudo-aristoi into a separate chamber of legislation where they may be hindered from doing mischief by their coordinate branches, and where also they may be a protection to wealth against the Agrarian and plundering enterprises of the Majority of the people. I think that to give them power in order to prevent them from doing mischief, is arming them for it, and increasing instead of remedying the evil. For if the coordinate branches can arrest their action, so may they that of the coordinates. Mischief may be done negatively as well as positively. Of this a cabal in the Senate of the U.S. has furnished many proofs. Nor do I believe them necessary to protect the wealthy; because enough of these will find their way into every branch of the legislation to protect themselves. From 15. to 20. legislatures of our own, in action for 30. years past, have proved that no fears of an equalisation of property are to be apprehended from them.

I think the best remedy is exactly that provided by all our constitutions, to leave to the citizens the free election and separation of the aristoi from the pseudo-aristoi, of the wheat from the chaff. In general they will elect the real good and wise. In some instances, wealth may corrupt, and birth blind them; but not in sufficient degree to endanger society.

To John Adams, October 28, 1813, *The Adams-Jefferson Letters,* ed. Cappon, II, 388–89.

Jefferson argues the case for man's possession of a moral instinct (Chapter XVII).

These good acts give us pleasure, but how happens it that they give us pleasure? Because nature hath implanted in our breasts a love of others, a sense of duty to them, a moral instinct, in short, which prompts us irresistibly to feel and to succor their distresses, and protests against the language of Helvetius, "what other motive than self-interest could determine a man to generous actions? It is as impossible for him to love what is good for the sake of good, as to love evil for the sake of evil." The Creator would indeed have been a bungling artist, had he intended man for a social animal, without planting in him social dispositions. It is true they are not planted in every man, because there is no rule without exceptions; but it is false reasoning which converts exceptions into the general rule. Some men are born without the organs of sight, or of hearing, or without hands. Yet it would be wrong to say that man is born without these faculties, and sight, hearing, and hands may with truth enter into the general definition of man. The want or imperfection of the moral sense in some men, like the want or imperfection of the senses of sight and hearing in others, is no proof that it is a general characteristic of the species. When it is wanting, we endeavor to supply the defect by education, by appeals to reason and calculation, by presenting to the being so unhappily conformed, other motives to do good and to eschew evil, such as the love, or the hatred, or rejection of those among whom he lives, and whose society is necessary to his happiness and even existence; demonstrations by sound calculation that honesty promotes interest in the long run; the rewards and penalties established by the laws; and ultimately the prospects of a future state of retribution for the evil as well as the good done while here. These are the correctives which are supplied by education, and which exercise the functions of the moralist, the preacher, and legislator; and they lead into a course of correct action all those whose disparity is not too profound to be eradicated. Some have argued against the existence of a moral sense, by saying that if nature had given us such a sense, impelling us to virtuous actions, and warning us against those which are vicious, then nature would also have designated, by some particular earmarks, the two sets of actions which are, in themselves, the one virtuous and the other vicious. Whereas, we find, in fact, that the same actions are deemed virtuous in one country and vicious in another. The answer is that nature has constituted *utility* to man the standard and test of virtue. Men living in different countries, under different circumstances, different habits and regimens, may have different utilities; the same act, therefore may be useful, and consequently virtuous in one country which is injurious and vicious in another differently circumstanced. I sincerely, then, believe with you in the general existence of a moral instinct. I think it the brightest gem with which the human character is studded, and the want of it as more degrading than the most hideous of the bodily deformities.

To Thomas Law, June 13, 1814, *The Complete Jefferson* ed. Saul K. Padover, pp. 1033–34.

Jefferson has altered his view concerning the importance of industry to the American economy (Chapter XVII).

But who in 1785 could foresee the rapid depravity which was to render the close of that century the disgrace of the history of man? Who could have imagined that the two most distinguished in the rank of nations, for science and civilization, would have suddenly descended from that honorable eminence, and setting at defiance all those moral laws established by the Author of nature between nation and nation, as between man and man, would cover earth and sea with robberies and piracies, merely because strong enough to do it with temporal impunity; and that under this disbandment of nations from social order, we should have been despoiled of a thousand ships, and have thousands of our citizens reduced to Algerine slavery. Yet all this has taken place. One of these nations interdicted to our vessels all harbors of the globe without having first proceeded to some one of hers, there paid a tribute proportioned to the cargo, and obtained her license to proceed to the port of destination. The other declared them to be lawful prize if they had touched at the port, or been visited by a ship of the enemy nation. Thus were we completely excluded from the ocean. Compare this state of things with that of '85, and say whether an opinion founded in the circumstances of that day can be fairly applied to those of the present. We have experienced what we did not then believe, that there exists both profligacy and power enough to exclude us from the field of interchange with other nations: that to be independent for the comforts of life we must fabricate them ourselves. We must now place the manufacturer by the side of the agriculturist. The former question is suppressed, or rather assumes a new form. Shall we make our own comforts, or go without them, at the will of a foreign nation? He, therefore, who is now against domestic manufacture, must be for reducing us either to dependence on that foreign nation, or to be clothed in skins, and to live like wild beasts in dens and caverns. I am not one of these; experience has taught me that manufactures are now as necessary to our independence as to our comfort; and if those who quote me as of a different opinion, will keep pace with me in purchasing nothing foreign where an equivalent of domestic fabric can be obtained, without regard to difference of price, it will not be our fault if we do not soon have a supply at home equal to our demand, and wrest that weapon of distress from the hand which has wielded it.

To Benjamin Austin, January 9, 1816, *Writings,* ed. Ford, X, 9–10.

Jefferson points out that constitutions and governments are only means of attaining freedom and happiness (Chapter XVII; cf., Chapter III).

Some men look at constitutions with sanctimonious reverence, and deem them like the arc [sic] of the covenant, too sacred to be touched. They ascribe to the men of the preceeding age a wisdom more than human, and suppose what they did to be beyond amendment. I knew that age well; I belonged to it, and labored with it. It deserved well of its country. It was very like the present, but without the experience of the present; and forty years of experience in government is worth a century of bookreading; and this they would say themselves,

were they to rise from the dead. I am certainly not an advocate for frequent and untried changes in laws and constitutions. I think moderate imperfections had better be borne
with; because, when once known, we accommodate ourselves
to them, and find practical means of correcting their ill effects. But I know also, that laws and institutions must go
hand in hand with the progress of the human mind. As that
becomes more developed, more enlightened, as new discover-
ies are made, new truths disclosed, and manners and opinions
change with the change of circumstances, institutions must
advance also, and keep pace with the times. We might as well
require a man to wear still the coat which fitted him when
a boy, as civilized society to remain ever under the regimen
of their barbarous ancestors. It is this preposterous idea
which has lately deluged Europe in blood. Their monarchs,
instead of wisely yielding to the gradual change of circumstances, of favoring progressive accommodation to progressive improvement, have clung to old abuses, entrenched
themselves behind steady habits, and obliged their subjects
to seek through blood and violence rash and ruinous innovations, which, had they been referred to the peaceful deliberations and collected wisdom of the nation, would have been
put into acceptable and salutary forms. Let us follow no such
examples, nor weakly believe that one generation is not as
capable as another of taking care of itself, and of ordering
its own affairs. Let us, as our sister States have done, avail
ourselves of our reason and experience, to correct the crude
essays of our first and unexperienced, although wise, virtuous, and well-meaning councils. And lastly, let us provide in
our constitution for its revision at stated periods. What these
periods should be, nature herself indicates. By the European
tables of mortality, of the adults living at any one moment
of time, a majority will be dead in about nineteen years. At
the end of that period, then, a new majority is come into
place; or, in other words, a new generation. Each generation
is as independent as the one preceding, as that was of all
which had gone before. It has then, like them, a right to
choose for itself the form of government it believes most
promotive of its own happiness; consequently, to accommodate to the circumstances in which it finds itself, that received
from its predecessors; and it is for the peace and good of

mankind, that a solemn opportunity of doing this every nine-teen or twenty years, should be provided by the constitution; so that it may be handed on, with periodical repairs, from generation to generation, to the end of time, if anything hu-man can so long endure. It is now forty years since the constitution of Virginia was formed. The same tables inform us, that, within that period, two-thirds of the adults then living are now dead. Have then the remaining third, even if they had the wish, the right to hold in obedience to their will, and to laws heretofore made by them, the other two-thirds, who, with themselves, compose the present mass of adults? If they have not, who has? The dead? But the dead have no rights. They are nothing; and nothing cannot own something. Where there is no substance, there can be no accident. This corporeal globe, and everything upon it, belong to its present corporeal inhabitants, during their generation.

To Samuel Kercheval, July 12, 1816, *Writings,* ed. Ford, X, 42–44.

Jefferson sums up his attitude toward organized religion (Chapter XVII).

The Priests, indeed, have heretofore thought proper to as-cribe to me religious, or rather anti-religious sentiments of their own fabric, but such as soothed their resentments against the Act of Virginia for establishing religious freedom. They wish him to be thought atheist, deist, or devil, who could advocate freedom from their religious dictations, but I have ever thought religion a concern purely between our God and our consciences for which we were accountable to him, and not to the priests. I never told my own religion nor scrutinized that of another. I never attempted to make a convert, nor wish to change another's creed. I have ever judged of the religion of others by their lives; and by this test, my dear Madam, I have been satisfied yours must be an excellent one, to have produced a life of such exemplary virtue and correctness, for it is in our lives and not from our words, that our religion must be read. By the same test the world must judge me.

But this does not satisfy the priesthood, they must have a positive, a declared assent to all their interested absurdities. My opinion is that there would never have been an infidel, if there had never been a priest. The artificial structure they have built on the purest of all moral systems for the purpose of deriving from it pence and power revolts those who think for themselves and who read in that system only what is really there. These, therefore, they brand with such nicknames as their enmity chooses gratuitously to impute. I have left the world in silence to judge of causes from their effects: and I am consoled in this course, my dear friend, when I perceive the candor with which I am judged by your justice and discernment; and that, notwithstanding the slander of the Saints, my fellow citizens have thought me worthy of trust. The imputations of irreligion having spent their force, they think an imputation of change might now be turned to account as a bolster for their duperies. I shall leave them as heretofore to grope on in the dark.

To Mrs. Samuel Harrison (Margaret Bayard) Smith, August 6, 1816, *The Complete Jefferson,* ed. Padover, pp. 955–56.

Appendix II
Excerpts from Hamilton's writings

Hamilton expresses his concern over the lack of power in the government of the Confederation (Chapter VI).

The fundamental defect is a want of power in Congress. It is hardly worth while to show in what this consists, as it seems to be universally acknowledged, or to point out how it has happened, as the only question is how to remedy it. It may however be said that it has originated from three causes—an excess of the spirit of liberty which has made the particular states show a jealousy of all power not in their own hands; and this jealousy has led them to exercise a right of judging in the last resort of the measures recommended by Congress, and of acting according to their own opinions of their propriety or necessity; a diffidence in Congress of their own powers, by which they have been timid and indecisive in their resolutions, constantly making concessions to the states, till they have scarcely left themselves the shadow of power; a want of sufficient means at their disposal to answer the public exigencies and of vigor to draw forth those means; which have occasioned them to depend on the states individually to fulfil their engagements with the army, and the consequence of which has been to ruin their influence and credit with the army, to establish its dependence on each state separately rather than *on them,* that is rather than on the whole collectively.

It may be pleaded, that Congress has never any definitive powers granted them and of course could exercise none— could do nothing more than recommend. The manner in which Congress was appointed would warrant, and the public good required, that they should have considered themselves as vested with full power *to preserve the republic from harm.* They have done many of the highest acts of sovereignty, which were always chearfully submitted to—the declaration of independence, the declaration of war, the levying an army, creating a navy, emitting money, making alliances with foreign powers, appointing a dictator &c. &c.—all these implications of a complete sovereignty were never disputed, and ought to have been a standard for the whole conduct of Administration. Undefined powers are discretionary powers, limited only by the object for which they were given—in the present case, the independence and freedom of America. The confederation made no difference; for as it has not been generally adopted, it had no operation. But from what I recollect of it, Congress have even descended from the authority which the spirit of that act gives them, while the particular states have no further attended to it than as it suited their pretensions and convenience. It would take too much time to enter into particular instances, each of which separately might appear inconsiderable; but united are of serious import. I only mean to remark, not to censure.

But the confederation itself is defective and requires to be altered; it is neither fit for war, nor peace. The idea of an uncontrolable sovereignty in each state, over its internal police, will defeat the other powers given to Congress, and make our union feeble and precarious. There are instances without number, where acts necessary for the general good, and which rise out of the powers given to Congress must interfere with the internal police of the states, and there are many instances in which the particular states by arrangements of internal police can effectually though indirectly counteract the arrangements of Congress.

To James Duane, September 30, 1780, *Papers,* ed. Syrett, II, 401–02.

Hamilton points out the danger of the dispersal of power in a federal system (Chapter VI).

In a single state, where the sovereign power is exercised by delegation, whether it be a limited monarchy or a republic, the danger most commonly is, that the sovereign will become too powerful for his constituents; in federal governments, where different states are represented in a general council, the danger is on the other side—that the members will be an overmatch for his common head, or in other words, that it will not have sufficient influence and authority to secure the obedience of the several parts of the confederacy. . . .

In federal governments, each member has a distinct sovereignty, makes and executes laws, imposes taxes, distributes justice, and exercises every other function of government. It has always within itself the means of revenue, and on an emergency can levy forces. If the common sovereign should meditate, or attempt any thing unfavourable to the general liberty, each member, having all the proper organs of power, can prepare for defence with celerity and vigour. Each can immediately sound the alarm to the others, and enter into leagues for mutual protection. If the combination is general, as is to be expected, the usurpers will soon find themselves without the means of recruiting their treasury, or their armies; and for want of continued supplies of men and money, must, in the end fall a sacrifice to the attempt. If the combination is not general, it will imply, that some of the members are interested in that which is the cause of dissatisfaction to others, and this cannot be an attack upon the common liberty, but upon the interests of one part in favour of another part; and it will be a war between the members of the federal union with each other, not between them and the federal government.

From the plainest principles of human nature, two inferences are to be drawn, one, that each member of a political confederacy, will be more disposed to advance its own authority upon the ruins of that of the confederacy, than to make any improper concessions in its favour, or support it in unreasonable pretensions; the other, that the subjects of each member, will be more devoted in their attachments and obedience to their own particular governments, than to that of the union.

It is the temper of societies as well as of individuals to be impatient of constraint, and to prefer partial to general interest. Many cases may occur, where members of a confederacy have, or seem to have an advantage in things contrary to the good of the whole, or a disadvantage in others conducive to that end. The selfishness of every part will dispose each to believe, that the public burthens are unequally apportioned, and that itself is the victim. These, and other circumstances, will promote a disposition for abridging the authority of the federal government; and the ambition of men in office in each state, will make them glad to encourage it. They think their own consequence connected with the power of the government of which they are a part; and will endeavor to encrease the one as the mean of encreasing the other.

The particular governments will have more empire over the minds of their subjects, than the general one, because their agency will be more direct, more uniform, and more apparent. The people will be habituated to look up to them as the arbiters and guardians of their personal concerns, by which the passions of the vulgar, if not of all men are most strongly affected; and in every difference with the confederated body will side with them against the common sovereign.

The Continentalist, II, July 19, 1781, *Papers,* ed. Syrett, II, 654–56, *passim.*

Hamilton explains that the new federal government will exercise its authority directly on the individual citizen (Chapter VII).

It has been urged in different shapes that a Constitution of the kind proposed by the convention cannot operate without the aid of a military force to execute its laws. This, however, like most other things that have been alleged on that side, rests on mere general assertion, unsupported by any precise or intelligible designation of the reasons upon which it is founded. As far as I have been able to divine the latent meaning of the objectors, it seems to originate in a presupposition that the people will be disinclined to the exercise of federal authority in any matter of an internal nature. Waiving any exception that might be taken to the inaccuracy of inexplicitness of the distinction between internal and external, let us inquire what ground there is to presuppose that disinclination in the people. Unless we presume at the same time that the powers of the general government will be worse administered than those of the State governments, there seems to be no room for the presumption of ill will, disaffection, or opposition in the people. I believe it may be laid down as a general rule that their confidence in and obedience to a government will commonly be proportioned to the goodness or badness of its administration. It must be admitted that there are exceptions to this rule; but these exceptions depend so entirely on accidental causes that they cannot be considered as having any relation to the intrinsic merits or demerits of a constitution. These can only be judged of by general principles and maxims.

Various reasons have been suggested in the course of these papers to induce a probability that the general government will be better administered than the particular governments: the principal of which are that the extension of the spheres of election will present a greater option, or latitude of choice, to the people, that through the medium of the State legislatures—who are select bodies of men and who are to appoint the members of the national Senate—there is reason to expect that this branch will generally be composed with peculiar care and judgment; that these circumstances promise greater knowledge and more comprehensive information in the national councils. And that on account of the extent of the country from which those, to whose direction they will be committed, will be drawn, they will be less apt to be tainted by the spirit of faction, and more out of the reach of those occasional ill humors, or temporary prejudices and propensities, which in smaller societies frequently contaminate the public deliberations, beget injustice and oppression of a part of the community, and engender schemes which, though they gratify a momentary inclination or desire, terminate in general distress, dissatisfaction, and disgust. Several additional reasons of considerable force to fortify that probability will occur when we come to survey with a more critical eye the interior structure of the edifice which we are invited to erect. It will be sufficient here to remark that until satisfactory reasons can be assigned to justify an opinion that the federal government is likely to be administered in such a manner as to render it odious or contemptible to the people, there can be no reasonable foundation for the supposition that the laws of the Union will meet with any greater obstruction from them, or will stand in need of any other methods to enforce their execution, than the laws of the particular members. . . .

One thing at all events must be evident, that a government like that proposed would bid much fairer to avoid the necessity of using force than the species of league contended for by most of its opponents; the authority of which should only operate upon the States in their political or collective capacities. It has been shown that in such a Confederacy there can be no sanction for the laws but force; that frequent delinquencies in the members are the natural offspring of the very frame of the government; and that as often as these happen, they can only be redressed, if at all, by war and violence.

The plan reported by the convention, by extending the authority of the federal head to the individual citizens of the several States, will enable the government to employ the ordinary magistracy of each in the execution of its laws. It is easy to perceive that this will tend to destroy, in the common apprehension, all distinction between the sources from which they might proceed; and will give the federal government the same advantage for securing a due obedience to its authority which is enjoyed by the government of each State, in addition to the influence on public opinion which will result from the important consideration of its having power to call to its assistance and support the resources of the whole Union. It merits particular attention in this place, that the laws of the Confederacy as to the *enumerated* and *legitimate* objects of its jurisdiction will become the SUPREME LAW of the land; to the observance of which all officers, legislative, executive, and judicial in each State will be bound by the sanctity of an oath. Thus the legislatures, courts, and magistrates, of the respective members will be incorporated into the operations of the national government *as far as its just and constitutional authority extends;* and it will be rendered auxiliary to the enforcement of its laws.

No. 27, *The Federalist,* ed. Cooke, pp. 171-175.

Hamilton points out that judicial review is inherent in the structure of the new government (Chapter VII).

Some perplexity respecting the rights of the courts to pronounce legislative acts void, because contrary to the Constitution, has arisen from an imagination that the doctrine would imply a superiority of the judiciary to the legislative power. It is urged that the authority which can declare the acts of another void must necessarily be superior to the one whose acts may be declared void. As this doctrine is of great importance in all the American constitutions, a brief discussion of the grounds on which it rests cannot be unacceptable.

There is no position which depends on clearer principles than that every act of a delegated authority, contrary to the tenor of the commission under which it is exercised, is void. No legislative act, therefore, contrary to the Constitution, can be valid. To deny this would be to affirm that the deputy is greater than his principal; that the servant is above his master; that the representatives of the people are superior to the people themselves; that men acting by virtue of powers may do not only what their powers do not authorize, but what they forbid.

If it be said that the legislative body are themselves the constitutional judges of their own powers and that the construction they put upon them is conclusive upon the other departments it may be answered that this cannot be the natural presumption where it is not to be collected from any particular provisions in the Constitution. It is not otherwise to be supposed that the Constitution could intend to enable the representatives of the people to substitute their *will* to that of their constituents. It is far more rational to suppose that the courts were designed to be an intermediate body between the people and the legislature in order, among other things, to keep the latter within the limits assigned to their authority. The interpretation of the laws is the proper and peculiar province of the courts. A constitution is, in fact, and must be regarded by the judges as, a fundamental law. It therefore belongs to them to ascertain its meaning as well as the meaning of any particular act proceeding from the legislative body. If there should happen to be an irreconcilable variance between the two, that which has the superior obligation and validity ought, of course, to be preferred; or, in other words, the Constitution ought to be preferred to the statute, the intention of the people to the intention of their agents.

Nor does this conclusion by any means suppose a superiority of the judicial to the legislative power. It only supposes that the power of the people is superior to both, and that where the will of the legislature, declared in its statutes, stands in opposition to that of the people, declared in the Constitution, the judges ought to be governed by the latter rather than the former. They ought to regulate their decisions by the fundamental laws rather than by those which are not fundamental.

No. 78, *The Federalist,* ed. Cooke, pp. 524-525.

Hamilton foresees the necessity for governmental aid in the development of industry in the United States (Chapter IX).

Experience teaches, that men are often so much governed by what they are accustomed to see and practice, that the simplest and most obvious improvements, in the [most] ordinary occupations, are adopted with hesitation, reluctance and by slow gradations. The spontaneous transition to new pursuits, in a community long habituated to different ones, may be expected to be attended with proportionably greater difficulty. When former occupations ceased to yield a profit adequate to the subsistence of their followers, or. when there was an absolute deficiency of employment in them, owing to the superabundance of hands, changes would ensue; but these changes would be likely to be more tardy than might consist with the interest either of individuals or of the Society. In many cases they would not happen, while a bare support could be ensured by an adherence to ancient courses; though a resort to a more profitable employment might be practicable. To produce the desireable changes, as early as may be expedient, may therefore require the incitement and patronage of government.

The apprehension of failing in new attempts is perhaps a more serious impediment. There are dispositions apt to be attracted by the mere novelty of an undertaking—but these are not always those best calculated to give it success. To this, it is of importance that the confidence of cautious sagacious capitalists both citizens and foreigners, should be excited. And to inspire this description of persons with confidence, it is essential, that they should be made to see in any project, which is new, and for that reason alone, if, for no other, precarious, the prospect of such a degree of countenance and support from government, as may be capable of overcoming the obstacles, inseperable from first experiments.

The superiority antecedently enjoyed by nations, who have preoccupied and perfected a branch of industry, constitutes a more formidable obstacle, than either of those, which have been mentioned, to the introduction of the same branch into a country, in which it did not before exist. To maintain between the recent establishments of one country and the long matured establishments of another country, a competition upon equal terms, both as to quality and price, is in most cases impracticable. The disparity in the one, or in the other, or in both, must necessarily be so considerable as to forbid a successful rivalship, without the extraordinary aid and protection of government.

Report on the Subject of Manufactures, December 5, 1791, *Papers,* ed. Syrett, X, 266–68.

Hamilton justifies the Bank of the United States as a valid exercise of "implied powers" (Chapter IX).

The whole turn of the clause containing it, indicates, that it was the intent of the convention, by that clause to give a liberal latitude to the exercise of the specified powers. The expressions have peculiar comprehensiveness. They are—"to make *all laws,* necessary & proper for *carrying into execution* the foregoing powers & all *other powers* vested by the constitution in the *government* of the United States, or in any *department* or *officer* thereof." To understand the word as the Secretary of State does, would be to depart from its obvious & popular sense, and to give it a *restrictive* operation; an idea never before entertained. It would be to give it the same force as if the word *absolutely* or *indispensibly* had been prefixed to it.

Such a construction would beget endless uncertainty & embarassment. The cases must be palpable & extreme in which it could be pronounced with certainty, that a measure was absolutely necessary, or one without which the exercise of a given power would be nugatory. There are few measures of any government, which would stand so severe a test. To insist upon it, would be to make the criterion of the exercise of any implied power a *case of extreme necessity;* which is rather a rule to justify the overleaping of the bounds of constitutional authority, than to govern the ordinary exercise of it.

It may be truly said of every government, as well as of that of the United States, that it has only a right, to pass such laws as are necessary & proper to accomplish the objects intrusted to it. For no government has a right to do *merely what it pleases.* . . .

It is no valid objection to the doctrine to say, that it is calculated to extend the powers of the general government throughout the entire sphere of State legislation. The same thing has been said, and may be said with regard to every exercise of power by *implication* or *construction.* The moment the literal meaning is departed from, there is a chance of error and abuse. And yet an adherence to the letter of its powers would at once arrest the motions of the government. It is not only agreed, on all hands, that the exercise of constructive powers is indispensible, but every act which has been passed is more or less an exemplification of it. One has been already mentioned, that relating to light houses &c. That which declares the power of the President to remove officers at pleasure, acknowledges the same truth in another, and a signal instance.

The truth is that difficulties on this point are inherent in the nature of the federal constitution. They result inevitably from a division of the legislative power. The consequence of this division is, that there will be cases clearly within the power of the National Government; others clearly without its power; and a third class, which will leave room for controversy & difference of opinion, & concerning which a reasonable latitude of judgment must be allowed.

But the doctrine which is contended for is not chargeable with the consequence imputed to it. It does not affirm that the National government is sovereign in all respects, but that it is sovereign to a certain extent: that is, to the extent of the objects of its specified powers.

It leaves therefore a criterion of what is constitutional, and of what is not so. This criterion is the *end* to which the measure relates as a *mean.* If the end be clearly comprehended within any of the specified powers, & if the measure have an obvious relation to that end, and is not forbidden by any particular provision of the constitution—it may safely be deemed to come within the compass of the national authority. There is also this further criterion which may materially assist the decision. Does the proposed measure abridge a preexisting right of any State, or of any individual? If it does not, there is a strong presumption in favour of its constitutionality; & slighter relations to any declared object of the constitution may be permitted to turn the scale.

Opinion on the Constitutionality of the Bank, February 23, 1791, *Papers*, ed. Syrett, VIII, 102–07, *passim*.

Hamilton discusses the question of morality versus national self-interest in diplomacy (Chapter X).

Indeed the rule of morality is in this respect not exactly the same between Nations as between individuals. The duty of making its own welfare the guide of its actions is much stronger upon the former than upon the latter; in proportion to the greater magnitude and importance of national compared with individual happiness, to the greater permancy of the effects of national than of individual conduct. Existing Millions and for the most part future generations are concerned in the present measures of a government: While the consequences of the private actions of an individual, for the most part, terminate with himself or are circumscribed within a narrow compass.

Whence it follows, that an individual may on numerous occasions meritoriously indulge the emotions of generosity and benevolence; not only without an eye to, but even at the expence of his own interest. But a Nation can rarely be justified in pursuing a similar course; and when it does so ought to confine itself within such stricter bounds. Good offices, which are indifferent to the Interest of a Nation performing them or which are compensated by the existence or expectation of some reasonable equivalent or which produce an essential good to the nation, to which they are rendered, without real detriment to the affairs of the nation rendering them, prescribe the limits of national generosity or benevolence.

It is not meant here to advocate a policy absolutely selfish or interested in nations; but to shew that a policy regulated by their own interest, as far as justice and good faith permit, is, and ought to be their prevailing policy: and that either to ascribe to them a different principle of action, or to deduce from the supposition of it arguments for self-denying and self-sacrificing gratitude on the part of a Nation, which may have received from another good offices, is to misconceive or mistake what usually are and ought to be the springs of National Conduct.

"Pacificus," No. IV, July 10, 1793, *Papers*, ed. Syrett, XV, 85–86.

Hamilton analyzes the reasons for the decline of popular support for the Federalist party (Chapters XIV and XV).

Nothing is more fallacious than to expect to produce any valuable or permanent results in political projects by relying merely on the reason of men. Men are rather reasoning than reasonable animals, for the most part governed by the impulse of passion. This is a truth well understood by our adversaries, who have practised upon it with no small benefit to their cause; for at the very moment they are eulogizing the reason of men, and professing to appeal only to that faculty, they are courting the strongest and most active passion of the human heart, *vanity!* It is no less true, that the Federalists seem not to have attended to the fact sufficiently; and that they erred in relying so much on the rectitude and utility of their measures as to have neglected the cultivation of popular favor, by fair and justifiable expedients. The observation has been repeatedly made by me to individuals with whom I particularly conversed, and expedients suggested for gaining good will, which were never adopted. Unluckily, however, for us, in the competition for the passions of the people, our opponents have great advantages over us; for the plain reason that the vicious are far more active than the good passions; and that, to win the former to our side, we must renounce our principles and our objects, and unite in corrupting public opinion till it becomes fit for nothing but mischief. Yet, unless we can contrive to take hold of, and carry along with us some strong feelings of the mind, we shall in vain calculate upon any substantial or durable results. Whatever plan we may adopt, to be successful, must be founded on the truth of this proposition. And perhaps it is not very easy for us to give it full effects; especially not without some deviations from what, on other occasions, we have maintained to be right. But in determining upon the propriety of the deviations, we must consider whether it be possible for us to succeed, without, in some degree, employing the weapons which have been employed against us, and whether the actual state and future prospect of things be not such as to justify the reciprocal use of them. I need not tell you that I do not mean to countenance the imitation of things intrinsically unworthy, but only of such as may be denominated irregular; such as, in a sound and stable order of things, ought not to exist. Neither are you to infer that any revolutionary result is contemplated. In my opinion, the present Constitution is the standard to which we are to cling. Under its banners, *bona fide,* must we combat our political foes, rejecting all changes but through the channel itself provides for amendments. By these general views of the subject have my reflections been guided.

To James A. Bayard, April ____, 1802, *Writings,* ed. Lodge, X, 433–34.

Notes

Chapter I   Virginia and the West Indies

1   Dumas Malone, *Jefferson the Virginian,* vol. I of *Jefferson and His Time,* pp. 90–92. Hereafter cited as Malone, *Virginian.*

2   Robert D. Meade, *Patrick Henry, Patriot in the Making,* pp. 166–75.

3   Malone, *Virginian,* pp. 92–94; "Journal of a French Traveller in the Colonies, 1765," *American Historical Review,* 26 (1921), 745–46.

4   Malone, *Virginian,* pp. 86–87.

5   Thomas Jefferson, *Autobiography,* ed. Paul Leicester Ford, pp. 3–5. Hereafter cited as Jefferson, *Autobiography.* Malone, *Virginian,* pp. 9–12, 21–27.

6   Malone, *Virginian,* pp. 12–20.

7   Ibid., pp. 17–21, 27; Fiske Kimball, "In Search of Thomas Jefferson's Birthplace," *Virginia Magazine of History and Biography,* 51 (1943), 313–25.

8   Jefferson, *Autobiography,* pp. 4–5.

9   Malone, *Virginian,* pp. 45–46.

10   Ibid., pp. 51–56; Jefferson, *Autobiography,* pp. 5–6.

11   Malone, *Virginian,* pp. 68–73.

12   Ibid., pp. 78–79.

13   Ibid., p. 87.

14   Alexander Hamilton to Edward Stevens, November 11, 1769, *The Papers of Alexander Hamilton,* ed. Harold C. Syrett, Jacob E. Cooke, *et al.,* I, 4. Hereafter cited as *Papers,* ed. Syrett.

15   Broadus Mitchell, *Alexander Hamilton, Youth to Maturity, 1755–1788,* vol. I of *Alexander Hamilton,* pp. 24–27. Hereafter cited as Mitchell, *Hamilton,* I.

16   Ibid., I, 24–25; Hamilton to Nicholas Cruger, November 12, 1771, *Papers,* ed. Syrett, I, 11; Hamilton to Tilemand Cruger, November 16, 1771, ibid., p. 13; Hamilton to Jacob Walton and J. H. Cruger, November 27, 1771, ibid., p. 18.

17   Hamilton to the *Royal Danish American Gazette,* Sep-

tember 6, 1772, quoted in *Papers,* ed. Syrett, I, 34–38.

18 Mitchell, *Hamilton,* I, 2–8.

19 Ibid., pp. 11–12.

20 Ibid., pp. 11, 13.

21 Ibid., pp. 9, 14; Hamilton to [Alexander?] Hamilton, May 2, 1797, *The Works of Alexander Hamilton,* ed. Henry Cabot Lodge, I, 261. Hereafter cited as *Works,* ed. Lodge.

22 Mitchell, *Hamilton,* I, 14, 16–18; *Papers,* ed. Syrett, I, 1–3.

23 Mitchell, *Hamilton,* I, 36–37, 38–40.

24 Ibid., pp. 40–43.

25 Ibid., pp. 45–49.

26 Nathan Schachner, ed., "Alexander Hamilton as Viewed by His Friends: The Narratives of Robert Troup and Hercules Mulligan," *William and Mary Quarterly,* 3rd ser., 4 (1947), 207. The quotation is Mulligan's.

27 Mitchell, *Hamilton,* I, 63; *Papers,* ed. Syrett, I, 45–79.

Chapter II   The Young Rebels

1 *The Papers of Thomas Jefferson,* ed. Julian P. Boyd, I, 24. Hereafter cited as *Papers,* ed. Boyd.

2 Henry S. Randall, *Life of Thomas Jefferson,* I, 53–57. Hereafter cited as Randall, *Jefferson. Thomas Jefferson's Farm Book,* ed. Edwin M. Betts, pp. 110–14. Hereafter cited as *Farm Book,* ed. Betts.

3 *Thomas Jefferson's Garden Book, 1766-1824,* ed. Edwin M. Betts, pp. 4–11, 70. Hereafter cited as *Garden Book,* ed. Betts. *Virginia Gazette,* ed. Purdie and Dixon, February 22, 1770.

4 Jefferson to Will Fleming, March 20, 1764, *Papers,* ed. Boyd, I, 16; *Garden Book,* ed. Betts, pp. 6, 10, 12; Malone, *Virginian,* pp. 150, 159–60, 153–55.

5 Malone, *Virginian,* pp. 156, 159–60, 153.

6 Ibid., pp. 130, 128, 158.

7 Ibid., pp. 131, 135–56; *Journal of the House of Burgesses of Virginia,* 1766–69, p. 174. Hereafter cited as *House of Burgesses.*

8 *House of Burgesses,* 1766–69, pp. 145–46, 174.

9   Ibid., pp. xxxix–xlii; *Papers,* ed. Boyd, I, 28–31.

10 *House of Burgesses,* 1766-69, p. 227; ibid., 1770–72, pp. xxvii–xxxi; *Papers,* ed. Boyd, I, 43–47.

11 Malone, *Virginian,* pp. 140–42, 160.

12 *House of Burgesses,* 1773–76, pp. 28, x.

13 Ibid., pp. ix–xi, 28; Malone, *Virginian,* pp. 169–70.

14 *House of Burgesses,* 1773–76, pp. 41–43.

15 Malone, *Virginian,* p. 171; Arthur M. Schlesinger, *The Colonial Merchants in the American Revolution,* pp. 262–64.

16 Malone, *Virginian,* p. 171.

17 Ibid., pp. 148, 171–72; *House of Burgesses,* 1773–76, pp. 124, xiv, 132.

18 *Virginia Gazette,* ed. Rind, August 4, 1774; ibid., eds. Purdie and Dixon, June 16, 1774; ibid., July 14, 1774; *Papers,* ed., Boyd, I, 135; Malone, *Virginian,* 180–81.

19 *Papers,* ed. Boyd, I, 117; Malone, *Virginian,* p. 182.

20 *Papers,* ed. Boyd, I, 121–31.

21 December 15, 1774, *Papers,* ed. Syrett, I, 67.

22 Ibid., pp. 45–78; John Locke, *Treatise of Civil Government and a Letter Concerning Toleration,* ed. Charles L. Sherman, chap. IX, sec. 123, 182. Hereafter cited as Locke, *Civil Government.* (Italics mine.)

23 John C. Miller, *Origins of the Revolution,* chap. IX; Jensen, *Founding of a Nation,* pp. 40–41, 453–60.

24 Mitchell, *Hamilton,* I, 63–64.

25 Edmund Cody Burnett, *The Continental Congress,* pp. 33–59. Hereafter cited as Burnett, *Continental Congress.* Nathan Schachner, *Alexander Hamilton,* p. 33. Hereafter cited as Schachner, *Hamilton.*

26 Mitchell, *Hamilton,* I, 66–73; E. E. Beardsley, *Life and Correspondence of Samuel Seabury,* pp. 38–47.

27 *Papers,* ed. Syrett, I, 47, 67.

28 Ibid., pp. 50–51.

29 *Papers,* ed. Syrett, I, 90–91.

30 Ibid., pp. 93–94.

31 Mitchell, *Hamilton,* I, 74–75.

32 Hamilton to John Jay, November 26, 1775, *Papers,* ed. Syrett, I, 176.

33 Mitchell, *Hamilton,* I, 79–80.

Chapter III "We Hold These Truths . . ."

1   Malone, *Virginian,* pp. 193–96.
2   William Wirt Henry, *Patrick Henry: Life Correspond-
    ence and Speeches,* I, 254–72; *Virginia Gazette,* ed. Dixon
    and Hunter, April 1, 1775.
3   Malone, *Virginian,* pp. 196–98.
4   Ibid., p. 195; *Garden Book,* ed. Betts, p. 66.
5   Jefferson, *Autobiography,* pp. 16–17; *Virginia Gazette,*
    ed. Dixon and Hunter, April 29, 1775, supplement; *The
    Correspondence and Works of the Earl of Chatham,* ed.
    W. H. Taylor and J. H. Pringle, IV, 402–03.
6   Jefferson, *Autobiography,* p. 17; Malone, *Virginian,* p.
    199; *Papers,* ed. Boyd, I, 171–72.
7   *Papers,* ed. Boyd, I, 173–74.
8   Malone, *Virginian,* pp. 201–02.
9   *Papers,* ed. Boyd, I, 207.
10 Ibid., p. 217; Malone, *Virginian,* p. 207.
11 John Adams, *Diary and Autobiography of John Adams,*
    ed. Lyman H. Butterfield, III, 322. Hereafter cited as
    Adams, *Diary.* Adams to Timothy Pickering, August 6,
    1822, *The Warren-Adams Letters: Being Chiefly a Corre-
    spondence Among John Adams, Samuel Adams, and
    James Warren,* ed. Worthington C. Ford, I, 199. Hereaf-
    ter cited as *Warren-Adams Letters,* ed. Ford.
12 Jefferson to Frances Eppes, November 7, 1775, *Papers,*
    ed. Boyd, I, 252; Malone, *Virginian,* p. 216.
13 Peter Force (ed.), *American Archives . . . A Documen-
    tary History of the American Colonies,* 4th ser., III,
    240–41. Hereafter cited as *Archives,* ed. Force.
14 16 George c. 5.
15 Thomas Paine, "Common Sense," *Tracts of the Ameri-
    can Revolution,* ed. Merrill Jensen, p. 428.
16 Malone, *Virginian,* p. 217.
17 *Archives,* ed. Force, 4th ser., VI, 1524.
18 Worthington C. Ford, *et al.* (eds.), *Journals of the Conti-
    nental Congress,* I, 364–68.
19 John Adams to James Warren, May 20, 1776, *Warren-
    Adams Letters.* ed. Ford, I, 249.

20 Jefferson, *Autobiography,* 18–19; Notes of Proceedings in the Continental Congress, *Papers,* ed. Boyd, I, 314.

21 Adams to Abigail Adams, July 3, 1776, *Adams Family Correspondence,* ed. Lyman H. Butterfield, II, 30.

22 *Papers,* ed. Boyd, I, 313, 314.

23 Carl Becker, *The Declaration of Independence,* pp. 212–26; *Papers,* ed. Boyd, I, 299–313.

24 Jefferson to Henry Lee, May 8, 1825, *The Writings of Thomas Jefferson,* ed. Paul Leicester Ford, X, 343. Hereafter cited as *Writings,* ed. Ford.

25 Thomas Jefferson, *Notes on the State of Virginia,* ed. William Peden, p. 159. Hereafter cited as Jefferson, *Notes on Virginia.* Jefferson to A.C.V.C. Destutt de Tracy, December 26, 1820, *Writings,* ed. Ford, X, 174.

26 Jefferson to Lee, May 8, 1825, *Writings,* ed. Ford, X, 343.

27 Locke, *Civil Government,* chap. II, secs. 95, 63. It should not be assumed that Jefferson had these or other specific phrases in mind. The purpose here is to show the general background of the Enlightenment, and Locke as one of its principal philosophers. Jefferson himself noted, "I turned to neither book nor pamphlet while writing it." Jefferson to Henry Lee, May 8, 1825, *Writings,* ed. Ford, X, 343.

28 Locke, *Civil Government,* chap. IX, secs. 124, 82.

29 Ibid., chap. XIX, secs. 214, 144.

30 Benjamin Franklin, *Writings,* ed. Albert H. Smythe, V, 115, 230.

31 *Papers,* ed. Syrett, I, 90–91.

32 Becker, *Declaration of Independence,* p. 6.

33 Carl Becker, *The Eve of the Revolution: A Chronicle of the Breach with England (Chronicles of America,* ed. Allen Johnson, vol. XI), p. 256.

Chapter IV   In the Service of the Nation

1 Mitchell, *Hamilton,* I, 89–99; Alfred Hoyt Bill, *The Campaign of Princeton,* pp. 112–13.

2 George Washington, *Writings,* ed. John C. Fitzpatrick, VII, p. 218. Hereafter cited as *Writings,* ed. Fitzpatrick.

3   George Washington to the President of Congress, May 23, 1776, ibid., IV, 306–07; Washington to Robert Harrison, January 9, 1777, ibid., VI, 487; Washington to Joseph Reed, January 23, 1776, ibid, IV, 269.

4   Martha Dangerfield Bland to Frances Bland Randolph, May 12, 1777, New Jersey Historical Society *Proceedings,* 51 (1933), p. 269.

5   George Washington Parke Custis, *Recollections and Private Memoirs of Washington,* pp. 345–46.

6   John C. Hamilton, *A History of the Republic Traced in the Writings of Alexander Hamilton,* I, 527–28; Hereafter cited as Hamilton, *Alexander Hamilton.* James Thomas Flexner, *George Washington in the American Revolution, 1775-1783,* p. 413. Hereafter cited as Flexner, *Washington in the Revolution.* Mitchell, *Hamilton,* I, 115; cf., Freeman, *Washington,* vols. IV and V in which Hamilton receives no more attention than the other aides.

7   Hamilton to Robert Livingston, June 28, 1777, *Papers,* ed. Syrett, I, 275; Hamilton to George Clinton, February 13, 1778, ibid., p. 425.

8   John C. Miller, *Alexander Hamilton: Portrait in Paradox,* pp. 37–40.

9   Ward, *Revolution,* I, chap. XLIV: Freeman, *Washington,* IV, 617–18.

10 Hamilton to Livingston, June 28, 1777, *Papers,* ed. Syrett, I, 275.

11 Freeman, *Washington,* IV, 217–18, 499–500; B. H. Liddell Hart, *Strategy,* chap. XIX, esp. pp. 334–35; Freeman, *Washington,* IV, 564–80; Flexner, *Washington in the Revolution,* pp. 267–68.

12 Freeman, *Washington,* IV, 419–24.

13 E.g., ibid., pp. 180–82, 236–40.

14 Washington to Patrick Henry, April 13, 1777, *Writings,* ed. Fitzpatrick, VII, 409.

15 Freeman, *Washington,* IV, 544–46; Mitchell, *Hamilton,* I, 130–38.

16 Freeman, *Washington,* IV, chap. XXII.

17 *Writings,* ed. Fitzpatrick, X, 30.

18 Hamilton to George Clinton, February 13, 1778, *Papers,* ed. Syrett, I, 428.

19 George Washington, *Writings,* ed. Jared Sparks, V, 512.
    Hereafter cited as *Writings of Washington,* ed. Sparks.

20 Mercy Warren to Mrs. Theoderick Bland, March 10,
    1778, *Warren-Adams Letters,* ed. Ford, II, 7.

21 Mitchell, *Hamilton,* I, 166; Miller, *Hamilton,* p. 31.

22 Freeman, *Washington,* IV, 18–44; Mitchell, *Hamilton,*
    I, 164–70. Lee is quoted in Miller, *Hamilton,* p. 31.

23 Miller, *Hamilton,* 35; Mitchell, *Hamilton,* I, 106.

24 James Thomas Flexner, *The Traitor and the Spy: Bene-
    dict Arnold and John André,* p. 371; Washington to Ro-
    chambeau, September 27, 1780, *Writings,* ed. Fitzpat-
    rick, XX, 97.

25 Hamilton to John Laurens, June 30, 1780, *Papers,* ed.
    Syrett, II, 348; Mitchell, *Hamilton,* I, 197–208.

26 Hamilton to Laurens, May 22, 1779, *Papers,* ed. Syrett,
    II, 52.

27 Freeman, *Washington,* V, 259–60; Hamilton to Philip
    Schuyler, February 18, 1781, *Papers,* ed. Syrett, II,
    563–65.

28 Freeman, *Washington,* V, 310; *Writings,* ed. Fitzpatrick,
    XXII, 438.

29 Miller, *Hamilton,* p. 77.

30 Freeman, *Washington,* V, 369–72; Mitchell, *Hamilton,*
    I, 256–59.

Chapter V   In the Service of Virginia

1 Jefferson to Thomas Nelson, May 16, 1776, *Papers,* ed.
   Boyd, I, 292.

2 Edmund Randolph to Jefferson, June 23, 1776, ibid.,
   407.

3 Drafts of Jefferson's constitution, Mason's plan, and the
   constitution as adopted in ibid., pp. 329–86.

4 Ibid., pp. 382, 385.

5 Ibid., pp. 363, 385.

6 Ibid., p. 362.

7 Jefferson to William Fleming, July 1, 1776, ibid., p. 412.

8 Jefferson to Pendleton, *ca.* June 30, 1776, ibid., p. 408;
   Jefferson to John Page, July 30, 1776, ibid., p. 483;
   George Wythe to Jefferson, November 18, 1776, ibid.,
   pp. 603–04.

9 Jefferson to John Hancock, October 11, 1776, ibid., p. 524.

10 Jefferson, *Autobiography,* pp. 58–59; Bill to Enable Tenants in Fee Tail to Convey Their Lands in Fee Simple, *Papers,* ed. Boyd, I, 560–61.

11 Malone, *Virginian,* pp. 261–63; *Papers,* ed. Boyd, II, 305–24 has full account of the evolution of the Virginia Code.

12 Jefferson to Pendleton, July 13, 1776, *Papers,* ed. Boyd, I, 492–93.

13 Anthony Marc Lewis, "Jefferson and Virginia's Pioneers, 1774–1781," *Mississippi Valley Historical Review,* 34 (1948), 551–58; Thomas Perkins Abernethy, *Western Lands in the American Revolution,* pp. 217–29.

14 *Papers,* ed. Boyd, VI, 613–615.

15 Bill No. 64, ibid., II, 493–95.

16 Bill No. 68, ibid., p. 513; Jefferson, *Autobiography,* p. 72.

17 Bill No. 64, *Papers,* ed. Boyd, II, 492; Bill No. 69, ibid., p. 515.

18 Ibid., p. 497.

19 Ibid., I, 363.

20 Bill No. 51 and notes, ibid., II, 470–73.

21 Jefferson to Adams, October 28, 1813, *Writings,* ed. Ford, IX, 426.

22 Jefferson, *Notes on Virginia,* p. 159.

23 Bill No. 82, *Papers,* ed. Boyd, II, 545–53.

24 Jefferson to Madison, December 16, 1786, ibid., X, 603.

25 Bill No. 79, ibid., II, 526.

26 Ibid., p. 527.

27 Jefferson to William Jarvis, September 28, 1820, *Writings,* ed. Ford, X, 161.

28 Bill No. 79, *Papers,* ed. Boyd, II, 527.

29 Jefferson to Madison, December 20, 1787, ibid., XII, 442.

30 Bill No. 79 and Bill No. 80 with notes, ibid., II, 526–43.

31 Jefferson, *Autobiography,* pp. 75–76; Jefferson, *Notes on Virginia,* p. 289.

32 Malone, *Virginian,* pp. 301–03; Page to Jefferson, June 6, 1779, and Jefferson's reply, June 3, 1779, *Papers,* ed. Boyd, II, 278–79.

33 Gordon S. Wood, *The Creation of the American Republic, 1776–1787,* pp. 146–50. Hereafter cited as Wood, *American Republic.* Margaret Burnham Macmillan, *The War Governors of the American Revolution,* chaps. III and IV.

34 January 8–19, 1781, *Journal of the Council of the State of Virginia,* ed. H. R. McIlwaine, II, 274–75.

35 Nathan Schachner, *Thomas Jefferson: A Biography,* p. 181. Hereafter cited as Schachner, *Jefferson.*

36 Jefferson to Fleming, June 8, 1779, *Papers,* ed. Boyd, II, 288; Jefferson to Benjamin Harrison, October 22, 1779, ibid., III, 109; Jefferson to Richard Henry Lee, June 17, 1779, ibid., II, 298.

37 Jefferson to Horatio Gates, November 10, 1780, ibid., IV, 108; Jefferson to Harrison, November 24, 1780, ibid., p. 150; Jefferson to the Chevalier de la Luzerne, August 31, 1780, ibid., III, 577.

38 See for example: Jefferson to the Committee of Congress, July 2, 1780, Jefferson to Samuel Huntington, same date, Jefferson to Washington, July 2 to July 27, 1780, ibid., III, 476–513, *passim.*

39 Gates to Jefferson, July 19, 1780, ibid., 496. For military events see Ward, *Revolution,* II, chaps. LXXXII–LXXXIV.

40 Page to Jefferson, September 22, 1780, *Papers,* ed. Boyd, III, 655; Mason to Jefferson, October 6, 1780, ibid., IV, 19.

41 Nathanael Greene to Jefferson, November 20, 1780, ibid., IV, 130–32; Jefferson to Harrison, November 24, 1780, ibid., 150–51.

42 Malone, *Virginian,* pp. 332–40; Schachner, *Jefferson,* pp. 199–204.

43 See for example Jefferson's correspondence, February 16–18, 1780, *Papers,* ed. Boyd, IV, 625–52, *passim.*

44 Jefferson to Baron von Steuben, February 12, 1781, ibid., p. 593.

45 Jefferson to von Steuben, February 13, 1781, ibid., p. 603; Jefferson to Richard Claiborne, March 10, 1781 and reply, March 30, 1781, ibid., V, 286–87.

46 Malone, *Virginian,* pp. 352–58.

47 Jefferson, *Autobiography,* p. 79.

Chapter VI   Hamilton and the Rise of Nationalism

1   Hamilton to Richard Kidder Meade, March _____, 1782,
    Papers, ed. Syrett, III, 70; Hamilton to John Laurens,
    August _____, 1782, ibid., p. 145.
2   Hamilton to Meade, August 27, 1782, ibid., pp. 150–51.
3   Hamilton to Meade, March _____, 1782, ibid., p. 69.
4   Hamilton to Robert Morris, May 18, 1782, ibid., p. 89;
    Mitchell, *Hamilton,* I, 268.
5   Hamilton to Morris, June 17, 1782, *Papers,* ed. Syrett,
    III, 93–94; Burnett, *Continental Congress,* pp. 492, 514.
6   Hamilton to Morris, July 22, 1782, *Papers,* ed. Syrett,
    III, 114; Hamilton to Morris, August 13, 1782, ibid., p.
    135.
7   Mitchell, *Hamilton,* I, 100-03; Publius Letter I, October
    16, 1778, *Papers,* ed. Syrett, III, 563.
8   Hamilton to James Duane, September 3, 1780, *Papers,*
    ed. Syrett, II, 401.
9   Hamilton to Morris, April 30, 1781, ibid., II, 604–35.
10 Hamilton to Morris, April 30, 1781, ibid., pp. 621, 622,
    625.
11 Merrill Jensen, *The New Nation: A History of the United
    States During the Confederation, 1781–1789,* pp. 60–63.
    Hereafter cited as Jensen, *The New Nation.*
12 Hamilton to Morris, April 4, 1781, *Papers,* ed. Syrett,
    II, 624, 626.
13 Hamilton to Morris, April 30, 1781, ibid., p. 618.
14 Ibid., pp. 629–30.
15 Hamilton to the Marquis de Lafayette, November 3,
    1782, ibid., p. 192.
16 Burnett, *Continental Congress,* pp. 482, 557–60; Hamil-
    ton to James Duane, September 3, 1780, *Papers,* ed.
    Syrett, II, 401.
17 The Continentalist, No. II, July 19, 1781, ibid., p. 656.
18 Burnett, *Continental Congress,* p. 533.
19 Madison as quoted in Irving Brant, *James Madison: Na-
    tionalist,* p. 228. Hereafter cited as Brant, *Nationalist.*
20 Congress to Governor William Greene of Rhode Island,
    December 11, 1782, *Papers,* ed. Syrett, III, 210; Burnett,
    Continental Congress, p. 533.
21 Stephen Higginson to Theophilus Parsons, Sr., April 7,

1783, Edmund Cody Burnett (ed.), *Letters of Members of the Continental Congress,* VIII, 123.

22. Hamilton to Washington, March 17, 1783, *Papers,* ed. Syrett, III, 292.

23 Ibid., p. 292; Burnett, *Continental Congress,* pp. 560–61, 568–71.

24 Hamilton to Morris, April 30, 1781, *Papers,* ed. Syrett, II, 635.

25 Hamilton to Washington, February 7, 1783, ibid., III, 254.

26 Hamilton to Washington, February 13, 1783, ibid., pp. 254–55.

27 Washington to Hamilton, March 4, 1783, *Writings,* ed. Fitzpatrick, XXVI, 186.

28 Ibid., p. 211 n.

29 Quoted in Miller, *Hamilton,* p. 94.

30 General Orders, March 11, 1783, *Writings,* ed. Fitzpatrick, XXVI, 208; Flexner, *Washington in the Revolution,* II, 501–07; Freeman, *Washington,* V, 433–36.

31 Hamilton to Washington, March 17, 1783, *Papers,* ed. Syrett, III, 290–93.

32 Hamilton to Washington, March 25, 1783, ibid., p. 306.

33 Washington to the Chevalier de la Luzerne, March 29, 1783, *Writings,* ed. Fitzpatrick, XXVI, 264; Freeman, *Washington,* V, 438–39.

34 Burnett, *Continental Congress,* p. 574; Freeman, *Washington,* V. 440–43.

35 Hamilton to John Dickinson, September 25–30, 1783, *Papers,* ed. Syrett, III, 455; Burnett, *Continental Congress,* pp. 576–81.

36 *Works,* ed. Lodge, I, 305–14; Mitchell, *Hamilton,* I, 323; Hamilton to John Jay, July 25, 1783, *Papers,* ed. Syrett, III, 417.

37 *Papers,* ed. Syrett, III, 471.

38 A Letter from Phocion to the Considerate Citizens of New York, January 1–27, 1784, ibid., pp. 484, 493–94.

39 *Treaties and Other International Acts of the United States,* ed. Hunter Miller, II, 155. Hereafter cited as *Treaties,* ed. Miller.

40 Letter from Phocion, January 1–27, 1784, *Papers,* ed. Syrett, III, 489.

41 Ibid., p. 484.

42 A Second Letter from Phocion, . . . April _____, 1784, ibid., p. 554.

43 Mitchell, *Hamilton,* I, 340–45.

44 *Select Cases of the Mayor's Court of New York City, 1674–1784,* ed. Richard Morris (*American Legal Records,* Vol. II), II, 312–13, 304–05, 309. Hereafter cited as *Mayor's Court,* ed. Morris.

45 As quoted in Miller, *Hamilton,* p. 107.

46 *Mayor's Court,* ed. Morris, II, 322–23; cf., *Bayard & Wife* v. *Singleton,* North Carolina Reports, 1 Martin, 42, 1797.

47 Mitchell, *Hamilton,* I, 344–45.

48 Hamilton to Gouverneur Morris, February 21, 1784, *Papers,* ed. Syrett, III, 512.

49 Hamilton to Robert Morris, August 27, 1782, ibid., p. 115; Hamilton to Nathanael Greene, June 10, 1783, ibid., p. 376; Hamilton to John Jay, August 25, 1783, ibid., pp. 416–17.

50 Burnett, *Continental Congress,* pp. 644–46.

51 Second Letter from Phocion, April _____, 1784, *Papers,* ed. Syrett, III, 557.

52 Burnett, *Continental Congress,* pp. 657–58.

53 Brant, *Nationalist,* chap. XXIV; Madison quoted in ibid., p. 381.

54 *Papers,* ed. Syrett, III, 665–66.

55 Madison to Jefferson, August 12, 1786, *Papers,* ed. Boyd, X, 223.

56 Address to the Annapolis Convention, September 14, 1786, *Papers,* ed. Syrett, III, 689.

57 Burnett, *Continental Congress,* pp. 663–64.

58 Richard J. Taylor, *Western Massachusetts in the Revolution,* chaps. V–VII; Wood, *American Republic,* pp. 325–26; Irving Brant, *James Madison: Father of the Constitution,* p. 116. Hereafter cited as Brant, *Father of the Constitution.*

59 Madison quoted in Wood, *American Republic,* p. 471.

60 Hamilton to Robert Livingston, April 25, 1785, *Papers,* ed. Syrett, III, 609.

61 Madison to Jefferson, October 24, 1787, *Papers,* ed. Boyd, XXVI, 276.

Chapter VII   Hamilton and the Constitution

1   Second Speech . . . on Governor Clinton's Message, *Papers,* ed. Syrett, IV, 15.
2   John Fiske, *The Critical Period in American History;* Jensen, *The New Nation,* p. xiii.
3   *Papers,* ed. Syrett, IV, 11, 95.
4   Hamilton to Washington, July 3, 1787, ibid., pp. 223–24.
5   Ibid., p. 108; Miller, *Hamilton,* pp. 151–52.
6   *Papers,* ed. Syrett, IV, 158–59, 223, 243.
7   George Mason to George Mason, Jr., June 1, 1787, Max Farrand (ed.), *The Records of the Federal Convention of 1787,* III, 32. Hereafter cited as *Federal Convention,* ed. Farrand.
8   Rossiter, *Grand Convention,* pp. 145–46.
9   Ibid., p. 242; *Federal Convention,* ed. Farrand, I, 125.
10 Hamilton to James Duane, September 10, 1780, *Papers,* ed. Syrett, II, 408, 407.
11 Hamilton to Robert Morris, April 30, 1781, ibid., II, 630; Address to the Annapolis Convention, September 14, 1786, ibid., III, 689.
12 *Federal Convention,* ed. Farrand, III, 567, 569.
13 Ibid., I, 13; George Mason to George Mason, Jr., May 27, 1787, ibid., III, 28; ibid., I, 15.
14 Jefferson to John Adams, August 30, 1787, *Papers,* ed. Boyd, XII, 347.
15 *Federal Convention,* ed. Farrand, I, 33, 35.
16 Ibid., pp. 94, 36, 193.
17 Ibid., p. 245.
18 Ibid., 282, 312.
19 Ibid., pp. 282–311; the quotations are on pp. 293, 300.
20 Ibid., p. 291; *Papers,* ed. Syrett, IV, 203.
21 *Federal Convention,* ed. Farrand, I, 364; ibid., II, 524–525, 560, 547, 645–46.
22 Ibid., I, 284, 287, 298.
23 James Madison quoted in Miller, *Hamilton,* p. 164; *Papers,* ed. Syrett, V, 39.
24 *Federal Convention,* ed. Farrand, I, 290.
25 Hamilton to Timothy Pickering, September 3, 1803, *Works,* ed. Lodge, X, 448; Hamilton to the Marquis de Lafayette, January 6, 1799, ibid., p. 337.

26 Hamilton to the Superiors of the City of Albany, February 18, 1789, *Papers,* ed. Syrett, V, 255.
27 *Federal Convention,* ed. Farrand, III, 622–23.
28 Ibid., I, 381–82.
29 The Farmer Refuted, December 15, 1775, *Papers,* ed. Syrett, I, 94–95; No. 76, Jacob E. Cooke (ed.), *The Federalist,* pp. 513–14. Hereafter cited as *Federalist,* ed. Cooke. *Papers,* ed. Syrett, I, 95.
30 *Federal Convention,* ed. Farrand, II, 531.
31 No. 8, *Federalist,* ed. Cooke, p. 44.
32 Mitchell, *Hamilton,* I, 415–16.
33 *Papers,* ed. Syrett, IV, 287–301.
34 Ibid., pp. 364–76, 377–90, 376–77.
35 No. 15, *Federalist,* ed. Cooke, p. 93.
36 No. 78, ibid., p. 525.
37 Learned Hand, *The Bill of Rights,* p. 15.
38 Clinton Rossiter, *Alexander Hamilton and the Constitution,* pp. 54–55, footnotes. Hereafter cited as Rossiter, *Hamilton.*
39 *Federal Convention,* ed. Farrand, III, 234.
40 *Papers,* ed. Syrett, IV, 650.
41 *Cohens* v. *Virginia,* 6 Wheaton, p. 418.
42 Hamilton to Washington, October 30, 1787, *Papers,* ed. Syrett, IV, 306.
43 E. Wilder Spaulding, *New York in the Critical Period, 1783–1789* ("New York State Historical Series," ed. Dixon Ryan Fox), p. 262. Hereafter cited as Spaulding, *New York.*
44 Hamilton to Madison, June 8, 1788, *Papers,* ed. Syrett, V, 3–4.
45 Spaulding, *New York,* pp. 251–52; Rossiter, *Hamilton,* pp. 63–65.
46 *Papers,* ed. Syrett, V, 100; *Federal Convention,* ed. Farrand, I, 297.
47 *Papers,* ed. Syrett, V. 135, 138.
48 Hamilton to Madison, July 8, 1788, ibid., pp. 147, 158.
49 Ibid., p. 185; Jonathan Elliot, (ed.), *The Debates in the State Conventions on the Adoption of the Federal Constitution,* II, 148. Hereafter cited as *Debates,* ed. Elliott.
50 *Federal Convention,* ed. Farrand, I, 288, 299.

Chapter VIII Jefferson and France

1   Jefferson to Edmund Randolph, September 16, 1781, *Papers,* ed. Boyd, VI, 18.

2   Archibald Cary to Jefferson, June 19, 1781, ibid., p. 97; Jefferson to Isaac Zane, December 24, 1781, ibid., p. 143.

3   Virginia General Assembly to Jefferson, December 12, 1781, ibid., p. 60.

4   Monroe to Jefferson, May 11, 1782, ibid., p. 83; Jefferson to Monroe, May 20, 1782, ibid., pp. 184–86.

5   Malone, *Virginian,* pp. 396–97; *Papers,* ed. Boyd, VI, 200.

6   Malone, *Virginian,* p. 399; Resolution of . . . Congress, November 13, 1782, *Papers,* ed. Boyd, VI, 202; Madison, quoted in ibid., p. 202 n; Jefferson to Madison, November 26, 1782, ibid., p. 207.

7   Malone, *Virginian,* p. 374. Jefferson to the Chevalier D'Anmours, November 30, 1780, *Papers,* ed. Boyd, IV, 167–68.

8   Jefferson, *Notes on Virginia,* pp. 84–85.

9   Ibid., pp. 164–65.

10   Report on Commerce, December 16, 1793, *Writings,* ed. Ford, VI, 482.

11   Jefferson, *Notes on Virginia,* pp. 211–12, 118–19, 161.

12   Ibid., p. 163.

13   Ibid, p. 143.

14   Malone, *Virginian,* pp. 399–400.

15   Ibid., pp. 400–01.

16   Ibid., pp. 403–04; Jefferson to Benjamin Harrison, November 11, 1783, *Papers,* ed. Boyd, VI, 351–53, 361–70.

17   Burnett, *Continental Congress,* pp. 580, 591–93; Ratification Proclamation, *Papers,* ed. Boyd, VI, 463.

18   Jefferson, *Autobiography,* p. 91; Jefferson to Martha Jefferson, February 18, 1784, *Papers,* ed. Boyd, VI, 456; Jefferson, *Autobiography,* p. 84.

19   Malone, *Virginian,* pp. 410–11; *Papers,* ed. Boyd, VII, 241, 252.

20   Ibid., VI, 611–12; ibid., VII, 118.

21   See especially Report on Arrears of Interest on the Na-

tional Debt, April 5, 1784, ibid., VII, 65 ff; ibid., pp. 150–204, *passim.*

22 Burnett, *Continental Congress,* p. 603; Jefferson to William Short, May 7, 1784, *Papers,* ed. Boyd, VII, 229.

23 Malone, *Virginian,* pp. 421–23.

24 Dumas Malone, *Jefferson and the Rights of Man* (*Jefferson and His Time,* vol. II), pp. 5–6, 7–9. Hereafter cited as Malone, *Rights of Man.*

25 Jefferson to Samuel Smith, August 22, 1798, *Writings,* ed. Ford, VIII, 276; Jefferson to Short, February 19, 1791, ibid., V, 292.

26 John Adams to James Warren, August 27, 1784, *Works,* ed. Adams, IX, 524; Adams to Jefferson, January 22, 1825, ibid., X, 414.

27 Malone, *Rights of Man,* p. 100.

28 Ibid., pp. 44, 88, 89–91.

29 Jefferson to Maria Cosway, October 12, 1786, *Papers,* ed. Boyd, X, 450.

30 Ibid., VII, 479–88.

31 Jefferson to Elbridge Gerry, November 11, 1784, ibid., VII, 502; Jefferson to Madison, February 8, 1786, ibid., IX, 264.

32 Malone, *Rights of Man,* Chap. II.

33 Gilbert Chinard, *Thomas Jefferson: Apostle of Americanism,* pp. 186–93. Hereafter cited as Chinard, *Jefferson.* Jefferson to John Jay, September 19, 1789, *Papers,* ed. Boyd, XV, 456–57.

34 Malone, *Rights of Man,* pp. 39–42, 46–48.

35 Jefferson to Lafayette, February 28, 1787, *Papers,* ed. Boyd, XI, 186; Jefferson to Jay, June 17, 1789, ibid., XV, 189, Jefferson to Madison, June 18, 1789, ibid, 196.

36 Jefferson to Lafayette, June 2, 1789, ibid., XV, 167–68; John Hall Stewart (ed.), *A Documentary History of the French Revolution,* p. 114.

37 Jefferson to Adams, November 13, 1787, *Papers,* ed. Boyd, XII, 350–51.

38 Madison to Jefferson, October 17, 1788, ibid., XIV, 20.

39 Madison to Jefferson, October 24, 1787, ibid., XII, 271–82; Jefferson to Madison, September 6, 1789, ibid., XV, 396; Jefferson to Washington, May 2, 1788, ibid., XIII, 128.

40 Jefferson to Edward Carrington, May 27, 1788, ibid., XIII, 208; Jefferson to Richard Price, January 8, 1789, ibid., XIV, 420; Jefferson to Madison, December 20, 1787, ibid., XII, 442.

41 Malone, *Rights of Man,* pp. 203–05, 209–10, 234–37.

42 Jefferson to Washington, December 15, 1789, *Papers,* ed. Boyd, XVI, 34.

43 Jefferson, *Autobiography,* p. 157.

Chapter IX The Hamiltonian System

1 Mitchell, *Hamilton,* II, 21–23; *Papers,* ed. Syrett, V, 365.

2 Mitchell, *Hamilton,* II, 22–23; Madison to Jefferson, May 27, 1789, *Papers,* ed. Boyd, XV, 153.

3 *Journal of the House of Representatives of the United States,* p. 117. *Debates and Proceedings in the Congress of the United States, 1789–1824,* 1st Cong., 1st sess., pp. 1044–55. Hereafter cited as *Annals.* The term "cabinet" did not come into general use until Jefferson's second administration. Although the attorney-general usually attended cabinet meetings, he was not considered a department head.

4 Report on Public Credit, January 9, 1790, *Papers,* ed. Syrett, VI, 84–88.

5 *Annals,* 1st Cong., 1st sess., pp. 366, 416, 46, 52.

6 Ibid., 1st Cong., 2nd sess., pp. 1180–82.

7 Defence of the Funding System, *Works,* ed. Lodge, VIII, 450–55; *Annals,* 1st Cong., 2nd sess., pp. 1345, 1354.

8 Report on Public Credit, January 9, 1790, *Papers,* ed. Syrett, VI, 78–83.

9 *Annals,* 1st Cong., 2nd sess., pp. 1533, 1543.

10 Malone, *Rights of Man,* pp. 246–53.

11 William Maclay, *Journal of William Maclay: United States Senator from Pennsylvania, 1789–1791,* ed. Edgar S. Maclay, p. 272. Hereafter cited as *Journal,* ed. Maclay.

12 Leonard D. White, *The Federalists: A Study in Administrative History, 1789–1801,* chap. IX. Hereafter cited as White, *Federalists.*

13 Ibid., chap. X.

14 Report on Weights and Measures, July 4, 1790, *Papers,*

ed. Boyd, XVI, 650–65; White, *Federalists*, pp. 136–39; Jefferson to William Short, May 27, 1790, *Papers*, ed. Boyd, XVI, 444.

15 *Annals*, 1st Cong., 2nd sess., p. 1525.

16 *Writings*, ed. Ford, VI, 172.

17 Jefferson to Monroe, June 20, 1790, ibid., V, 189.

18 Ibid., VI, 173–74.

19 *Annals*, 1st Cong., 2nd sess., pp. 1679–80, 1712.

20 *Writings*, ed. Ford, VI, 174.

21 See chap. X below.

22 *Journal*, ed. Maclay, p. 177; Mitchell, *Hamilton*, II, 154–64.

23 Hamilton to Henry Lee, December 1, 1789, *Papers*, ed. Syrett, VI, 1.

24 Washington to Lafayette, June 3, 1790, *Writings*, ed. Fitzpatrick, XXXI, 46.

25 Report on a National Bank, December 14, 1790, *Papers*, ed. Syrett, VII, 305–42.

26 *Annals*, 1st Cong., 2nd sess., pp. 1960, 1894, 1902.

27 *Writings*, ed. Ford, V, 286–87.

28 U.S. Constitution, Art. I, sec. 8.

29 *Writings*, ed. Ford, V, 289.

30 Hamilton to Robert Morris, April 30, 1781, *Papers*, ed. Syrett, II, 604–35.

31 Ibid, VIII, 98.

32 *Writings*, ed. Ford, V, 285–86.

33 *Papers*, ed. Syrett, VIII, 105.

34 Ibid., X, 230–40.

35 Jefferson, *Notes on Virginia*, p. 165.

36 Hamilton to Robert Morris, April 30, 1781, *Papers*, ed. Syrett, II, 635; Hamilton to _____, _____, 1790, ibid., p. 244.

37 Hamilton to Edward Carrington, May 26, 1792, ibid., XI, 427.

38 King to Hamilton, August 15, 1791, ibid., IX, 60.

39 Mitchell, *Hamilton*, II, chap. II.

40 Miller, *Hamilton*, pp. 353–59; Jefferson to Monroe, June 23, 1792, *Writings*, ed. Ford, VI, 93–94.

41. Jefferson to Edward Rutledge, August 29, 1791, ibid., p. 376.

42 Malone, *Rights of Man*, pp. 359–63; Jefferson to Martha

Randolph, May 31, 1791, *Writings,* ed. Ford, V, 337–38; Jefferson to Thomas Mann Randolph, June 5, 1791, ibid., p. 340–42.

43 Jefferson to Adams, July 17, 1791, ibid., pp. 354–55.

44 Jefferson to Washington, June 19, 1796, ibid., VII, 82.

45 Jefferson to Thomas Mann Randolph, May 15, 1791, ibid., V, 336; Lewis Leary, *That Rascal Freneau: A Study in Literary Failure,* pp. 193–97. Hereafter cited as Leary, *Freneau.*

46 See *Works,* ed. Lodge, VII, 230–303, *passim.*

47 Jefferson to Washington, September 6, 1792, *Writings,* ed. Ford, VI, 106.

48 Hamilton to Edward Carrington, May 26, 1792, *Papers,* ed. Syrett, XI, 429–32.

49 Jefferson to Washington, May 23, 1792, *Writtings,* ed. Ford, VI, 3, 4.

50 *Annals,* 2nd Cong., 2nd session pp. 835–40; for Hamilton's reports, ibid., p. 1199, ff.; for Giles' resolutions and the House vote, ibid., pp. 900–05; Dumas Malone, *Jefferson and the Ordeal of Liberty* (*Jefferson and His Time,* vol III), chap. II. Hereafter cited as Malone, *Ordeal of Liberty.* Schachner, *Hamilton,* pp. 310–14.

51 Malone, *Ordeal of Liberty,* pp. 26–33; Fisher Ames to Timothy Dwight, Jan, ___, 1793, *Works of Fisher Ames,* ed. Seth Ames, I, 127.

52 *Gazette of the United States* (Philadelphia), March 6, 1793; Memorandum, February 7, 1793, *Writings,* ed. Ford, VI, 215; Hamilton to William Short, February 5, 1793, *Works,* ed. Lodge, VIII, 293.

53 Jefferson to Francis Hopkinson, March 13, 1789, ibid., V, 76; *Works,* ed. Adams, II, 152; *Papers,* ed. Syrett, V, 85.

54 No. 10, *Federalist,* ed. Cooke, p. 58; James Madison, *Writings,* ed. Gaillard Hunt, VI, 104–05. Hereafter cited as *Writings of Madison,* ed. Hunt.

55 Cunningham, *Jeffersonian Republicans,* p. 23 n.

56 Ibid., p. 33.

57 Ibid., p. 22.

58 Eugene P. Link, *The Democratic-Republican Societies, 1790–1800,* p. 19.

59 William Nisbet Chambers, *Political Parties in the New*

Nation, pp. 44–45. Hereafter cited as Chambers, *Political Parties.*

60 Leland Baldwin, *The Whiskey Rebellion: The Story of a Frontier Uprising.*

61 Hamilton to Rufus King, October 30, 1794, *Works,* ed. Lodge, X, 77.

62 Jefferson to Madison, December 28, 1794, *Writings,* ed. Ford, VI, 518; Washington to Hamilton, October 26, 1794, *Writings,* ed. Fitzpatrick, XXXIV, 8; Jefferson to Madison, *loc cit.*

63 Cunningham, *The Jeffersonian Republicans,* p. 109–15.

64 Ibid., p. 96–97.

65 Ibid., p. 94.

66 Chambers, *Political Parties,* p. 127.

Chapter X   The French Menace

1   *Treaties,* ed. Miller, II, 3.

2   "Anas," October 1, 1792, *Writings,* ed. Ford, I, 204.

3   Ibid., pp. 204–05.

4   Hamilton to Washington, September 9, 1792, *Papers,* ed. Syrett, XII, 347–48.

5   Freeman, *Washington,* VI, 378–79.

6   Jefferson to Washington, December 15, 1789, *Papers,* ed. Boyd, XVI, 34; Washington to Jefferson, January 21, 1790, ibid., p. 90.

7   "Anas," *Writings,* ed. Ford, I, 160.

8   See William K. Manning, "The Nootka Sound Controversy," American Historical Association *Annual Report for 1904,* pp. 279–478; see also Samuel Flagg Bemis, *Jay's Treaty: A Study in Commerce and Diplomacy,* p. 71 ff. Hereafter cited as Bemis, *Jay's Treaty.*

9   Schachner, *Jefferson,* pp. 408–09.

10 Opinion on the Course of the United States towards Britain and Spain, August 28, 1790, *Writings,* ed. Ford, V, 239.

11 Jefferson to Thomas Mann Randolph, January 7, 1793, ibid., VI, 157; Charles D. Hazen, *Contemporary American Opinion of the French Revolution* (Johns Hopkins University "Studies in Historical and Political Science," vol. XVI), pp. ix–x, 140–43, 170.

12 Hamilton to ____, May 18, 1793, *Papers,* ed. Syrett, XIV, 475–76.

13 Jefferson to T. M. Randolph, January 7, 1793, *Writings,* ed. Ford, VI, 157.

14 Charles M. Thomas, *American Neutrality in 1793: A Study in Cabinet Government,* pp. 38–40. Hereafter cited as Thomas *American Neutrality. Papers,* ed. Syrett, XIV, 367–96.

15 Hammond to Lord Grenville, March 7, 1793, British Correspondence, America, Henry Adams Transcripts, Library of Congress. Quoted in Freeman, *Washington,* VII, 45 n.

16 Jefferson to Madison, June 23, 1793, *Writings,* ed. Ford, VI, 315–16.

17 "Anas," April 18, 1793, *Writings,* ed., Ford, I, 227.

18 *American State Papers: Documents, Legislative and Executive, Foreign Relations,* selected and edited, under the authority of Congress by Walter Lowrie and Matthew St. Clair Clarke, I, 140. Hereafter cited as *ASP, FR.* See also *Messages and Papers of the Presidents, 1789–1897,* compiled by James D. Richardson, I, 148–49. Hereafter cited as *Messages and Papers,* ed. Richardson.

19 Thomas, *American Neutrality,* pp. 60–65; Opinion on the French Treaties, April 18, 1793, *Writings,* ed. Ford, VI, 230–31.

20 DeConde, *Entangling Alliances,* pp. 169–70.

21 For the Haitian Revolt, C. L. R. James, *The Black Jacobins: Toussaint L'Ouverture and the San Domingo Revolution.*

22 For Genet's career see Meade Minnigerode, *Jefferson, Friend of France;* . . . Greville Bathe, *Citizen Genêt, Diplomat and Inventor;* George Clinton Genêt, *Washington, Jefferson and Citizen Genêt.*

23 Frederick Jackson Turner, "Origins of Citizens Genêt's Attack on Louisiana and the Floridas," *American Historical Review,* 3 (1898), 651–70; also Frederick Jackson Turner, "The Policy of France toward the Mississippi Valley in the Period of Washington and Adams," *American Historical Review,* 10 (1905), 249–79.

24 Thomas, *American Neutrality,* pp. 81–84.

25 Freeman, *Washington,* VII, 75 and note.

26 Ibid., pp. 76–77.

27 Genet to Foreign Minister LeBrun, June 19, 1793, Frederick Jackson Turner, (ed.), "Correspondence of French Ministers to the United States, 1791–97, American Historical Association *Annual Report for 1903*, II, 217. Hereafter cited as "Correspondence," ed. Turner.

28 Jefferson to Madison, May 19, 1793, *Writings*, ed. Ford, VI, 260–61.

29 Jefferson to Monroe, July 14, 1793, ibid., p. 348.

30 Summary of content of Hammond's note in Jefferson to Hammond, May 15 and June 5, 1793, ibid., pp. 252–57, 282–87.

31 Hamilton to Washington, May 15, 1793, *Papers*, ed. Syrett, XIV, 454–60; Opinion of Treaties, April 28, 1793, *Writings*, ed. Ford, VI, 230 ff.

32 Freeman, *Washington*, VII, 77–78.

33 Thomas, *American Neutrality*, pp. 171–75; Charles Warren, *The Supreme Court in United States History*, I, 112–15. Hereafter cited as Warren, *Supreme Court. ASP, FR*, I, 455.

34 Genet to Jefferson, May 23, 1793, *ASP, FR*, I, 147.

35 Opinion of Treaties, April 18, 1793, *Writings*, ed. Ford, VI, 225.

36 Genet to Jefferson, June 8, 1793, *ASP, FR*, I, 151.

37 Jefferson to Monroe, June 28, 1793, *Writings*, ed. Ford, VI, 323.

38 Jefferson to Gouverneur Morris, August 16, 1793, ibid., VI, 382.

39 *National Gazette* (Philadelphia), June 5, 1793, quoted in Freeman, *Washington*, VII, 86.

40 "Anas," July 10, 1793, *Writings*, ed. Ford, I, 237.

41 Minutes of a Conversation between Mr. Jefferson . . . and Mr. Genet, July 10, 1793, *Writings of Washington*, ed. Sparks, X, 539.

42 Jefferson to Genet, July 9, 1793, *ASP, FR*, I, 163.

43 Reasons for Dissent, July 8, 1793, *Writings*, ed. Ford, I, 356–69.

44 *Gazette of the United States*, July 13, 1793, quoted in *Works*, ed. Lodge, IV, 472–73. This volume contains entire series.

45 Freeman, *Washington*, VI, 108; Thomas, *American Neu-*

trality, pp. 148–51; Rules for Belligerents, *Writings,* ed. Ford, VI, 358–59 n.

46 Instructions to Collectors of Customs, August 4, 1793, *Works,* ed. Lodge, IV, 236–41.

47 Jefferson to Madison, August 25, 1793, *Writings,* ed. Ford, VI, 398.

48 DeConde, *Entangling Alliances,* p. 299; Freeman, *Washington,* VII, 111–14. Genet's recall is requested in *ASP, FR,* I, 167–72.

49 Minister of Foreign Affairs to Genet, July 30, 1793, "Correspondence," ed. Turner, p. 230.

50 Genet to Jefferson, September 18, 1793, *ASP, FR,* I, 172–74.

51 Freeman, *Washington,* VII, 154.

52 Hamilton to Rufus King, August 13, 1793, *Works,* ed. Lodge, X, 50–53.

53 The phrase is quoted in DeConde, *Entangling Alliances,* p. 300.

54 Freeman, *Washington,* VII, 114–15.

55 Hamilton to Washington, June 21, 1793, *Works,* ed. Lodge, X, 48–49.

56 "Anas," August 6, 1793, *Writings,* ed. Ford, I, 256; Washington to Jefferson, August 12, 1793, *Writings,* ed. Fitzpatrick, XXXIII, 45.

57 Freeman, *Washington,* VII, 119–23.

58 John Quincy Adams, *Writings,* ed. Worthington C. Ford, I, 148. Hereafter cited as *Writings of J. Q. Adams,* ed. Ford.

Chapter XI   The British Menace

1 *Le Moniteur Universel* (Paris), February 7, 1794.

2 Edmund Burke, *Reflections on the Revolution in France,* p. 21.

3 Jefferson to Angelica Church, November 27, 1793, *Writings,* ed. Ford, VI, 455.

4 Jefferson to Hammond, December 15, 1793, ibid, pp. 467–69.

5 Report on . . . the Commerce of the United States, . . . December 16, 1793, ibid., pp. 470–84.

6   Opinion on Neutral Trade, December 20, 1793, ibid., pp.
    485–88; *The Statistical History of the United States from
    Colonial Times to the Present,* prepared by the United
    States Bureau of the Census and the Social Science Re-
    search Council, p. 455. Hereafter cited as *Statistical His-
    tory.*

7   Jefferson to Dr. Enoch Edwards, December 30, 1793,
    Writings, ed. Ford, VI, 495.

8   Hammond to Jefferson, September 12, 1793, *ASP, FR,*
    I, 240.

9   Fulmer Skipworth to the Secretary of State, March 7,
    1794, ibid., p. 429.

10 *Annals,* 3rd Cong., 1st sess., pp. 155–56.

11 Ibid., p. 176.

12 Hamilton to Washington, March 8, 1794, *Works,* ed.
    Lodge, X, 63–65.

13 Jefferson to Madison, April 3, 1794, *Writings,* ed. Ford,
    VI, 501–03.

14 *Annals,* 3rd Cong., 1st sess., pp. 529–30; *ASP, FR,* I, 431.

15 Hamilton to Washington, April 14, 1794, *Works,* ed.
    Lodge, V, 97–115. The quotation is on p. 106.

16 Jefferson to Adams, May 25, 1794, *Writings,* ed. Ford,
    VI, 505.

17 Memorandum titled "R. King Manuscript," Rufus
    King, *Life and Correspondence,* ed. Charles R. King, I,
    517–23. Hereafter cited as *Correspondence of King,* ed.
    King.

18 For Jay's career, see Frank Monaghan, *John Jay, De-
    fender of Liberty.*

19 Hamilton to Washington, April 14, 1794, *Works,* ed.
    Lodge, V, 114.

20 "Franklin," in *Independent Gazeteer* (Philadelphia),
    March 11 and June 10, 1795, quoted in DeConde, *En-
    tangling Alliances,* p. 103 n.

21 *Correspondence of King,* ed. King, I, 521.

22 "Anas," *Writings,* ed. Ford, I, 220.

23 DeConde, *Entangling Alliances,* p. 104.

24 Hamilton to Washington, May 23, 1794, and Hamilton
    to Jay, May 6, 1794, *Works,* ed. Lodge, 115–31, *passim.*

25 Randolph's instructions to Jay, *ASP, FR,* I, 472–74.

26 Hammond to Grenville, April 17, 1794, Public Records

Office, Foreign Office, ser. 5, vol. 5, quoted in Bemis, *Jay's Treaty,* p. 277.

27 Hamilton to Randolph, July 8, 1794, *Works,* ed. Lodge, V, 135.

28 Randolph's instructions to Jay, *ASP, FR,* I, 473.

29 Grenville to Hammond, October 2, 1794, Bernard Mayo (ed.), *Instructions to British Ministers to the United States, 1791–1812* American Historical Association *Annual Report for 1936,* p. 67. Hereafter cited as *Instructions,* ed. Mayo.

30 Jay to Hamilton, September 11, 1794, Alexander Hamilton, *Works,* ed. John C. Hamilton, V, 27. Hereafter cited as *Works,* ed. Hamilton.

31 *The Manuscripts of J. B. Fortescue, Esq., Preserved at Dropmore,* Historical Manuscripts Commission Report, II, 578.

32 Bemis, *Jay's Treaty,* p. 318.

33 Ibid., pp. 318–73, *passim.*

34 Text of treaty in ibid., pp. 453–84. The quotation is on p. 480.

35 Jay to Hamilton, November 19, 1794, *Works,* ed. Hamilton, V, 54.

36 *Virginia Herald and Fredericksburg Advertiser,* August 11, 1795, quoted in DeConde, *Entangling Alliances,* p. 115 n.

37 Washington to Randolph, July 29, 1795, *Writings,* ed. Fitzpatrick, XXXIV, 245–57.

38 Madison to Jefferson, February 15, 1795, quoted in Nathan Schachner, *The Founding Fathers,* p. 359. Hereafter cited as Schachner, *Founding Fathers.*

39 The Public Conduct and Character of John Adams, Esq., President of the United States, *Works,* ed. Lodge, VII, 359.

40 Jefferson to Madison, September 27, 1796, *Writings,* ed. Ford, VII, 69.

41 DeConde, *Entangling Alliances,* p. 113 and n.

42 Schachner, *Founding Fathers,* pp. 364–66; DeConde, *Entangling Alliances,* pp. 111–20; Miller, *Hamilton,* pp. 442–46; Mitchell, *Hamilton,* II, 341–43. The quotations are *seriatim.*

43 Washington to Hamilton, July 14, 1795, *Writings,* ed.

Fitzpatrick, XXXIV, 241–42; Randolph to Jay, August 16, 1795, *Works,* ed. Hamilton, VI, 31–33. Hereaftei cited as *Works,* ed. Hamilton.

44   Schachner, *Founding Fathers,* pp. 371–78; Irving Brant, "Edmund Randolph, Not Guilty," *William and Mary Quarterly,* 3rd ser., 7 (1950), 190.

45   Jefferson to W. B. Giles, December 31, 1795, *Writings,* ed. Ford, VII, 42–43.

46   Hamilton to Washington, November 5, 1795, *Works,* ed. Lodge, X, 129–32.

47   John Adams to Abigail Adams, February 8, 1796, John Adams, *Letters . . . Addressed to His Wife,* ed. Charles Francis Adams, II, 195.

48   Washington to Hamilton, July 29, 1795, *Writings,* ed. Fitzpatrick, XXXIV, 263–64.

49   Jefferson to Madison, September 21, 1795, *Writings,* ed. Ford, VII, 32–33.

50   Camillus, *Works,* ed. Lodge, V, 189—VI, 197. The quotation is in V, 95.

51   Ibid., pp. 206–07.

52   Ibid., VI, 106–07.

53   Ibid., V, 203.

54   Ibid., p. 205.

55   Ibid., p. 190.

56   *Annals,* 3rd. Cong., 2nd sess., pp. 400–01, 426.

57   Hamilton to Oliver Wolcott, Jr., April 20, 1796, *Works,* ed. Lodge, X, 161–62.

58   Hamilton to Washington, March 28, 1796, *Works,* ed. Hamilton, VI, 97–98.

59   Washington to Hamilton, March 31, 1796, *Writings,* ed. Fitzpatrick, XXXV, 6.

60   Samuel Flagg Bemis, *Pinckney's Treaty, A Study in America's Advantage from Europe's Distress, 1783–1800,* pp. 343–62. The quotation is on p. 302.

61   *Annals,* 3rd Cong., 2nd sess., p. 1280.

62   Madison to Jefferson, May 9, 1796, *Letters and Other Writings of James Madison,* Published by order of Congress, II, 100; see also Madison's letters of April 18 and 23, and May 1 and 14, ibid., pp. 95–105.

63   Jefferson to Monroe, July 10, 1796, *Writings,* ed. Ford, VII, 89.

64 DeConde, *Entangling Alliances,* pp. 127–32.
65 Report on Commerce, . . . *Writings,* ed. Ford, VI, 481.
66 Camillus, *Works,* ed. Lodge, V, 200.
67 Hamilton to Jay, May 6, 1794, ibid., pp. 125–26.

Chapter XII   The Alien and Sedition Acts

1 Hamilton to Washington, September 4, 1795, *Works,* ed. Lodge, VI, 205.
2 Isaac Weld, Jr., *Travels Through the States of North America and Canada,* p. 58.
3 Following the treaty controversy the President received letters, petitions, etc., most of which he tried to answer. However, those that employed language that he felt to be objectionable he marked, "Tenor indecent: No answer returned." *Writings,* ed. Fitzpatrick, XXXV, 254 n.
4 Freeman, *Washington,* VII, 381–82, 398–99, 400–03.
5 Text in *Writings,* ed. Fitzpatrick, XXXV, 214–238. Despite its title, the address was a "press release" to David Clay of Poole's *American Daily Advertiser,* September 19, 1796.
6 The quotations, in the order in which they appear, are in *Writings,* ed. Fitzpatrick, XXXV, 218, 220–21, 224, 223, 225–26, 231, 233–35, 232–33.
7 Hamilton to Washington, July 5, 1796, *Works,* ed. Lodge, X, 181; Madison to Monroe, September 29, 1796, quoted in Irving Brant, *James Madison: Father of the Constitution, 1787–1800,* p. 442. Hereafter cited as Brant, *Father of the Constitution.*
8 Jefferson to Archibald Stuart, January 4, 1797, *Writings,* ed. Ford, VII, 101.
9 Adet to Minister of Foreign Relations, October 12, 1796, "Correspondence," ed. Turner, 954.
10 Monroe to Randolph, August 25, 1794, James Monroe, *Writings,* ed. Stanislaus M. Hamilton, II, 33–34. Hereafter cited as *Writings of Monroe,* ed. Hamilton. *ASP, FR,* I, 672–75.
11 *Writings of Monroe,* ed. Hamilton, II, 1–9. The quotation is on p. 8. Italics are Monroe's.
12. Randolph to Monroe, December 5, 1794, February 15,

1795, March 8, 1795, April 7, 1795, *ASP, FR,* I, 690–701, *passim.*

13 Monroe to the Committee of Public Safety, December 27, 1794, *Writings of Monroe,* ed. Hamilton, II, 163.

14 Monroe to Madison, September 8, 1795, ibid., pp. 347–49.

15 Monroe to Secretary of State Pickering, February 16, 1796, ibid., p. 455; Monroe to the Minister of Foreign Affairs, February 17, 1796, quoted in Samuel Flagg Bemis, "Washington's Farewell Address: A Foreign Policy of Independence," *American Historical Review,* 34 (1934), p. 258.

16 Hamilton to Wolcott, June 15, 1796, *Works,* ed. Hamilton, VI, 130.

17 Adams to Tristram Dalton, January 19, 1797, *Writings,* ed. Ford, VII, 108.

18 Jefferson to Madison, January 22, 1797, ibid., pp. 107–08.

19 Hamilton to Tobias Lear, January 2, 1800, *Works,* ed. Hamilton, VI, 215.

20 Stephen Higginson to Hamilton, January 12, 1797, ibid., p. 191.

21 Jefferson to Phillip Mazzei, April 24, 1796, *Writings,* ed. Ford, VII, 75–76.

22 Ibid., pp. 72–78, contain entire letter and translations.

23 Mitchell, *Hamilton,* II, 399–422; Miller, *Hamilton,* pp. 468–74. Pertinent documents are in *Works,* ed. Lodge, VII, 369–479.

24 Jefferson to Edward Rutledge, June 24, 1797, *Writings,* ed. Ford, VII, 154–55.

25 DeConde, *The Quasi-War,* pp. 8–10.

26 Hamilton to Wolcott, April 5, 1797, *Works,* ed. Hamilton, VI, 230.

27 Adams to Congress, May 16, 1797, *Messages and Papers,* ed. Richardson, I, 223–28.

28 *Annals,* 5th Cong., 2nd sess., pp. 239–86, *passim.*

29 Jefferson to Thomas Pinckney, May 29, 1797, *Writings,* ed. Ford, VII, 128–30; Jefferson to Elbridge Gerry, June 21, 1797, ibid., p. 149.

30 Jefferson to Peregrine Fitzhugh, February 23, 1798, ibid., p. 211.

31 Hamilton to Pickering, May 11, 1797, *Works,* ed. Hamilton, VI, 246–47.

32 *ASP, FR,* II, 161–63; Albert Beveridge, *Life of John Marshall,* II, 272–75.

33 DeConde, *Quasi-War,* chap. V; Eugene F. Cramer, "Some New Light on the XYZ Affair: Elbridge Gerry's Reasons For Opposing War with France," *New England Quarterly,* 39 (1956), p. 512.

34 Hamilton to Pickering, March 17, 1798, *Works,* ed. Hamilton, VI, 270.

35 Adams to Congress, March 19, 1798, *Messages and Papers,* ed. Richardson, I, 254–55; Page Smith, *John Adams,* II, 953–55. Hereafter cited as Smith, *Adams.* Jefferson to Monroe, February 21, 1798, *Writings,* ed. Ford, VII, 221.

36 Robert Troup to Rufus King, June 3, 1798, *Correspondence of King,* ed. King, II, 329.

37 Smith, *Adams,* II, 962–63.

38 Ibid., p. 965.

39 *Annals,* 5th Cong., 2nd sess., pp. 1473–76, 1566–68.

40 Madison to Jefferson, May 13, 1798, *Writings of Madison,* ed. Hunt, II, 141.

41 Washington to Hamilton, May 27, 1798, *Works,* ed. Hamilton, VI, 290.

42 For the text of the Naturalization Act and the Alien and Sedition Acts see *U.S. Statutes at Large,* I, 566 ff.

43 Jefferson to John Taylor of Caroline, June 1, 1798, *Writings,* VII, 265.

44 Schachner, *Founding Fathers,* pp. 461–62.

45 Jefferson to Madison, June 7, 1798, *Writings,* ed. Ford, VII, 267.

46 Jefferson to Taylor, June 1, 1798, ibid., pp. 264–65.

47 Schachner, *Founding Fathers,* p. 482; John C. Miller, *Crisis in Freedom,* pp. 214–20. Hereafter cited as Miller, *Crisis in Freedom.*

48 Schachner, *Founding Fathers,* p. 483; Miller, *Crisis in Freedom,* pp. 185–86.

49 Hamilton to Wolcott, June 29, 1798, *Works,* ed. Lodge, X, 295.

50 Hamilton to Jonathan Dayton, ——, 1799, *Works,* ed. Hamilton, VI, 383 ff.

51 Adrienne Koch, *Jefferson and Madison: The Great Collaboration*, pp. 185–90. Hereafter cited as Koch, *Jefferson and Madison*. See also Adrienne Koch and Harry Ammon, "The Virginia and Kentucky Resolutions: An Episode in Jefferson's and Madison's Defense of Civil Liberties," *William and Mary Quarterly*, 3rd ser., 5 (1948), pp. 45–76. Jefferson to John Cabell Breckinridge, December 11, 1821, *Writings*, ed. Ford, VII, 290–91.

52 No. 46, *Federalist*, ed. Cooke, pp. 315–23; No. 28, ibid., p. 179.

53 A facsimile and Jefferson's rough draft in *Writings*, ed. Ford, VII, 288–309. Quotations on pp. 292, 293, and 305; *Debates*, ed. Elliot, IV, 529.

54 Jefferson to Madison, August 23, 1799, quoted in Koch, *Jefferson and Madison*, pp. 197–98.

55 Ibid., p. 201.

56 Jefferson to Robert Livingston, February 23, 1799, *Writings*, ed. Ford, VII, 369.

Chapter XIII   The Election of 1800

1 Jefferson to Archibald Rowan, September 26, 1798, *Writings*, ed. Ford, VII, 280.

2 Hamilton to Washington, May 19, 1798, *Works*, ed. Hamilton, VI, 289.

3 Mary E. Clark, *Peter Procupine in America: The Career of William Cobbett, 1792–1800*, pp. 94–125; Leary, *Freneau*, pp. 271–306.

4 Hamilton to Rufus King, May ____, 1798, *Works*, ed. Lodge, X, 283–84.

5 *Statistical History*, pp. 551–53.

6 King to Hamilton, May 12, 1798, *Works*, ed. Hamilton, VI, 284.

7 John C. Miller, *The Federalist Era, 1789–1801*, p. 215.

8 George Cabot to Wolcott, October 25, 1789, George Gibbs (ed), *Memoirs of the Administrations of Washington and John Adams, Edited from the Papers of Oliver Wolcott, Secretary of the Treasury*, II, 109. Hereafter referred to as *Memoirs*, ed. Gibbs.

9 *Annals*, 5th Cong., 2nd sess., pp. 2128–32.

10 DeConde, *Quasi-War*, pp. 104–05.

11 Washington to Hamilton, July 14, 1798, *Works,* ed.
    Hamilton, VI, 322.

12 Adams to James McHenry, August 14, 1798 and August
    29, 1798, *Works,* ed. Adams, VIII, 588–90; see also
    C. F. Adams' notes pp. 580–590.

13 Washington to Pickering, August 11, 1798, *Works,* ed.
    Hamilton, VI, 319.

14 Washington to Adams, September 25, 1798, *Writings,*
    ed. Fitzpatrick, XXXVI, 453–62.

15 Adams to Washington, October 9, 1798, *Works,* ed.
    Adams, VII, 600–01.

16 Adams to James Lloyd, February 17, 1815, ibid., X, 124.

17 Washington to McHenry, September 30, 1798, *Writings,*
    ed. Fitzpatrick, XXXVI, 474–75.

18 Jefferson to Washington, January 26, 1799, *Writings,* ed.
    Ford, VII, 328.

19 An Act for the Better Organization of the Troops of the
    United States, . . . March 3, 1799, *Works,* ed. Hamilton,
    V, 223–32.

20 Hamilton to Washington, May 3, 1799; Hamilton to
    McHenry, August 19, 1799, *Works,* ed. Lodge, VII,
    78–79, 108.

21 Memorandum, _____, 1799, ibid., pp. 55–56.

22 Memorandum, _____, 1799, ibid., p. 49; Hamilton to
    McHenry, January 21, 1799, ibid., pp. 58–59.

23 Hamilton to Washington, May 3, 1799, ibid., p. 79.

24 Hamilton to McHenry, March 18, 1799, ibid., p. 69.

25 George Cabot to Hamilton, July 23, 1800, *Works,* ed.
    Hamilton, VI, 461.

26 Hamilton to James Gunn, December 22, 1798, *Works,*
    ed. Lodge, VII, 46.

27 Hamilton to Harrison Gray Otis, January 26, 1799,
    Works, ed. Hamilton, VI, 391.

28 William Spencer Roberson, *Life of Miranda,* I, 42–44,
    168–70.

29 Hamilton to King, July 22, 1798, *Works,* ed. Hamilton,
    VI, 347 Hamilton to Miranda, July 22, 1798, ibid, p. 348.
    This letter was sent to King to be delivered or not to
    Miranda as he say fit. Hamilton to Otis, January 26,
    1799, ibid., pp. 390–91.

30 Hamilton to Washington, February 15, 1799, *Works,* ed.

Lodge, VII, 67. Hamilton may have meant "ulterior" as simply "further" or "future."

31 Washington to Hamilton, September 15, 1799, *Writings,* ed. Fitzpatrick, XXXVII, 364.

32 DeConde, *Quasi-War,* pp. 162–74.

33 Theodore Sedgewick to Hamilton, February 7, 1799, *Works,* ed. Hamilton, VI, 394.

34 Quoted in Miller, *Hamilton,* p. 508.

35 For details of naval activity, see Gardner W. Allen, *Our Naval War with France.*

36 For Logan see Frederick B. Tolles, *George Logan of Philadelphia.*

37 King to Hamilton, September 23, 1798, *Works,* ed. Hamilton, VI, 359.

38 Adams to Washington, February 19, 1799, *Works,* ed. Adams, VIII, 624–25.

39 Jefferson to Madison, February 19, 1799, *Writings,* ed. Ford, VII, 363.

40 Pickering to Hamilton, February 25, 1799 and February 25, 1799, *Works,* ed. Hamilton, VI, 396–99.

41 Washington to Adams, March 3, 1799, *Writings,* ed. Fitzpatrick, XXXVII, 143–44.

42 Hamilton to Sedgewick, February 21, 1799, *Works,* ed. Hamilton, VI, 397; Smith, *Adams,* II, 1002–11, *passim;* Sedgewick to Hamilton, February 19, 1799, *Works,* ed. Hamilton, VI, 396–97.

43 Hamilton to McHenry, June 27, 1799, *Works,* ed. Lodge, VII, 97–98.

44 Benjamin Stoddert to Adams, September 13, 1799, *Works,* ed. Adams, IX, 25–29.

45 Smith, *Adams,* II, 1012–16; DeConde, *Quasi-War,* pp. 218–22.

46 DeConde, *Quasi-War,* pp. 221–23; Miller, *Hamilton,* p. 503.

47 Cunningham, *Jeffersonian Republicans,* pp. 181–82; Jefferson to Monroe, January 12, 1800, *Writings,* ed. Ford, VII, 400–03.

48 Jefferson to Monroe, January 12, 1800, *Writings,* ed. Ford, VII, 401.

49 Ibid., pp. 401–03.

50 Schachner, *Founding Fathers,* pp. 531–34; Miller, *Hamilton,* pp. 512–13.

51 Jefferson to Thomas Lomax, March 12, 1799, *Writings,* ed. Ford, VII, 373–74.

52 *Hartford* (Connecticut) *Courant,* September 8, 1800, quoted in Cunningham, *Jeffersonian Republicans,* p. 217.

53 Smith, *Adams,* pp. 1027–29.

54 Hamilton to Adams, August 1, 1800 and October 1, 1800, *Works,* ed. Lodge, VII, 364–65.

55 Hamilton to Pickering, May 14, 1800, and to Wolcott, July 1, 1800, ibid., X, 376–77.

56 Public Conduct and Character of John Adams, Esq., President of the United States, ibid., VII, 309–64. The quotations are on pp. 320, 363–64.

57 Robert Troup to King, November 9, 1800, *Correspondence of King,* ed. King, III, 331.

58 Public Conduct, . . . *Works,* ed. Lodge, VII, 320–21.

59 McHenry to Wolcott, July 22, 1800, *Memoirs,* ed. Gibbs, II, 384–85.

60 Schachner, *Founding Fathers,* pp. 542–43; DeConde, *Quasi-War,* pp. 228–53, *passim.*

61 Cunningham, *Jeffersonian Republicans,* pp. 236–56.

62 Chambers, *Political Parties,* p. 161.

63 U.S. Constitution, Art. II, sect. 1.

64 *The Federalist* (Washington, D.C.), December 31, 1800.

65 Aaron Burr to Samuel Smith, December 29, 1800, quoted in John S. Pancake, "Aaron Burr: Would-Be Usurper," *William and Mary Quarterly,* 3rd ser., 8 (1951), pp. 205–06. Hereafter cited as Pancake, "Aaron Burr."

66 Burr to Smith, January 16, 1801, quoted in ibid., p. 207.

67 Bayard to Hamilton, January 7, 1801, *Works,* ed. Hamilton, VI, 506.

68 George Christie to Smith, n.d., 1804, quoted in Pancake, "Aaron Burr," p. 208.

69 J. Fairfax McLaughlin, *Mathew Lyon, The Hampden of Congress,* p. 386.

70 Robert Goodloe Harper, "To His Constituents," *Correspondence of James A. Bayard,* ed. Elizabeth Donnan

American Historical Association *Annual Report, 1913,* II, 136.

71 Hamilton to Robert Morris, December 26, 1800, *Works,* ed. Lodge, X, 401.

72 Hamilton to James A. Bayard, December 27, 1800; to John Rutledge, December __, 1800; to James Ross, __, 1801; to Bayard, January 6, 1801, ibid., pp. 402–19, *passim.*

73 George Baer to R. H. Bayard, April 19, 1830, printed in *Congressional Globe, Containing the Debates and Proceedings . . . 1833–1873,* Appendix XXXI, p. 138.

74 Hamilton to John Rutledge, December __, 1800, *Works,* ed. Lodge, X, 405.

Chapter XIV   Jefferson in Power

1 Jefferson to Benjamin Rush, January 16, 1811, *Writings,* ed. Ford, IX, 296–97.

2 *Writings,* ed. Ford, VIII, 3–6, *passim.* This and subsequent quotations are from Jefferson's "first draft" with abbreviations spelled out. Cf., Dumas Malone, *Jefferson the President: First Term, 1801–1805* (vol. IV of *Jefferson and His Time*), p. 18 n. Hereafter cited as Malone, *Jefferson: First Term.*

3 Margaret Bayard Smith, *The First Forty Years of Washington Society,* ed. Gaillard Hunt, pp. 25–26. Hereafter cited as Smith, *Forty Years of Washington.*

4 Jefferson to Benjamin S. Barton, February 14, 1801, *Writings,* ed. Ford, VII, 489–90; Jefferson to Joseph Fay, March 22, 1801, quoted in Noble E. Cunningham, *The Jeffersonian Republicans in Power: Party Operations, 1801–1809,* p. 8. Hereafter cited as Cunningham, *Republicans in Power.*

5 Address to the Electors of New York State, __, 1801, *Works,* ed. Lodge, VIII, 240.

6 Cunningham, *Republicans in Power,* pp. 4–6; Noble E. Cunningham, "The Virginia Jeffersonians' Victory Celebration in 1801," *Virginia Cavalcade,* 8 (1958), pp. 4–9.

7 Malone, *President, First Term,* pp. 58–63; Leonard D. White, *The Jeffersonians: A Study in Administrative History, 1801–1829,* pp. 77–80; Circular to Heads of De-

partments, November 6, 1801, *Writings,* ed. Ford, VIII, 99–101.

8   Jefferson to William Duane, July 24, 1803, *Writings,* ed. Ford, VIII, 258.

9   Malone, *President, First Term,* pp. 70–72; Jefferson to Monroe, March 7, 1801, *Writings,* ed. Ford, VIII, 8–10.

10 Jefferson to W. C. Nicholas, June 11, 1801, *Writings,* ed. Ford, VIII, 64; Cunningham, *Republicans in Power,* pp. 44–49.

11 Jefferson to Elias Simpson and Others, A Committee of Merchants of New Haven, July 12, 1801, *Writings,* ed. Ford, VIII, 70.

12 Jefferson to Duane, July 24, 1803, ibid., pp. 257–58; Cunningham, *Republicans in Power,* pp. 69–70.

13 Jefferson to Benjamin Rush, December 20, 1801, *Writings,* ed. Ford, VIII, 128.

14 First Annual Message, December 8, 1801, ibid., pp. 109–25.

15 Raymond Walters, Jr., *Albert Gallatin: Jeffersonian Financier and Diplomat,* pp. 145–46. Hereafter cited as Walters, *Gallatin.*

16 Examination of Jefferson's Message to Congress of December 7, 1801, No. II, December 21, 1801, *Works,* ed. Lodge, VIII, 253; Jefferson to Rush, December 20, 1801, *Writings,* ed. Ford, VIII, 128.

17 Walters, *Gallatin,* p. 146–47.

18 Examination of Jefferson's Message, . . . No. IV, December 26, 1801, *Works,* ed. Lodge, VIII, 265.

19 Jefferson to Madison, March 22, 1803, *Writings,* ed. Ford, VIII, 221–22; for details of the Barbary Wars see Gardner W. Allen, *Our Navy and the Barbary Corsairs.*

20 *Statistical History,* pp. 711–12.

21 Jefferson to Henry Knox, March 7, 1801, *Writings,* ed. Ford, VIII, 37.

22 Examination of Jefferson's Message, . . . No. V, December 29, 1801, *Works,* ed. Lodge, VIII, 271; Jefferson to Abigail Adams, June 13, 1804, *Writings,* ed. Ford, VIII, 307.

23 Warren, *Supreme Court,* I, 249–52.

24 Cranch (U.S.), 180 (1803); Cf., No. 78, *Federalist,* ed. Cooke, pp. 524–526.

25　Jefferson to Madison, May 25, 1810, *Writings*, ed. Ford, IX, 276.

26　Merrill Peterson, *Thomas Jefferson and the New Nation*, pp. 692, 698. Hereafter cited as Peterson, *Jefferson*. Edward S. Corwin, *Court Over Constitution*, pp. 66–76.

27　Jefferson to Gallatin, September, 27, 1810, *Writings*, ed. Ford, IX, 285.

28　Lynn W. Turner, "The Impeachment of John Pickering," *American Historical Review*, 54 (1949), pp. 485–507.

29　*Annals*, 8th Cong., 2nd sess., pp. 726–63.

30　Malone, *President, First Term*, pp. 464–83; William Cabell Bruce, *John Randolph of Roanoke, 1773–1833*, II, 200–21. Hereafter cited as Bruce, *Randolph*. *Annals*, 8th Cong., 2nd sess., pp. 664–69.

31　King to Jefferson, March 29, 1801, quoted in Arthur Burr Darling, *Our Rising Empire*, p. 399.

32　Frances Gardiner Davenport (ed.), *European Treaties Bearing Upon the History of the United States and Its Possessions*, IV, 181.

33　Carl L. Lokke, "Jefferson and the LeClerc Expedition," *American Historical Review*, 33 (1928), 322–28; Irving Brant, *James Madison: Secretary of State*, pp. 74–75, 90–91. Hereafter cited as Brant, *Secretary of State*.

34　Jefferson to Monroe, November 24, 1801, *Writings*, ed. Ford, VIII, 105.

35　George Dangerfield, *Chancellor Robert R. Livingston of New York, 1746–1813*, pp. 309–14. Hereafter cited as Dangerfield, *Livingston*. Madison to Livingston, September 28, 1801, *ASP, FR*, II, 510–11.

36　King to Madison, October 2, 1801, *ASP, FR*, II, 424; King to Madison, November 20, 1801, ibid., p. 511.

37　Malone, *President, First Term*, pp. 253–54; Brant, *Secretary of State*, pp. 74–75.

38　Jefferson to Du Pont de Nemours, April 25, 1802, *The Correspondence of Jefferson and Du Pont de Nemours*, ed. Gilbert Chinard, p. 47.

39　Jefferson to Livingston, April 8, 1802, *Writings*, ed. Ford, VIII, 144–45.

40　Livingston to Tallyrand, August 10, 1802, and to Madison, same date, *ASP, FR*, II, 520–24.

41 Livingston to Madison, September 1, 1802, ibid., p. 525.
42 King to Livingston, March 23, 1802, *Correspondence of King,* ed. King, IV, 87.
43 Livingston to Jefferson, October 28, 1802, *ASP, FR,* II, 525–26.
44 Malone, *President, First Term,* pp. 253–54; Jefferson to Livingston, October 10, 1802, *Writings,* ed. Ford, VIII, 174; Brant, *Secretary of State,* pp. 89–92.
45 Arthur P. Whitaker, *The Mississippi Question, 1795–1803: A Study in Trade, Politics, and Diplomacy,* pp. 189–99. Hereafter cited as Whitaker, *The Mississippi Question.*
46 *Writings,* ed. Ford, VIII, 183–85.
47 Hamilton to C. C. Pinckney, December 29, 1802, *Works,* ed. Lodge, X, 445–46.
48 Jefferson to Monroe, January 13, 1803, *Writings,* ed. Ford, VIII, 190.
49 Whitaker, *The Mississippi Question,* pp. 205–06.
50 *Annals,* 7th Cong., 2nd, sess., p. 370; Jefferson to Monroe, January 10, 1803, *Writings,* ed. Ford, VIII, 188.
51 *Annals,* 7th Cong., 2nd sess., p. 83; Livingston to Madison, April 11, 1803, *ASP, FR,* II, 552; Madison to Monroe and Livingston, March 2, 1803, ibid., p. 540.
52 Wilson Lyon, *Louisiana in French Diplomacy, 1759–1804,* p. 194.
53 Livingston to Jefferson, March 12, 1803, *ASP, FR,* II, 547; King to Madison, March 17, 1803, ibid., p. 548; Pichon to Tallyrand, January 24, 1803, quoted in Brant, *Secretary of State,* p. 117.
54 Barbé-Marbois, *Histoire de Louisiane,* p. 298.
55 Livingston to Madison, April 11, 1803, *ASP, FR,* II, 552.
56 Monroe and Livingston to Madison, May 13, 1803, ibid., pp. 558–59, 507–08.
57 Livingston to Madison, May 20, 1803, ibid., pp. 560–61.
58 Bernard Mayo, "A Peppercorn for Mr. Jefferson," *Virginia Quarterly Review,* 19 (1943), pp. 221–26.
59 Jefferson to John Dickinson, August 9, 1803, *Writings,* ed. Ford, VIII, 262.
60 Jefferson to Wilson Cary Nicholas, September 7, 1803, ibid., p. 262.

61 Jefferson to Levi Lincoln, August 8, 30, 1803, ibid., p. 246.
62 Jefferson to John C. Breckinridge, August 12, 1803, ibid., p. 243.
63 Jefferson to Breckinridge, August 12, 1803, ibid., p. 243–44.
64 Confidential Message on an Expedition to the Pacific, January 18, 1803, ibid., p. 201.
65 Jefferson to Meriwether Lewis, April 27, 1803, ibid., pp. 195–96.
66 Malone, *President, First Term,* pp. 342–63; *Messages and Papers,* ed. Richardson, I, 367.
67 Examination of Jefferson's Message, . . . No. I, *Works,* ed. Lodge, VIII, 247.
68 Malone, *President, First Term,* p. 325.
69 Peterson, *Jefferson,* pp. 724–29.
70 Jefferson to James Sullivan, May 21, 1805, *Writings,* ed Ford, VIII, 355; Jefferson to Lafayette, November 4, 1823, ibid., X, 280.
71 Smith, *Forty Years of Washington,* p. v.
72 Jefferson to Michael Leib, August 12, 1805, *Writings,* ed. Ford, VIII, 354.
73 Jefferson to Gallatin, June 19, 1802, ibid., p. 158.
74 Examination of Jefferson's Message, . . . No. XVI, *Works,* ed. Lodge, VIII, 346.

Chapter XV A Giant Passes

1 Hamilton to Gouverneur Morris, February 27, 1802, *Works,* ed. Lodge, X, 425–26.
2 Mitchell, *Hamilton,* II, 496–98; Troup to King, December 5, 1801, *Correspondence of King,* ed. King, IV, 28
3 Mitchell, *Hamilton,* II, 501–02; Hamilton to C. C. Pinckney, December 29, 1802, *Works,* ed. Lodge, X, 444.
4 Mitchell, *Hamilton,* II, 547–49.
5 *Works,* ed. Lodge, VIII, 388 n.
6 Brief and arguments in the Croswell case are in ibid., pp. 383, 407, 340, 422, 391.
7 Quoted in Mitchell, *Hamilton,* II, 495.
8 Ibid., pp. 494–95; Schachner, *Hamilton,* p. 405.

9 Schachner, *Hamilton,* p. 403–04.

10 Address to the Electors of New York, 1801, *Works,* ed. Lodge, VIII, 225, 240; Adams is quoted in Miller, *Hamilton,* p. 539.

11 Hamilton to James A. Bayard, April __, 1802, *Works,* ed. Lodge, X, 436.

12 Pickering to King, March 4, 1804, *Correspondence of King,* ed. King, IV, 364; Hamilton to Gouverneur Morris, February 27, 1802, *Works,* ed. Lodge, X, 428.

13 Pickering to King, March 4, 1804, *Correspondence of King,* ed. King, IV, 365.

14 *Works,* ed. Lodge, VIII, 375; Mitchell, *Hamilton,* II, 523 ff.

15 Hamilton to Burr, June 20, 1804, *Works,* ed. Lodge, X, 461.

16 Burr to Hamilton, June 18, 1804, ibid., p. 460; Statement by Hamilton, n.d., ibid., p. 474.

17 Douglass Adair and Marvin Harvey, "Was Alexander Hamilton a Christian Statesman?" in Jacob E. Cooke (ed.), *Alexander Hamilton, A Profile,* p. 254; *Works,* ed. Lodge, X, 474.

18 *Works,* ed. Lodge, X, 474.

19 Hamilton to _____, April 12, 1804, ibid., p. 456.

Chapter XVI Commercial Warfare

1 Cunningham, *Republicans in Power,* pp. 103–04.

2 *Annals,* 8th Cong., 1st sess., pp. 1305–07.

3 *Statistical History,* pp. 685, 692.

4 March 4, 1805, *Writings,* ed. Ford, VIII, 343–47, *passim.*

5 Jefferson to Gallatin, March 28, 1803, ibid., pp. 222–23.

6 Opinion on the Powers of the Senate, n.d., (1790?), ibid., V, 161.

7 *Annals,* 8th Cong., 1st sess., pp. 1257–58; Brant, *Secretary of State,* pp. 192–94; Don Pedro Cevallos to Monroe, July 8, 1804, *ASP, FR,* II, 620–21; *id.* to *id.,* February 24, 1805, ibid., pp. 644–46.

8 Jefferson to Monroe, December 13, 1803, *Writings,* ed. Ford, VIII, 288–89; Jefferson to Madison, September 16, October 11 and October 25, 1805, ibid., 379–81.

9 Jefferson to James Bowdoin, April 27, 1805, ibid., p. 351.

10   December 3, 1805, ibid., p. 391; *Annals,* 9th Cong., 1st
      sess., 266, 444.

11   Brant, *Secretary of State,* pp. 234–40.

12   Bruce, *Randolph,* I, 228–32; *Annals,* 9th Cong., 1st sess.,
      pp. 1226–27.

13   Arthur P. Whitaker, *The United States and Latin Ameri-
      can Independence, 1800–1830,* pp. 28–34.

14   Thomas P. Abernethy, *The Burr Conspiracy,* pp. 38–40,
      55–56 (Yrujo); pp. 36, 56 (Merry); chaps. II and III,
      passim (Livingston and Clark). Hereafter cited as
      Abernethy, *Burr Conspiracy.*

15   James R. Jacobs, *The Tarnished Warrior;* Royal O.
      Shreve, *The Finished Scoundrel.*

16   Abernethy, *Burr Conspiracy,* pp. 67–79.

17   Jefferson to George Morgan, September 19, 1806, *Writ-
      ings,* VIII, 473–74.

18   Abernethy, *Burr Conspiracy,* pp. 158, 219–24; *Writings,*
      ed. Ford, VIII, 481.

19   Abernethy, *Burr Conspiracy,* chap. XIV. For Jefferson's
      response to the court's subpoenas see Dumas Malone,
      letter to the editor of the *New York Times,* November
      26, 1973.

20   Perkins, *Prologue to War,* pp. 90–91; *Statistical History,*
      pp. 451, 538.

21   Jefferson to Gallatin, June 26, 1806, *Writings,* ed. Ford,
      VIII, 458.

22   James F. Zimmerman, *Impressment of American Sea-
      man* (Columbia University "Studies in History, Eco-
      nomics and Public Law"), pp. 255–56; Cf., Perkins, *Pro-
      logue to War,* pp. 91–93.

23   *Independent Chronicle* (Boston), May 27, 1811.

24   A. L. Burt, *The United States, Great Britain, and British
      North America,* pp. 218–22; Perkins, *Prologue to War,*
      pp. 77–82.

25   Smith to _____, January 30, 1806, quoted in John S.
      Pancake, "The Invisibles: A Chapter in the Opposition
      to Madison," *Journal of Southern History,* 21 (1955), pp.
      21–22. Hereafter cited as Pancake, "Invisibles." See also
      Eli F. Hecksher, *The Continental* System.

26   Monroe to Madison, February 12, 1806, *ASP, FR,* III,
      112.

27 Jefferson to Monroe, January 8, 1804, *Writings,* ed. Ford, VIII, 291; Brant, *Secretary of State,* pp. 162–69; Smith, *Forty Years of Washington,* pp. 46–47.

28 Perkins, *Prologue to War,* pp. 12–14; Jefferson to William Duane, November 13, 1810, *Writings,* ed. Ford, IX, 287.

29 Perkins, *Prologue to War,* pp. 19–24.

30 Monroe to Madison, April 18, 20, and May 17, 1806, *ASP, FR,* III, 116–26.

31 Proclamation concerning the *Leander,* May 3, 1806, *Writings,* ed. Ford, VIII, 445–46.

32 *Annals,* 9th Cong., 1st sess., p. 851; ibid., 9th Cong., 1st sess., p. 877.

33 Jefferson to Monroe, March 10, 1808, *Writings,* ed. Ford, IX, 179.

34 Madison to Monroe, May 15, 1806, *ASP, FR,* III, 119.

35 Madison to Monroe and Pinckney, May 17, 1806, ibid., 119–24.

36 Monroe to Madison, June 9, 1806, ibid., pp. 126–27; Monroe to Jefferson, March 22, 1808, *Works of Monroe,* ed. Hamilton, V, 30.

37 *ASP, FR,* III, 147–52.

38 Jefferson to Monroe, March 21, 1807, *Writings,* ed. Ford, IX, 36; S. Smith to Madison, April 18, 1807, quoted in Pancake, "Invisibles," p. 21.

39 S. Smith to Wilson Cary Nicholas, March 4, 1807, quoted in Pancake, "Invisibles," p. 22.

40 Jefferson to Madison April 21, 1807, *Writings,* ed. Ford, IX, 47; Jefferson to Monroe, March 21, 1807, ibid., p. 37.

41 Zimmerman, *Impressment,* pp. 135–37; Perkins, *Prologue to War,* pp. 140–42.

42 Nicholas to Jefferson, July 7, 1807, quoted in Pancake, "Invisibles," p. 23; *Enquirer* (Richmond), July 21, 1807.

43 Turreau to Tallyrand, July 18, 1807, quoted in Henry Adams, *A History of the United States During the Administrations of Thomas Jefferson and James Madison, 1801–1817,* IV, 36. Hereafter cited as Adams, *History.* Jefferson to Barnabas Bidwell, July 11, 1807, *Writings,* ed. Ford, IX, 106–07.

44 December 8, 1801, *Writings,* ed. Ford, VIII, 121.

45 An Act for Classing Militia, December __, 1805, ibid., pp. 409–12.

46 Peterson, *Jefferson*, pp. 832–39.

47 Jefferson to Adams, April 27, 1813, *The Adams-Jefferson Letters*, ed. Lester Cappon, II, 324. Hereafter cited as *Adams-Jefferson Letters*, ed. Cappon.

48 Madison to Monroe, July 6, 1807, *ASP, FR*, III, 183–85.

49 Ibid., pp. 29–31.

50 Ibid., pp. 290–91.

51 *Annals*, 10th Cong., 1st sess., pp. 1221–22.

52 Reginald Horseman, *The Causes of the War of 1812*, pp. 30–34.

53 Adams, *History*, IV, 201–03; cf., Louis Martin Sears, *Jefferson and the Embargo*; Walter Jennings, *The American Embargo, 1807–1809* (University of Iowa "Studies in the Social Sciences," Vol. VIII, No. 1), chaps. V and VI.

54 *Annals*, 10th Cong., 2nd sess., pp. 138 ff., 230.

55 Jefferson to James Sullivan, August 12, 1808, *Writings*, ed. Ford, IX, 205.

56 November 3, 1808, ibid., pp. 213–25.

57 *The Repertory* (Boston), July 15, 1808.

58 Jefferson to Monroe, March 21, 1807, *Writings*, ed. Ford, IX, 37; E. Wilder Spaulding, *His Excellency, Governor Clinton*, pp. 287–94.

59 Cunningham, *Republicans in Power*, pp. 110–19.

60 *Annapolis Gazette* (Maryland), December 8, 1808; *Statistical History*, pp. 691–92.

61 Jefferson to Levi Lincoln, November 13, 1808, *Writings* ed. Ford, IX, 227.

62 *Annals*, 10th Congress, 2nd sess., pp. 1798–1804; *Federal Republican and Commercial Gazette* (Baltimore), January 18, 1809.

63 Jefferson to Thomas Mann Randolph, February 7, 1809, *Writings*, ed. Ford, IX, 244.

64 Jefferson to Henry Dearborn, July 16, 1810, ibid., p. 277.

65 *Annals*, 10th Cong., 2nd sess., p. 1541.

66 Erskine to Canning, November 5, 1808, quoted in Adams, *History*, IV, 384–85; *id.* to *id.*, November 26, 1808, ibid., p. 392; *id.* to *id.*, December 4, 1808, ibid., pp. 386–87.

67 Canning to Erskine, May 30, 1809, *Instructions to Ministers,* ed. Mayo, p. 264–66.
68 *ASP, FR,* III, 295–97.
69 Canning to Erskine, May 30, 1809, *Instructions to Ministers,* ed. Mayo, p. 276
70 Pinkney to Madison, August 19, 1809, quoted in Perkins, *Prologue to War,* p. 234.
71 *Annals,* 11th Cong., 1st session part 1, p. 608.
72 Jefferson to Dearborn, July 16, 1810, *Writings,* ed. Ford, IX, 278.
73 *Correspondence of Du Pont,* ed. Chinard, p. 122.
74 Smith, *Forty Years of Washington,* p. 410.

Chapter XVII   The Sage of Monticello

1 Thomas T. Waterman, *The Mansions of Virginia, 1706–1776,* p. 387–94.
2 *Farm Book,* ed. Betts, pp. 426–28, 337–38, 421–22, 456.
3 Peterson, *Jefferson,* pp. 926–27.
4 Jefferson to Madison, February 17, 1826, *Writings,* ed. Ford, X, 376–77.
5 *Farm Book,* ed. Betts, pp. 5, 310 ff.; Peterson, *Jefferson,* p. 924.
6 Quoted in Peterson, *Jefferson,* p. 927.
7 Smith, *Forty Years of Washington,* pp. 34–35; Jefferson to Vine Utley, March 21, 1819, *Writings,* ed. Ford, X, 126.
8 *Writings,* ed. Ford, IX, 248.
9 Jefferson to Monroe, May 5, 1811, ibid., p. 324.
10 Jefferson to John Wayles Eppes, September 11, 1813, ibid., p. 396; Jefferson to Madison, November 6, 1812, ibid., p. 370.
11 Jefferson to Baron Humbolt, December 6, 1813, ibid., 431; Jefferson to Thomas Leiper, June 12, 1815, ibid., 52.
12 Jefferson to Monroe, May 14, 1820, ibid., X, 159.
13 Jefferson to William Johnson, October 27, 1822, ibid., 223–24.
14 Jefferson to Benjamin Austin, January 9, 1816, ibid., p. 10.

15 *Farm Book,* ed. Betts, pp. 218–220; Jefferson to Richard
    Rush, June 22, 1819, *Writings,* ed. Ford, X, 133–34.
16 Jefferson to John Holmes, April 22, 1820, *Writings,* ed.
    Ford, X, 157.
17 Ibid., pp. 349–52.
18 Jefferson, *Notes on Virginia,* p. 163.
19 Ibid., pp. 142–43, 139.
20 *Messages and Papers,* ed. Richardson, I, 408.
21 Malone, *President, First Term,* pp. 494–98; cf., Winthrop
    D. Jordan, *White Over Black: American Attitudes To-
    ward the Negro, 1550–1812,* pp. 464–69.
22 Jefferson to the Marquis de Condorcet, August 30, 1791,
    Writings, ed. Ford, V, 379.
23 Jefferson, *Notes on Virginia,* p. 121.
24 Jefferson to Edward Coles, August 25, 1814, *Writings,*
    ed. Ford, IX, 478; Jefferson to Jared Sparks, February
    4, 1824, ibid., X, 289–93.
25 Jefferson to Frances Wright, August 7, 1825, ibid., X,
    344–45.
26 Jefferson to John Tyler, May 26, 1810, ibid., IX, 277.
27 Jefferson to John Adams, July 5, 1814, ibid., p. 464.
28 Jefferson to George Ticknor, November 25, 1817, ibid.,
    X, 95–96; Jefferson to Joseph Cabell, January 14, 1818,
    ibid., pp. 98–102.
29 Philip Alexander Bruce, *History of the University of Vir-
    ginia, 1819–1919,* I, 88–94. Hereafter cited as Bruce,
    University of Virginia.
30 Ibid., pp. 188–89.
31 Ibid., pp. 178–87, 240–51.
32 Ibid., pp. 256–57.
33 Jefferson to Thomas Cooper, November 2, 1822, *Writ-
    ings,* ed. Ford, X, 242–44.
34 Jefferson to Cooper, December 11, 1823, ibid., pp.
    285–86; Bruce, *University of Virginia,* I, 200–06.
35 Bruce, *University of Virginia,* I, 356–76.
36 Jefferson to Benjamin Waterhouse, January 8, 1825,
    Writings, ed. Ford, X, 335–36; Jefferson to George
    Loyall, February 22, 1826, ibid., p. 380.
37 Jefferson to Giles, December 26, 1825, ibid., p. 357.
38 Jefferson to Adams, September 18, 1825, ibid., p. 347.
39 *Adams-Jefferson Letters,* ed. Cappon, II, 318.

40 Peterson, *Jefferson,* pp. 1006–07.
41 Jefferson to Roger Weightman, June 24, 1825, *Writings,* ed. Ford, X, 391.
42 Photographic reproduction of Jefferson's memorandum, Peterson, Jefferson, following p. 912.

Chapter XVIII   The Verdict of History

1 *Messages and Papers of the Presidents, 1789–1897,* compiled by James D. Richardson, I, 311. Since this chapter is a historiographical essay, the full name of the author and full title are given all works even though they have been cited elsewhere.
2 James Madison, *Writings,* ed. Gaillard Hunt, IV, 204.
3 A. B. Norton, *Reminiscences of the Log Cabin and Hard Cider Campaign,* p. 298.
4 Anyone who has read Merrill Peterson's *The Jefferson Image in the American Mind* will recognize my indebtedness to his outstanding scholarship. The quotation is from page 171. Hereafter cited as Peterson, *Jefferson Image.*
5 Abraham Lincoln, *Complete Works,* ed. J. G. Nicolay and John Hay, I, 88.
6 Roscoe Pound, *et. al., Federalism as a Democratic Process,* pp. 82–90.
7 Thomas Jefferson, *Memoirs, Correspondence and Private Papers,* ed. Thomas Mann Randolph.
8 George Tucker, *Life of Thomas Jefferson, Third President of the United States, . . .* I, xi.
9 George Gibbs (ed.), *Memoirs of the Administrations of George Washington and John Adams. . . .*
10 William Sullivan (ed.), *Familiar Letters of Public Characters and Public Events.*
11 Theodore Dwight, *The Character of Thomas Jefferson.*
12 Richard Hildreth, *A History of the United States of America,* VI, 141; IV, 108, 298.
13 Henry S. Randall, *Life of Thomas Jefferson.* The description of Randall's study is in Peterson, *The Jefferson Image,* p. 151.
14 Macauley to Randall, May 23, 1860, Francis Coleman Rosenberger (ed.), *The Jefferson Reader,* p. 262.

15   Speech in New York, March 10, 1831, Daniel Webster,
      Writings, ed. J. W. McIntyre, II, 50.

16   James O. Bennett, *Chicago Tribune*, December 20, 1931,
      quoted in Peterson, *Jefferson Image*, p. 260.

17   Theodore Roosevelt to Gouverneur Morris, November
      28, 1910, Theodore Roosevelt, *Letters*, ed. Elting E.
      Morison, VII, 175.

18   Gertrude Atherton, *The Conqueror*, p. 392.

19   Herbert Croly, *The Promise of American Life*, p. 40.

20   Theodore Roosevelt, *Works*, comp. Herman Hagedorn,
      XVII, 6.

21   Henry Cabot Lodge, *Alexander Hamilton;* Alexander
      Hamilton, *Works*, ed. Henry Cabot Lodge.

22   Albert J. Beveridge, *Life of John Marshall*.

23   William Graham Sumner, *Alexander Hamilton*.

24   Alfred T. Mahan, *Sea Power and Its Relations to the War
      of 1812*.

25   A. Mitchell Palmer (Pennsylvania), in *Congressional
      Record*, 62nd Cong., 3rd sess., pp. 178–79 (December
      5, 1912).

26   Woodrow Wilson, *A History of the American People*, III,
      74.

27   *Princeton Alumni Weekly*, April 28, 1906, quoted in
      Peterson *Jefferson Image*, p. 343.

28   George Bancroft, *A History of the United States from the
      Discovery of the American Continent*.

29   John Bach MacMaster, *A History of the People of the
      United States*, I, 125; II, 51.

30   Frank L. Owsley, remark to the author, April 1951.

31   Irving Brant to the author shortly after the publication
      of *James Madison: Secretary of State;* see pp. 330–31;
      James Madison: President, p. 510; cf., William Jorfy,
      Henry Adams, Scientific Historian, pp. 59–68.

32   Henry Adams, *A History of the United States During the
      Administrations of Thomas Jefferson and James Madi-
      son, 1801–1817*, IV, 461–65.

33   James Schouler, *The History of the United States under
      the Constitution*, II, 71–72.

34   Edward Channing, *A History of the United States; idem.,
      The Jeffersonian System* ("The American Nation Se-
      ries," ed. A. B. Hart).

35 C. J. Riethmüller, *Alexander Hamilton and His Contemporaries.*

36 John C. Hamilton, *History of the Republic of the United States as Traced in the Writings of Alexander Hamilton and His Contemporaries.*

37 John T. Morse, *Life of Alexander Hamilton;* see also his *Thomas Jefferson.*

38 Sarah Nicholas Randolph, *The Domestic Life of Thomas Jefferson.*

39 James Parton, *Life of Thomas Jefferson, Third President of the United States;* see also Milton E. Fowler, *James Parton, The Father of Modern Biography.*

40 Thomas Jefferson, *Writings,* ed. Paul Leicester Ford.

41 Ibid., I, xviii.

42 Charles A. Beard, *The Economic Interpretation of the Constitution.*

43 Ibid., preface to 1935 ed., p. xvi.

44 Charles A. Beard, *The Economic Origins of Jeffersonian Democracy,* p. 467.

45 Beard, *Economic Interpretation of the Constitution,* p. 19.

46 Vernon L. Parrington, *Main Currents of American Thought: The Colonial Mind,* p. i.

47 Carl Becker, *The Declaration of Independence,* p. 278.

48 Albert Jay Nock, *Jefferson,* pp. 267–72, 310–14.

49 Arthur H. Vandenburg, *If Hamilton Were Alive Today,* p. vii.

50 John W. Davis, "Thomas Jefferson, Attorney at Law," address to the Virginia State Bar Association, August 4, 1926, reprinted in Rosenberg (ed.), *The Jefferson Reader,* p. 117.

51 Nicholas Murray Butler, *Building the American Nation.*

52 James Truslow Adams, *The Epic of America,* p. 306.

53 Claude G. Bowers, *Jefferson and Hamilton: The Struggle for Democracy in America.*

54 Frank Freidel, *Franklin Roosevelt: The Ordeal,* p. 205.

55 Franklin Roosevelt, *Public Papers and Addresses,* ed. Samuel I. Rosenman, I, 746.

56 *The New York Times,* February 13 and July 5, 1938.

57 Twelve Southern Authors, *I'll Take My Stand: The South and the Agrarian Tradition.*

58   Sidney Kingsley, *The Patriots*, p. 141.
59   Elmer Davis, *By Elmer Davis*, ed. Robert Lloyd Davis, p. 42.
60   Claude G. Bowers, *Jefferson in Power*, p. vi.
61   James Truslow Adams, *The Living Jefferson*, p. 394.
62   Gilbert Chinard, *Thomas Jefferson: The Apostle of Americanism*.
63   Marie Kimbell, *The Jefferson Cook Book*.
64   Marie Kimbell, *Thomas Jefferson: The Road to Glory*, pp. 3–6, 7–26.
65   Parks, *Symposium*, 3 (July, 1933); Owsley, *Hound and Horn*, 6 (October, 1932); Beard, *Yale Review*, 25 (December, 1935); Malone *Scribner's Magazine*, 93 (June, 1933).
66   Broadus Mitchell, *Heritage from Hamilton*, pp. 29–30.
67   Rexford Tugwell and Joseph Dorfman, "Alexander Hamilton: Nation Maker," *Columbia University Quarterly*, 29 (1937), pp. 221, 225.
68   Address at the dedication of the Jefferson Memorial, April 13, 1943, *Public Papers*, ed. Rosenman, XI, 164.

Chapter XIX   Jefferson, Hamilton, and the Living Generation

1   Nathan Schachner, *Alexander Hamilton*, p. 409. Cf., chap. XVIII, note 1.
2   Richard B. Morris (ed.), *Alexander Hamilton and the Founding of the Nation*, pp. viii, ix, xii–xiii.
3   Louis M. Hacker, *Alexander Hamilton in the American Tradition*, pp. 6–7, 18.
4   Ibid., 254–55.
5   Hans Morganthau, *In Defense of the National Interest: A Critical Examination of American Foreign Policy*, pp. 14, 18–19.
6   Alfred H. Bowman, "Jefferson, Hamilton, and American Foreign Policy," *Political Science Quarterly*, 71 (1956), pp. 19, 40–41.
7   Broadus Mitchell, *Alexander Hamilton*.
8   Broadus Mitchell, *Heritage from Hamilton*, pp. 66–67, 68, 93.

9 John C. Miller, *Alexander Hamilton: Portrait in Paradox,* pp. xi–xii.

10 Clinton Rossiter, *Alexander Hamilton and the Constitution.*

11 Samuel D. Konefsky, *John Marshall and Alexander Hamilton: Architects of the Constitution,* p. 76.

12 Julian P. Boyd, *Number 7: Alexander Hamilton's Secret Attempts to Control American Foreign Policy.*

13 Leonard D. White, *The Federalists: A Study in Administrative History, 1789–1801,* pp. 125–26.

14 Cecelia Kenyon, "Alexander Hamilton: Rousseau of the Right," *Political Science Quarterly,* 73 (1958), p. 178.

15 Alexander Hamilton, *The Mind of Alexander Hamilton,* ed. Saul K. Padover, pp. 12–13, 27.

16 Alexander Hamilton, *Reports,* ed. Jacob E. Cooke, p. xxii.

17 Bernard Mayo, *Jefferson Himself: A Personal Narrative of a Many-Sided American,* p. vi.

18 Bernard Mayo, *Myths and Men: Patrick Henry, George Washington, and Thomas Jefferson,* p. 70.

19 Dumas Malone, *Jefferson and His Time* (through Jefferson's second term as President).

20 Malone, *President, First Term,* pp. xx–xxi.

21 Nathan Schachner, *Thomas Jefferson, A Biography,* p. viii.

22 Merrill D. Peterson, *Thomas Jefferson and the New Nation,* p. ix.

23 Max Beloff, *Thomas Jefferson and American Democracy,* p. 255.

24 Sidney Hook, *The Paradoxes of Freedom,* p. 6.

25 Carl Becker, "What Is Still Living in the Philosophy of Thomas Jefferson?" in *Thomas Jefferson: A Profile,* ed. Merrill D. Peterson, p. 58.

26 John Dos Passos, "A Portico Facing the Wilderness" (from Dos Passos, *The Ground We Stand On*), in ibid., p. 84.

27 Robert R. Palmer, "The Dubious Democrat: Thomas Jefferson in Bourbon France," in ibid., pp. 102–103.

28 William Grampp, "A Re-examination of Jeffersonian Economics," in ibid., p. 162.

29 Julian P. Boyd, "Thomas Jefferson's Empire For Liberty," in ibid., p. 186.

30 Irving Brant, *James Madison: Father of the Constitution, 1787–1800,* pp. 332–33, 351–52; *idem, James Madison: Commander-in-Chief, 1812–1836,* pp. 526–27.

31 Adrienne Koch, *Jefferson and Madison: The Great Collaboration,* p. [v].

32 Daniel Boorstin, *The Lost World of Thomas Jefferson.*

33 Merrill D. Peterson, *The Jefferson Image in the American Mind,* pp. 8, 14.

Bibliography

PRIMARY SOURCES

Writings of Hamilton:

Alexander Hamilton and the Founding of the Nation, ed. Richard B. Morris. New York: The Dial Press, 1957, Pbk., Harper and Row/Torchbooks.

The Mind of Alexander Hamilton, ed. Saul K. Padover. New York: Harper and Row, 1958.

The Papers of Alexander Hamilton, ed. Harold C. Syrett, Jacob E. Cooke, *et. al.* 15 vols. (to 1794). New York: Columbia University Press, 1961–69.

The Reports of Alexander Hamilton, ed. Jacob E. Cooke. New York: Harper and Row, 1964.

The Works of Alexander Hamilton, ed. Henry Cabot Lodge. 12 vols. New York: G. P. Putnam's Sons, 1904.

The Works of Alexander Hamilton, ed. John C. Hamilton. 7 vols. New York: C. S. Francis and Co., 1850–51.

Writings of Jefferson:

The Adams-Jefferson Letters, ed. Lester Cappon. 2 vols. Chapel Hill, N.C.: University of North Carolina Press, 1959.

The Autobiography of Thomas Jefferson, ed. Paul Leicester Ford. New York: G. P. Putnam's Sons, 1914. Pbk.

The Correspondence of Jefferson and Du Pont de Nemours, ed. Gilbert Chinard. Baltimore: Johns Hopkins Press, 1931.

The Memoirs, Correspondence and Private Papers of Thomas Jefferson, ed. Thomas Jefferson Randolph. 4 vols. Charlottesville, Va.: F. Carr and Co., 1829.

Notes on the State of Virginia, ed. William Peden. Chapel Hill, N.C.: University of North Carolina Press, 1955. Pbk.

The Papers of Thomas Jefferson, ed. Julian P. Boyd. 18 vols. (to 1790). Princeton, N.J.: Princeton University Press, 1950–72.

Thomas Jefferson's Garden Book, 1766–1824, ed. Edwin M.
  Betts. Philadelphia: American Philosophical Society, 1944.
Thomas Jefferson's Farm Book, ed. Edwin M. Betts. Prince-
  ton, N.J.: Princeton University Press, 1953.
The Writings of Thomas Jefferson, ed. Paul Leicester Ford.
  10 vols. New York: G. P. Putnam's Sons, 1892–99.

Government Documents:

*American State Papers: Documents, Legislative and Execu-
  tive, Foreign Relations,* selected and edited under the authority of Congress by Walter Loworie and Mathew St.
  Clair Clarke. 38 vols. Washington, D.C.: Gales and Seaton,
  1836–61.
Annals of Congress. See Debates and Proceedings of the Congress. . . .
*Congressional Globe, Containing Debates and Proceedings,
  1833–1873,* eds. Blair and Rives, John C. Rives, F. and J.
  Rives and George A. Bailey. Washington, D.C.: Printed
  at the *Globe* office for the editors, 1833–73.
Congressional Record, Containing Proceedings and Debates.
  Washington: Government Printing Office, 1875– .
*Debates and Proceedings in the Congress of the United States,
  1789–1824.* 42 vols. Washington, D.C.: Gales and Seaton,
  1834–56.
*European Treaties Bearing Upon the History of the United
  States and Its Dependencies,* ed. Frances Gardiner Daven-
  port. 4 vols. Washington, D.C.: Carnegie Institution,
  1917–1937.
Journal of the House of Representatives of the United States.
  Washington: Government Printing Office, 1789– .
Journals of the House of Burgesses of Virginia, 1766–69,
  1773–76. Richmond, Va.: Virginia State Library, 1905–06.
Journals of the Council of State of Virginia, ed. H. R. McIlwaine. 2 vols. Richmond, Va.: Virginia State Library,
  1931–32.
Messages and Papers of the Presidents, 1789–1897, compiled
  by James D. Richardson. 10 vols. Washington, D.C.: Bureau of National Literature, 1897–1907.
Select Cases from the Mayor's Court of New York City, ed.

Richard B. Morris. New York: New York University School of Law, 1941.

Treaties and Other International Acts of the United States, ed. Hunter Miller. 8 vols. Washington, D.C.: Government Printing Office, 1931–48.

Statutes at Large of the United States of America, 1789–1873. 17 vols. Boston: Little, Brown and Co., 1850–73.

Writings of Contemporaries:

Adams, John. *Diary and Autobiography,* ed. Lyman H. Butterfield. 4 vols. Cambridge, Mass.: Belknap Press of Harvard University, 1961.

    Letters . . . Addressed to His Wife, ed. Charles Francis Adams. 2 vols. Boston: Little, Brown and Co. 1841.

    Life and Works, ed. Charles Francis Adams. 10 vols. Boston: Little, Brown and Co., 1856.

Adams, John Quincy. *Writings,* ed. Worthington Chauncey Ford. 7 vols. New York: The Macmillan Co., 1913–17.

Barbé-Marbois [Francois, Marquis de]. *Histoire de Louisiane.* Paris: Imprin. de Firmin Didot, 1829.

Burke, Edmund. *Reflections on the Revolution in France.* London: J. Dodsley, 1790. Pbk., Penguin Books.

Burnett, Edmund Cody (ed.). *Letters of Members of the Continental Congress.* 8 vols. Washington, D.C.: Carnegie Institution, 1934.

Butterfield, Lyman H. (ed.). *The Adams Family Correspondence.* 2 vols. Cambridge, Mass.: Belknap Press of Harvard, 1963.

Cooke, Jacob E. (ed.). *The Federalist.* Middletown, Conn.: Wesleyan University Press, 1961. Pbk., World Publishers.

Custis, George Washington Parke. *Recollections and Private Memoirs of Washington.* New York: W. H. Moore, 1859.

Elliot, Jonathan (ed.). *The Debates in the State Conventions on the Adoption of the Federal Constitution.* 2 vols. Philadelphia: printed by the editor, 1836, 1841.

Farrand, Max (ed.). *The Records of the Federal Convention of 1787.* 4 vols. New Haven, Conn.: Yale University Press, 1911–37. Pbk.

Force, Peter (ed.). *American Archives: Fourth Series, Contain-*

ing a Documentary History of the English Colonies. . . . 6 vols. Washington, D.C.: Printed by P. Force, 1837–46.

Manuscripts of J. B. Fortescue, Esq., Preserved at Dropmore. 10 vols. Mss. Hist. Comm., London: H. M. Stationery Office, 1892–1927.

Franklin, Benjamin. *Writings,* ed. Albert H. Smythe. 10 vols. New York: The Macmillan Co., 1905–07.

Gibbs, George. *Memoirs of the Administrations of Washington and John Adams, Edited from the Papers of Oliver Wolcott, Secretary of the Treasury.* 2 vols. New York: W. Van Norden, 1846.

Jensen, Merrill (ed.). *Tracts of the American Revolution.* Indianapolis: The Bobbs-Merrill Co., 1967. Pbk.

King, Rufus. *Life and Correspondence,* ed. Charles R. King. 4 vols. New York: G. P. Putnam's Sons, 1894–97.

Lincoln, Abraham. *Complete Works,* eds. J. G. Nicolay, John Hay. 12 vols. New York: Francis D. Tandy, 1905.

Locke, John. *Treatise of Civil Government and A Letter Concerning Toleration,* ed. Charles Sherman. New York: Appleton-Century Co., 1937. Pbk., Appleton-Century-Crofts.

Maclay, William. *Journals of William Maclay, Senator from Pennsylvania, 1789–91,* ed. Edgar S. Maclay, intro. Charles A. Beard. New York: Albert and Charles Boni, 1927.

Madison, James. *Writings,* ed. Gaillard Hunt. 9 vols. New York: G. P. Putnam's Sons, 1900–10.

Letters and Other Writings of James Madison, Fourth President of the United States, published by order of Congress. 4 vols. Philadelphia: J. B. Lippincott, 1865.

Mayo, Bernard (ed.). *Instructions to British Ministers to the United States, 1791–1812,* American Historical Association *Annual Report for 1936.* III. Washington, D.C., 1941.

Monroe, James. *Writings,* ed. Stanislaus M. Hamilton. 7 vols. New York: G. P. Putnam's Sons, 1893–1903.

Pitt, William. *Correspondence of William Pitt, Earl of Chatham,* ed. John H. Pringle and J. S. Taylor. 4 vols. London: John Murray, 1838–40.

Roosevelt, Franklin. *Public Papers and Addresses,* ed. Samuel I. Rosenman. 13 vols. New York: Random House, 1938–40.

Roosevelt, Theodore. *Letters,* ed. Elting E. Morison. 8 vols. Cambridge, Mass.: Harvard University Press, 1951–54.

Works, Compiled by Herman Hagedorn. 24 vols. New York: Charles Scribner's Sons, 1923–26.

Schachner, Nathan (ed.). "Alexander Hamilton as Viewed by His Friends: The Narratives of Robert Troup and Hercules Mulligan," *William and Mary Quarterly,* 3rd ser., 4 (1947), pp. 203–25.

Smith, Mrs. Samuel Harrison [Margaret Bayard]. *The First Forty Years of Washington Society,* ed. Gaillard Hunt. New York: Charles Scribner's Sons, 1906.

Stewart, John Hall, ed. *A Documentary History of the French Revolution.* New York: The Macmillan Co., 1951.

Sullivan, William, ed. *Familiar Letters of Public Characters and Public Events.* Boston: Russell, Odiorne and Metcalfe, 1834.

Turner, Frederick Jackson (ed.). "Correspondence of French Ministers to the United States, 1791–1797," American Historical Association *Annual Report for 1903.* Washington, D.C., 1904.

The Warren-Adams Letters: Being Chiefly a Correspondence Among John Adams, Samuel Adams, and James Warren, Massachusetts Historical Society *Collections,* 72 (1917) and 73 (1925). Boston, 1917.

Washington, George. *Writings,* ed. John C. Fitzpatrick. 39 vols. Washington, D.C.: Government Printing Office, 1931–40.

Writings, ed. Jared Sparks. 12 vols. Boston: F. Andrews, 1839.

Webster, Daniel. *Writings,* ed. J. W. McIntyre. 6 vols. Boston: Little, Brown and Co., 1903.

Weld, Isaac Jr. *Travels Through the States of North America and Canada.* London: J. Stockdale, 1799.

Newspapers:

The Annapolis Gazette (Maryland). 1808.

The Enquirer (Richmond). 1807, 1808.

The Federalist (Washington). 1800.

The Federal Republican and Commercial Gazette (Baltimore). 1808, 1809.

The Independent Chronicle (Boston). 1811.

Le Moniteur Universel (Paris). 1794.

The Repertory (Boston). 1808.

The Virginia Gazette (Williamsburg). Ed. at various times, often concurrently, by William Rind, Purdie and Dixon, and Dixon and Hunter. 1770, 1774.

SECONDARY SOURCES

Books about Hamilton:

Boyd, Julian P. *Number 7: Alexander Hamilton's Secret Attempts to Control American Foreign Policy.* Princeton, N.J.: Princeton University Press, 1964.

Cooke, Jacob E. (ed). *Alexander Hamilton: A Profile.* New York: Hill and Wang, 1967. Pbk.

Hacker, Louis M. *Alexander Hamilton in the American Tradition.* New York: McGraw Hill, 1957.

Hamilton, Allen McLean. *Intimate Life of Alexander Hamilton.* New York: Charles Scribners' Sons, 1910.

Lodge, Henry Cabot. *Alexander Hamilton.* Boston: Houghton Mifflin Co., 1898.

Looze, Helene Johnson. *Alexander Hamilton and the British Orientation of American Foreign Policy.* The Hague and Paris: Mouton, 1969.

Lycan, Gilbert L. *Alexander Hamilton & American Foreign Policy: A Design for Greatness.* Norman, Okla.: University of Oklahoma Press, 1970.

Miller, John C. *Alexander Hamilton: Portrait in Paradox.* New York: Harper, 1959. Harper and Row/Torchbooks.

Mitchell, Broadus. *Alexander Hamilton: Youth to Maturity, 1755–1788.* New York: The Macmillan Co., 1957.
Alexander Hamilton: The National Adventure, 1788–1804. New York: The Macmillan Co., 1962.
Heritage from Hamilton. New York: Columbia University Press, 1957.

Morse, John T. *Life of Alexander Hamilton.* 2 vols. Boston: Little, Brown and Co., 1876.

Riethmuller, C. J. *Alexander Hamilton and His Contemporaries.* London: Bell and Daldy, 1864.

Rossiter, Clinton. *Alexander Hamilton and the Constitution.* New York: Harcourt, Brace and World, 1964.

Schachner, Nathan T. *Alexander Hamilton.* New York: D. Appleton-Century Co., 1946. Pbk., A. S. Barnes, Inc.

Stourzh, Gerald. *Alexander Hamilton and the Idea of Republican Government.* Stanford, Cal.: Stanford University Press, 1970.

Sumner, William Graham. *Alexander Hamilton.* New York: Dodd, Mead and Co., 1890.

Vandenburg, Arthur. *If Hamilton Were Alive Today.* New York: G. P. Putnam's Sons, 1923.

Books About Jefferson:

Adams, James Truslow. *The Living Jefferson.* New York: Charles Scribner's Sons, 1936.

Beloff, Max. *Thomas Jefferson and American Democracy.* London: Holder and Stoughton, 1948. Pbk., Macmillan Co.

Boorstin, Daniel J., *The Lost World of Thomas Jefferson.* New York: H. Holt, 1948. Pbk., Beacon Press.

Bowers, Claude G. *The Young Jefferson, 1743–1789.* Boston: Houghton Mifflin Co., 1945. Pbk.

Jefferson and Hamilton: The Struggle for Democracy in America. Boston: Houghton Mifflin and Co., 1925. Pbk.

Jefferson in Power: The Death Struggle of the Federalists. Boston: Houghton Mifflin Co., 1936. Pbk.

Bullock, Helen D. *My Head and My Heart: A Little History of Thomas Jefferson and Maria Cosway.* New York: G. P. Putnam's Sons, 1945.

Chinard, Gilbert. *Thomas Jefferson: Apostle of Americanism.* New York: Little, Brown and Co., 1929. Pbk., University of Michigan Press.

Daniels, Jonathan. *Ordeal of Ambition: Jefferson, Hamilton and Burr.* Garden City, N.Y.: Doubleday, 1970.

Dwight, Theodore. *The Character of Thomas Jefferson.* Boston: Weeks, Jordan and Co., 1839.

Fleming, Thomas. *The Man from Monticello: An Intimate Life of Thomas Jefferson.* New York: Morrow, 1969.

Kimball, Marie. *Jefferson: The Road to Glory.* New York: Coward-McCann, Inc., 1943.

Jefferson: War and Peace. New York: Coward-McCann, Inc., 1947.

Jefferson: The Scene of Europe. New York: Coward-McCann, Inc. 1950.

Koch, Adrienne. *Jefferson and Madison: The Great Collaboration.* New York: A. A. Knopf, 1950. Pbk., Oxford University Press.

Levy, Leonard. *Jefferson and Civil Liberties.* Cambridge, Mass.: Belknap Press of Harvard, 1963.

Malone, Dumas. *Jefferson and His Time.* 5 vols. (to 1809), as follows:

Jefferson the Virginian. Boston: Little, Brown and Co., 1948. Pbk.

Jefferson and the Rights of Man. Boston: Little, Brown and Co., 1951. Pbk.

Jefferson and the Ordeal of Liberty. Boston: Little, Brown and Co., 1962. Pbk.

Jefferson the President: First Term, 1801–1805. Boston: Little, Brown and Co., 1970.

Jefferson the President: Second Term, 1805–1809. Boston: Little, Brown and Co., 1974.

Mayo, Bernard. *Jefferson Himself: A Personal Narrative of A Many-Sided American.* New York: Houghton Mifflin Co., 1941. Pbk., University of Virginia Press.

Minnigerode, Meade. *Jefferson, Friend of France.* New York: G. P. Putnam's Sons, 1928.

Morse, John T. *Thomas Jefferson.* Boston: Houghton Mifflin Co., 1886.

Nock, Albert J. *Jefferson.* New York: Harcourt Brace and Co., 1926. Pbk., Hill and Wang, Inc.

Parton, James. *The Life of Thomas Jefferson, Third President of the United States.* New York: J. R. Osgood, 1874.

Peterson, Merrill D. *The Jefferson Image in the American Mind.* New York: Oxford University Press, 1970. Pbk.

(ed.). *Thomas Jefferson: A Profile.* New York: Hill and Wang, 1967. See entries for Becker, Boyd, Dos Passos and Palmer. Pbk.

Thomas Jefferson and the New Nation. New York: Oxford University Press, 1970.

Randall, Henry S. *The Life of Thomas Jefferson.* 3 vols. New York: J. B. Lippincott, 1858.

Randolph, Sarah Nicholas. *The Domestic Life of Thomas Jefferson.* New York: Harper and Brothers, 1871.

Rosenberger, Francis Coleman (ed.). *The Jefferson Reader.* New York: E. P. Dutton, 1953.

Schachner, Nathan. *Thomas Jefferson: A Biography.* 2 vols. New York: Appleton-Century-Crofts, 1951.

Tucker, George. *The Life of Thomas Jefferson, Third President of the United States.* Philadelphia: Carey, Lea and Blanchard, 1837.

Wiltse, Charles M. *The Jeffersonian Tradition in American Democracy.* Chapel Hill, N.C.: University of North Carolina Press, 1935. Pbk., Hill and Wang, Inc.

Other Books:

Abernethy, Thomas Perkins. *The Burr Conspiracy.* New York: Oxford University Press, 1954.
    Western Lands in the American Revolution. New York: D. Appleton-Century Co., 1937.

Adams, Henry. *A History of the United States During the Administrations of Thomas Jefferson and James Madison, 1801–1817.* 9 vols. New York: Charles Scribner's Sons, 1889–91. Pbk., University of Chicago Press.

Adams, James Truslow. *The Epic of America.* Boston: Little, Brown and Co., 1937.

Allen, Gardner W. *Our Naval War with France.* Boston: Houghton Mifflin Co., 1909.
    Our Navy and the Barbary Corsairs. Boston: Houghton Mifflin Co., 1905.

Atherton, Gertrude. *The Conqueror.* New York: The Macmillan Co. 1902.

Baldwin, Leland. *The Whiskey Rebellion: The Story of a Frontier Uprising.* Pittsburg, Pa.: University of Pittsburg Press, 1939. Pbk.

Bancroft, George. *A History of the United States from the Discovery of the American Continent.* 10 vols. Boston: Little, Brown and Co., 1834–74. Pbk., abr. University of Chicago Press.

Bathe, Greville. *Citizen Genêt, Diplomat, and Inventor.* Philadelphia: Press of Allen, Lane and Scott, 1946.

Beard, Charles A. *The Economic Interpretation of the Constitution of the United States.* New York: The Macmillan Co., 1913. Rev. ed., 1935. Pbk., Free Press.

The Economic Origins of Jeffersonian Democracy. New York: The Macmillan Co., 1913. Pbk., Free Press.

Beardsley, E. E. *Life and Correspondence of Samuel Seabury.* Boston: Houghton Mifflin Co., 1881.

Becker, Carl Lotus. *The Declaration of Independence: A Study in the History of Political Ideas.* New York: Harcourt, Brace and World, 1922. Pbk., Vintage/Random House, Inc.

The Eve of the Revolution: A Chronicle of the Breach with England. Vol. XI. "Chronicles of America," ed. Allen Johnson. New Haven, Conn.: Yale University Press, 1918.

Bemis, Samuel Flagg. *Jay's Treaty: A Study in Commerce and Diplomacy.* New York: The Macmillan Co., 1923. Pbk., Yale University Press.

Beveridge, Albert J. *Life of John Marshall.* 4 vols. Boston: Houghton Mifflin Co., 1916–19.

Bill, Alfred Hoyt. *The Campaign of Princeton.* Princeton, N.J.: Princeton University Press, 1948.

Boyd, Julian P. *The Declaration of Independence: The Evolution of the Text. . . .* Washington, D.C.: The Library of Congress, 1943.

Brant, Irving S. *James Madison: The Virginia Revolutionist, 1751–1780.* Indianapolis: The Bobbs-Merrill Co., 1941.

James Madison: Nationalist, 1780–1787. Indianapolis: The Bobbs-Merrill Co., 1948.

James Madison: Father of the Constitution, 1787–1800. Indianapolis: The Bobbs-Merrill Co., 1950.

James Madison: Secretary of State, 1801–1809. Indianapolis: The Bobbs-Merrill Co., 1953.

James Madison: President, 1809–1812. Indianapolis: The Bobbs-Merrill Co., 1956.

James Madison: Commander in Chief, 1812–1836. Indianapolis: The Bobbs-Merrill Co., 1961.

Brown, Roger. *The Republic in Peril: 1812.* New York: Columbia University Press, 1964.

Bruce, Philip A. *History of the University of Virginia, 1819–1919.* 2 vols. New York: The Macmillan Co., 1920.

Burnett, Edmund Cody. *The Continental Congress.* New York: The Macmillan Co., 1941. Pbk., Norton Co.

Burt, A. L. *The United States, Great Britain, and British*

North America. New Haven, Conn.: Yale University Press, 1940.

Butler, Nicholas Murray. *Building the American Nation.* New York: Charles Scribner's Sons, 1923.

Caldwell, Lynton. *The Administrative Theories of Thomas Jefferson and Alexander Hamilton.* Chicago: University of Chicago Press, 1944.

Carroll, John A., and Mary W. Ashworth. See Freeman, Douglas Southall.

Chambers, William Nisbet. *Political Parties in the New Nation.* New York: Oxford University Press, 1963. Pbk.

Channing, Edward. *A History of the United States.* 6 vols. New York: The Macmillan Co., 1905–1925.
   The Jeffersonian System. Vol. VIII in "The American Nation," ed. Albert Bushnell Hart. New York: Harper and Brothers, 1906.

Charles, Joseph. *The Origins of the American Party System.* Williamsburg, Va.: Institute of Early American History and Culture, 1956. Pbk., Oxford University Press.

Clark, Mary E. *Peter Porcupine in America: The Career of William Cobbett, 1792–1800.* Philadelphia: Times and News Publishing Co., 1939.

Corwin, Edward S. *Court Over Constitution.* New York: Peter Smith, 1950.

Cresson, William P. *James Monroe.* Chapel Hill, N.C.: University of North Carolina Press, 1946.

Croly, Herbert. *The Promise of American Life.* New York: The Macmillan Co., 1909. Pbk. Bobbs-Merrill Co. or E. P. Dutton Co.

Cunningham, Noble E. *The Jeffersonian Republicans: The Formation of Party Organization, 1789–1801.* Chapel Hill, N.C.: University of North Carolina Press, 1957. Pbk.
   The Jeffersonian Republicans in Power, 1801–1809. Chapel Hill, N.C.: University of North Carolina Press, 1963. Pbk.

Dangerfield, George. *Chancellor Robert Livingston of New York, 1743–1813.* New York: Harcourt, Brace and Co., 1960.

Darling, Arthur B. *Our Rising Empire.* New Haven, Conn.: Yale University Press, 1940.

Dauer, Manning J. *The Adams Federalists*. Baltimore: Johns Hopkins Press, 1953.

Davis, Elmer. *By Elmer Davis,* ed. Robert L. Davis. Indianapolis: The Bobbs-Merrill Co., 1964.

DeConde, Alexander. *Entangling Alliances: Politics and Diplomacy Under Washington*. Durham, N.C.: Duke University Press, 1958.

    The Quasi-War: The Politics and Diplomacy of the Undeclared War with France, 1797–1801. New York: Charles Scribner's Sons, 1966. Pbk.

Dorfman, Joseph. *The Economic Mind in American Civilization*. 3 vols. New York: The Macmillan Co., 1946–49.

Fiske, John. *The Critical Period in American History*. Boston: Houghton Mifflin Co., 1888.

Flexner, James Thomas. *George Washington and the American Revolution*. Boston: Little, Brown and Co., 1968.

    The Traitor and the Spy: Benedict Arnold and John André. New York: Harcourt, Brace and Co., 1953.

Fowler, Milton E. *James Parton: The Father of Modern Biography*. Durham, N.C.: Duke University Press, 1951.

Freeman, Douglas Southall. *George Washington: A Biography*. 7 vols. (Volume VII by John A. Carroll and Mary W. Ashworth.) New York: Charles Scribner's Sons, 1948–51.

Freidel, Frank. *Franklin Roosevelt: The Ordeal*. Boston: Little, Brown and Co., 1954.

Gay, Peter. *The Enlightenment: An Interpretation. The Rise of Modern Paganism*. New York: A. A. Knopf, 1966. Pbk., Vintage/Random House.

Genêt, George Clinton. *Washington, Jefferson, and "Citizen" Genêt, 1793*. New York, 1889.

Hamilton, John C. *A History of the United States Traced in the Writings of Alexander Hamilton and His Contemporaries*. 6 vols. New York: D. Appleton and Company, 1857–64.

Hand, Learned. *The Bill of Rights*. Cambridge, Mass.: Harvard University Press, 1958. Pbk., Atheneum.

Hazen, Charles D. *Contemporary American Opinion of the French Revolution*. ("Johns Hopkins University Studies in Historical and Political Science," Vol. XVI.) Baltimore: Johns Hopkins Press, 1897.

Hecksher, Eli F. *The Continental System*. London: H. Milford, 1922.

Henry, William Wirt. *Patrick Henry: Life, Correspondence and Speeches.* 3 vols. New York: Charles Scribner's Sons, 1891.

Hildreth, Richard. *The History of the United States of America.* 6 vols. New York: Harper and Brothers, 1849–56.

Hook, Sydney. *The Paradoxes of Freedom.* Berkeley, Cal.: University of California Press, 1962. Pbk.

Horsman, Reginald. *The Causes of the War of 1812.* Philadelphia: University of Pennsylvania Press, 1962. Pbk., A. S. Barnes and Co.

Jacobs, James R. *The Tarnished Warrior.* New York: The Macmillan Co., 1938.

James, C. L. R. *The Black Jacobins: Toussaint L'Ouverture and the San Domingo Revolution.* New York: Dial Press, 1938.

Jennings, Walter. *The American Embargo: 1807–1809.* Iowa City: The University of Iowa Press, 1921.

Jensen, Merrill. *The New Nation: A History of the United States During the Confederation, 1781–1789.* New York: A. A. Knopf, 1950. Pbk., Vintage/Random House.
The Founding of a Nation. New York: Oxford University Press, 1968.

Jordan, Winthrop D. *White Over Black: American Attitudes Toward the Negro, 1550–1815.* Chapel Hill, N.C.: University of North Carolina Press, 1968. Pbk., Penguin Books.

Kimball, Marie. *Thomas Jefferson's Cook Book.* Richmond, Va.: Garrett, Massie, 1938.

Kingsley, Sydney. *The Patriots.* New York: Random House, 1943.

Konefsky, Samuel J. *John Marshall and Alexander Hamilton: Architects of the Constitution.* New York: The Macmillan Co., 1964.

Leary, Lewis. *That Rascal Freneau: A Study in Literary Failure.* Brunswick, N.J.: Rutgers University Press, 1941.

Liddell Hart, Basil H. *Strategy.* New York: Praeger, 1954. Pbk., Frederick A. Praeger Inc.

Link, Eugene P. *The Democratic-Republican Societies, 1790–1800.* New York: Columbia University Press, 1942.

Lyons, Wilson. *Louisiana in French Diplomacy, 1759–1804.* Norman, Okla.: University of Oklahoma Press, 1934.

MacDonald, Forrest. *We the People: An Economic Interpreta-*

tion of the Constitution. Chicago: University of Chicago Press, 1958. Pbk.

McLaughlin, James Fairfax. *Matthew Lyon, the Hampden of Congress.* New York: Wynkoop, Hallenbech, Crawford Co., 1900.

MacMaster, John Bach. *A History of the People of the United States from the Revolution to the Civil War.* 8 vols. New York: D. Appleton and Company, 1883–1913.

Macmillan, Margaret Burnham. *The War Governors in the American Revolution.* Gloucester, Mass.: Peter Smith, 1943.

Mahan, Alfred Thayer. *Sea Power in its Relations to the War of 1812.* Boston: Little, Brown and Co., 1919.

Mayo, Bernard. *Myths and Men: Patrick Henry, George Washington, and Thomas Jefferson.* Athens, Ga.: University of Georgia Press, 1959. Pbk., Harper and Row/Torchbooks.

Meade, Robert D. *Patrick Henry: Patriot in the Making.* Philadelphia: Lippincott, 1957.

Miller, John C. *Crisis in Freedom.* Boston: Little, Brown and Co., 1951. Pbk.
　　The Federalist Era. New York: Harper and Row, 1960. Pbk., Harper and Row/Torchbooks.
　　Origins of the American Revolution. Boston: Little, Brown and Co., 1943. Pbk., Stanford University Press.

Monaghan, Frank. *John Jay: Defender of Liberty.* Indianapolis: The Bobbs-Merrill Co., 1935.

Morgan, Edmund S. *Birth of the Republic, 1763–1789.* Chicago: University of Chicago Press, 1956. Pbk.

Morganthau, Hans. *In Defense of the National Interest: A Critical Examination of American Foreign Policy.* New York: A. A. Knopf, 1951.

Norton, A. B. *Reminiscences of the Log Cabin and Hard Cider Campaign.* Mount Vernon, Ohio: A. B. Norton and Co., 1888.

Palmer, Robert R. *The Age of Democratic Revolution.* Princeton: Princeton University Press, 1959–64. Pbk.

Parrington, Vernon L. *Main Currents in American Thought.* 3 vols. New York: Harcourt, Brace and Company, 1927–30. Pbk., Harcourt Brace and Jovanovich, Inc.

Perkins, Bradford. *Prologue to War: England and the United*

States, 1805–1812. Berkeley, Cal.: University of California Press, 1961. Pbk.

Pound, Roscoe, *et. al., Federalism as a Democratic Process.* New Brunswick, N.J.: Rutgers University Press, 1942.

Robertson, William Spencer. *Life of Miranda.* 2 vols. Chapel Hill, N.C.: University of North Carolina Press, 1929.

Rossiter, Clinton. *1787: The Grand Convention.* New York: The Macmillan Co., 1966. Pbk., New American Library.

Schachner, Nathan. *The Founding Fathers.* New York: G. P. Putnam's Sons, 1954.

Schlesinger, Arthur M. *The Colonial Merchants in the American Revolution.* New York: Columbia University, 1918. Pbk., Atheneum.

Schouler, James. *The History of the United States under the Constitution.* 7 vols. Washington, D.C.: W. H. and O. H. Morrison, 1880–1913.

Sears, Louis Martin. *Jefferson and the Embargo.* Durham, N.C.: Duke University Press, 1927.

Shreve, Royal O. *The Finished Scoundrel.* Indianapolis: The Bobbs-Merrill Co., 1933.

Smith, Page. *John Adams.* 2 vols. Garden City, N.Y.: Doubleday, 1962.

Spaulding, E. Wilder. *His Excellency, Governor Clinton.* New York: The Macmillan Co., 1938.

New York in the Critical Period ("New York State Historical Association Series"), ed. Dixon Ryan Fox. New York: Columbia University Press, 1932.

Taylor, Robert J. *Western Massachusetts in the Revolution.* Providence, R.I.: Brown University Press, 1954.

Thomas, Charles Marion. *American Neutrality in 1793: A Study in Cabinet Government.* New York: Columbia University Press, 1931.

Tolles, Frederick B. *George Logan of Philadelphia.* New York: Oxford University Press, 1953.

Twelve Southern Authors. *I'll Take My Stand.* New York: Harper and Brothers, 1930. Pbk., Harper and Row/Torchbooks.

United States Bureau of the Census and the Social Sciences Research Council. *The Statistical History of the United States from Colonial Times to the Present.* Stamford, Conn.: Fairfield Publishers, 1965.

Walters, Raymond J., Jr. *Albert Gallatin: Jeffersonian Financier.* New York: The Macmillan Co., 1957. Pbk., University of Pittsburgh Press.

Ward, Christopher C. *The War of the Revolution.* 2 vols. New York: The Macmillan Co., 1952.

Warren, Charles. *The Supreme Court in United States History.* 2 vols. Boston: Little, Brown and Company, 1922.

Waterman, Thomas T. *The Mansions of Virginia, 1706–1776.* Chapel Hill, N.C.: University of North Carolina Press, 1946.

Whitaker, Arthur P. *The Mississippi Question, 1795–1803: A Study in Trade, Politics and Diplomacy.* New York: D. Appleton-Century Co., 1934.

The United States and The Independence of Latin America, Baltimore: Johns Hopkins Press, 1941.

White, Leonard D. *The Federalists: A Study in Administrative History, 1789–1801.* New York: The Macmillan Co., 1948. Pbk., The Free Press.

The Jeffersonians: A Study in Administrative History, 1801–1809. New York: The Macmillan Co., 1951. Pbk., The Free Press.

Wilson, Thomas Woodrow. *A History of the American People.* 5 vols. New York: Harper and Brothers, 1902.

Wish, Harvey. *The American Historian.* New York: Oxford University Press, 1960.

Wood, Gordon S. *The Creation of the American Republic, 1776–1787.* Chapel Hill, N.C.: University of North Carolina Press, 1969. Pbk.

Zimmerman, James F. *Impressment of American Seamen* ("Columbia University Studies in History, Economics and Public Law"). New York: Columbia University, 1925.

Articles and Essays:

Adair, Douglass, and Henry Marvin. "Was Alexander Hamilton a Christian Gentlemen?" *Hamilton: A Profile,* ed. Cooke, pp. 230–255.

Beard, Charles A. "Jefferson in American Law," *Yale Review,* 35 (1935), pp. 241–57.

Becker, Carl Lotus. "What is Still Living in the Philosophy of Thomas Jefferson?" *Jefferson: A Profile,* ed. Peterson, pp. 41–60.

Bemis, Samuel Flagg. "Washington's Farewell Address," *American Historical Review,* 38 (1932) pp. 250–68.

Bowman, Alfred H. "Jefferson, Hamilton, and American Foreign Policy," *Political Science Quarterly,* 71 (1956), pp. 18–41.

Boyd, Julian P. "Thomas Jefferson's Empire for Liberty," *Jefferson: A Profile,* ed. Peterson, pp. 178–194.

Brant, Irving. "Edmund Randolph, Not Guilty," *William and Mary Quarterly,* 3rd ser., 7 (1950), pp. 179–98.

Cramer, Eugene. "Some New Lights on the XYZ Affair: Elbridge Gerry's Reasons for Opposing War with France," *New England Quarterly,* 29 (1956), pp. 509–13.

Cunningham, Noble E. "The Virginia Jeffersonians' Victory Celebration in 1801," *Virginia Cavalcade,* 8 (1958), pp. 4–9.

Dos Passos, John. "A Portico Facing the Wilderness," *Jefferson: A Profile,* ed. Peterson, pp. 61–85.

Grampp, William. "A Re-examination of Jeffersonian Economics," *Jefferson: A Profile,* ed. Peterson, pp. 135–163.

"Journal of a French Traveller in the Colonies, 1765," *American Historical Review,* 26 (1921), 729–47.

Kenyon, Cecelia. "Alexander Hamilton: Rousseau of the Right," *Political Science Quarterly,* 73 (1958), pp. 161–78.

Kimball, Fiske. "In Search of Thomas Jefferson's Birthplace," *Virginia Magazine of History and Biography,* 51 (1943), pp. 313–25.

Koch, Adrienne, and Harry Ammon, "The Virginia and Kentucky Resolutions: An Episode in Jefferson's and Madison's Defense of Civil Liberties," *William and Mary Quarterly,* 3rd ser., 5 (1948), pp. 145–76.

Lewis, Anthony Marc. "Jefferson and Virginia's Pioneers, 1774–1781," *Mississippi Valley Historical Review,* 34 (1949), pp. 551–88.

Lokke, Carl. "Jefferson and the LeClerc Expedition," *American Historical Review,* 33 (1928), pp. 322–28.

Malone, Dumas. "Jefferson and the New Deal," *Scribner's Magazine,* 93 (June, 1933), pp. 356–59.

Letter to the editor of the *New York Times,* November 26, 1973.

Manning, William K. "The Nootka Sound Controversy," American Historical Association *Annual Report for 1904* (Washington, 1905), pp. 279–438.

Mayo, Bernard. "A Peppercorn for Mr. Jefferson," *Virginia Quarterly Review,* 19 (1943), 221–26.

Owsley, Frank Lawrence. "Two Agrarian Philosophers: Jefferson and Du Pont," *Hound and Horn,* 6 (1932), pp. 166–72.

Palmer, Robert R. "The Dubious Democrat: Thomas Jefferson in Bourbon France," *Jefferson: A Profile,* ed. Peterson, pp. 86–103.

Pancake, John S. "Aaron Burr: Would-Be Usurper," *William and Mary Quarterly,* 3rd. ser., 8 (1951), pp. 204–13.
"The Invisibles: A Chapter in the Opposition to Madison," *Journal of Southern History,* 21 (1955), pp. 17–37.

Parks, Henry Bamford. "Jeffersonian Democracy," *Symposium,* 3 (1933), pp. 26–31.

Tugwell, Rexford G., and Joseph Dorfman. "Alexander Hamilton: Nation-Maker," *Columbia University Quarterly,* 29 (1937), pp. 209–26.

Turner, Frederick Jackson. "Origins of Genêt's Attack on Louisiana and the Floridas," *American Historical Review,* 3 (1898), pp. 651–71.
"The Policy of France toward the Mississippi Valley in the Period of Washington and Adams," *American Historical Review,* 10 (1905), pp. 249–79.

Turner, Lynn W. "The Impeachment of John Pickering," *American Historical Review,* 54 (1949), pp. 485–507.

Index